Jesus and Paul before Christianity

Jesus and Paul before Christianity

Their World and Work in Retrospect

∽

V. GEORGE SHILLINGTON

CASCADE Books • Eugene, Oregon

JESUS AND PAUL BEFORE CHRISTIANITY
Their World and Work in Retrospect

Copyright © 2011 V. George Shillington. All rights reserved. Except for brief quotations in critical publications or reviews, no part of this book may be reproduced in any manner without prior written permission from the publisher. Write: Permissions, Wipf and Stock Publishers, 199 W. 8th Ave., Suite 3, Eugene, OR 97401.

Cascade Books
An Imprint of Wipf and Stock Publishers
199 W. 8th Ave., Suite 3
Eugene, OR 97401

www.wipfandstock.com

ISBN 13: 978-1-60899-694-0

Unless otherwise indicated, Scripture quotations are from the New Revised Standard Version of the Bible, copyright © 1989 by the National Council of the Churches of Christ in the USA. Used by permission. All rights reserved.

The map of Palestine and the map of the New Testament World are from The Believers Church Bible Commentary, *Mark*, © 2001. Herald Press, Scottdale PA 15683. Used by permission.

Cataloging-in-Publication data:

Shillington, V. G. (V. George)

    Jesus and Paul before Christianity : their world and work in retrospect / V. George Shillington.

    p. ; cm. — Includes bibliographical references and index(es).

    ISBN 13: 978-1-60899-694-0

    1. Jesus Christ—Historicity. 2. Paul, the Apostle, Saint. I. Title

BS2361.3 S45 2011

Manufactured in the U.S.A.

for Connal

. . . latest grandchild,
delightful addition to our family

Contents

Preface / ix
Abbreviations / xi

Part I: Groundwork

1 Invitation to Read this Book / 3
2 Before Christianity / 6
3 Beyond the Jesus-Paul Debate / 13

Part II: Jesus

4 Where to Look for Jesus / 23
5 The Crux of the Matter / 33
6 Growing Up in Lower Galilee / 40
7 From John to Jesus / 55
8 Enacting the Kingdom of God / 65
9 Speaking of the Kingdom of God / 90
10 The Last Days in Jerusalem / 111

Part III: Paul

11 Interface: Between Jesus and Paul / 135
12 Prophetic Call in Jewish Context / 154
13 Gathering the Nations into Jesus Messiah / 164
14 Life Together in the Fellowship of Jesus Messiah / 182
15 Universal Restoration: God, Israel, and the Nations / 201

16 Conclusion: Jesus First and also Paul / 217

Bibliography / 227
Ancient Documents Index / 235
Author Index / 245
Subject Index / 247

Preface

MY INTEREST IN FINDING HELPFUL WAYS OF VIEWING THE HISTORICAL FIGURES of Jesus and Paul began in 1978 at McMaster University in Hamilton, Ontario. I had written an essay in a seminar on Paul, under the tutelage of E. P. Sanders, and found myself bewildered by the strange presence (or absence) of Jesus in the letters of Paul. The essay eventually turned into a full-length dissertation, "The Figure of Jesus in the Typological Thought of Paul." I was not impressed with the century-long scholarly debate in which the two figures were either pitted against each other, or seen as pleasantly living in the same social and theological space.

Since that first encounter with the issue, I have since taught courses on Jesus and the Gospels, and on Paul and the Letters, and have written articles and books related to one or the other. I discovered along the way that the differences between Jesus and Paul were not merely those of scholarly observations of New Testament specialists, but also the impression of non-specialist readers. In group-discussions with lay people I found that a number objected to the character of Paul for one reason or another: he is arrogant, talks about himself too much, refuses to listen to the good counsel of his friends, dishonors women. Jesus, on the other hand, is "meek and lowly of heart," likable and kind. Somehow the people who find Jesus so attractive fail to notice that the people responsible for running the affairs of the society in which Jesus lived crucified him.

My toying with the idea of writing a book about both historical figures came to a head in 2002. That year Professor Seán Freyne was the guest lecturer for the J. J. Thiessen Lectures in Winnipeg, Canada. In the course of conversation with him about my ongoing conversation about Jesus and Paul, he suggested I commit to writing a book about the two figures for the benefit of others. Now, in the spring of 2011, the work is done. I hope the readers, both specialist and non-specialist alike, will find something worthwhile for their life and thought from the picture I have painted in the following pages of the two most formidable figures at the gateway of what was to become Christianity.

I have many people to thank, too many to mention, all of them mentors and coaches in their own right. Some deserve recognition here for their direct involvement in my work. My son, Ralph, listened to my many musings, read some questionable discussions, and offered advice for revisions. I have valued his insight, enthusiasm, and

Preface

personal support for the project. Part way through the writing of the book, Eckhard Goerz invited me to present four lectures in a class of thoughtful adults on the world and work of Jesus. The participants offered helpful feedback, some of which comes through in the ensuing discussions.

A number of friends and colleagues agreed to read the manuscript, and graciously allowed their names to be associated with my work. For that generous gift I offer sincere gratitude: William Campbell, Philip Esler, Seán Freyne, Tim Rogalsky, Arthur Walker-Jones, Mark Nanos, Gordon Zerbe, and Rev. Tony Davidson. Thank you all!

Editor, Chris Spinks, saw the project through from an initial conversation at the Society of Biblical Literature, to the finished product. He, along with the efficient staff at Wipf & Stock Publishers, have my unqualified vote of thanks for a job well done.

Finally, I congratulate my wife, Grace, for putting up with my endless talk about Jesus and Paul over the last few years. I could not have a better conversation partner. Thank you!

—Winnipeg, April 2011

Abbreviations

SCRIPTURES

Gen.	Genesis	Mic.	Micah
Exod.	Exodus	Nah.	Nahum
Lev.	Leviticus	Hab.	Habakkuk
Num.	Numbers	Zeph.	Zephaniah
Deut.	Deuteronomy	Hag.	Haggai
Josh.	Joshua	Zech.	Zechariah
Judg.	Judges	Mal.	Malachi
Sam.	1–2 Samuel	Matt.	Matthew
Kgs.	1–2 Kings	Rom.	Romans
Chron.	1–2 Chronicles	Cor.	1–2 Corinthians
Neh.	Nehemiah	Gal.	Galatians
Ps.	Psalms	Eph.	Ephesians
Prov.	Proverbs	Phil.	Philippians
Eccl.	Ecclesiastes	Col.	Colossians
Isa.	Isaiah	Thess.	1–2 Thessalonians
Jer.	Jeremiah	Tim.	1–2 Timothy
Lam.	Lamentations	Tit.	Titus
Ezek.	Ezekiel	Phlm.	Philemon
Dan.	Daniel	Heb.	Hebrews
Hos.	Hosea	Pet.	1–2 Peter
Obad.	Obadiah	Rev.	Revelation

Abbreviations

OTHER REFERENCED WORKS

Ant	Josephus, *Jewish Antiquities*
ASV	American Standard Version
BBR	*Bulletin for Biblical Research*
BI	*Biblical Interpretation*
BJRL	*Bulleting of the John Rylands Library.*
BTB	*Biblical Theological Bulletin*
CEB	Common English Bible
DSS	Dead Sea Scrolls
Gos. Eb.	*Gospel of the Ebionites*
Gos. Heb.	*Gospel of the Hebrews*
Gos. Naz.	*Gospel of the Nazarenes*
Gos. Thom.	*Gospel of Thomas*
HTR	*Harvard Theological Review*
Int	*Interpretation*
J. W.	Josephus, *Jewish War*
JBL	*Journal of Biblical Literature*
JSNT	*Journal for the Study of the New Testament*
KJV	King James Version, (otherwise Authorized Version)
Macc.	1–2 Maccabees
NASB	New American Standard Bible
NEB	New English Bible
NRSV	New Revised Standard Version
NTS	*New Testament Studies*
Ps. Sol.	*Psalms of Solomon*
USQR	*Union Seminary Quarterly Review*
Wis.	Wisdom of Solomon

Part I
Groundwork

whoever plows should plow in hope
(1 Cor. 9:10)

1

Invitation to Read This Book

"IN TRUTH, THERE WAS ONLY ONE CHRISTIAN AND HE DIED ON THE CROSS."[1] Thus spoke Friedrich Nietzsche in 1888. Maybe he spoke tongue-in-cheek. Maybe not. Either way, the statement is false. Jesus was not a Christian. Nor did Jesus ever project the word forward to later generations of Christians.

Paul "is the genius in hatred . . . , in the relentless logic of hatred. . . he falsified the history of Israel, so as to make it appear as a prologue to *his* mission."[2] Nietzsche again in 1888, talking out of the abyss of his own anti-Christian experience. How could the Apostle who wrote the celebrated love song in First Corinthians 13 be so accused of hatred?

What we find in the sources, instead, is an extraordinary meeting of two Jewish minds in two different contexts in the first century, without any actual meeting having taken place between the two historical persons. The subject of Jesus and Paul has been around for a long time. And I have been deeply interested in the subject for about forty years. In churchly settings, in my experience, some people pit the two historical figures against each other. Others try to harmonize the two by picking out scraps of texts from any book of the New Testament and pasting the scraps into a contrived collage on a piece of bristle board. To date I have not observed a title over the collage saying, "The Life and Mission of Two Jewish Radicals." I dare not take the metaphor any further. I suggest, rather, that you delve into the chapters that follow to find out how these two remarkable Jewish men, each in his own time and place, shaped a movement that grew into a colossal institutional religion beyond their wildest dreams.

One of the problems I faced—the main one actually—in writing this book was to transcend the influence of the later religion, Christianity, to allow the voice and vision of the two historical figures to come through with as little interference from later language and theology, with which I am all too familiar. Henry Cadbury stated the matter well: "The patterns of thought change as do the patterns of clothes from land to land

---

1. Nietzsche, *Antichrist*, 111.
2. Ibid., 119–20.

Part 1: Groundwork

and from age to age, and the thoughts of a first century Jew like Jesus or Paul are not the thoughts of a twentieth century Englishman or German or American."[3] With this in mind, I try throughout the chapters to use terms of reference more in keeping with the time and situation and meaning in which Jesus and Paul lived and spoke. Later on in this "invitation to read this book" I will list terms commonly used in books such as this, terms I consider anachronistic, or laden with connotations from a later time and situation. For each term listed I will provide a more appropriate alternate that I use in my discussions.

Another decision I had to face as I approached the writing of this work was the readership. Should I write for esteemed colleagues in the guild of New Testament scholarship? Or should I write for a more general readership interested in the "inside story" of these two towering figures of the first century? I chose the latter, with some qualification. I wanted the writing to be insightful, fresh, informed, readable, but also subject to the scrutiny of my peers in New Testament studies. That meant that the language would not be so popular as to trivialize the project, and not so technically cumbersome as to disengage the reader. I find that balance difficult to strike. I try it anyway. Whether successful or not remains for you to decide.

Related to readership, I deliberately keep footnotes to a minimum. The sources of quotations have to be provided. But I try to keep the number in check, using only those I deem truly pertinent. Anyone wanting to pursue a topic further should consult the bibliography.

Each reader brings to the reading table everything they are: gender, heritage, social status, religious affiliation, education—formal and informal, and level of interest in the subject. It cannot be otherwise. Supporting all of these mental and emotional qualities is the dynamic human self: *a reasonable and responsible reader*. To that person I appeal and invite to engage the material surrounding Jesus and Paul.

Fifteen chapters follow this one. I trust your reading of them will be as rewarding for you as my writing of them was for me. There are three main parts to the book. You are already in Part I, the "groundwork." Part II is all about Jesus. My approach is to picture Jesus in his own time and place, acting and speaking uniquely out of his setting. As Wright admits, "the search for Jesus in his historical context is possible, vital, and urgent."[4] Part III is all about Paul. He too should be allowed to speak and act from within his own context. By setting up the two figures side by side we are in a position to compare their roles and contributions to human history. That comparison forms the conclusion to the work as a whole. I suggest that you not cheat yourself by reading the conclusion to the exclusion of the chapters leading up to it.

Now we come to commonly used terms of reference that I find unhelpful to the project of positioning the two Jewish figures of Jesus and Paul in their rightful contexts. In the left column of the table below are terms traditionally used, especially by Christian interpreters, to identify persons or groups of people. In the right column

---

3. Cadbury, *Modernizing*, 3.
4. Wright, "Five Gospels," 115.

Invitation to Read This Book

are alternate terms to help keep later categories out of the picture. Even though the alternate is sometimes more cumbersome, it preempts the encroachment of ideas and connotations alien to the time and context of Jesus and Paul. One concession I have to make: in citing secondary sources and translations of the Bible I do not change the given terms.

Commonly used terminology	Alternate terminology
• Christ	• Messiah (Hebraic)/Christ (Hellenistic) used alternately. Basic meaning of both, "anointed one."
• Christian/Christians, Early Christians	• Christ-follower/s, believers in Jesus/Christ, people of faith in Jesus Messiah.
• Church/churches	• Christ-community/communities, new community of Christ, called-out group(s).
• Jew/Jews	• Judean/Judeans/Jewish people.
• Gentiles/pagans	• Nations (Gk. *ethnē*), non-Jewish people.

One final topic to ponder before moving ahead to the rest of the "groundwork": *the anticipated outcome from reading the book.* I hereby confess that in the process of preparing to write what you are about to read I had some mind-changing experiences. After getting over the discomfort of changing position, or insight, I had the joy of new discovery and new direction. And there can be no turning back. I wish the same exhilaration for you. Now I must let you proceed with the rest of the groundwork: "Before Christianity" and "Beyond the Jesus-Paul Debate."

2

Before Christianity

IN THE EARLY STAGES OF PREPARING TO WRITE THIS BOOK, A CHRISTIAN woman asked about the subject matter. When I told her the proposed title of the book, *Jesus and Paul Before Christianity*, she expressed some puzzlement. "How could Jesus and Paul exist before Christianity, since they were the first Christians?" On second thought she realized Jesus was not a "Christian." But he was "Christ," so everyone who believed in him from that time forward were surely "Christians." Paul especially was a "Christian," the woman insisted. "He converted from his old religion of Judaism to Christianity. Wouldn't that make him a Christian"? She is not alone in her thinking. A multitude of Christian people today accept that anachronistic proposition.

Professor Eisenbaum's point is well taken: "The image of Paul as the first true Christian also requires him to be the first true convert to Christianity. . . Once converted, he realized the futility of Judaism, with its endless demands of the law, and rejected it."[1] With the world religion of Christianity being as pervasive as it is, and its two foundational heroes as pronounced as they are in historic confessions of faith, it is hard for professing Christians today to imagine a time when believers in Jesus of Nazareth would refer to themselves by any other name than "Christians," and to their religion by any other name than "Christianity."

Herein lies the challenge of both writing and reading this book. How can we keep in check the multiple elements of Christian confessions of faith, grounded as they are in a two-thousand-year history that we so easily associate with the two principal figures of the New Testament?

WHEN BELIEVERS IN JESUS WERE FIRST CALLED "CHRISTIANS"

The adjective-become-noun appears only three times in the New Testament, as we shall see in a moment. Nowhere in the four canonical gospels are the disciples of Jesus called "Christians." As "disciples" they were *learning* the Jesus-way of life and thought. As "apostles" they were *sent out* to practice the Jesus-way of life and thought in relation

---

1. Eisenbaum, *Paul*, 2.

Before Christianity

to others. But they were not called "Christians" by Jesus, or by anyone else, and certainly not by themselves. If they had been so called, surely the gospel writers would have made use of the term in writing their respective gospels.

What about Paul's letters that occupy the largest space within the New Testament? The letters express his new vision of the Jewish Messiah (Gk. *Christos* = "anointed one"), written as they were during those critical years of mission in which he called non-Jewish people into community under the banner of Jesus the anointed of God for the salvation of the world. Yet not once does he refer to himself or to the members in those communities as "Christian." My plea, therefore, for the discourse of this book, is that we, both writer and reader, refrain from imposing the deeply embedded self-designation of later members of Christianity on the texts and contexts surrounding the two historical figures of Jesus and Paul. Later in this chapter I will expand the reasons for the restraint.

Meanwhile, consider how the term "Christian(s)" occurs at three places in the New Testament, twice in Acts and once in 1 Peter. In Acts 11:26 it appears out of the blue, as a tag already in circulation at the time of writing Acts: "So it was that for an entire year they met with the church and taught a great many people, and it was in Antioch that the disciples were first called 'Christians.'" Acts was written at the end of the first century. By that time the groups of believers in Jesus, scattered throughout the Mediterranean world, were talking about him as "the Anointed" (Gk. *Christos*), the one ordained of God to save the world. Outsiders coined the adjective, *christianoi*, probably with derogatory undertones, to match the outspoken confession of the followers of Jesus. The writer of Acts affirms (1) that the term was used first at Antioch, and implies (2) that the term was applied to the disciples by persons other than themselves. The *time* of the first use of the word "Christians" is not stated, only that it was used first at Antioch. It may have come into use around the time of writing Acts, ca. 95–100 CE.

The second occurrence of the term in Acts comes in the dialogue between Paul and Agrippa II in Acts 26:28-29. Agrippa said to Paul, "Are you so quickly persuading me to become a Christian"? Paul replied, "Whether quickly or not, I pray to God that not only you but also all who are listening to me today might become such as I am—except for these chains." This time "Christian" clearly comes from the mouth of an outsider, an accuser with political power in Judea. His question is more a sarcastic taunt than a sincere inquiry. Notice that Paul's reply does not repeat the name "Christian" from Agrippa's mouth. Paul, the ridiculed and accused believer in Jesus, is in chains. At the time of writing Acts, "Christian" was not a title attached to people in polite society, people like Agrippa. It was more a term of shame than honor. In Paul's case in the narrative of Acts 26, the shame of chains.

By far the most striking of the three places where "Christian" is used in the New Testament is that of First Peter 4:15-16: "But let none of you suffer as a murderer, a thief, a criminal, or even as a mischief maker. Yet if any of you suffers as a Christian, do not consider it a disgrace, but glorify God because you bear this name." Apparently, when people were labeled "Christian" for believing in Jesus as the Anointed of God

Part 1: Groundwork

in the socio-political context of First Peter, the label was not a badge of honor, but of disgrace. There was no conventional *Christos* to save believers from their suffering. Yet they continued to confess Jesus as the Messiah. Their accusers thus employed the derisive "Christian" label to degrade and persecute them. But the suffering believers in the context of First Peter are encouraged to bear the name, ironically, to glorify God.[2]

The general epistle of First Peter was probably written within the same time frame as Acts, towards the end of the first century CE.[3] Moreover, the name "Christian" was not yet part of the positive self-definition of members of the community of Jesus, much less the religious name "Christianity" as applied to the aggregate communities.

CONSTANTINE, COUNCILS, CREEDS AND CANONS

As the various groups of believers moved forward through the second and third centuries many of them experienced persecution, tension between the groups, struggles with self-identity, even the threat of extinction. Local people of the cities had their gods and shrines, all of them sanctioned by the imperial power of Rome. And there was the Emperor himself, also expecting honor due a divinity. All of these factors facing the Jesus-movement of the first three centuries put the developing communities always at risk. At the same time, there were those in the movement endowed with intellectual ability, educated, able to speak and write and lead the beleaguered communities forward undaunted.

All the while, the new Jesus-movement was becoming more and more non-Jewish in composition and theological orientation. Increasingly the borderline separating formative Rabbinic Judaism from the Jesus-communities became more and more fixed. By the end of the third century Jewish synagogues and Christ communities had parted company. One man from the Christ-movement in the mid-second century went so far as to deny any connection between his congregations and the Jewish religion. His name was Marcion. He rejected the entire Scriptures of the Jewish people in favor of a new reading-list made up of Paul's letters and the Gospel of Luke. This was the earliest "canon"—a select list of documents for use in worship and teaching in the communities of Jesus Christ.

The religion of Judaism had had a long history. Rome tolerated its existence in the Empire. Judaism could survive as long as it refrained from subversive activity against Rome, a difficult row for the Jewish people to hoe. The uprising of the second century under the leadership of a Jewish leader, Bar Kochba (132–135 CE), constituted rebellion against Rome. Emperor Hadrian had initially given permission to Bar Kochba to rebuild the Temple of Jerusalem, but went back on his word. Rebellion ensued. Bar Kochba was viewed as a kind of Messiah by the Jewish people of Palestine. But Hadrian brought the legions down upon the enterprise in Jerusalem, replacing the emerging Jewish shrine with one dedicated to Hadrian's deity instead.

---

2. Horrel, "Label," 361-81.
3. Shillington, *Context*, 139.

Before Christianity

I draw attention to this event to make the point that any sign of subversion from any quarter cannot stand the scrutiny of Rome. Jesus-people were implicitly doing just that: they were hailing their leader as Messiah/Christ, Savior, and Lord. They spoke of another kingdom and another king, namely Jesus (cf. Acts 17:7). No wonder they suffered persecution in a political environment governed by only one supreme ruler, the Roman Emperor. Had the situation of the first 300 years continued as it was, the Jesus-movement may not have become the highly regarded world religion known today as "Christianity."

A seismic shift came in the first quarter of the fourth century. A man now known as Constantine the Great fought against Emperor Maxentius under the banner of the cross of Jesus the Christ.[4] His interest in the Jesus-movement probably came from his mother Helena, who had adopted the message proclaimed by the followers of Jesus. After Constantine's victory over Maxentius on October 28, 312 CE, Constantine came to faith in Jesus as the Christ. The next year he issued the Edict of Milan, which officially recognized the "Christian" religion as acceptable within the Empire. Persecution of Christians under his predecessor, Diocletian, ceased immediately. Buildings were erected in honor of Jesus. Sacred sites in Palestine were discovered and monuments built in honor of the founder of the religion, forever after called "Christianity." The Church of the Holy Sepulchre in Jerusalem remains to this day as a lasting symbol of the efforts of Emperor Constantine to establish Christianity in its native homeland.

Following the conversion of Constantine the designations "Christian" and "Christianity" took on positive connotations, and became part of the *self-definition* of the Jesus-movement. Doctrine was hammered out in an effort to unite the Christian Church. Heretics were detected and excluded from the ranks of orthodoxy— conformity to the established rule of faith. Official councillor documents were issued for the purpose of bringing all members of the one Christian Church together in one mind. The first Council of Nicea of 325 CE is a classic example of the move to make the Christian Church catholic. At issue especially was the nature of Jesus as the Christ, the Son of God. The Nicean Creed was the first of several that attempted to spell out the doctrine of the divine nature of Jesus. Once the statement of faith was settled by a council of bishops it became church law by which to include converts and exclude heretics. Here is one part of the Nicean Creed with respect to the nature of Jesus:

> We believe in one Lord, Jesus Christ,
> the only son of God,
> eternally begotten of the Father,
> God from God, Light from Light,
> true God from true God,
> begotten, not made,
> of one being with the Father.
> Through him all things were made.
> For us and for our salvation
> he came down from heaven:

---

4. Eusebius, *Constantine*, 37-41.

Part 1: Groundwork

> by the power of the Holy Spirit
> he became incarnate from the Virgin Mary,
> and was made man.

With creedal statements such as this in mind, Christians henceforth have found it easy to say "Jesus is God," and from that position take the next logical step: Mary is the mother of God. What confessing Christians should realize is that the propositions in a creed are *statements of faith*, not verifiable facts of history. Someone asked me recently: "When did Jesus know he was God?" To which I could only reply: "He didn't say." What believers in Jesus confess about Jesus in creeds coming out of the established church of the post-Constantine era should not pre-determine the method and results of historical inquiry into Jesus of Nazareth during the first thirty years of the Common Era.

Creed and canon together have the effect of setting the bounds of a religion. Nowhere is that more true than in the Christianity of the fourth century. In the year 367 CE, bishop Athanasius of Alexandria, who had also served on the first Council of Nicea, wrote an Easter letter in which he listed twenty-seven documents that could be read in churches for public worship and instruction. He called the list a *kanōn*, a Greek word meaning "rule." Only the twenty-seven on the list, from among many others in circulation in the churches, could be used as the authoritative rule of faith and life in the churches. The same twenty-seven then became the Christian New Testament scripture throughout the world to this day.

By the end of the fourth century Christianity had quickly become the ascendant religion over Judaism. Whatever forces the church faced thereafter, nothing could stop its forward march in making history for good or ill. From the militant Crusades of the Middle Ages to the Reformation and Counter Reformation of the sixteenth and seventeenth centuries, to the modern evangelical movement(s), to Vatican Council II, all of them owe much of their life of faith to people and events of the fourth century when Constantine, councils, creeds and canon set Christianity on a power track that marks much of its belief and practice in the present time. With all the history and tradition of Christianity embedded in western culture as deeply as it is, one has to exercise a concerted effort to keep the tenets and predispositions of Christianity from short-circuiting the project of rediscovering Jesus and Paul *before Christianity*.

THE PRESENT SHAPE OF CHRISTENDOM

The world religions of Judaism and Christianity have not only survived their respective ordeals throughout their long history, but are also now speaking to each other through their representatives. Still, the long history of animosity between members of the two religions has some distance to go before the chasm that has separated them for so long is bridged securely.

As Christians came to occupy center stage in western civilization in the post-Constantine world, the Jewish people increasingly felt the sting of anti-Jewish sentiment, which came to a ferocious head during Adolf Hitler's Nazi purge of undesirables from

Before Christianity

the "superior" Aryan race. Hitler's hatred for the Jewish people stemmed as much from Christian sources as from any other. For example, he had watched the Passion play at Oberammergau in Bavaria in 1930 and 1934 and concluded in 1942 that . . .

> it is vital that the Passion play be continued at Oberammergau; for never has the menace of Jewry been so convincingly portrayed as in this presentation of what happened in the time of the Romans. There one sees Pontius Pilate, a Roman racially and intellectually so superior, that he stands out like a firm, clean rock in the middle of the whole muck and mire of Jewry.[5]

The play, based on a selection of passion narratives from the gospels of the New Testament, portrays Pilate as a kind of hero figure who wanted to save Jesus from crucifixion. Instead of portraying him as the callous, cruel Roman procurator that he was at the time of Jesus' death, later followers of Jesus tried to make him into something of a "Christian," and the Jewish people all into "Jesus killers." The death camps of the Nazi regime are a grim testimony to the rancor of anti-Semitism so egregiously active through the twentieth century and even into the twenty-first. One would like to think that Christians have overcome their insidious hostility towards the Jewish people. To the extent that anti-Judaism remains part of Christian consciousness, to that extent it inhibits the quest for the historical figures of Jesus and Paul, both of whom were Jewish until their death.

Christianity itself has had a rather chequered history, the remains of which are odiously evident in the present post-Reformation, post-modern industrial world. The bitter name-calling between some Christian groups, or a quiet indifference among others, in no way helps the enterprise of rediscovering Jesus and Paul in their time and place. Nothing worthwhile is gained by parochialism or sectarianism: our group is right and the others are not. Much is achieved by cooperation. Labelling one group liberal and another conservative, one group Catholic and another Protestant, one group evangelical and the other traditional, serves no one well in the pursuit of knowing the life and thought of the two principal figures behind the sacred texts common to all Christians.

Images of Jesus are manifold today. It borders on the absurd to ask, as many do today when faced with a critical situation, "What would Jesus do?" Answers flowing from a stream of consciousness scarcely meet the challenge. How much better it would be to ask rather, what *did* Jesus do and say in his time. From an understanding of the answer to that question one can begin to imagine what Jesus' vision would look like in present-day situations. Jesus and Paul lived and worked and spoke within a particular context before Christianity entered the world-stage. Disinterest, or minimal interest, in their historic life and world renders the repetition of their names in the present time of little consequence. It would be better not to use their names at all than to utter them inauthentically.

There is as well in contemporary Christendom an element of individualist existentialism: a kind of personal, interior experience of Jesus and/or Paul. Albert

---

5. In Crossan and Reed, *Excavating*, 229.

Part 1: Groundwork

Schweitzer's conclusion to his classic book about the old quest of the historical Jesus of the nineteenth century signals well the beginning of a trend that has continued through the twentieth century and into the present time:

> [Jesus] comes to us as One unknown, without a name, as of old, by the lake-side, He came to those men who knew Him not. He speaks to us the same word: "Follow thou me!" and sets us to the tasks which He has to fulfill for our time. He commands. And to those who obey Him, whether they be wise or simple, He will reveal Himself in the toils, the conflicts, the sufferings which they shall pass through in His fellowship, and, as an ineffable mystery, they shall learn in their own experience Who He is.[6]

Many modern gospel songs echo the same sentiment. Jesus lives in the present time in the hearts of people of faith. And this experiential Jesus is said to be the Jesus of Paul's life and gospel as well. For example, here is a line from a hymn written in 1933: "He walks with me and talks with me along life's narrow way."

For many sincere Christian people today, the Jesus of this hymn and of Schweitzer's concluding statement is "the real Jesus." Any attempt to recover Jesus of history behind the rather thick veil of Christianity, including also the thinner veil of the Gospels, is an unnecessary and even futile undertaking. At the same time, personal inner faith is not to be discounted. Faith properly informed by honest historical inquiry can weather many a storm. Uninformed faith, on the other hand, is shaky at best, and vulnerable at worst. Thus the invitation is here put forward to join in the rediscovery of who Jesus was: what he thought and said and did in his time and place and world before the later creedal architects had drawn their blueprints for how "Christians" should think world-wide for ever.

---

6. Schweitzer, *Quest*, 403.

3

Beyond the Jesus-Paul Debate

A COMPREHENSIVE SURVEY OF THE JESUS-PAUL DEBATE THAT STARTED IN THE middle of the nineteenth century and continued into the twenty-first would go beyond the purpose and scope of this book. At the same time, something should be stated about the nature of the debate,[1] at least, before we can get beyond it to something more productive.

THE NATURE OF THE DEBATE

The debate about Paul's relationship to Jesus can be summed up in to two words: *continuity* versus *discontinuity*. Prompted by the paucity of historical Jesus material in Paul's letters, the debate is not likely to subside completely.

Professor F. C. Baur of Tübingen University first raised the notion that Paul espoused and acted out a Christocentric theology independent of the Jerusalem apostles, and therefore independent of the Jesus-tradition handed down by them. That position put into sharp focus the idea that Paul minted new terminology and ideology commensurate with his call to gather people of the nations into community under the name of the risen Christ. Paul was not a disciple of the earthly Jesus, but claimed the status of "apostle" of the resurrected Jesus Messiah who had revealed himself to Paul (Gal. 1:16).

The meeting(s) Paul had with the Jerusalem apostles, Peter in particular, were not to gain instruction in the ways and words of the historical Jesus, but rather to have the Jerusalem apostles recognize his status as an apostle of the Christ whom God raised from the dead (Gal. 1:18; 2:1-10). Paul did not need anything more than the crucifixion and resurrection-vindication of Jesus to win converts from the nations to faith and gather them into community.

Of course, not all agreed with Baur's sharp distinction between Paul's mission and the mission of the apostle Peter, former disciple of the historical Jesus. At the turn of the twentieth century Adolf von Harnack, for example, pushed for the continuity

---

1. See Furnish, "Jesus-Paul," 342-81.

Part 1: Groundwork

of Paul's message and mission with that of Jesus. Paul was "Christ's disciple," said von Harnack, "who understood the Master and continued his work . . . It was Paul who delivered the Christian religion from Judaism."[2] Here in plain view is the misguided notion that Paul founded "the Christian religion" in opposition to the religion of Judaism. In these words we see a blatant retrojection of von Harnack's Christian thought, and with that also anachronistic terminology foisted onto the thought and mission of Paul. The "Christian religion" was not yet a reality, nor did Paul, by his own testimony, wish to separate himself, or his new communities of believers in Jesus as Messiah, from Judaism (Rom. 9:1–5; 11:24–26).

For every argument for the *continuity* side of the debate, counterarguments rose up in defense of *discontinuity*. Paul Wernle went so far as to coin the slogan, "back from Paul to Jesus." The thought was that Paul had abandoned, or ignored, the piety and moral teaching of Jesus evident in the gospels. This situation, so it was said, arose out of Paul's doctrine of justification by faith alone. "Whoever examines St. Paul's doctrine of justification," said Wernle, "is bound to reckon it one of his most disastrous creations."[3]

Notably, this sharp dichotomy between the vision and message of Paul and that of Jesus is not peculiar to scholars of the turn of the twentieth century. At the turn of the twenty-first century I have heard non-scholarly Christians openly express their displeasure with Paul in his letters, and their delight with Jesus in the gospels. One wonders how some words of Jesus in the Gospel of John, for example, are more delightful than the words of Paul. Of "the Jews" the Johannine Jesus says, "You are from your father the devil, and you choose to do your father's desires" (John 8:44). In whose ears would that statement sound a note of delight or pleasure? Certainly not among Jewish people. Or who would feel inner delight to hear these words applied to them: "You are like whitewashed tombs, which on the outside look beautiful, but inside they are full of the bones of the dead and of all kinds of filth"? (Matt. 23:27). Even against his most bitter opponents Paul scarcely reaches this level of vitriol attributed to Jesus in Matthew. Even so, some readers of the two bodies of New Testament literature in the present time sense discontinuity, or dissonance, between Paul in his letters and Jesus in the four gospels.

Back and forth the momentum of the debate has moved between *continuity* and *discontinuity*. A man named Richard Drescher countered the radical discontinuity set forth by Wernle and others. Drescher believed Paul had Jesus on his side in his battle to reinterpret the Law in keeping with Paul's mission to the nations. Jesus did the same in his time, so Drescher thought. And sure enough a non-critical reading of Mark 7:19 could support that view: Jesus "declared all foods clean." If this declaration in Mark 7 came straight from the belief and practice of the historical Jesus, and not from the narrator in Mark, then indeed Jesus could be seen as one who challenged the food Law along the same lines as Paul (1 Cor. 8:1–6; 10:25–30). But Mark was written years after

---

2. Von Harnack, *Christianity?* 176.
3. Wernle, *Christianity*, 255

Beyond the Jesus-Paul Debate

Paul's mission had taken hold, and so encodes that experience in his narrative about Jesus declaring all foods clean.

One of the most radical proponents of the *discontinuity* between Paul and Jesus came from Wilhelm Wrede in 1905. Paul was not a disciple of Jesus in any historical sense. An "enormous gulf" existed between the two figures. Paul's faith was anchored not in the life and teaching of Jesus of history but in a divine Christ in a celestial realm. A number of people found Wrede's argument quite compelling, while others found the insight wanting in evidence. But Wrede's proposal gave rise to the question that circulates to this day: Who founded Christianity? Jesus or Paul?

Arnold Meyer asked that question in 1907 with good reason. What evolved into the world religion called Christianity owes a great deal to the world vision of Paul. Yet he himself did not hold out much hope for a long history of the world, much less the conversion of Emperor Constantine and the creation of an institutional religion completely separate from historic Israel represented in Judaism. "The present form of this world is passing away," writes Paul (1 Cor. 7:31). Not much sign of a powerful this-world religion in that statement. But in the relatively short time he had to spread the word about Jesus Messiah crucified and resurrected, Paul managed to break through barriers that had separated the Jewish people from non-Jewish people of the world for centuries.[4]

Johannes Weiss in 1909 tried to bridge the gap between the two figures of Jesus and Paul, and thus also between scholars engaged in the debate. His observation was simple. The only significant difference between Jesus and Paul was in their eschatological outlook. For Paul the resurrection experience signaled the beginning of the end. Final salvation was drawing near, and along with salvation also judgment. Jesus had no such experience, at least not in the same way, and could not therefore preach such a gospel. The two historical figures lived in two time zones, as it were. For the historical Paul the fullness of time had come (Gal. 4:4). For the historical Jesus it had yet to come.

Rudolf Bultmann was a student of Weiss, and followed his lead in some measure. Bultmann asked three probing questions: 1) How far was Paul directly or indirectly dependent on Jesus of history? 2) How was Paul's theology related to the teaching and preaching of Jesus? 3) What significance did the fact of the historical Jesus have for Paul? The third question was key for Bultmann. He distinguished between the "what" of Jesus and the "that" of Jesus for Paul. *What* Jesus said and did during his ministry was of little consequence for Paul's preaching of the gospel among the nations. In Bultmann's words, the teaching of Jesus was "irrelevant for Paul."[5] *That* Jesus lived and died by crucifixion was at the heart of Paul's preaching. The resurrection was the redemptive sequel to crucifixion that completed the gospel for the world. Paul needed nothing more, as evidenced in his letters.

---

4. Dix describes the cultural differences, *Jew and Greek*.
5. Bultmann, "Significance," 223.

Part 1: Groundwork

Second Corinthians 5:16 became critical for Bultmann's view: "From now on, therefore, we know no one according to the flesh; even though we once knew Christ according to the flesh, we know him no longer in that way."[6] Bultmann took this to mean that Paul had no interest in knowing the historical Jesus, "Christ according to the flesh." But other scholars, J. L. Martyn especially, pointed out that the phrase does not describe the historical Jesus, but *the way Paul knows*: no longer by ordinary human standards. Even so, Bultmann maintained the end result is the same. Paul did not need historical information about Jesus of Nazareth to make his preaching good news for the nations.

Numerous articles and monographs continued to come out in the post-Bultmann period, most of them in search of harmony between Paul and Jesus. Two eminent scholars will illustrate this harmonizing approach, C. H. Dodd and W. D. Davies. Both men argued that Paul and Jesus both adopted a new law, which Paul identifies in Galatians 6:2 as "the law of Christ." Dodd viewed Matthew's sermon on the mount as representative of "the law of the kingdom of God," with its roots in the historical Jesus and its expression in the early Christ-community. The "new law" can be summed up in the word "love" (*agapē*), which both Jesus and Paul preached and taught as the character of their common gospel.[7]

Davies criticized the Bultmannian view that the historical Jesus had no significance for Paul. On the contrary, said Davies, "the words and life of Jesus were normative for Paul"[8] after his experience of the resurrected Christ. "Paul is steeped in the mind and words of his Lord."[9] And thus ensued a search for parallels between the words of Jesus in the gospels and Paul's instructions to his churches in the letters. Davies found numerous ideas in the letters that he thought had some connection with Jesus' words in the gospels. And he was not alone in this quest. Dale Allison, for example, believed he could detect patterns of "sayings" in Paul's letters similar to those in the gospels.[10] Unlike direct citations of sayings, allusions and echoes are slippery "parallels" at the best of times.

Two problems arise out of these attempts at lining up sayings of Jesus with elements in Paul's letters, as though Paul were consciously drawing on a body of material related to Jesus. The first is that the gospel writers post-date Paul and his mission, so that the parallel ideas—if they really exist—could have run in the opposite direction. That is, the tradition that grew out of Paul's preaching was deep and influential in the mind of the developing Christ-communities. The gospels that arose out of those communities had Paul's thoughts already in circulation, which may in turn have entered the texture of the gospel stories about Jesus. The second problem with digging up parallels between the letters of Paul and the gospels is that

---

6. More literal than NRSV.
7. Dodd, *Gospel and Law*, 71.
8. Davies, *Paul*, 195.
9. Ibid., 140.
10. Allison, "Pauline Epistles," 1–32.

most of the "parallel" ideas, or sayings, could be found in many ethical schools of the day, both in Judaism and in Hellenism.

The literary, textual fact remains: very few authentic sayings from the Synoptic tradition appear in Paul's arguments in the letters (1 Cor. 7:19; 9:14; 11:23–25; possibly 1 Thess. 4:15). These most likely would have circulated piecemeal and orally in the pre-Pauline communities. Paul would have picked them up on his visits. But the few recognizable sayings he cites he does not attribute to Jesus of history, but to "the Lord," the same resurrected Lord who appeared to him. Even then he quickly sets aside the quoted saying in favor of his own conviction (e.g., 1 Cor. 9:14–15), or he adds his own judgment as equally authoritative (e.g., 1 Cor. 7:12, 25).

Concerning these identifiable references to the Synoptic tradition in Paul's letters, David Dungan wrote an insightful monograph. He concentrated on the two commands in First Corinthians 9:4–18 and 7:10–11. From these two examples Dungan concluded that Paul depended on the sayings material only allusively and indirectly, but used the material for the regulation of church life. Given these two cases of using command-sayings from the tradition, Dungan was convinced that Paul was totally allied with the primitive Jesus-community that transmitted the synoptic materials:

> The alleged contrast between Pauline Christianity and that branch of the early Church which preserved the Palestinian Jesus-tradition that finally ended up in the Synoptic gospels is a figment of the imagination. In fact, they are one and the same branch.[11]

Rather than prolong the exploration from one side to the other, suffice it to say that the debate has persisted to the present time. In 2004 A. J. M. Wedderburn published a collection of essays that highlight the nature of the debate. Wedderburn himself wrote two of the essays in an effort to trace a variety of connections between Paul and Jesus.[12] For Wedderburn, "the question of . . . links and of continuity between the two men is nevertheless a necessary one that cannot and should not be avoided."[13] What is puzzling about this statement is the fact that the debate over continuity or discontinuity between the two figures has run for more than 150 years with no more final resolution at the end than at the beginning, as evidenced in the multi-authored volume of 2007, edited by Todd Still under the title, *Jesus and Paul Reconnected*. To my mind, the two figures are no more "reconnected" in this volume than they have been in the myriad books and articles that preceded this one. It seems to me, rather, that this, or any other collection of disparate essays related to Jesus and/or Paul, lacks the persuasive steam to propel the question to its final destination, if such exists. Perhaps the question needs to be framed differently.

It is time, surely, to move beyond the debate to a frank and open identification of the two figures in their time and place and mission without polarizing them, on the one hand, or forcing a fusion between them on the other.

---

11. Dungan, *Sayings*, 150.
12. Wedderburn, *Paul and Jesus*, 117–18.
13. Ibid., 118.

Part 1: Groundwork

BEYOND DEBATE: LOCATING JESUS AND PAUL IN THEIR RESPECTIVE PLACES

In November 1993 Victor Paul Furnish delivered the presidential address at the Society of Biblical Literature on the topic, "On Putting Paul in His Place."[14] Furnish made the point that churchly people who followed Paul put him in a place that would serve the later church on its way through at least sixteen hundred years of self-definition. In the modern period historical critical scholars have sought to put Paul in his historical place by reconstructing a place for him, and calling him the historical Paul. This latter effort Furnish considered equally inadequate. One wonders what other approach there could be that would not be reconstruction. The test in the end is whether the reconstruction meets the challenge of authenticity. *Is it true to the available evidence?*

The same could be said of Jesus of Nazareth. The later churchly officers who came after Jesus put him in his place in accordance with their confessions of faith and ecclesiastical structures. And as with Paul so with Jesus, modern biblical scholars have aimed at putting Jesus in his historical place using the canons of the historical-critical method. The result is reconstruction of the figure of Jesus. Again, the issue is whether the reconstruction efforts are "honest to Jesus," to use the title of Robert Funk's book.[15] The results discussed in the remainder of this book are subject to the same test: *Do they reflect an honest reading of the relevant evidence available?*

A major challenge in locating the two figures of Jesus and Paul in their respective places will be to do so without prejudice and beyond debate. However difficult it will be to refrain from seeing the two somehow together, connected in some ideological, theological, canonical, or religious way, we must refrain. Connection seems so obviously right, and disconnection so clearly wrong. The aim should be, rather, to allow each of the figures to be who they were where they were, doing and saying what they were driven to say and do in the situation and experience that informed their vision and action. Let Jesus be the figure he was in Galilee and Jerusalem, and Paul the figure he was elsewhere in the world. History, by its very nature, cannot be seamless any more than it can be an incongruous heap of disparate events and unrelated people. Human beings intend something beyond the present, and seek to achieve something that did not exist previously. Jesus and Paul were two historical figures, each with his own experience and aims, each one making another piece of historical tapestry.

Once the two figures are genuinely located in their history-making places, then a comparison can be made. There will be differences between them, just as there will be similarities. If that were not so, then neither of them would be the respective history-maker that he was. The question that seems to have troubled Christian scholars throughout the debate concerns Paul's relation to Jesus. If Paul went out on his own, crafting a gospel commensurate with his own aims, with little or no forthright attempt to relate to the ministry of Jesus of history, then perhaps he was indeed the real founder of the world religion, Christianity. That possibility does not sit well with

---

14. Furnish, "On Putting Paul in His Place," 3–17.
15. Funk, *Honest to Jesus*.

Beyond the Jesus-Paul Debate

many people of Christian persuasion. Frankly, I believe it would not sit well with the Apostle Paul either, for different reasons. The discussions in Part III will explain why the latter would be so.

The question at the end of the day is not, Who founded Christianity? At the close of his long article on the Jesus-Paul debate, Furnish pointed a way forward, one that could take us out of debate mode into a more acceptable way of thinking about the historical movement from one frame of reference to another. Here is his comment:

> In the future scholars must concentrate not on what or how Paul knew about the historical Jesus, but rather on the way he employed and applied the knowledge he did have, and what place the Jesus of history had in relation to the heart and center of his preaching.[16]

Implicit in this otherwise helpful pointer forward is the notion that Paul had a body of knowledge about the earthly figure of Jesus in his time, and that he tied that historical knowledge into the heart of his preaching. I think this assumes more than the textual evidence will sustain. Paul used two or three short sayings that can be traced to the Synoptic tradition about Jesus. How many of these sayings Paul knew cannot be proven. If he did know many more sayings he did not use them in support of his arguments, or as content for his gospel. But Paul knew the radical, self-giving *character* of Jesus "who died for our sins in accordance with the scriptures" (1 Cor. 15:3), a character that God honored and vindicated. The vindicated Jesus constituted God's Messiah for Paul, Messiah who would deliver the faithful "when God's righteous judgment will be revealed" (Rom. 2:5). Jesus was radical in his vision of God's rule; so also was Paul, as Crossan and Borg discovered in their investigation of the undisputed letters of Paul. The subtitle of their book is striking: "Reclaiming the Radical Visionary Behind the Church's Conservative Icon."[17]

Moreover, the project articulated in Furnish's conclusion to his article is not exactly the goal of this study. The issue here is not so much about how Paul used material from the historical ministry of Jesus in his preaching among the nations, but about the social, historical, geographical, religious, and theological space each of the two figures occupied, and how that space shaped their thinking and impelled their respective missions. This approach, I submit, can become an exodus from endless debate into fruitful conversation.

With that in mind, the next two major parts of the book are dedicated to the two major figures of New Testament literature and history: Jesus (Part II) and Paul (Part III).

---

16. Furnish, "Jesus-Paul," in Wedderburn, *Jesus and Paul*, 50.
17. Borg and Crossan, *First Paul*, iii.

Palestine at the time of Jesus

Part II
Jesus

". . . something more than Solomon is here!"

(Q 11:31 = Matt. 12:42)

4

Where to Look for Jesus

GREAT FIGURES OF HISTORY USUALLY LEAVE BEHIND A LEGACY OF LITERATURE, or other art forms, from which to glean their thoughts, aspirations, and actions. Their works are cited in speeches, essays, and books. Shakespeare is lauded because of his plays and poems. Luther is remembered and studied by virtue of the shelf-full of theological treatises he left behind. The same is true for Aquinas, Augustine, Plato, Aristotle, and a host of others. These all wrote their thoughts for successive generations to ponder and debate. Not so with Jesus. He did not *write* a single word that has survived.

WISHFUL THINKING

Imagine how different our understanding of Jesus would be had he kept a journal of his daily life over a period of twenty years, and bequeathed the journal to his inner circle of friends to pass down to their friends, and ultimately down to us. What a treasure that would be!

I would rejoice even to have a few sermons Jesus wrote out in preparation for preaching them. Later preachers, said to follow in the footsteps of Jesus, have written their sermons out in full, and filed them away for future reference. Some have even published their sermons. Then other preachers quote from the written text, assured that they are quoting the very words of the earlier preacher. But not so with the homilies of Jesus. By all accounts Jesus did not write his ideas and visions, or keep a journal, much as we wish he had.

Even a few letters that Jesus might have written to family or friends would be a treasure. From his letters we could connect directly with his emotions, his plans and his conflicts. None of this we have directly from the mind and hand of Jesus.

Nor did the disciples carry note pads (much less iPads!) with them on their travels with Jesus. Had they taken notes on the spot about the places, and events, and persons, and sayings of Jesus, and passed them on to their successors unchanged, we could come very close to the personality of Jesus in his time and place. But even this

Part II: Jesus

much from the disciples is wishful thinking. Unlike our text-based society, the society in which Jesus and his disciples lived was oral-based and communal. The people remembered the stories in their communal life, and passed them on in oral form for generations. Jewish rabbis of the time are fine examples of this mind-set. A Jewish rabbi would gather willing listeners around him, and teach the Law by *spoken word and personal example*, not from textbooks or written lecture notes. Much as the rabbis taught the Law, Jesus taught "the rule of God" to his disciples. Some gospel narratives even refer to him as "rabbi," a term reminiscent of an educated Pharisee (e.g., Mark 9:5; 11:21; John 1:49; 3:2, 26; 4:31; 6:25; 9:2; 11:8).

Nevertheless, we do have sources from which to recover a credible image of the historical figure of Jesus. To them we now turn our attention.

RELEVANT LITERARY SOURCES

The earliest surviving documents of the primitive Jesus-community come from a man who did not know Jesus in the flesh. He believed in Jesus, of course, having heard about him from the preaching of others. The man in question is the Apostle Paul, and the documents are his personal letters to congregations he called into being in the name of Jesus Messiah. These letters come from the decade of the fifties CE, but information in them about the historical life and ministry of Jesus in Galilee and Judea two to three decades earlier is limited to these few facts: that Jesus had a human birth (Gal 4:4); that he was Jewish (Gal 4:4); that he was betrayed at night (1 Cor. 11:23); that he instituted a Eucharistic meal of bread and wine (1 Cor. 11:23–25); that he said (1) preachers of the gospel should be paid (1 Cor. 9:14), and (2) a wife and husband should not divorce (1 Cor. 7:10 11); and that he was crucified by (unidentified) earthly rulers (1 Cor. 2:8). These few facts, while important, are devoid of narrative context. They are, instead, woven into the arguments of Paul's letters. However much Paul may have learned about the earthly Jesus from the Apostles during his two visits to Jerusalem (Gal 1:18; 2:1), he left the pre-Easter ministry of Jesus very much out of sight in his letters to his congregations. His motivation for doing so is not revealed in his correspondence. One can only guess that such narrative material from Jesus would have been secondhand to Paul, proving only that he was dependent on the Apostles who had been with Jesus. When Paul does cite the three sayings from the tradition of Jesus, he refers to them as coming from "the Lord" (1 Cor. 7:10; 9:14; 11:23).

Gospels

While gospels are the main sources of information about Jesus, even they fall under the category of "according to." They are not gospels *by* Jesus, but gospels *about* Jesus, according to persons other than Jesus, persons writing many years after Jesus' life in Roman-occupied Palestine. Four of these gospels are canonical: they were deemed worthy of inclusion in the body of New Testament literature adopted by the later church. All of them are anonymous. The familiar title-names were added some time after their composition.

Where to Look for Jesus

Many other "gospels" have survived, and are valuable in their own right for understanding Jesus. Notable among these other gospels are the sayings gospels of *Thomas* and of *Mary*, the fragmentary *Gospel of Peter*, and the Jewish-oriented gospels of the *Hebrews* and of the *Nazoreans*.[1] All of these appear to be later accretions of the canonical gospels.

While these extra-canonical gospels contain material traceable to the tradition of Jesus, the four *narrative* gospels of the New Testament constitute the principal sources of information and insight pertaining to Jesus. Yet these four, Matthew, Mark, Luke, and John, do not paint the same narrative picture of the pre-Easter Jesus. The Gospel of John is unabashedly evangelistic and theological by its own testimony: "these [signs] are written so that you may come *to believe* that Jesus is the Messiah, the Son of God, and that through *believing* you may have life in his name" (John 20:30–31). This Fourth Gospel was written primarily to promote and strengthen faith among members in a community living in the last decade of the first century, at least sixty years after the death of Jesus. Yet the Fourth Gospel has pieces of historical information textured into the theological discourses characteristic of this gospel. For example, the day of the crucifixion of Jesus in John — the day before the special Passover Sabbath (John 19:14, 31)—could be more probable than "the day before the [weekly] Sabbath" implied in the other three gospels (Mark 15:42). Whether the day before the Passover Sabbath or the weekly Sabbath, one would expect the Jewish authorities of Jerusalem to have better things to do than call a trial leading to an execution on such a special day of Preparation.

The first three narrative gospels in the New Testament, called *synoptic* because they share material in common, present images of Jesus in Galilee and Judea that are less interwoven with post-Easter theology than the narratives in John. For this reason, among others, the synoptic gospels are primary sources in the search for Jesus of history.

At many points in the three synoptic narratives the wording is identical. Because of this peculiar overlap between Matthew, Mark, and Luke, scholars are convinced that the three evangelists used sources independently of each other to create their respective narratives about the ministry of Jesus. Mark was almost certainly written first, perhaps in the late sixties or early seventies, and Matthew and Luke some years later, after Mark had been in circulation among the primitive communities of believers in Jesus.

Both Matthew and Luke used Mark's narrative structure, and much of Mark's text, as the base for their respective gospels. Matthew contains about ninety per cent of Mark; Luke not nearly as much.

But Matthew and Luke have material in common not found in Mark. Most of this common text consists of *sayings*. For example, Matthew's "Sermon on the Mount" (chapters 5–7) and Luke's "Sermon on the Plain" (chapter 6) are made up of sayings that these two gospels hold in common. Yet the sayings are not in the same order or

---

1. See Miller, *Complete Gospels*; and Cameron, *Other Gospels*.

Part II: Jesus

context in each gospel. Thus it appears that their common source consisted of sayings with little or no narrative context. This sayings source embedded in Matthew and Luke is identified simply as Q. A German scholar made the identification, and called the source document simply *Quelle*, "source." Hence the letter Q for ever after.[2]

A mammoth amount of scholarly work has gone into the identification of the original Q,[3] which is said to be earlier than Mark. Its place of origin cannot be established with certainty. It may have originated in Galilee among a group of people who maintained the tradition of Jesus in that area. Matthew's narratives, in which Q is embedded, manifest close ties with a Galilean context. James Robinson credits the author of Matthew with preserving the very early, and very valuable "Sayings Gospel Q" from which we learn so much about the thought and ministry of Jesus. Robinson's recent book, *Jesus: According to the Earliest Witness,* pays high tribute to Q.[4] It is now common practice to cite a saying in Q by using the reference numbering in Luke. For example, the Lord's Prayer is cited as Q 11:2–4, which is found redacted in Luke 11:2–4.

Painstaking scholarly labor has gone into determining the most primitive form of the sayings in Q, all in the cause of hearing more clearly the voice of Jesus in his time and situation. By calling Q a Say*ings* Gospel, as a number of scholars do, the implication is that Q never did have a passion-resurrection narrative in the manner of the four canonical gospels. Yet the community that preserved the collection of sayings of Jesus must have sensed the ongoing presence of his spirit among them as they meditated on his promising and provocative words.

In addition to Q-material embedded in Matthew and Luke, each of these two gospels contains Jesus-material peculiar to itself. Not knowing the origin of the distinctive material, scholars have simply assigned it respectively "M" (Matthew) and "L" (Luke). The Gospel of Luke has a large body of "L" material gathered together in the middle, chapters 10–18. The well-known parables of the Good Samaritan (Luke 10:30–37) and the Prodigal Son (Luke 15:11–32) belong to the special Lukan material, while the parable of the Laborers in the Vineyard is special Matthew (Matt 20:1–15). It should be noted also that each of the two birth-and-infancy narratives about Jesus in Matthew and Luke is distinctive to the respective gospel. For example, Luke accents lowly shepherds and a stable, while Matthew accents regal wise men (magi) and a house. The tendency of later Christian churches to harmonize these two introductory narratives detracts from the metaphoric power of each of them.

The narrative gospels, one would think, would be highly valuable in the effort to recover the historical context of Jesus. And they are. But those sources are "gospels," not histories, and not biographies. Written in post-Easter contexts to strengthen communities of faith in challenging situations in the Roman world, the narrative gospels bring the crucified-resurrected Jesus to meaningful expression in the new setting. The

---

2. Citations of Q Sayings hereafter are taken from Robinson, *Sayings Gospel Q in English.*
3. Two notable Q scholars are Kloppenborg, *Formation of Q*; and Robinson, *Collected Essays.*
4. A collection of essays written over two decades, Robinson, *Jesus,* 1–201.

respective aims of their authors were not identical with the aims of Jesus[5] so many years earlier in another place. Gospels primarily are timely tracts in memory of Jesus for people in need of encouragement and hope. The Gospel of Mark, for example, devotes more than one-third of its text to the last week of Jesus' life. By narrating the trial and death of Jesus as it does, Mark holds out hope of God's deliverance for people in tough circumstances.

All of this to say that while the gospels provide the principal sources for recovering Jesus in his time and place among the people of Galilee and Judea, the material pertinent to Jesus is lodged within a gospel-word for another generation in another time and place. Moreover, gospel texts call for critical analysis in keeping with their respective aims. This is not to denigrate the gospels. On the contrary, it simply recognizes the nature of gospel literature as "good news" on target for audiences in need of sustaining grace in the name and memory of Jesus. Thus the gospels carry two levels of blended history: that of Jesus in the last few years of his life, and that of the communities of faith in Jesus at another time and situation. Where the interest is in the first level, the task is one of sorting out the first from the last.

All of the gospels appear to have been written originally in Greek. Majority opinion is that Jesus spoke Aramaic, the language native to Jewish Palestine. He may have learned Greek from interaction with the non-Jewish population in Galilee, but his language among his Jewish disciples, and with other Jewish compatriots, would almost certainly have been Aramaic. While this language difference from Jesus to the gospels is not a major obstacle, it does raise a question: To what extent does the translation of Jesus' language into another language-culture conceal his Aramaic-based thought pattern? In the mid-twentieth century Joachim Jeremias, among others, wrestled with this issue, to the point of re-translating some of the Greek words in the synoptic gospels back into Aramaic.[6] For example, the word of address in the Lord's Prayer in Aramaic is deemed to have been "*Abba*." Would "*Abba*" carry the same emotive quality as the Greek, *Patēr hēmōn*, "Our Father"?

Tanakh and Mishnah

The canonical gospels often quote from the Scriptures of the Jewish people, and cite Jesus as quoting from them. But the quotations in the gospels are from a Greek translation of the Hebrew Scriptures called the Septuagint (LXX). This translation was carried out in Alexandria in Egypt about two hundred years before Jesus, and was used by Jewish communities living outside Palestine. In the Temple and the synagogues within Palestine, however, Jewish leaders would have used the Hebrew text of the Jewish Scriptures. The Hebrew term, *Tanakh*, is a three-consonant acronym (T-N-K) for the three divisions of the Jewish Scriptures: 1. Torah, "instruction," consisting of the five books attributed to Moses; 2. Nevi'im, consisting of the "prophets," including also the narrative books in which prophets such as Elijah and Elisha are found; 3. Ketuvim,

---

5. See Meyer, *Aims*, 1–315.
6. E.g., Jeremias, *Eucharistic Words*, 62–66, 184.

Part II: Jesus

consisting of the "writings," psalms and the wisdom literature. The Hebrew *Tanakh* would have been the Scriptures Jesus heard in his youth and then used in his ministry. His Galilean disciples likewise would have viewed the *Tanakh* as the Scriptures of their faith and life, not the Greek translation used by the Evangelists.

Any search for Jesus that does not take the *Tanakh* into account misses the mark. The Hebrew Scriptures shaped Jesus' religious thought and life in the first three decades of the first century. From hearing them read/recited he shaped his vision of the "kingdom of God," a term of reference that distinguished the ministry of Jesus. More on that subject in chapter 6.

The *Mishnah*, meaning "review" or "study by repetition," implies "oral Torah" that needs to be recalled and reapplied to life. The teachers within Judaism developed the oral Torah during the Second Temple period (536 BCE–70 CE). With every new situation in every new generation the oral Torah was brought to bear and interpreted further as the need arose. With the fall of Jerusalem in 70 CE, and ongoing persecution of the Jewish people in the second century, Rabbi Judah, president of the rabbinic school in Palestine, felt compelled to commit the oral Torah of the Pharisees to written form and publish it in 200 CE. Moreover, the Mishnah *contains* beliefs and practices and debates dating back to first century Palestinian Judaism within which Jesus lived and worshipped; "contains" implies redaction. Rabbi Judah redacted the oral teaching, and arranged it into six orders as follows:

- *Zeraim* ("seeds") deals with prayers and blessings related variously to the rules of agriculture;
- *Moed* ("festival") discusses the rules of Sabbath and other Jewish festivals;
- *Nashim* ("women") deals with rules about marriage and divorce, and about taking oaths and committing to the nazarite vow;
- *Nezikin* ("damages") describes how the Jewish courts function in the execution of civil and criminal justice;
- *Kodashim* ("holy matters") focuses on sacrificial rituals, the Temple and dietary regulations;
- *Tohorot* ("purity") pertains to purity/impurity of the body and of food, and the impurity of the dead.

Each of the six orders is further divided into tractates and paragraphs for easy reference. Valuable as the Mishnah can be for recovering something of the religious and practical aspects of the Judaism of Jesus' time, it still needs to be read with a critical eye to the editorial embellishments that come with such an enterprise. What was said above for the gospels, holds also for the Mishnah.

As time went by, following the publication of the Mishnah in 200 CE, other rabbis made their contributions to the various tractates. The additional commentary is called Gemara ("study of tradition"). The resulting compilation is Talmud. Two Talmudic traditions came to the fore over the course of time, one from the Jewish scholars at

Babylonia, and the other from the rabbinic school in Palestine. The latter is usually referred to as the Jerusalem Talmud, even though it was not created in that city. Again, Talmudic commentary, whether Babylonian or Jerusalem, reflects some traditions of the first century, but these require careful scrutiny in reconstructing historical images from the first half of the first century.

Many other relevant Jewish sources are available, including some Aramaic Targums (commentaries on the Hebrew Scriptures written from the time of the Second Temple to the Middle Ages); the Dead Sea Scrolls written from *ca.* 165 BCE to 70 CE; the treatises of Philo of Alexandria, a Jewish scholar and contemporary of Jesus, among many others. Scholars have searched diligently through all the available sources of Judaism for beliefs and practices during the Second Temple period, and that by no more eminent scholar than E. P. Sanders. The result from his research, *Jewish Law from Jesus to the Mishnah*, and *Judaism: Practice and Belief, 63 BCE–66 CE*,[7] provides ready access to reliable insights into the religious and social life in which Jesus would have participated. Sanders has argued for a common pattern of religion among Jewish communities, both in Palestine and in the Hellenistic world. He called the pattern "covenantal nomism": belief in a covenant relationship initiated by God with the people of Israel, including the gift of the Law (*nomos*) to be obeyed, "while providing means of atonement for transgression."[8]

Yet Judaism of the first century CE was not undifferentiated altogether. Religion takes on a particular hue in relation to the environment in which it is practiced. First-century Judaism was no exception. Groups of Jewish people rallied around some features of their religion, while other groups were more relaxed about the same features. The Jewish covenanters at Qumran, for example, withdrew from the Temple rituals in Jerusalem believing them to be corrupt, along with the priests who performed them. Outside Palestine, Judaism flourished in a Hellenistic environment, and took on some of the characteristics of Greco-Roman culture, not least the Greek language and education. Philo of Alexandria in Egypt is a fine example.

A number of scholars find solid information about the religious matrix of first century Judaism in the New Testament itself.[9] The writers of the New Testament documents were most likely of Jewish heritage, and knew the commonality as well as the diversity that existed among the Jewish communities around the Mediterranean basin. The earliest Jesus movement was part of that Jewish diversity, which eventually opened the door to include people from other religions and cultures. The author of the book of Acts seems well aware of differences between Jewish groups who hold to the same basic view of covenantal nomism. Acts 6–7 describes a clash between two Jewish worldviews, one seemingly more liberal than the other. The narrative of Acts 7 ends with Jewish leaders in Jerusalem stoning a Hellenistic Jewish man, Stephen, because of his unconventional views of the Temple and the holy land on which the Temple stood.

---

7. Sanders, *Jewish Law*, 1–331; *Practice and Belief*, 1–595.
8. Sanders, *Paul and Palestinian Judaism*, 75, 422.
9. Chilton and Neusner, *Judaism*, 1–18; 129–159.

Part II: Jesus

Flavius Josephus

Josephus was born a few years after the death of Jesus (ca. 37–100 CE). A Palestinian Jewish man of noble birth and priestly stock, Josephus believed his religion to be consistent with Greek and Roman life and thought. When the Roman legions under general Titus invaded his land through Galilee to the north in response to the first Jewish revolt, Josephus and his Jewish resistance fighters held them off for as long as they could, but eventually had to surrender to the more powerful imperial forces.

Josephus is remembered, not for his Jewish resistance movement, but for his education and ability to write Jewish history. His two most notable and most quoted works are *The Jewish War* and *Antiquities of the Jews*. The *War* is the story of the first battle of the Jewish people against the Roman military prior to and after the fall of Jerusalem in 70 CE. The war broke out in 66 and continued after 70 until all the pockets of Jewish resistance were eradicated. The *Antiquities* is a history of Israel among the nations viewed through Jewish eyes. Both of these volumes were written during the last quarter of the first century.

Josephus does not narrate much about the life and ministry of Jesus. What he does say specifically appears at two places in the available manuscripts. But the manuscripts exhibit some later Christian additions to Josephus' own reporting: (1) "Now, there was about this time Jesus, a wise man, *if it be lawful to call him a man*, for he was a doer of wonderful works—a teacher of such men as receive the truth with pleasure. He drew over to him both many of the Jews, and many of the Gentiles. *He was [the] Christ.*[10] (2) [Ananus] assembled the Sanhedrin of judges, and brought before them the brother of Jesus, *who was called Christ*, whose name was James, and some others; and when he had formed an accusation against them as breakers of the law, he delivered them to be stoned."[11] I have identified the later "Christian" additions in italics. The likelihood that Josephus would declare Jesus to be the Messiah and more than human is scarcely tenable. He was a Jewish historian who made no claim to be a follower of Jesus, much less to confess him to be the Jewish Messiah.

The value of the writings of Josephus lies in his insights into the social and political contexts of Jewish life in Roman-occupied Palestine around the time of Jesus. He was a Jewish compatriot who understood the need to work out compromises with Rome for the sake of the survival of the Jewish people. Of course, he was not a critical historian of modern vintage; at points he exaggerates his description of events, including the inflation of numbers. Even so, his narration about events and people in Palestine together with his insights into his own religion and culture—which were also that of Jesus—make Josephus a worthy resource for the enterprise of recovering Jesus in his time and place.

---

10. *Ant.* 18.3.3.63;
11. *Ant.* 20.9.1.200

Geography

Jesus lived in a particular place in a particular time and situation. As with all places populated by human inhabitants, the place Jesus occupied for thirty years had a name and a politics associated with its topography. Geography identifies a people as much as language and culture does. Borderlines enable inhabitants to name a territory, and thus also to name themselves. A geographical boundary also enables outsiders to characterize (or caricature) the inhabitants of the territory by the name of the geography. In the Gospel of Matthew "Jesus the Galilean" is the label by which Jesus was known to a woman of Jerusalem in a conversation with one of his disciples (Matt. 26:69; cf. Luke 22:59). Similarly, the Jewish authorities of Jerusalem in the Gospel of John are convinced that "no prophet is to arise from Galilee" (John 7:52).

Self-identity is shaped very much by living within a particular geography, inasmuch as non-residents label a territory and its people positively or negatively. Politics enters into geography. Herod Antipas ruled Galilee, and sought to put his stamp on the place by building (or re-building) two Hellenistic cities on the landscape, Sepphoris and Tiberias. But Galilee had a sizable population of Jewish people, whose religious history and experience called upon them to honor the city of Jerusalem in Judea to the south, and especially the holy Temple that symbolized their relationship to the God of Israel. Thus, part of the self-identity of Jewish Galileans included their Judean heritage and the festivals orchestrated around the central symbol of the Temple. More on this topic in chapter 6.

That there was some tension between Jewish religionists in Galilee and those of Jerusalem seems likely. How serious the tension was is debatable. Professor Seán Freyne—whose research on Galilee during the Hasmonean and Herodian periods is second to none[12]—has argued persuasively that relations between the Jewish people of Galilee and Jerusalem at the time of Jesus were far from hostile.[13] People from both geographical locations aspired to the restoration of Israel in terms of the originating "tribal confederation of Israel."[14] They were thus of one mind about the heritage of the land that included both Galilee and Judea. Moreover, "a Jewish ethnic identity and hope . . . was shared by Galileans and Judeans alike."[15] Even so, the geo-political history of the Second Temple period tended to differentiate one group from the other. All of them came under the domination of Rome to be sure, but Jerusalem Judaism had become more tightly tied to the Roman system by Rome's appointment of the high priest of the Temple, and by the appointment of a Roman prefect to govern the affairs of Judea. The Galileans, for all their disaffection with the rule of Herod Antipas, could at least claim as their chief politician the son of Herod the Great who built the Temple in Jerusalem.

---

12. Freyne, *Galilee*, 3–380.
13. Freyne, "Restoration," 289–311.
14. Ibid., 292.
15. Ibid., 304.

Part II: Jesus

Political geography is a potent mix at any time, and nowhere more so than in the land of Palestine, to this day. If geography shapes human identity and vision, as history attests, then the geography of Galilee within of the Roman province of Palestine is a place to look for Jesus.

Archaeology

Archaeology is the stratigraphic study of cultural remains left by human habitation.[16] Hunters and gatherers leave little or no cultural remains, in that they are always on the move. Sedentary life, on the other hand, deposits artifacts of culture in one place or another within a geographical area. Most modern archaeological excavations are carried out on mounds, called tells or khirbets, in which lie buried materials from past inhabitants. Such excavation sites can be many feet deep, representing many layers of generations of human endeavor. What makes modern archaeology scientific is the stratigraphic method. Each layer of artifacts—potsherds, buttons, parts of walls, floors, lamps, etc.—is carefully removed, and the artifacts dated and labeled by comparative study. Eventually, the archaeologist offers an interpretation of the excavated layers of cultural remains.

Many of the villages of Galilee, along with two major cities of Tiberas and Sepphoris, have been excavated significantly. The results have shed light on the way of life of the different levels of Galilean society. The recent archaeological work of Jonathan Reed,[17] among others, in Lower Galilee has opened new windows onto the world of Jesus in that area in the first thirty years of the first century.

As one would expect, excavations in Jerusalem are ongoing and difficult. So many of the ancient ruins in that city lie beneath important structures that serve the current community. Yet much has been recovered, with illuminating results for understanding the character of the people who lived in the social structures of the city in the first century CE,[18] the city in which the earthly life of the Galilean Jesus came to a violent end.

An investigation of these fields together—relevant literary sources, geography and archaeology—helps yield a cumulative, viable image of the figure of Jesus in his time and place. However much we may mourn the lack of the written word from Jesus himself, the available evidence is sufficient for the challenge of knowing Jesus for who he was and what he did in Galilee and Jerusalem.

---

16. Lawrence Toombs' definition in a lecture in 1973.
17. Reed, *Galilean Jesus*, 1–220.
18. Hanson and Oakman, *Palestine*, 57–89; 123–45.

5

The Crux of the Matter

I BEGIN EXPLORING THE MISSION OF JESUS WHERE IT CAME TO AN END: AT his crucifixion. I do so not because the crucifixion of the man, Jesus, is the best attested of all the information about him, but because the crucifixion captures, paradoxically, the meaning of his ministry. Strange as that may seem, the bloody, awful, crucifixion of Jesus energized his followers, moving them to form a community in honor of his name, his vision, his word, and his work. They might have been expected to forget the man they followed in hope, and go back to their old lives. He had, after all, been found guilty of a crime, and was sentenced to a shameful death by the highest court in the land. What could possibly impel his followers to remember him, to talk about him, to trust in him? They did all of these, and that publicly.

Ben F. Meyer, reflecting on his study of the *Aims of Jesus*, summarizes his findings judiciously as follows:

> It is probable that [Jesus] conceived his death in sacrificial terms. It is probable that despite a powerful instinct of recoil he went willingly to his death. But what, in the end, made Jesus operate in this way, what energized his incorporating death into his mission, his facing it and going to meet it? . . . It is above all in the tradition generated by Jesus that we discover what made him operate in the way he did, what made him epitomize his life in the single act of going to his death: He "loved me and handed himself over for me" (Gal 2:20; cf. Eph 5:2); "having loved his own who were in the world, he loved them to the end" (John 13:1); he "freed us from our sins by his own blood" because "he loves us" (Rev 1:5). If authenticity lies in the coherence between word (Mark 12:28–43 par.) and deed (Gal 2:20; Eph 5:2; John 13:1; Rev 1:5), our question has found an answer.[1]

COHERENCE

Not all scholars take the position that Meyer lays out in his book, as summarized in this quotation. What energized his followers after his death, some would say, was the

---

1. Meyer, *Aims*, 252–53.

Part II: Jesus

"resurrection experience" wherein the Jesus they knew became present to them again.[2] Thus the disciples picked up the torch that Jesus had carried in his time with them. But the image of torch bearing hardly squares with the evidence. The restored group carried, instead, the cross in their mind and message (1 Cor. 1:17–23; Gal. 2:19–20), and understood the meaning of Jesus' word and deed *in light of the crucifixion*.[3]

Moreover, the end result of Jesus' ministry in Palestine, namely a community of believers who hailed the crucifixion as the pivotal saving act of Jesus for them and for the world, makes little sense if the pre-Easter Jesus did not speak and act *towards* that end along the way. Separation of the pre-crucifixion ministry of Jesus from the crucifixion, and from the community that resulted from it, leaves the project of recovering Jesus behind Easter lacking in coherence. Meyer's question, moreover, is the crux of the matter: Did Jesus know that his vision, actions, and words had the mark of crucifixion written on them? The surviving disciples, looking back, thought so. Why else would they remember and preach Jesus' word and deed in keeping with his crucifixion if they could see no coherence between them?

An objection could be raised. To construe the crucifixion of Jesus as consistent with his word and deed beforehand is theological, not historical. To use the later preaching of the Apostles to answer the historical question about what led to the crucifixion of Jesus lacks critical credibility. The crucifixion of their leader was imprinted indelibly on their minds, and called for explanation beyond the harsh political reality of a trial and a Roman execution. Their explanation can only be construed as theological—or more precisely, Christological—and should not encroach on the historical investigation of pre-crucifixion activities of Jesus with his disciples.

The objection has some merit. Yet it falls short of accounting for the interconnection between the religious, theological, historical, political, economic, and social dimensions of an ancient society such as that of Jewish Palestine. Jesus lived and breathed the total atmosphere in which he lived, which included all of those elements listed above. The question is not how Jesus conformed to the norms of his society, but how he deviated from the norms. Something in his action and word provoked the authorities to bring him to trial, find him guilty of some crime, and sentence him to death by crucifixion. To isolate a single action-and-word from the last days in Jerusalem that would have led to Jesus' crucifixion strains credulity. That position assumes that Jesus moved around the country with his disciples in a conventional Jewish manner, without offense, until one unexpected situation thrust him into an offensive mode. More likely, however, the words and actions of Jesus with his disciples from the beginning were unconventional, implicitly and explicitly calling ruling elitist authorities into question in favor of an alternate rule of life ordained by the God of Israel. Such a course of action in the religious, social, political world of Judeo-Roman Palestine could hardly escape trial and crucifixion. That conviction remains to be demonstrated in the chapters that follow.

2. Johnson, *Real Jesus*, 134–35.
3. Shillington, "Parables," 505–23.

THE SEARCH FOR OFFENSE

Some people on the quest for the historical Jesus examine the sources for possible offences in Jesus' word and deed. The issue is two-pronged because of the two powers operating in Palestine at the time: What would the Jewish leaders have found so offensive in Jesus to bring him to trial? And what would the Roman prefect, Pilate, have found offensive to Roman jurisprudence?

Concerning the first question, what would Jewish leaders have found offensive, E. P. Sanders has marshaled his extensive research into Jewish Law to meet the challenge. Sanders scoured the synoptic gospels to find every instance that could be construed as offensive to Palestinian Jewish sensibilities, and evaluated each instance against a corresponding article of Jewish law and practice.[4]

While Sanders' analytical work is very impressive, his conclusion scarcely answers the question posed about the connection between Jesus' word-and-deed and his crucifixion. Here is Sanders' conclusion after perusing the synoptic gospels alongside all relevant Jewish legal literature:

> Even if each conflict narrative were literally true, however, [and not the work of the synoptic redactors] it would be seen that Jesus did not seriously challenge the law as it was practiced in his day, not even by the strict rules of observance of pietistic groups—except on the issue of food. The subsequent debate on that issue in the early church, however (Gal. 2; Rom. 14; Acts 10; 15), makes this the point that may be denied to the historical Jesus with most confidence. He may have been in minor disagreement with one group or another about some legal observances, but prior to the attack on the Temple I cannot find a single issue which would have been the occasion of a serious charge.[5]

Sanders' judgment on matters of Jewish law deserves respect. His work in the area stands up to the scrutiny of his peers. And I am also inclined to subscribe to his understanding that Jesus did not go around breaking Jewish law. It would be difficult indeed for Jesus to proclaim the rule of God apart from a deep respect for the divine origin of his Jewish Scriptures. Matthew's Jesus unequivocally affirms the law: "Do not think that I have come to abolish the law or the prophets; I have come not to abolish but to fulfill. For truly I tell you, until heaven and earth pass away, not one letter, not one stroke of a letter, will pass from the law until all is accomplished" (Matt. 5:17–18). Jesus' way of adhering to the Torah regulations may not have been as rigid as that of others, but the offence was not punishable be crucifixion. The schools of Shammai and Hillel disagreed with each other on how to practice points of Jewish law. But the disagreements did not result in a trial before a Roman prefect, resulting in execution of the leader of the school. There had to be something in Jesus' word and behavior beyond deliberate breaking of this or that article of the Jewish law of the land to account for his crucifixion.

---

4. Sanders, *Jewish Law*, 1–96.
5. Ibid., 96.

Part II: Jesus

According to Sanders, "Jews killed one another when government was at stake, not over legal disagreements which had no overtones of civil or government control. To explain bloodshed we must have something other than *purely* legal disagreements."[6] And Sanders finds the "something other" in the "attack on the Temple" in the last week of Jesus' life. And here is where I have a problem: pinning the cause of Jesus' death by crucifixion on a single act of rebellion tends to dissociate that act from the life and ministry that preceded it. Behind and before that precipitous act, among others in the last week, were activities and words of the same character. To illustrate the point, I elicit an example that Sanders used to demonstrate Jesus' attitude towards purity regulation in Judaism: the parable of the Good Samaritan. Sanders cites the implied criticism of the priest and the Levite for passing by the person on the side of the road. "Jesus' implied criticism is serious, since in effect it asks priests to risk transgression when there is a chance . . . of helping an injured person."[7] True as this analysis may be, the stinging affront of the parable comes not from the passersby, but from the geographically labeled character of the one who stops to lavish compassion on the injured person. I submit that this kind of storytelling in a Jewish context has the mark of crucifixion written on it. Granted, there is not enough to indict, but there surely is enough to offend. Speech and action of this sort bespeak a vision and mission that is destined to come to a head. When it does, crucifixion ensues.

Cause and effect are difficult to ascertain at the best of times. In the matter of the earthly ministry of Jesus that came to an end on a Roman cross we have to rely on second-hand information about the case that came before the authorities in Jerusalem. The synoptic evangelists were almost certainly not eyewitnesses to the events leading up to Jesus death. Why would they rely on sources for their narratives if they were eyewitnesses? Furthermore, each of the synoptic evangelists had interests and aims that were their own. They did not write their gospels to enable scholars two thousand years later to do research into the life and work of Jesus.

For example, the centurion's confession at the foot of the cross in the Gospel of Luke is worded differently from the parallel narrative in Mark and Matthew. Luke's Roman centurion says, "Certainly this man was innocent" (*ontōs ho anthrōpos houtos dikaios ēn*), whereas Mark's centurion declares: "Truly this man was God's Son!" (*alēthōs houtos ho anthrōpos huios theou ēn*). The difference is significant. Luke's centurion declares the crucified Jesus judicially innocent of the crime that sent him to the cross, without any indication what the crime might have been. Mark and Matthew, on the other hand, cite the centurion as recognizing divinity in the crucified Jesus, implying that this had something to do with the charge brought against him: "this man *was indeed* son of God." The point to this little exercise with synoptic texts is to exemplify the difficulty of finding cause and effect relationship from sources that have their own agenda after the fact.

---

6. Ibid., 89.
7. Sanders, *Jewish Law*, 42.

The Crux of the Matter

To focus on a single act-and-word of Jesus as the immediate offense that caused his trial and execution is to truncate the end of Jesus' ministry from its origin and aim. At the same time, it would be inappropriate to suggest that Jesus deliberately orchestrated his own death to become a martyr. There had to be a cause and purpose beyond self-interest. His death is better seen as having redemptive, restorative purpose behind it and in it. Only a comprehensive analysis and understanding of the various pieces of the puzzle of Jesus' activity in Galilee and Judea will be sufficient to meet the challenge of the question: *What crucified Jesus?* This question will come up again for final discussion in the last chapter of this section on Jesus.

THE EXTREME PENALTY

Neither suicide nor martyrdom was the aim of Jesus. Nor did he provoke the authorities to bring him to trial and crucifixion for the sake of being provocative. On the contrary, Jesus knew the pain and shame that came with crucifixion, and recoiled from it in his humanness (Mark 14:32–6). Unlike cultured people of the modern world, Jesus doubtless saw his share of crucifixions, or at least heard of them, and knew the utmost humiliation crucifixion brought to the victim and the family in that society. No wonder the Apostle Paul calls the "word of the cross" foolishness to Greeks and a scandal to Jews (1 Cor. 1:23). Crucifixion in the Roman world was the extreme penalty meted out to convicted criminals, most of whom were low class, slaves especially. In that social context of crucifixion, the early hymn to Christ in Philippians 2:6–11 finds its significance. In that hymn the Messiah figure in the form of God descends to the lowest strata of society, becomes a slave, and obeys the call to take his place with condemned slaves in their horrendous death, "even death on a cross."

The classic work on crucifixion in the Greco-Roman world is that of Martin Hengel, *Crucifixion*. His meticulous research into Persian, Greek, Roman, and Jewish literature on the subject reveals at once the widespread use of the punishment, the abject shame that accompanied it, and those most likely to suffer the despicable death. I owe much of the insight in this discussion to Hengel's work.

The Romans were not the first to use crucifixion as an extreme penalty. Before the Roman general, Pompey, invaded Palestine, the Jewish Hasmonean state was embroiled in civil war. The Jewish people, especially the Pharisees, resented the powerful Hasmonean priest-king system of Jewish government. Josephus describes the ruthless way the Hasmonean leader, Alexander Jannaeus (103–76 BCE), punished the Pharisees who opposed his rule: "[Alexander] brought them to Jerusalem, and did one of the most barbarous actions in the world to them; for as he was feasting with his concubines, in the sight of all the city, he ordered about eight hundred of them to be crucified; and while they were living, he ordered the throats of their children and wives to be cut before their eyes."[8] Crucifixion served not only as the most severe penalty on the victim, but also as a form of bizarre entertainment for those in charge of carrying out the execution. In the case of the eight hundred Pharisees, they were forced to witness

---

8. *Ant.* 13.14.2.380.

Part II: Jesus

the cruel deaths of their families from their place on their crosses, while spectators had their fun. Jewish philosopher, Philo of Alexandria, a contemporary of Jesus, witnessed something of the theatre of execution by crucifixion on his own people at the command of Flaccus, the Roman prefect in Egypt at the time:

> [Flaccus] commanded living men to be crucified; and he did this after they had been beaten by scourgings in the middle of the theatre; and after he had tortured them with fire and sword; and the spectacle of their sufferings was divided; for the first part of the exhibition lasted from the morning to the third or fourth hour, in which the Jews were scourged, were hung up, were tortured on the wheel, were condemned, and were dragged to execution through the middle of the orchestra; and after this beautiful exhibition came the dancers, and the buffoons, and the flute-players, and all the other diversions of the theatrical contests.[9]

Philo's description of the "beautiful exhibition . . . and all the other diversions" that accompanied the crucifixion of his Jewish compatriots in the city of Alexandria squares with the description of the masquerade that went with the crucifixion of Jesus in the city of Jerusalem around the same time. All four gospels affirm the entertainment aspect of crucifixion. Here is Mark's description:

> The soldiers of the governor took Jesus into the governor's headquarters, and they gathered the whole cohort around him. They stripped him and put a scarlet robe on him, and after twisting some thorns into a crown, they put it on his head. They put a reed in his right hand and knelt before him and mocked him, saying, "Hail, King of the Jews!" They spat on him, and took the reed and struck him on the head. After mocking him, they stripped him of the robe and put his own clothes on him. Then they led him away to crucify him. (Mark 15:16–20)

It is often inferred that Jewish leaders did not practice crucifixion as a form of punishment. But I have shown above that a Jewish Hasmonean ruler had no qualms about crucifying those who interfered with affairs of government. The Romans brought the Hasmonean system of Jewish rule in Judea to an end in 63 BCE, but the Romans continued the penalty of crucifixion of criminals in Palestine. In the course of the take-over of the Jewish state, the Romans crucified many Jewish insurgents. The same happened at the end of the First Jewish War against Rome in 70 CE. Josephus records a large number of crucifixions. Where then does the notion come from that the Jewish people did not practice crucifixion?

The answer has a particular twist to it. After the Romans had taken control of Judea, a certain Herod, son of Antipater of Idumea, aspired to becoming king of the Judeans, and won the prize for himself from the Roman senate, influenced by Mark Anthony who supported Herod.[10] Herod was not known for his compassionate character. Far from it. He murdered even members of his own family for the least offence. But for whatever reason, Herod banned crucifixion as a form of Jewish punishment for offenders. He may have been influenced by the Pharisees to abandon the practice.

---

9. Philo, *In Flaccum*, 83–5.
10. *J. W.* 1.14.4.284.

The Crux of the Matter

The Pharisees knew the law of Deuteronomy 21:23: "anyone hung on a tree is under God's curse. You must not defile the land that the LORD your God is giving you for possession." Imagine, then, how difficult it would be for a law observant Jewish person to accept a messiah condemned to hang on a tree! The term is an oxymoron. If the Jewish authorities in Jerusalem called for the crucifixion of Jesus by the Romans, as Mark 15:13 claims, they did so believing that he was "under God's curse" (cf. Gal. 3:13). That is one possible interpretation.

Moreover, at the time of Jesus the extreme penalty of crucifixion was the domain of the Romans overlords. "Crucifixion was and remained a political and military punishment."[11] That did not necessarily mean that the victim had committed a crime of treason or rebellion against the state. A lawbreaker in the Roman world could be sentenced to crucifixion for a number of crimes, including robbery, rebellion, murder, and insurrection. Crucifixion served not only as extreme punishment for a crime, but also as a deterrent. Crucifixions were carried out in a public place, beside a road, on a hill, near the entrance to a city, any place where a passersby could witness the horror and shame of the victim thus condemned. The idea was that the onlookers would say to themselves: "That must never happen to me."

In summary, the crucifixion of Jesus was, and remains, a mystery. Not that the event is beyond historical verification. It is one of the best-attested facts about the earthly Jesus. It is a mystery insofar as it stands out from all the thousands of crucifixions carried out in the ancient Jewish-Roman world. Crucifixion was a great shame, not only on the victim, but also on his family and friends. To be associated with such a figure was to be considered party to his shame. Why then would his followers continue to talk about their time with this particular figure? Not only that, why would they continue to honor him as *the crucified Messiah*? One would expect them to play down the ignominious way his life and work came to an end, and play up, instead, the way he was before the crucifixion. But they did the opposite. They hailed Jesus crucified as the Messiah, and set that figure at the center of their preaching and their life. Somehow they saw in that horrible, shameful act perpetrated on their leader and friend by the Romans the very act of God on behalf of the world. And more, they looked back on his mission in Galilee and Judea from the consciousness of his final act of going to the cross without violence or reprisal. The foolishness of the cross became the saving power of God to those able to overcome the scandal (1 Cor. 1:23).

---

11. Hengel, *Crucifixion*, 87.

6

Growing up in Lower Galilee

THERE WAS A TIME WHEN CHRISTIAN SEMINARIES LISTED COURSES ON "THE life of Jesus," or "the life of Christ." By the end of the twentieth century, however, such course titles had all but disappeared from curricula, out of a sober recognition that virtually no literary or archaeological evidence exists for twenty-seven years of the thirty-year life of Jesus in Galilee. One gospel of the New Testament (John) implies three years of *ministry*, while the other three narrate less than two. Luke does tell a theologically weighted story of Jesus at twelve years leaving his parents in favor of a conversation with teachers in the Temple of Jerusalem during a Passover (Luke 2:41–50). Beyond that one brief narrative about Jesus in the years prior to his ministry in Galilee and Judea, we have nothing of historical note. Why then attempt a chapter about Jesus growing up in Galilee?

PLACE AND IDENTITY

The answer, in a word, is *context*. Place plays an important role in shaping identity, as noted already in chapter 4. Galilee was the place-name of Jesus during his lifetime. However much the Jewish Galileans interacted with Judea to the south out of a shared religious heritage, the home place of Jesus was Galilee, particularly lower Galilee. From the relevant sources available, it is possible to explore imaginatively the space and place that Jesus occupied in the formative years of his life leading up to the activation of his vision and mission in the company of others.[1]

Imagination, however necessary for such a project, must not be allowed to roam beyond the scope of the facts in evidence. For example, there is nothing in the record about Jesus to suggest that he entered the two principal cities of Galilee, Sepphoris and Tiberias, during his ministry. To propose that he did so prior to his ministry is a breach of trust in the evidence in favor of creative imagination. Surprisingly, a reputable scholar in the person of Jerome Murphy-O'Connor has done just that. Here is a sample of how he envisions Jesus in his formative years:

---

1. See Chilton, *Rabbi Jesus*, 3–22.

> To a village boy the city [of Sepphoris] held the attraction of a theme park, a cornucopia of sights and sounds that excited wonder and inspired questions. Why did an arch stay up when the carpenters removed the scaffolding? How could a couple of men with a crane raise a large block of stone? How did masons ensure that a wall was absolutely vertical? How did engineers transfer a line of sight to paper? Sepphoris seethed with a vitality he could almost reach out and touch. Home was unbearably dull by comparison.[2]

Murphy O'Connor then goes on to say that it would be "a great mistake to imagine Jesus did not spend what time he could in Sepphoris from the moment he was free to explore with his friends."[3] Why it would be a "great mistake" is curious. If Jesus was fascinated with cities during his formative years he must have spurned that attraction when he launched his ministry. Nothing in the record suggests he entered any city of Galilee. Even when he took the rather long trip north to the city of Caesarea Philippi, he visited *the villages* of the area, as Mark is careful to report (Mark 8:27). What, then, moves Murphy-O'Connor to paint a picture of Jesus involved with the cities of Galilee, Sepphoris in particular? The answer seems to be that he seeks to create parallel lives between Jesus and Paul, as the title of his recent book affirms, *Jesus and Paul: Parallel Lives*. It seems to me, however, that "a great mistake" would be to force a parallelism between Jesus and Paul that does not exist in the available sources. Jesus was "Jesus of Nazareth," a small village; Paul was "Paul of Tarsus," a large city. One can assume, as a matter of course, that both men shared common human experiences: consumption of food, excretion of waste, pain, work, laughter, sorrow, etc. They also shared the same religion, Judaism, but *they did not share the same place*, the same politics, the same education, the same social network. It would be a mistake to create a place for Jesus that was not truly his, and likewise also for Paul.

THE LANDSCAPE

The region known as Galilee ("circle of the peoples"[4]) lies in the northern part of what was the ancient nation of Israel. At the time of Jesus certain areas of Galilee were further specified. Josephus makes repeated reference to upper and lower Galilee, by which he means the northern and southern areas of the region respectively. The Mishnah tractate, *Shebiith*, however, describes three parts of Galilee: "The Galilee is divided into upper Galilee, lower Galilee and the Valley. From Kfar Hananiah and northward, all places where the sycamore does not grow are regarded as upper Galilee. And from Kfar Hananiah and southwards, all places where the sycamores do grow are regarded as lower Galilee. And the region of Tiberias is regarded as the Valley."[5] The Valley would have included the Lake of Genneseret, also called the Sea of Galilee and the Sea of Tiberias (Luke 5:1; Mark 1:16; John 6:1). Jesus grew up neither in the Valley,

---

2. Murphy-O'Connor, *Jesus and Paul*, 25.
3. Ibid.
4. Horsley, *Galilee*, 20, 159.
5. Mishnah, *Shebiith* 9:2.

Part II: Jesus

nor in upper Galilee where the sycamores do not grow, but in lower Galilee where the sycamores do grow.

The Mishnah's mentioning the growth properties of the regions of Galilee illustrates the interest the Rabbis had in the life-sustaining gift of the land, and the rich harvest of blessing it provided to the people. As Sean Freyne has demonstrated admirably, Jesus likewise valued the land that the Lord God of Israel had given in trust. Freyne's insightful re-reading of the sources with respect to Jesus' attitude toward the land and its natural resources as covenant gift and place of identity deserves serious consideration, much more than this brief treatment allows. "It is somewhat surprising," he says, "that very little has been written about [Jesus'] attitudes to the natural environment." A number of modern studies have focused on "concerns about justice for the marginalized" without paying attention to "eco-justice" at the same time.[6] Freyne explores the likelihood of Jesus knowing the creation stories of Genesis, along with the covenant promise of blessing to Abraham and to his descendents from the same sacred book of origins in the Hebrew Bible. The land of promise included the land of lower Galilee on which Jesus walked and worked, and from which he sustained his earthly life. The line from "the Lord's Prayer" in Matthew, "your will be done on earth," could just as well be translated "your will be done on the land" (*epi gēs* Matt. 6:10). In the chapters that follow, Jesus' concern for the land and its trustees will be explored in more detail.

Water supply for the whole of Israel flowed from the headwaters of Mount Hermon in upper Galilee through the region of Caesarea Philippi into the Sea of Galilee, and south via the Jordan River to Judea, emptying ultimately into the Dead Sea. Water was life-giving for humans and animals, an environment for fish, and a means of purification and blessing. All Israel benefited from the rich water resource that Galilee had to offer.

Galilee had on its western side the Great Sea, with the port of Ptolemais (Acco) available for the import and export of goods—import more than export. Galilee was not a large manufacturing region. Its people were mostly peasants engaged in the production of food supplies for their families, and for the payment of taxes and tribute to the various levels of government centered in the cities.

The landscape of Galilee was varied, with mountains, valleys, plains, and waterways. The two most notable mountains were Mount Hermon in the far north, and Mount Tabor southwest of the Sea of Galilee. Mountains were considered sacred by the ancient people. Mount Hermon had a long history of worship to various gods, from Ba'al to Pan. Mount Tabor too was viewed as a sacred site, probably the mountain implied in Mark 9:2 as the site of the transfiguration of Jesus. In addition to these two well-known mountains of Galilee were mountain ranges throughout the region between the Mediterranean Sea and the Jordan River, among them the Nazareth range, which Jesus would surely have explored, lying as it did on his doorstep for most of his life. Fertile plains included the Plain of Acco along the western shore of the Mediterranean, the Plain of Esdraelon southwest of Mount Tabor, the Plain of

---

6. Freyne, *Jesus*, 24–25.

Growing up in Lower Galilee

Gennesar northwest of the Sea of Galilee, and the Plain of Bethsaida to the northeast of the Sea of Galilee.

All of these would have been familiar to Jesus. Peasants made their living from the fertile land in the plains and valleys. When peasants lost their land to wealthy city dwellers because of debt, they effectively lost their livelihood. There was no social system, beyond the village community-network, to sustain them and their families. Jesus knew the way of life of Galilean peasants, as his parables illustrate, and he knew also the promise God made to Israel at the founding of the nation. It was a good land "flowing with milk and honey" (Ex. 3:8; Lev. 20:24; Deut. 6:3; 11:9). The land was God's gift of life to the elect people, a land to be held in trust, an inheritance to be used with respect to the divine donor.

GALILEAN POPULATION

Who were the Galileans of the first century? That question has occupied scholars for some time. Archaeology has helped answer the question. Various artifacts, especially pottery and coins, are used to identify the cultural and ethnic configuration of a given area. However, most of the excavations have been carried out at city sites or large towns. Village sites do not yield as much artifactual information as the city sites, with the result that information from city sites is sometimes assumed for village populations. Still, with the help of literary evidence it is possible to have a fairly secure sense of the ethnic background of the people who occupied the land of Galilee where Jesus lived.

The biblical story of the conquest and settlement of the Promised Land is well known. The Deuteronomic narrative-tradition of the Hebrew Bible (the books of Deuteronomy through Kings) describes the Israelite take-over of various areas of the land east and west of the Jordan River. The narratives are not easily interpreted, produced as they were from different sources. Some place names are hard to identify precisely. But the allotments of land for the clans of Israel during and following the conquest, recorded in Joshua and Judges especially, can be stated with assurance. The clan of Dan received the area to the far north, at the headwaters of the Jordan River. Asher occupied the coastal plain from Mount Carmel to the city of Tyre. Naphtali was east of Asher, bounded by the Jordan and the sea of Galilee to the east. Zebulon lay to the south west of Naphtali, and Issachar to the south east of Naphtali, next to Zebulon. Manasseh had a lion's share in the territory in the middle of the land of Israel west of Jordan. Ephraim, Benjamin, and Judah were allotted portions in the southern part of the country. The tribes were consolidated under the political and military leadership of kings Saul, David, and Solomon from the eleventh to the tenth century BCE. When Solomon's son, Rehoboam, refused to reduce the burden of taxation after his father's death, the northern tribes separated from Judah and Benjamin to form a separate coalition of Israel under a non-Davidic king (1 Kings 11–12).

Two kingdoms of Israel thus came into being, Israel to the north and Judah to the south. Both coalitions had inherited the same ethnic, cultural, and religious

Part II: Jesus

traditions, but they formed two governments in two centers. Judah continued to view Jerusalem as the holy city of David, while the northern government established the city of Samaria in the center of the land, and set up its own shrine there. The prophet Amos challenged the religion and ethics of Samaria, together with its priests and king: "Hear this word, you cows of Bashan who are on Mount Samaria, who oppress the poor, who crush the needy, who say to their husbands, 'Bring something to drink!' The Lord GOD has sworn by his holiness: The time is surely coming upon you, when they shall take you away with hooks, even the last of you with fishhooks" (Amos 4:1–2).

After a number of invasions of the northern tribes, Israel fell to Assyria in 722 BCE. The leaders and other elites were carried off from Samaria into Assyria. There is no record of their official return to Samaria. Powerless Israelite peasants of Galilee and Samaria were probably allowed to remain in their village settlements after the captivity of the elites. Remaining Samaritans rallied around the sacred site of Mount Gerizim, and practiced their religion based on their version of the "five books of Moses" (Pentateuch).

Then in 586 BCE King Nebuchadnezzar of Babylon took Judeans captive to the Tigris-Euphrates region. The Judeans lived in Babylonia until the new ruler, Cyrus of Persia, assisted their return to the land of Judah in 538 BCE to rebuild their lives in relation to their God revealed in their religious traditions. A number remained in Babylonia, but kept faith with their heritage in Judah. With the help of funds from the treasury of Cyrus, the returnees built a new temple in Jerusalem on the rubble of Solomon's great temple destroyed in 586 BCE (Ezra 1:2–11, 6:3–5). The people of Judah maintained their separation from the Samaritans, and the Samaritans also from them (Neh. 2:17–20).

The Greek occupation, headed up first by Alexander the Great (330 BCE), brought significant change to the political landscape of Samaria and Judah, and at no time more striking than when the Seleucids of Syria in the second century BCE were in control. Antiochus IV forced Greek culture and religion onto the people of Judah, to the point of converting the Jewish Temple in Jerusalem into a Greek shrine with all the attending rituals. The upshot was revolt led by the family of a loyalist man of Judah, Mattathias. His sentiment and conviction as a Jewish loyalist are expressed poignantly in the text of 1 Maccabees:

> Mattathias answered and said in a loud voice: "Even if all the nations that live under the rule of the king (Antiochus IV) obey him, and have chosen to obey his commandments, everyone of them abandoning the religion of their ancestors, I and my sons and my brothers will continue to live by the covenant of our ancestors. Far be it from us to desert the law and the ordinances. We will not obey the king's words by turning aside from our religion to the right hand or to the left."
> (1 Macc. 2:19–22)

His sons, Judas, Simon, and Jonathan gathered a band of rebels around them, and successfully recaptured the Temple of Jerusalem from the hands of Antiochus and his soldiers. They were successful also in liberating much of the land that had earlier belonged to Israel, including Galilee. While Judas Maccabee ("hammerer"?) led the successful revolt against the Syrian king in 165 BCE, it was Simon who instituted the priest-king system about twenty years later. Thus the Hasmonean dynasty was born. Effectively Simon and his brothers established an independent Jewish state based in Jerusalem, but encompassing much of the land to the north that had been occupied by the tribes of Israel. The city of Sepphoris in lower Galilee, a few miles northwest of Nazareth, became a Hasmonean stronghold for the governance of the people who lived in Galilee for at least two generations before the Roman take-over. Hasmonean coins found at Sepphoris confirm the presence of that regime in the Galilean city.[7]

Some kings of the Hasmonean dynasty ruled with a heavy hand. John Hyrcanus, son of Simon Maccabee, withstood successfully the incursion from the Seleucid king, Antiochus VII, but he also attacked Samaria with a vengeance, and subjected the Samaritans to his rule. Many of the Judeans themselves, especially the Pharisees, objected strongly to the Hasmoneans arrogating to themselves the right of kingship. They were not of Davidic lineage. Furthermore, the combining of the two offices of high priest and king in one person went against Israelite tradition. "Hyrcanus" was a Greek name, which John applied to himself when he came to power, probably in an effort to ingratiate himself to the surrounding Hellenized states. Some of the Judeans themselves were so outraged by the corruption and collusion they perceived in the Hasmonean kingdom that they withdrew from Jerusalem altogether. The Qumran community northwest of the Dead Sea is a fine example of this response.

The independent rule of the Hasmoneans effectively came to an end in 63 BCE when the Roman General, Pompey, invaded and seized the land. But Jerusalem was not destroyed at that time, nor were the Temple functions halted, so the Hasmonean rule continued in some respects until the Roman senate appointed Herod the Great as "king of the Jews" in 37 BCE. During Herod's thirty-three-year reign he continued to control and expand the territory of the Hasmoneans.[8] Thus, Galilee became part of Herod's kingdom as it had been part of the kingdom of David and Solomon a thousand years earlier.

Returning now to the opening question, who were the Galileans of the first century? Were they Judeans who migrated to Galilee during the Hasmonean period? There is no hard evidence to suggest that they did, although the likelihood of their doing so is high. Some Judeans had remained in Babylonia after permission to return to Jerusalem had been granted. Others migrated to Alexandria in Egypt, and still others to various centers around the Mediterranean. It would be surprising not to find Judeans migrating to Galilee, and settling there, during the time of the Hasmonean kingdom. At the same time, descendents of the tribes of Israel that had settled in Galilee much earlier may have been part of the population of the region as well. Horsley argues that point:

> Thus, since critical interpretation of Assyrian records clearly suggests that the deportations were mainly of officials and skilled personnel, we must conclude that much of the Israelite population of Galilee must have remained in their vil-

---

7. Horsley, *Archaeology*, 47.
8. See Smallwood, *The Jews*, 44–59.

lages or perhaps withdrew into rugged interior. Continuity of the Israelite population into later times therefore seems the most likely historical conclusion.[9]

Granting Horsley's conclusion, the remaining Israelite descendents would likely have identified with their Judean neighbors who had escaped Assyrian captivity in 722 BCE, and would also likely not have sided with the Samaritans. Questions come to mind: If there were, in fact, Galilean descendents of the northern tribes of Israel at the time of Jesus, would they have been loyal to Jerusalem and the Temple, as their ancestors had been at the time of kings David and Solomon? Or did they have their own local expression of Israelite religion? Did they have their own version and interpretation of the Law of Moses? There is nothing in the literary or archaeological record to signify that people of Galilee with Israelite heritage were hostile to the Temple authority in Jerusalem when Jesus was growing up in the area.

There were revolts, indeed, originating in Galilee during Jesus' early years. One of the most noteworthy was the rebellion led by Judas the Galilean, as he was called. It was not a revolt against Jerusalem and the Temple, but against the Romans on the matter of taxation. The event is recalled in Acts 5:37 of the New Testament: "Judas the Galilean rose up at the time of the census and got people to follow him; he also perished, and all who followed him were scattered." Josephus also records the event.[10] It happened in 6 or 7 CE when Quirinius, Rome-appointed governor of Syria at the time, took account of the property belonging to those aligned with Jerusalem and the Temple. Judas the Galilean had gathered a significant number of Zealots around him, and proclaimed the state of the Judeans independent of Rome. Conflict with the Roman security militia ensued. Rome won that round. Jesus would have been twelve or thirteen at the time.

Judas perished in the conflict, but the spirit of his movement did not. His sons carried on the Zealot philosophy. Josephus credits Judas the Galilean with the founding of the Zealot philosophy, the chief tenet of which was freedom from external overlords.[11] Some scholars have tried to forge a link between the thinking of Judas the Galilean and that of Jesus the Galilean, but with little evidentiary success (cf. Luke 6:15). The point to be made here, however, is that this rebel leader was known as a Galilean, yet he defended the independence of the Judean state centered in Jerusalem and the Temple. If Judas the Galilean is representative of Galilean attachment to Jerusalem in the first century CE, then the idea of a Galilean hostility against the rule of Jerusalem and the Temple is ill founded. It would seem rather, as Sean Freyne has demonstrated, that the Hebraic population of Galilee was favorably disposed to Jerusalem rule. How many Judeans had migrated to Galilee during the Hasmonean period cannot be known with certainty. And how many others of Israelite ancestry were still resident in Galilee is equally uncertain. This much is evident from the literary sources, the Gospels especially: *Galileans of Israelite origin were Judean in orientation.*

9. Horsley, *Archaeology*, 23
10. *Ant.* 18.1.1.1.
11. *Ant.* 18.23.

Growing up in Lower Galilee

Also in Galilee were residents of non-Israelite heritage and ethnicity. The prophet Isaiah refers to the region as "Galilee of the nations" (Isa. 9:1; cf. Matt. 4:15; and 1 Macc. 5:14). Palestine was a gateway between east and west, north and south. When Jesus was growing up in lower Galilee Roman soldiers were stationed at key points in the region, as elsewhere, to ensure the *Pax Romana* (Roman peace) that Caesar Augustus had promulgated during his long reign (31 BCE–14 CE). The Q document (7:1, 3, 6b–9), for example, affirms the presence of a Roman centurion in Capernaum. But in addition to Roman soldiers, other non-Judean residents lived and worked in Galilee, as the archaeological records from the city sites affirm. There is no way of knowing how much contact Jesus had with non-Jewish residents in his region. From what we know of their village community meetings (*sunagôgai*), the Jewish Galileans met by themselves, and worshipped in keeping with the dictates of their Jewish Law. Presumably the non-Judeans had their own meetings and their own shrines. One thing is reasonably clear: when Jesus launched his mission in Galilee he did not make a point of reaching out to those of non-Israelite heritage. His was a mission of restoration of *all Israel*, as both Matthew and Q imply: "I was sent only to the lost sheep of the house of Israel" (Matt. 15:24); "You who have followed me will sit . . . on thrones judging the twelve tribes of Israel" (Q 22:28, 30). The story of Jesus' (rather disturbing) meeting with a non-Israelite woman of Syro-Phoenecia is reserved for later discussion.

The population of Galilee, while diverse ethnically, was divided also between village and city residents. Before expanding that point, however, something of the political situation in Galilee during Jesus' lifetime needs to be highlighted.

GALILEAN POLITICS

Herod the Great died in 4 BCE. According to the gospels of Matthew and Luke, Jesus was born a short time before the death of Herod (Matt. 2:1–15; Luke 1:5). His birth is thus calculated at about 6 BCE. Jesus was too young to have known Herod the Great, but he certainly knew his son, Herod Antipas, at one point reportedly labeling Antipas "that fox" (Luke 13:32).

At the death of Herod the Great his kingdom was divided up between Herod's sons. Antipas received Galilee and Perea (east of the Jordan) as his inheritance. Rome approved. Antipas was tetrarch of Galilee from 4 BCE until 39 CE, at which time Rome exiled him to Gaul. Jesus grew up under the rule of Herod Antipas, whose aspirations, like those of his father, were grandiose, as we shall see in a moment. It was this same Herod that John the Baptist opposed for marrying his brother Philip's divorced wife, thus breaking Jewish Law (Mark 6:16–18). Josephus also reports the same situation, and accuses Antipas of violating "ancestral laws."[12] Herod had John imprisoned, and later beheaded for his prophetic affront.

Like his father before him, Antipas made a name for himself by building (or rebuilding) cities and putting his own stamp on them, while recognizing the authority of Rome. Sepphoris was operating as a city during the Hasmonean period. When

---

12. *Ant.* 18.5.4.136.

Part II: Jesus

Herod the Great was setting up his kingdom he took Sepphoris during a snowstorm, against the rebellious efforts of the citizens.[13] After Herod's death another revolt broke out, but the Roman general, Gaius, set fire to the city, and committed the surviving inhabitants into slavery. This was the city that Antipas determined to rebuild, using various Hellenistic and Roman architecture and ornamentation, while recognizing the Jewish tradition that had been present there for many years. Interestingly, during the First Jewish War of 66–70 CE the inhabitants of Sepphoris chose not to engage in the revolt against Rome.

For many years now, excavation on the site of Sepphoris has been conducted with illuminating results. The work of Carol L. Meyers and Eric M. Meyers of Duke University, along with Ehud Netzer of the Hebrew University has been ongoing at the site since 1987. In that year the excavators discovered a colored mosaic floor with strong Hellenistic influence, including a beautiful woman wearing a wreath on her head. The mosaic floor belonged to what looks like a dining room belonging to a large two-story mansion. The archaeologists have dated the mosaic in the second century. Some coins were also discovered dated 67/68 CE, bearing the imprint *Eirenopolis*, "city of peace." Not a wealth of archaeological material has emerged from the first half of the first century. Enough has been discovered, however, to know that Herod's Sepphoris could boast a resplendent city environment, attractive to a good cross-section of people interested in such an urban way of life. A theatre seating about five thousand spectators was situated at the northeast section of the city, and may have been the product of Antipas' vision. Aqueducts and water reservoirs were also discovered, which also appear to be part of Herod's plan. Some water structures may have been used as recreational or ritual baths. Josephus confirms what archaeology has revealed about the splendor of Herod's city, referring to Sepphoris as "the ornament of all Galilee."[14]

Only three and a half miles from the village of Nazareth, Sepphoris was well endowed with Greek and Roman culture alongside Jewish synagogues and artifacts. In this respect it was cosmopolitan. Sepphoris survived the onslaught of the First Jewish War against Rome. Its citizens refrained from the rebellion that broke out elsewhere in Galilee in 66/67, and were therefore spared the horrors that befell Jerusalem. So attractive was this city as a safe place to live that Jewish rabbis moved their headquarters to Sepphoris some years after the War (66–70 CE). It was in Sepphoris that Rabbi Judah the Prince compiled and published the Mishnah, ca. 200 CE.

What is the significance of Herod's Sepphoris for an understanding of the environmental influence on Jesus? The city is ironically noteworthy by its absence from the available records about the ministry of Jesus. How could such an important city be missing from reports about the word and work of Jesus? There seems to be only one explanation from this deafening silence: Jesus did not conduct his ministry in the principal city of Galilee, Sepphoris. If that be true, as seems likely, then it is also likely that Jesus did not have much time for city life growing up, despite Murphy O'Connor's

---

13. *J. W.* 1.16.2.304.
14. *Ant.* 18.2.1.27.

Growing up in Lower Galilee

fanciful idea that the city environment of Sepphoris would have been irresistible to him as a youth. Sepphoris represented the ornament and security of Herod's kingdom when Jesus was growing up, a walled city so unlike the village of Nazareth, and so unlike the kingdom of God. I submit that Jesus knew very early in his life the great difference between the reign of Herod in Galilee and the reign of God over all Israel and the world.

One more observation about Sepphoris needs to be made. As "the city of the king" (*autokratorida*), with all the attendant amenities, Sepphoris attracted mostly the elite from the various cultures, including Judean religious leaders and wealthy landowners. The services available in Sepphoris for those who could afford them were the best in the country. Such a city offered the best in education to the upper class, involving especially the ability to read and write. With these cultured skills came power to influence the shaping of ideas and the society that enshrined them. Only the privileged of the society could afford the services of a teacher to develop such skills, and the place to find such an instructor was the city. The city of Sepphoris was a place of high politics, manufacturing, erudition, religion, entertainment, and recreation. None of these belonged to a small village community made up mostly of peasant farmers, from whom came the resources through taxation for building and maintaining such a city as Sepphoris.

Jesus doubtless knew about Sepphoris, and may have witnessed it first hand on more than one occasion, but his home was in the village of Nazareth a few miles southeast. There is nothing to suggest that he left his village home as an adult to join the citizens of Sepphoris or any other major city.

As mentioned above, Herod Antipas took up residence in Sepphoris after his father's death in 4 BCE, and lived there until 19/20 CE, at which time Antipas decided to build a new city on the western shore of the Sea of Galilee. He moved his court and his retinue to that site. He named the city in honor of the reigning Roman Emperor, Tiberias (14–37 CE). The name of the city appears in the Gospel of John. Not at all in the three Synoptics. Twice the name is used in John to identify the Sea of Galilee (John 6:1; 21:1), and once to identify the site from which some boats came to the place where Jesus had provided bread for the crowd (John 6:21). Apart from these three oblique references to Tiberias, the city does not figure in the gospel record of the life and ministry of Jesus.

With hot springs nearby (used to this day), Tiberias had the potential of attracting visitors and residents. However, as the foundations were being laid, an ancient burial ground was discovered, which rendered the new city unclean for prospective Jewish residents. Antipas continued to build regardless, with the result that observant Judeans in Galilee would not inhabit the city (cf. Q 11:44). Josephus describes the project thus:

> Herod the tetrarch, who was in great favor with [Emperor] Tiberius, built a city of the same name . . . He built it in the best part of Galilee, at the lake of Gennesareth. There are warm baths at a little distance from it, in a village named Emmaus. Strangers came and inhabited this city; a great number of the inhabit-

Part II: Jesus

> ants were Galileans also; and many . . . were by force compelled to be its inhabitants; some of them were persons of high standing. He also admitted poor people . . . and a great many slaves to whom he granted freedom, but obliged them not to forsake the city . . . To make this place a habitation was to transgress the Jewish ancient laws, because many sepulchers were to be taken away, in order to make room for the city Tiberias; whereas our law pronounces, that such inhabitants are unclean for seven days.[15]

Included among the principal buildings of Tiberias was a palace erected on an elevated site, a fortress on the north side, and a synagogue (a meeting place for observant Jewish Galileans). Ironically, a synagogue built on a necropolis is not a place for observant Jewish people. Eventually, after the Second Jewish War against Rome (132–135 CE), Tiberias became an important center for Rabbinic Judaism. The presidents of the highest Jewish court took up residence in Tiberias. It was there that the two Talmuds were compiled, and there also where the invention of vowel pointing was appended to the Hebrew consonants. All of this, while noteworthy, takes us well beyond the time of Jesus.

There is a point to be made from the foregoing, however. Judging from the silence concerning the city of Tiberias in the Synoptic Gospels, Jesus did not conduct any work in the new city situated on the shore of the Sea of Galilee on which Jesus frequently sailed with his friends. Likewise the writer of the Gospel of John, who clearly knows the city by name, stops short of saying that Jesus entered Tiberias. He circled around it, but did not perform a single act or word that we know of inside its boundary.

Excavation continues at the site of first-century Tiberias. One of the most significant remains was a gate and a street leading into the city from the south. The gate seems to have been set between two towers, styled as fortifications after the manner of Late Hellenistic or Early Roman architecture. Jesus would have witnessed the elegance of the gate and towers, but probably did not frequent the city. He too was an observant Jewish Galilean, and as such would have considered the city unclean. By all accounts Jesus did not have much time for the kind of power and glory embodied in Herod Antipas, who had John the Baptist killed.

One final word about the politics of Galilee: who paid for the massive building projects? Rich donors may have contributed out of their abundance. More likely than not, however, the funds came from taxation. The majority of Jewish Galileans were villagers, with plots of ground used to sustain their lives. Some were tenant farmers who paid rent in the form of land produce to rich landowners living in cities such as Sepphoris and Tiberias. Others were craftsmen who used their skills to provide products in wood, stone, pottery, and metals for people who could afford to buy such items. All of these people were subject to forced taxation imposed arbitrarily on the people of the land of Galilee. Jesus experienced the politics (city rule) firsthand, and eventually raised his voice against it by presenting the alternate rule of God, easily accessible to the powerless poor (Q 6:20).

---

15. *Ant.* 18:2.3.36, 38.

HOME, EDUCATION AND OCCUPATION.

Today the city of Nazareth is the most adored Christian city in Galilee, with a population of about 65,000. But it was not so during the lifetime of Jesus. Beneath the elaborate Christian structures, some of them dating back to the Byzantine period, lies the scant remains of a small village from the first century with a population of 200 to 500 persons. So insignificant was the village of Nazareth that Josephus, who knew Galilee well, does not mention it. He names many other villages and towns, but not Nazareth. Its importance springs into focus in the gospels of the New Testament by virtue of the fact that this small village was the home of Jesus and his family for most of his life. Regrettably, the remains of the first-century village are few: no signs of elaborate buildings, tiled roofs, baths, or exquisite mosaics, all symbols of elitist values of a city.

If there was a Jewish synagogue building in Nazareth, it was not an imposing building like the one there today. There may not have been a building at all. A "synagogue" was the name for a group of Jewish people gathered together with a purpose. The agenda of such a village meeting may have included prayers, reflections on the ancestors, story telling, recitation of scriptures, instruction in right living, discussion of the situations in the life of the people, and singing. Such a gathering of the Jewish Galilean village people could have happened in the outdoors (cf. Acts 16:13), or in a dedicated building made from perishable materials similar to those used for the village houses. If so, the synagogue building would have fitted the simple style of the village population. But no such building is evident in the remains of first-century Nazareth.

One of the caves at Nazareth that exists to this day is known as "Mary's Well." It received its name long after the time of Jesus and his family, but doubtless provided Jesus and the people of Nazareth with their water supply.

Nazareth lies in a fertile valley beside a mountain range, with the rich Netofa valley to the north and the great Plain of Esdraelon to the south. The land could produce olives, grapes, grain, and support some livestock. Native villagers were mostly peasant farmers with enough land to provide subsistence for the family. Otherwise a village man might ply a trade or craft in addition to working a plot of land, or even apart from the land. Jesus is said to have been a craftsman (*tektōn*) in Mark 6:3. Matthew qualifies Mark by reporting Jesus to have been the son of a craftsman, perhaps to elevate Jesus above the lowly status of a villager who works with his hands. A *tektōn* could mean carpenter or mason, someone engaged in making or repairing implements or buildings. It is believed that such a village worker would have travelled to different places to work, especially cities. Nazareth would have been too small for a *tektōn* to make a living. On the strength of this assumption, some have suggested that Jesus was probably involved in the building of nearby Sepphoris and even Tiberias. He may have travelled even further afield to support himself. One rather questionable source from the second century claims to know that Jesus "hired himself out as a servant in Egypt on account of his poverty."[16] All of these conjectures have one element in common: *Jesus grew up in a humble social status characteristic of residents of a small village community.*

---

16. Celsus, in Chadwick, *Contra Celsum* I, 28.

Part II: Jesus

Very little is stated in the gospels about the education of Jesus. Luke alone gives some indication of his intellectual development: "The child grew and became strong, *filled with wisdom*; and the favor of God was upon him" (2:40); "And Jesus *increased in wisdom* and in years, and in divine and human favor" (2:52). Both statements point to the integration of physical growth, understanding of life in the world, and relationship to God. Beyond this brief and broad indication of the early life of Jesus in Nazareth in Luke there is nothing on record about any special schooling in which the young Jesus engaged. And that is not surprising. Parents living in Galilean villages did not have the means to sponsor their children in a formal, much less literary education in the city. That privilege belonged to the elite minority. "Those who had learned to read and write in antiquity were the rulers, the wealthy, or their scribes."[17] Jesus was none of these.

Education in a Jewish Galilean village community was centered mainly in the home, and additionally in the synagogue. Unlike the government regulation pursuant to education in modern western and northern cultures, education in ancient Galilee was not required. Parents instructed their children in the ways of their God as passed down from the ancestors and practiced in the community. Conventions and values were picked up along the way by observation and imitation, in the same way a child learns a language through repeated listening and performing the intelligible sounds. Eventually the linguistic facility becomes part of the child's thought and way of life. Beyond learning their native language, boys imitated the behavior of their fathers, and girls their mothers. Deviation from the community norms met with censure of one kind or another, depending on the nature of the deviance. Luke's story of Jesus at twelve exemplifies parental censure for deviation: "Child, why have you treated us like this? Look, your father and I have been searching for you in great anxiety . . . Then he went down with them and came to Nazareth, and was obedient to them" (2:48–51).

Teachers of the Jewish Law (from the group known as Pharisees) doubtless visited the community meetings (synagogues) dotted around the country, and gave oral instruction to the villagers. But the effective learning of traditions and conventions happened at home and in day-to-day life in the village community. The Aramaic Targums (translations) of the Hebrew Scriptures were memorized and used as a guide for living a righteous life. Aramaic was the common language among Jewish families in Galilee and elsewhere in Palestine. Knowledge of the Targums was expected of Jewish children, especially boys, in observant families. Schools that provided more sophisticated education were few, and were located in cities. The social location of Jesus, on the other hand, was the Jewish village of Nazareth in lower Galilee.

A number of scholars[18] believe Jesus was born in Nazareth, or in Bethlehem of Galilee,[19] but not in Bethlehem of Judea. The town of Bethlehem in Matthew and Luke is a theological location marking the beginning of Jesus' life in the world. Bethlehem

---

17. Crossan and Reed, *Excavating*, 19.
18. E.g., Bornkamm, *Jesus*, 53; Bultmann, *Synoptic Tradition*, 32.
19. Chilton, *Rabbi Jesus*, 8.

Growing up in Lower Galilee

of Judea was the "city of David," symbolic of the messianic lineage of Jesus. But Jesus was known not as "Jesus of Bethlehem," but as "Jesus of Nazareth." It is striking, for example, that in the Gospel of John Philip introduces Jesus to Nathaniel as "Jesus son of Joseph from Nazareth" (1:45; cf. 7:41-42). A person in the ancient world was identified by birthplace as well as paternity. Be that as it may, this much is unequivocal: Jesus grew up in the small peasant hamlet of Nazareth, and was identified even in his death by that epithet, "Jesus of Nazareth" (John 19:19).

We have some names of Jesus' family members, but not much more than that. His father's name was Joseph (John 1:45; Matt. 1:18-25); he was a *tektōn* (Matt. 13:55). Joseph may have died while Jesus was still a young person, judging from the absence of Joseph's name from the gospel record of the ministry of Jesus. His mother, Mary, appears to have outlived her husband and her son, Jesus. That Jesus had brothers and sisters is evident from Mark 6:3. How many siblings there were altogether we do not know. Mark 6 names his brothers "James and Joses and Judas and Simon" but does not give the names or the number of "his sisters."

It is likely that this Jewish family practiced the Jewish way of life, from the circumcision of infant boys (cf. Luke 2:21), to the eating of kosher food, to the practice of purification rituals. There can be little doubt that Jesus grew up in an observant Jewish village home in Galilee, with religious ties to the holy city of Jerusalem and the sacred Temple on Mount Zion. The family probably made some pilgrimages to Jerusalem on the high holidays, Passover especially, bringing with them appropriate offerings, or purchasing such from the officials in the Temple. At the Temple they would have heard and recited the prayers of the people in Hebrew or Aramaic, particularly the *shema*: "Hear, O Israel: The LORD (*YAHWEH*) is our God (*Elohim*), *YAHWEH* alone. You shall love *YAHWEH* your God with all your heart, and with all your soul, and with all your might" (Deut. 6:4-5).

In addition to his occupation as a craftsman, Jesus must have had time to explore places and encounter people beyond his native village. Judging from the significant number of times Jesus is found in a boat on the Sea of Galilee in the gospel narratives, he must have frequented the lake and joined the fishermen in their boats. The Sea of Galilee is 15 miles from Nazareth, and covers an area of about 40,000 acres. It is 13 miles north to south, and 8 miles east to west, reaching a depth of about 150 feet. At the time of Jesus the Lake may have been somewhat longer and narrower than it is today.

If Jesus walked the fifteen miles to the region of the Lake, as seems likely, he probably stayed with friends in the neighborhood rather than return home on the same day. His call to the sons of Zebedee to leave their fishing trade and their father to follow him could hardly have happened without prior relationship with them. It is hard to imagine the fishermen leaving everything to follow someone they had just met for the very first time (Mark 1:19). Similarly, brothers Simon and Andrew (Mark 1:16). Jesus likely went fishing frequently on the Sea of Galilee with these friends, and brought some fish back to his family in Nazareth.

Part II: Jesus

Fishing was a business on the Sea of Galilee. Fish and bread were "the staple diet of the average small householder (Mark 6:38)."[20] Fish could be preserved by using salt, and could in turn be exported. The ancient town of Magdala (tower of fish) on the western shore of the Sea of Galilee was given the Greek name, Tarichaeae, (center for salting fish).[21] Moreover, fishing was more than a sustenance activity. It was probably also a moneymaking industry, as indicated by the note in the gospel of Mark that Zebedee had "hired men" (1:20). A fisherman may have been a notch higher on the social register than a peasant farmer or a craftsman. There is little to suggest that Jesus was involved in fishing as a means of livelihood before he embarked on his itinerant ministry, only that he was familiar with the Sea of Galilee and with some of the people who sailed the Sea in search of fish for food and market. As an industry, however, fishing on the Sea of Galilee was probably "no financial bonanza."[22]

A very interesting discovery was made in 1986. That year Galilee suffered a severe drought that lowered the water level in the Sea of Galilee significantly. While two brothers from the Kibbutz Ginnosar were walking along the shore they noticed the outline of a boat in the mud near Magdala. When the object was investigated it was determined that it was indeed a boat from the first century CE. It may have been wrecked in a storm, its reusable parts salvaged, and the hull abandoned to the bottom of the Lake. The remains were well preserved in the "mud pack." The craftsman (*tektōn*) who first made the fishing boat used various timber products, including cedar from Lebanon. Its underside was covered with a bitumen product. The boat measures 8'x12', and is located in the museum of the Kibbutz Ginnosar. It would have been in such a boat as this that Jesus sailed on the Sea of Galilee with his friends on numerous occasions (Mark 3:9; 4:1, 36–37; 5:2, 18, 21; 6:32, 45).

At almost thirty years of age, Jesus, having grown up in the humble Jewish village of Nazareth in lower Galilee, launched a time-honored ministry, the character of which will be explored in the chapters that follow.

20. Freyne, *Jesus*, 52.
21. Ibid., 50.
22. Crossan and Reed, *Excavating*, 85.

7

From John to Jesus

LIVING QUIETLY IN A GIVEN PLACE, SUCH AS NAZARETH OF GALILEE, DOES not bequeath historical prominence to the inhabitant. Stepping outside the conventional boundary of the place, acting intentionally in an unconventional way, that is the stuff of history-making. Jesus is known to us today, not by living anonymously in a tiny village community, but by speaking out and acting out his vision of another way of life beyond the accepted norms.

But first there was John the Baptizer, catalytic forerunner to the subsequent ministry of Jesus. Of all the "evidence which is most secure"[1] about Jesus of Nazareth, none is any more firm than Jesus' baptism by John in the Jordan River. Before approaching the implications of Jesus' baptism, however, the figure of John himself should be brought to light.

A DESERT PROPHET

Attempts have been made to connect John with the group at Qumran in the Judean desert. Members of that Jewish sect practiced an ascetic life-style in reaction to the religious system centered in the Temple of Jerusalem, which they perceived as corrupt. In order to enter this sectarian Jewish community the applicant had to convert to the way of life set out in the charter document of the group. That meant taking a stand against the priestly rituals going on in the Temple of Jerusalem. Here is a sample from the "Community Rule," the name commonly used to refer to the charter scroll:

> This is the rule for the men of the community (*Yahad*) who *volunteer to repent* from all evil and to hold fast to all that [God], by His good will, has commanded. They are to *separate from the congregation of perverse men*. They are to come together as one with respect to Law and wealth. Their discussions shall be under the oversight of the Sons of Zadok—priests and preservers of the Covenant—and according to the majority rule of the men of the community, who hold fast to the Covenant. These men shall guide all decisions on matters of Law, money,

---

1. Sanders, *Jesus and Judaism*, 10.

Part II: Jesus

> and judgment ... These are the regulations that govern when they are gathered together as a community. Every initiant into the society of the community is to enter the Covenant in full view of all the volunteers ... None of the perverse men is to *enter purifying waters* used by the Men of Holiness and so contact their purity ... Each one who thus enters the Covenant by oath is to *separate himself from all of the perverse men*, those who walk in the wicked way, for such are not reckoned a part of His Covenant.[2] (Italics added).

I have highlighted some phrases in this extract to illustrate how John the Baptizer shows signs of association with this Jewish sectarian movement. Entrance is voluntary, not by birthright or rank, but by repentance. Repentance is not merely a spiritual, ethical conversion, but a renunciation of any association with a "perverse" society, a veiled allusion to the priesthood in Jerusalem. An initiation ritual seems to be implied by excluding "perverse men" from entering the "purifying waters." Beside the rules there is the place: a desert. These elements can be found variously in the preaching and action of John.

The desert was a deeply embedded theme in Jewish history. The ancient Hebrews, including the leaders Moses, Aaron, and Joshua, wandered in the desert for forty years. In the desert they received the Law of God, and prepared themselves thereby to enter the Promised Land flowing with milk and honey. The desert was a purifying experience, a time of testing before becoming the Israel of God. John the Baptizer chose the desert of Perea, part of the realm of Herod Antipas, not because he had nowhere else to preach, but more likely because it conjured up a deeply rooted Jewish tradition. His choice of the desert echoes the prophetic word of Isaiah 40:3: "A voice cries out: 'In the wilderness prepare the way of the LORD (*Yahweh*), make straight in the desert a highway for our God.'" John's diet and attire, as given in Mark, bespeak a desert prophet like Elijah: John was "clothed with camel's hair, with a leather belt around his waist, and he ate locusts and wild honey" (1:6). Nurtured in the desert, there may also be an echo of Deuteronomy 32 involved, which tells of the Lord caring for the elect people: "the LORD'S own portion was his people, Jacob his allotted share. He sustained him in a desert land, in a howling wilderness waste; he shielded him, cared for him, guarded him as the apple of his eye. The LORD alone guided him; no foreign god was with him; ... he nursed him with honey from the crags, with oil from flinty rock" (Deut. 32:9–14).

John's place in the desert east of Jordan, together with his practice of baptizing, made a statement, the content of which can only be given as a best guess from the available evidence. Majority opinion holds that John perceived unfaithfulness among the Jewish people of Palestine, leaders included, and called them to repent of their sins and seal their penitent hearts with the purifying water of baptism in the Jordan. And this view is supported by no lesser source than Josephus, contemporary with the Evangelists.

Josephus links John's preaching, baptism, and execution with Herod Antipas, all in one passage:

---

2. 1QS 5, in Wise et al., *Scrolls*, 131–32.

> Now, some of the Jews thought that the defeat of Herod's army came from God ... as a punishment for what he did against John, called the Baptizer; for Herod killed him, though [John] was a good man, and called upon the Jews to exercise virtue, to do right towards their neighbors, and to practice piety towards God, and so to enter baptism. For the purification [with water] would be acceptable to God ..., not for putting away of some sins, but for the consecration of the body, implying that the soul was already purified by right behavior. When others joined the crowds around him, for they were greatly moved by his words, Herod was troubled. He feared the great influence John had over the people might lead to a rebellion. The people seemed ready to do anything he asked, so Herod thought it best to put John to death. By so doing Herod hoped to prevent any uprising he might cause ... John was brought in chains to prison in the stronghold of Machaerus, where he was put to death. But the Jews believed that the destruction of Herod's army was God's punishment on Herod for what he did to John.[3]

By this account John's mission was ethical. He called the people to purify their souls and live just lives before God and neighbor. But that view leaves several key questions unanswered. Why conduct this ethical mission in the desert of Perea? Why would John's ethical preaching draw such crowds as to lead Herod to put him to death? Why carry out the baptism in the Jordan River specifically? Why not send the people to the historic Temple in Jerusalem to have their sins forgiven by the priests? Adequate answers to these questions could illuminate our understanding, not only of John the Baptizer, but also of Jesus baptized by him.

MORE THAN A PROPHET

It could be that John chose the desert and the Jordan for his ministry as a strike against the Temple religion in Jerusalem. Morton Smith calls the practice of baptism in the Jordan "John's great invention"[4] for the Jewish people, in place of going to the Temple of Jerusalem to have their sins forgiven. The Temple was the traditional and legal center for attaining such forgiveness. The new idea was that ordinary Jewish people could prepare for the coming kingdom through repentance and baptism without offering costly sacrifices to the priests. Commendable as this interpretation is, it leaves the question of the desert and the Jordan somewhat up in the air.

I find Dominic Crossan's analysis promising.[5] John was not merely imitating the activity of the Jewish sect at Qumran, but much more than that. He was reenacting the original Israelites crossing the Jordan into the Promised Land. John's was an eschatological ministry with apocalyptic overtones. God was about to restore the fortunes of Israel by overcoming the present oppressive rule in the Land, with judgment also falling on those who practiced injustice on the people of God. Herod Antipas may have picked up this strand of John's ominous preaching, a sampling of which comes from the Q Source:

---

3. *Ant.* 116–19.
4. Smith, *Clement*, 208.
5. Crossan, *Historical Jesus*, 227–64; *Revolutionary*, 29–53.

Part II: Jesus

> Snakes' litter! Who warned you to run from the impending rage? So bear fruit worthy of repentance, and do not presume to tell yourselves: We have as forefather Abraham! For I tell you: God can produce children for Abraham right out of these rocks! And the ax already lies at the root of the trees. So every tree not bearing healthy fruit is to be chopped down and thrown on the fire. (Q 3:7–9 = Matt. 3:7–10)

> I baptize you in water, but the one to come after me is more powerful than I, whose sandals I am not fit to take off. He will baptize you in the Holy Spirit and fire. His pitchfork is in his hand, and he will clear his threshing floor and gather the wheat into his granary, but the chaff he will burn on a fire that can never be put out. (Q 3:16–17 = Matt. 3:11–12)

Final judgment is central to these two examples of John's prophetic word to the people who came out to the desert to hear him. The "wrath to come" and the "One to Come" are both strong eschatological signals in apocalyptic dress. Such visionary preaching arises out of a current situation of injustice and oppression of the people of God. The note of judgment on the wicked comes through also in the two images of the ax lying at the root of the trees and the winnowing fork on the threshing floor. Rulers, like the trees that stand tall, will soon be brought down to ground zero. The good wheat and the worthless chaff will soon be separated. The grain will be saved and the chaff destroyed. But John does not see himself as the one to bring about the change in the Land. Instead, he anticipates the just action of the Lord (*Yahweh*), which his preaching merely announces as happening soon. His is only a prophetic voice, and his baptism in the Jordan merely the act of preparing the people for the impending judgment of the One to Come. Divine judgment, and only divine judgment, will open up the way to a new order of life for the people.

Returning now to the desert and the Jordan River. Jewish people would have caught the significance of the desert and the Jordan, and relished the thought of restoration. "People from the whole Judean countryside," says Mark, "and all the people of Jerusalem were going out to [John], and were baptized by him in the river Jordan" (Mark 1:5). Crossan imagines the direction of the movement of the people as highly significant. John stands on the east bank of the Jordan in the desert region of Perea, and calls the people over to him there. "People cross over into the desert and are baptized in the Jordan as they return to the Promised Land." This, says Crossan, was "politically explosive"[6] insofar as the action signaled not merely the people reclaiming the Land promised to them long ago, but the God of Israel about to reclaim it out of the hands of the current rulers, particularly Herod Antipas. "A Transjordanian desert location and a baptism in the Jordan, precisely the Jordan, had overtones, explicit and implicit, of political subversion . . . Desert and Jordan, prophet and crowds, were always a volatile mix calling for immediate preventive strikes."[7] John was a fearless apocalyptic prophet who envisioned the eschatological Coming One doing for the people what they could not do for themselves.

6. Crossan, *Historical Jesus*, 231.
7. Ibid., 235.

JOHN BAPTIZES JESUS

Puzzling as the baptism of Jesus may have been for the gospel writers—and it was rather puzzling as we shall see—its solid place in the Jesus tradition leaves the gospel writers little choice but to include the event in their narratives. Each of the writers tells the story of the baptism in their own way, which is testimony to their problem with Jesus being baptized by John: the one baptizing is superior to the one being baptized. Furthermore, if John's baptism was about repentance from transgressions, that would put Jesus in the same sinful state as the other candidates for baptism. By the time the gospels were written, forty to seventy years after the event, Jesus-Christology had declared Jesus the sinless Son of God; hence their problem with Jesus being baptized by John in the Jordan. A survey of the various renderings in the gospel sources should help focus the issue.

Mark, the earliest of the Synoptics, is the most straightforward: "In those days Jesus came from Nazareth of Galilee and was baptized by John in the Jordan" (1:9). Immediately preceding this one-line comment, Mark describes John as "proclaiming a baptism of repentance for the forgiveness of sins" (1:4). Mark seems to be able to hold these two in tension, qualified only by the extraordinary voice from the heavens immediately following the baptism: "You are my Son, the Beloved; with you I am well pleased" (1:11).

The fragmentary Gospel of the Hebrews, probably originating in Egypt some sixty years after Mark, delivers Jesus from complicity with the sinners: "The mother of the Lord and his brothers said to him, 'John the Baptist baptized for the forgiveness of sins. Let's go and get baptized by him.' But he said to them, 'How have I sinned? So why should I go and get baptized by him? Only if I am ignorant of what I speak" (*Gos. Heb.* 2; *Gos. Naz.* 2 has the same wording). In this text Jesus is self-consciously without sin, unless his self-knowledge is ignorance. The tenor of the statement implies that Jesus did not submit to John's baptism.

The Gospel of the Ebionites reads like Mark: "When the people were baptized, Jesus also came and got baptized by John" (*Gos Eb.* 4:1). There is no effort made to qualify the baptism of Jesus, compared to the baptism of the others who came, except that Jesus' baptism is followed by the heavenly declaration as in Mark.

When we come to the Gospel of Matthew, however, the problem of Jesus' baptism by John becomes more sharply focused. Notice the qualifiers that come through in the dialogue between John and Jesus: "Then Jesus came from Galilee to John at the Jordan, to be baptized by him. John would have prevented him, saying, 'I need to be baptized by you, and do you come to me?' But Jesus answered him, 'Let it be so now; for it is proper for us in this way to fulfill all righteousness.' Then he consented" (Matt. 3:13–15). Matthew ties in the act of baptism with a prevailing theme in that gospel: righteousness. While Matthew follows Mark elsewhere in the narrative about John's baptism, the writer weaves in a resolution to the two problems cited above —superiority of the baptizer, and the sins of the baptized. First, John declares Jesus superior to

Part II: Jesus

him, so he does not at first consent to the baptism, and second, Jesus declares John's baptism an act of righteousness, and therefore something to which he should submit.

Luke simply mutes the baptism by putting it in a subordinate clause in the context of Jesus' praying, thematic in Luke. "Now when all the people were baptized, and when Jesus also had been baptized and was praying, . . ." Thus the focus falls not on the baptism, but on prayer, the descent of the Spirit, and the voice out of the heavens.

The Gospel of John, while making much of John the Baptizer, makes sure also to put him in a secondary position to Jesus. John is simply "witness" and "voice," not the light-bringer or life-giver that Jesus is (John 1:6-9, 20-21). The Fourth Gospel does not even acknowledge that Jesus was baptized by John, only that the Baptizer witnessed the descent of the Spirit on Jesus: "And John testified, 'I saw the Spirit descending from heaven like a dove, and it remained on him'" (1:32). More than that, the Baptizer in the Fourth Gospel points to Jesus as the one who takes away the sin of the world (1:29), making John's baptism for the remission of sins insignificant by its absence from the narrative. Add to that the transfer of two of John's disciples to the followers of Jesus (1:37). As "witness" only, John is a minor actor who must eventually move off the stage to allow for the grand performance of Jesus: "He must increase, but I must decrease" (3:30).

Despite diminishing the status of John the Baptizer in the presence of the Christology in the Fourth Gospel, the evidence overall points to the fact that Jesus went out to the desert where John was baptizing, and submitted to his baptism. By so doing he was affirming John's vision and preaching, identifying with his mission of purification, and joining with the people awaiting the Coming One who will put things right. In short, both John and Jesus were preparing the people for the coming kingdom of God.

JOHN IMPRISONED AND EXECUTED

"The more clearly we understand John," states Paula Fredriksen, "the more clearly we might understand Jesus."[8] One thing is clearly evident from the sources: John was not preaching and baptizing in a corner. The whole country, including Herod Antipas, knew about John's word and work. Crowds went out to the desert not only to hear him, but also to do as he said. But "crowds, as we know, were dangerous and could get out of hand."[9] Josephus, quoted above, points to John's popularity and influence as the reason for Herod's determination to silence him. Jesus was present with John, was baptized by him, but was not thrown in prison with him. One can only extrapolate, then, that Jesus had not started his ministry while John was active in his.

Mark also tells his version of the story about John's preaching that resulted in his imprisonment and execution. In that version John confronts Herod Antipas directly about his adulterous marriage to Herodias, his brother's Philip's wife. Herodias, in turn, had her daughter ask for John's head on a platter. Antipas was reluctant to honor their

---

8. Fredriksen, *Jesus*, 185.
9. Rivkin, *Crucified?* 49.

request, but was bound by his oath to the daughter of Herodias to give her whatever she asked, and so orders John's death (Mark 6:18–27). As we saw in chapter 6, Josephus also knows about the adulterous marriage of Herod, and condemns it as a violation of Jewish law. Josephus, however, finds the cause behind John's imprisonment and subsequent execution not merely in a personal affront against Herod and Herodias, but in the larger problem of John's attracting crowds to his preaching and baptism.

The two accounts, Mark's and Josephus', have one important element in common. Both of them agree that John's preaching had a moral core. He called the people to repent of their sins, to change their hearts and their ways, and purify their bodies in baptism in the Jordan. Presumably Herod and Herodias knew the ethical character of John's preaching, but did not submit to his word or his baptism. With John out of the way they were able to continue in their power positions without fear of recrimination.

Mark avers that Jesus did not launch his own ministry until John was imprisoned: "Now after that John was put in prison, Jesus came into Galilee, preaching the gospel of the kingdom of God" (Mark 1:14). Did Jesus simply carry on the vision and work of John? Or did he dissociate himself and his work from that of John? The answer seems to lie somewhere between these two. Jesus continued to preach repentance, and offer good news about the arrival of the kingdom of God. But, in the word and deed of Jesus, the kingdom had "come near," as near as Jesus himself (Mark 1:15). While John announced the cataclysmic judgment of God for which people should prepare themselves, Jesus acted out its arrival in his word and work. There is no record of John having performed any miracle, healing or otherwise. Jesus, on the other hand, is known for his acts of compassion and restoration as representative of the reign of God.

There is a very telling story in the Q Source that illuminates the similarity and difference between the vision-and-ministry of John and that of Jesus about the expected reign of God. The story is set at a time when John is in prison. He has heard about the ministry of Jesus, and wonders how it corresponds to his own, so he sends two disciples to inquire.

> And John, on hearing . . . about all these things, sending through his disciples, said, to him: "Are you the one to come, or are we to expect someone else?" And in reply he said to them: "Go report to John what you hear and see: The blind regain their sight and the lame walk around, the skin-diseased are cleansed and the deaf hear, and the dead are raised, and the poor are given good news. And blessed is whoever is not offended by me." (Q 7:18–23 Matthew 11:2–6)

John had been preaching about the Coming One in expectation of the in-breaking of the great Day of the Lord. Now Jesus is making a name for himself among the people, not by calling them to purification and baptism in the Jordan, but by offering them the gift of God where they live. John's query through his two disciples is one of hope more than doubt. He recognizes in the word and work of Jesus something other than his own. Hence his question: "Are you the one who is to come, or are we to wait for another?" The response Jesus sends back to John is affirmative. The evidence of the reign of God—as compared to the reign of Herod who threw John in prison—is this:

Part II: Jesus

"the blind receive their sight, the lame walk, the lepers are cleansed, the deaf hear, the dead are raised, the poor have good news brought to them." The offense might be that the list does not include the release of prisoners. John might rightly have expected the arrival of the Coming One to bring an end to the unjust rule of Herod, and the opening of the prison doors for all those wrongfully incarcerated. John remained in Machaerus prison until his bloody execution. Jesus would suffer a similar fate in another stronghold in due course. All the while the kingdom was active despite the injustice meted out by the political rulers.

JESUS ADDS A CODICIL TO HIS PRAISE OF JOHN

That John had a group of disciples is taken for granted in the gospels (Mark 2:18; Luke 5:33). Whether Jesus was among them at any time is not so clear. If his baptism and his profound respect for John are signs of discipleship, it is also evident that he did not continue with the group that was following John. After John was arrested Jesus began his own preaching, and called his own disciples (Mark 1:14–19). That did not mean that he opposed John's word and work, but only that he went beyond them to perform his own. The attitude of Jesus towards John comes through in three very probing sayings, each of which calls for comment.

The first, found in the Q Source, is an extraordinary word of praise for the person of John and for what his represents. "I tell you: There has not arisen among women's offspring anyone who surpasses John" (Q 7:28 = Matt. 11:11). Even if this is hyperbole —"the greatest human in history"[10]—it leaves no doubt about the enormously high regard Jesus had for the character of the man and the effects of his ministry.

Yet this word of praise does not stand alone. It forms the basis for one of the most provocative sayings of Jesus, a codicil to his testament about John: "Yet the least significant in God's kingdom is more than he." This qualification of the commendation for John is subject to more than one interpretation. J. C. O'Neill believes Jesus "is contrasting the present state of the greatest of men with the future state of the least in the coming kingdom."[11] With respect, I fail to see O'Neill's "present state" and "future state" in the diction of the saying. Nor is "*coming* kingdom" a qualifier in Jesus' word. It would seem rather, that two realms of "greatness" are compared. John was a highly influential human being in the world of Palestine. He had the raw courage to confront Herod, enough popularity to bring down Herod's wrath upon him, great *human* attributes that Jesus recognizes. But the greatness of the kingdom of God, whether present or future, operates by a different standard. The least are recognized; *they* are "great" by the rule of God.

A striking variation of this saying appears in the *Gospel of Thomas* 46, which makes the saying about the least in the kingdom even more poignant. "Jesus said, 'From Adam to John the Baptist, among those born of women, not one is so much greater than John the Baptist that his eyes should not be averted. But I have said that

---

10. Sanders, *Jesus and Judaism*, 93.
11. O'Neill, *Messiah*, 10–11.

whoever among you becomes *a child* will recognize the (Father's) imperial rule and will become greater than John.'" This saying is reminiscent of another in Mark, the narrative context of which tells something of the social context. People were bringing little children to Jesus, but the disciples "spoke sternly" to the ones who brought the little ones. They were acting out of the social convention that views children as insignificant, unworthy of notice. Jesus responds indignantly, "Let the little children come to me; do not stop them; for it is to such as these that the kingdom of God belongs."

Little children in the ancient world were the weakest of the weak. From evidence in papyrus fragments, Crossan discovered that infants, non-Jewish infants especially, were at the mercy of their parents for good or ill. Infants could be "abandoned at birth by their parents and saved from the rubbish dumps to be reared as slaves . . . To be a child was to be a nobody, with the possibility of becoming a somebody absolutely dependent on parental discretion and parental standing in the community."[12] It would have been an insult in an ancient society—or even a modern one—for an adult to be compared to a child. But that is exactly the comparison that highlights the character of the kingdom of God in the new word of Jesus. The kingdom of God is made up entirely of children: dependent, defenseless, powerless children. Anyone who thinks otherwise, according to the saying, does not belong in the kingdom of God in the present or the future.

The second provocative saying in praise of John comes from the same Q Source. Addressing the crowds, Jesus said, "What did you go out into the wilderness to look at? A reed shaken by the wind? If not, what *did* you go out to see? A person arrayed in finery? Look, those wearing finery are in kings' houses. But then what did you go out to see? A prophet? Yes, I tell you, even more than a prophet! This is the one about whom it has been written: Look, I am sending my messenger ahead of you, who will prepare your path in front of you" (Q 7:24–28 = Matt. 11:7–11). The questions are sarcastically humorous. No one would go out to a desert to look at a reed, nor would they expect to find someone in that locality dressed fashionably and living in luxury. Herod Antipas dressed in royal robes and lived in his luxurious palace in Tiberias, but his kingdom did not reflect the kingdom of God. John's abode in the desert, on the other hand, together with his attire of camel's hair, sets him apart as one who speaks for God for the benefit of the people. The crowds can expect to find God in John's desert-world, not in the world of those who dress fashionably and live in luxury at the expense of others who have no such life. Only one group in the crowd, if they happen to be there, would find offense in Jesus' saying: the ones living in luxury in royal palaces.

The third saying of Jesus about the kingdom of God since the time of John is one of the most difficult to understand. "No saying of Jesus has been the subject of more disagreement"[13] than this one from the Q Source: "The law and the prophets were until John. From then on the kingdom of God is violated and the violent plunder it" (Q 16:16 = Matt. 11:12). Matthew's rendering is even more problematic than Luke's: "From the days of John the Baptist until now the kingdom of heaven has suffered

---

12. Crossan, *Historical Jesus*, 269.
13. Chilton, *Pure*, 94.

Part II: Jesus

violence, and the violent take it by force." The difference may be reckoned as coming from two versions of the Q Source used by Matthew and Luke respectively. If not that, then the two evangelists, in their own way, have tried to make sense of their source for their readers and thus rendered the saying differently. The difficulty remains. Why is the kingdom of God associated with violence?

I find Bruce Chilton's analysis of this saying convincing. An expert in Aramaic, Chilton came upon the term *têqêp*, which Jesus probably used in his telling of this saying. The Greek word in Q, used by Matthew and Luke, lacks the flexibility of the Aramaic *têqêp*. "*Têqêp*, whose basic meaning is 'take' or 'grasp', may refer both to prevailing over something or someone and to the intensification of effort in order to prevail."[14] If Luke best represents the saying in Q, then the problem of "violence" occurs only in the third part of the saying: "everyone tries to enter [the kingdom] violently" (Gk. *biazetai*). The NRSV has "by force." With the flexibility of the Aramaic *têqêp* in mind, Chilton uses the English "avail" to resolve the "violence" associated with the kingdom of God. Thus he renders the three parts of the saying as follows:

a) the law and the prophets were until John, and then

b) the kingdom of God avails itself (it has force or imposes itself)

c) and everyone avails himself of it (takes advantage).

Effectively the saying pinpoints the arrival of the kingdom of God in the preaching of John, and its expansion in the preaching of Jesus and his disciples. The inference is, I believe, that the kingdom of God, by its very nature, is an irresistible force in the world. People will *grasp* it; they will *avail* themselves of it by virtue of its divine intrusion into their human lives in the world. In this respect, then, the kingdom of God is not associated with human violence, a negative evil force in the world, but with the unstoppable life-giving dynamism that is by nature, the rule of God. Another way of construing the saying might be this: the kingdom of God is not dependent on any human power to make it effective in the world. It imposes itself on human society, and people grasp it there as an alternate to the conventional rule of human power brokers.

In conclusion, Jesus had more than a detached respect for John the Baptizer. He submitted to John's preaching and his baptism, thus placing himself squarely within a revolutionary movement that appealed to the crowds. Herod had John imprisoned and later executed to prevent subversion of his rule in Galilee and Perea. Jesus, having endorsed John and his ministry, launched his own mission when John was imprisoned at Machaerus. The theme of the kingdom of God continued with Jesus, not merely as a coming reign for which people should prepare themselves, but as one already *at hand*, active in the lives of the people through healings, exorcisms, and the proclamation of good news to the destitute poor. The ministry of John that sent him to prison and death intensified in the ministry of Jesus, with at least as much offense, and with the same prospect of arrest and execution. But the kingdom of God prevails invariably, despite the human rulers of the age, and people take advantage of its paradoxical presence in their world.

14. Ibid., 95.

8

Enacting the Kingdom of God

HARDLY ANY SCHOLAR OF THE NEW TESTAMENT WOULD DISPUTE THE FACT that Jesus talked about the kingdom of God. Many see the term of reference as the centerpiece of the ministry of Jesus. What he meant by the term exactly has occupied his interpreters for many years. Within the purpose and scope of this study of Jesus and Paul I can devote only this chapter and the next to the significance Jesus attached to "the kingdom of God" through his action and his word as transmitted through the gospels.

BACKGROUND

It may be overstatement to say that Jesus minted the phrase "kingdom of God" (*basileia tou theou*). The idea was already present in the Hebrew Scriptures and in the Aramaic Targums, although not precisely in the form found in the Gospels. The nation of Israel had its physical, political kings, but there was no mistaking who was the king of Israel's kings. The Psalms proclaimed repeatedly "the Lord (*Yahweh*) is king" (e.g., Ps. 10:16; 93:1; 96:10). Even the charismatic king David himself had to take his position under the sovereign rule of *Yahweh*, Lord. Prophets, such as Nathan, saw to it that he did (2 Sam. 12:1–10). In First Chronicles 16 the scope of the kingship of the Lord extends beyond Israel: "Let the heavens be glad, and let the earth rejoice, and let them say *among the nations*, 'The LORD is king!'" (1 Chron. 16:31).

There can be little doubt that refrains such as these from the history and tradition of Israel informed the preaching of Jesus. Jewish leaders were equally familiar with the traditional religious concept that their one God was king of the whole of creation. As O'Neill points out, "We have to ask ourselves, then, whether or not Jesus held a view of the Kingdom that differed from the current Jewish views."[1]

Before moving in that direction, however, it should be stated that the proclamation of Jesus found an audience in the more immediate context of the kingdom of Herod Antipas in Galilee and Perea, and the rule of Pilate in Judea, both of them

---

1. O'Neill, *Messiah*, 13.

Part II: Jesus

subject to the imperial rule of Rome. For Jesus to proclaim the kingdom *of God* as the supreme alternative to the existing political rule in the Land, would court the charge of subversion. Implicitly he did just that, as the evidence will show.

It seems very unlikely that Jesus hoped for a revival of the Hasmonean priest-king system. That kingdom had come to an ignominious end, and had little chance of returning to power. Its demise upon the arrival of imperial Rome in 63 BCE begs several questions about the nature of the "kingdom of God" that Jesus envisioned and proclaimed. Would it be political? Would it be centered in Jerusalem? Would it have a human ruler? Was it a visionary kingdom of the future? Or would it be forever elusive, mysteriously breaking into the human state of affairs?

THE LANGUAGE

"Kingdom" may not be the best English translation of the Greek word, *basileia*. "Kingdom" implies a realm, a geographically bounded place where people live under the rule of a political leader and a government. In the case of an empire, smaller territories could be granted some degree of self-government with a ruler appointed from among their own people, but sanctioned and supervised always by the imperial ruler and his government. In this scenario the local king would be a pawn in the hands of the super power. This describes, in brief, the political situation into which Jesus of Nazareth projected his language about another rule of life and law, one that did not simply blend in with the existing rule of Herod and Rome, nor, for that part, with the authority of the Temple in Jerusalem. Perhaps "rule of God" would capture Jesus' idea better than "kingdom of God," but the latter has so etched itself into the psychological map of readers of the New Testament that it seems best to retain it in the current discussion. I will, at times, interchange "kingdom of God" with "rule of God."

SYMBOL

It would make the job of discovering Jesus' meaning much easier—although not necessarily more rewarding—if he had explained his terms of reference in unambiguous speech. What he meant by "kingdom" is left open to interpretation. As I mentioned above, "kingdom" is generally associated with a geographic piece of earth in which people live, governed by a ruler. The ruler of an earthly kingdom in the ancient world was not elected by popular vote of the people, but appointed by virtue of his/her heredity, charisma, and experience. The realm was then subject to the laws established by the ruler in collaboration with an authoritative body, such as a senate. If Jesus did not have this kind of kingdom in view when he spoke of the "Kingdom of God," then we are bound to ask how we are to understand his use of the term "kingdom."

The term stands in the sayings of Jesus virtually undefined, as though it needed no such thing. If "kingdom" was *a symbol* in the vision and voice of Jesus, that does not diminish its potency. As symbol, the meaning is open to a variety of possibilities, but not so open that anything goes. Terms, specifically loaded terms such as "kingdom," convey meaning in keeping with their accepted use. "Kingdom of God" in the language of Jesus was meant to evoke first the basic ideas of "kingdom" in circulation at the time and place in which Jesus lived, then qualified by the genitive construction, "*of God*." Therein lies the distinctive feature of the work and word of Jesus.

Moreover, it is game-playing to think of the symbolic use of the "kingdom" as somehow devoid of real meaning. Symbols are not arbitrary images and artifacts and vocabulary constructed to spellbind people. People—especially religious people—live within a system of symbols. When a symbol is nuanced, the people involved in its performance need to know its origin and how its nuance affects their lives. Sanders puts the matter of Jesus' meaning of "*kingdom* of God" sharply: "I propose that *we know perfectly well what [Jesus] meant in general terms: the ruling power of God*."[2] How and when that "ruling power of God" would come into effect is a matter of some debate among New Testament scholars. To read it as a future reality entirely, devalues the acts and words of Jesus, including his act of facing death by crucifixion. The value of the ministry of Jesus in first-century Palestine lay in his variegated demonstration of "the ruling power of God" in what he did and said on behalf of the people in the company of his disciples.

RELIGIOUS POWER

On the religious side, the Temple of Jerusalem wielded its own kind of political power over the people. Even though the Hasmoneans had lost their power to rule by the time of Jesus, the High Priest, in conjunction with the Jewish court made up of priests, scribes, and Pharisees, was still very much in charge of the religious life of the Jewish people in the Roman province of Palestine. Jewish religious life of that time was not an adjunct entity tacked onto their social reality. Ancient societies were religious at core. The Law under which Jewish people of the time lived their lives was religious. The notion of a secular legal system is a modern construct. God ordained the Jewish Law, and appointed the priesthood to ensure that the people obey its precepts in every aspect of their lives. In this respect, therefore, the priests serving in the Temple of Jerusalem were the custodians responsible for the rule of God's Law in Jewish society. And Rome allowed that much self-government to the occupied peoples, provided their self-government did not interfere with Roman jurisprudence, conscription to the Roman military, and taxation from the occupied people in support of the imperial system.

Scribes and Pharisees were the experts in the interpretation of God's Law for the people, but the priests executed its proper ritual observance, reflected especially in the bringing of tithes and offerings of various kinds to the priests of the Temple. To be in a right relationship with the Temple meant a right relationship with God, the supreme benefactor of the elect people of the covenant. In this religious environment, the rule of God came to expression in the proper observance of the Law of God inscribed in the scrolls of the Torah and enshrined in the precincts of the Temple.

2. Sanders, *Jesus and Judaism*, 127.

Part II: Jesus

In view of this way of life and thought in Palestinian Judaism, the "kingdom of God" may not have sounded strange to the ears of the Jewish people of Galilee and Judea. They had learned through story, Targum, and ritual how their God ruled their lives. Yet Jesus, himself a Jewish resident of Galilee familiar with this way of life, stepped outside the embedded conventions to announce the arrival of "the kingdom of God," as though *not* present in the existing way of Jewish life, much less in Roman occupation of the Land.

In the next chapter I will examine how Jesus gives verbal expression to the "kingdom of God" in selected sayings transmitted through the gospels, canonical and non-canonical. Meanwhile, in this chapter I will try to capture from the sources the ways in which Jesus *enacted* the kingdom of God.

THE CALL OF DISCIPLES

Of all the well-attested historical facts about Jesus, none carries greater weight than his call of disciples to be with him, the call of the four fishermen being the best known (Mark 1:16–20). Too often in modern Christian parlance, however, the call of disciples points to Jesus as teacher, or rabbi, not as the active agent of the kingdom of God. Granted, Jesus is addressed sometimes in the gospels as "rabbi" (e.g., Mark 9:5; Matt. 26:25; John 1:49). But that title should not be confused with the later Rabbinic Academy that held sway after the destruction of the Temple in 70 CE. Jesus was not an official Rabbi of that school, so it can be misleading to call him *Rabbi Jesus*,[3] as though he were in the same league as Rabbi Jochanan Ben Zakkai or Rabbi Judah the Prince of the post-Temple era. "Rabbi" was a title of respect at the time of Jesus, much like "Sir" in the present time. It did carry the connotation of "teacher of students," but the title had not yet reached the particular nuance of a professional instructor-leader from an established school. Jesus' call of disciples "to be with him" and "to be sent out to proclaim the message" (Mark 3:14) *enacted the coming of the kingdom of God* in the towns and villages of Palestine. More on that subject later in the next chapter.

Beyond Discipleship

In some Protestant denominations, with which I am familiar, discipleship is nothing short of a doctrine. The doctrine grew out of a reading of the gospels about the disciples who followed Jesus. The term "disciple" (*mathētēs*) in this case is understood simply as "student," one who learns from a master-teacher. Hence the people who emphasize discipleship as a doctrine believe they are adhering to the model of Jesus who called disciples around him to teach them to obey the will of God. In this thinking everyone who is a believer is by that confession also a disciple of Jesus. In this understanding, discipleship happens by reading, or hearing, the ethical teaching of Jesus in the gospels especially, and by putting those learned precepts into practice.

Viewing Jesus' call of disciples from this confessional stance, the radical nature of Jesus' call to *certain people* to follow him, literally follow after him, could be lost

---

3. Chilton, *Rabbi Jesus*.

under the doctrinal veil of discipleship. Paul, for example, did not teach "discipleship," nor did he use the term "disciple" in his letters to congregations. His aim in bringing people to faith in Jesus as the Messiah of God was not to have them "follow Jesus"—certainly not literally!—but to have them incorporated into the Spirit of the crucified-resurrected Jesus resident in the new community. True, he encouraged them to be "imitators": imitators of himself (1 Cor. 4:16; 11:1); imitators of the Lord (1 Thess. 1:6); imitators of the congregations of God in Judea (1 Thess. 2:14). But imitators are not disciples in the sense that Jesus called certain people to *follow after* him wherever he went. Following after (*akolouthein*) Jesus, I submit, involved much more than learning patterns of thought and behavior, however worthy. "To walk behind or follow after is a Biblicism . . . denoting allegiance."[4] It meant a radical new order of social existence that signaled the in-breaking of the unconventional kingdom of God, headed up by Jesus.

A distinction should be made between those who believed in Jesus and disciples he called to follow after him. Mark introduces the ministry of Jesus as follows: "The time is fulfilled, and the kingdom of God has come near; repent, and believe in the good news" (Mark 1:14). "Repent" (*metanoein*) need not imply, and in this text does not imply, that the hearers were sinners in need of purification and forgiveness. At heart the verb implies "change of mind," a turn-around. The change in direction means believing that the opportune time (*kairos*) has come for the kingdom of God to be manifest. This is good news. People in the audience are asked to "believe" this good word, and to act upon it. The act of believing means being persuaded in heart and mind that the word is worthy of trust. "Repent" and "believe" belong together. The arrival of the kingdom of God in the word and deed of Jesus involved a turn-around in thinking and living on the part of those persuaded by the announcement. But this proclamation was not a call for all believers to *follow after* Jesus physically.

The Twelve

The importance of "the Twelve" for understanding the mission of Jesus in bringing the kingdom of God to bear in Palestinian society cannot be overstressed. Before tackling that subject specifically a word about the radical nature of the call to follow after Jesus would be in place.

Unconditional Following

The call to follow Jesus was unequivocal, unconditional, and unconventional. Example after example could be summoned to illustrate the point. Instead of doing that, I will follow the lead of Hengel in his treatment of one text as paradigmatic of the nature of Jesus' call to follow him.[5] The text comes from Q (= Matt. 8:21–22): "But another said to him: Master, permit me first to go and bury my father. But he said to him: Follow me, and leave the dead to bury their own dead" (9:59–60). The man's request, in response to Jesus' call to follow him, appears to be well within

---

4. Meyer, "Language," 93.
5. Hengel, *Charismatic*, 3–15.

Part II: Jesus

reason, and certainly within longstanding Jewish tradition. Respect for one's parents was not simply a matter of social contract, an accepted norm in Jewish communities. It was an act of obedience to one of the Ten Commandments: "Honor your father and your mother, so that your days may be long in the land that the LORD your God is giving you" (Exod. 20:12).

Jewish tradition, carried forward in the Talmud, sets respect for a deceased relative, especially a parent, high on the list of obligations. "One whose dead [relative] lies before him is exempt from saying the Shema' and from the prayers and blessings and from all precepts laid down in the Torah."[6] Exemption from these very important Jewish rituals for the sake of burying a relative illustrates the overriding importance of the duty of attending the funeral of a father. On compassionate grounds alone, the man's request was legitimate. But the man was Jewish. To attend the Jewish funeral of one's father was the duty of an honorable son. The man in question was asking only that he be allowed to fulfill his filial Jewish duty. Jesus' response to his request was harsh and completely out of normal expectation. With this kind of response to a would-be disciple, "Jesus stood outside *any discoverable uniform teaching tradition of Judaism*."[7]

Quite apart from the offence in the saying, it is hard to know how the man would have understood the reply. How could physically dead people bury other dead people? The ones doing the burying may be understood as spiritually dead, as many interpreters believe. I am not altogether satisfied with the "spiritually dead" interpretation. In the context of Jesus' proclamation of the kingdom of God, the dead buriers of the dead would be those outside the values of the kingdom to which Jesus is calling the candidate for the position of disciple. In Hengel's words, "dead buriers of the dead are those who do not allow themselves to be affected by Jesus' message or by the nearness of the Kingdom."[8]

This is the kind of saying the evangelists, or their sources, would likely not create. The saying puts Jesus in a rather bad light by normal standards. But there it stands, transmitted in Matthew and Luke without polish or polity. The uncanny break with the norm in the saying signals the urgency of the oncoming kingdom of God in the person and ministry of Jesus. A call to join him in such an unconventional endeavor requires nothing less than unconditional acceptance of the call, or else be rejected from the ranks of the disciples of Jesus. "The unconditional nature of following [Jesus] . . . is to be explained only on the basis of his unique authority as the proclaimer of the *imminent Kingdom of God*."[9]

Immediately preceding this provocative Q saying in Matthew 8 and Luke 9 is another of similar vintage: "And someone said to him: I will follow you wherever you go. And Jesus said to him: Foxes have holes, and birds of the sky have nests; but the son of humanity does not have anywhere he can lay his head" (9:57–58 = Matt. 8:19–20).

6. Talmud, *Berakoth* 3:1.
7. Hengel, *Charismatic*, 49.
8. Ibid., 8.
9. Ibid., 15.

Enacting the Kingdom of God

Jesus had a home and family in Nazareth. He could have remained in the home and continued his association with his family. But he chose instead an itinerant, charismatic ministry, a life of total submission to the unplanned provision and mercy of his God. Foxes and birds have their respective places to live on the earth, but the One representing Humanity has no place to rest his head. That One belongs to another realm, which he calls "the kingdom of God." To become a disciple of this One will require complete and unconditional abandonment to the rule of God in the presence of Jesus.

One final example of the nature of the call to be a disciple of Jesus must suffice. It comes from Mark 10:17–22 (Matt. 19:16–23; Luke 18:18–23). A man came to Jesus and asked how he might attain eternal life. Jesus prescribed the keeping of the commandments of God, to which the man replied, "Teacher, I have kept all these since my youth" (Mark 10:20). Jesus loved the man, and wanted him to *follow after* him. To do so the man would have to sell his possessions, which were many, and give the proceeds to the poor. When the man heard this "he was shocked and went away grieving" (10:22). This was not merely Jesus' invitation to turn and believe the good news of the kingdom of God; it was a call to be *engaged with Jesus* in bringing the kingdom into effect. To do so would mean giving up everything for the privilege of belonging to the disciple-group. As O'Neill puts it, "the demand made on the rich young ruler was not meant as a demand automatically made by Jesus on all rich [people]; it was a demand made on this man to enter the special number of those commissioned to preach the gospel."[10]

Before moving on to the special number, Twelve, a word about Jesus' relationship to his biological family, vis-à-vis his disciples.

A New Family

The Gospel of Mark, the earliest narrative gospel, makes very little mention of the family of Jesus. The three places where they do appear in the narrative (3:21; 3:31–35; 6:1–3) they come across in a rather negative light. None of the family members, not even the mother of Jesus, appears in the narrative about the trial and crucifixion of Jesus. Other mothers are present at the narrative scene, but not the mother of Jesus (15:40, 47; 16:1).

In the first narrative, Mark 3:21, a crowd had gathered to hear Jesus, and to benefit from his healing power. "When his family heard it, they went out to restrain him, for the people were saying he has gone out of his mind." The family's restraint of Jesus was meant to pull him back into the safe, conventional way of the family and the village in which he had previously lived and worked. In addition, their restraint points to their distance from his revolutionary way of speaking and acting.[11] They wanted no part of a family member who was perceived to be "out of his mind." The third narrative in Mark 6 sends a similar signal. The people of Nazareth, where Jesus had grown up, reject his "wisdom" with the note that his mother and brothers and sisters belong to their village community. The family stands with the village community, and the community with

10. O'Neill, *Messiah*, 88.
11. See Hengel, *Revolutionist?* 19–36.

Part II: Jesus

the family. They do not stand with Jesus, because he has stepped outside the norms of Jewish village life in Galilee, and thus also outside his biological family ties.

By far the most pointed of the three narrative pieces in Mark is in 3:31–35. It bears directly on the nature of the call to become a disciple of Jesus the kingdom-bringer. Again, a crowd was sitting around Jesus listening to his words. His mother and his brothers came on the scene, but they were standing *outside* the circle. Someone sent word to Jesus that his mother and brothers and sisters were *outside* asking for him. His reply is peculiar: "Who are my mother and brothers?" As though he did not know his biological family! The question opens the way for a new family quotient. Looking at those close to him, he said, "Here are my mother and my brothers! Whoever does the will of God is my brother and sister and mother." Sociologists call this a fictive family. In the context of the gospels, the new family is, above all, a circle of disciples who have left behind the ordinary affairs of life, even their families, to be part of the eschatological kingdom of God in the person and power of Jesus.

In this light, the saying in Q about "hating" family members in order to follow Jesus makes some sense. The stark hyperbole is shocking: "The one who does not hate father and mother cannot be my disciple; and the one who does not hate son and daughter cannot be my disciple" (Q 14:26 =Matt. 10:37–39; cf. *Gos. Thom.* 55). The question is one of exclusive sovereignty: Who rules the person's life? There cannot be two masters for one slave (Q 16:13 = Matt. 6:24).

The Number Twelve

We come now to the significance of twelve disciples specifically. Even though twelve names are attached to the number in the Synoptic Gospels, their names are not as important as the number itself. There is even slight disagreement between Mark and Luke about their names (Matt. 10:2–4; Mark 3:16–19; Luke 6:14–16). The Gospel of John speaks of the Twelve, but does not give their names (6:67, 70, 71; 20:24). In fact, two of the inner circle of three—Simon (Peter), James and John—are not mentioned by name in the Fourth Gospel. One of them, Simon Peter, is prominent in that Gospel, as he is in the Synoptics, although Simon is not as worthy in the Fourth Gospel as the unnamed "disciple whom Jesus loved" (John 13:23; 21:7, 20).

The symbolic significance of the Twelve carried over into the tradition of the post-Easter community, even after Judas Iscariot had handed Jesus over to the authorities and was no longer numbered with the Twelve. Paul, for example, drawing on the tradition about the appearances of the resurrected Jesus, said, "he appeared to Cephas, then to the twelve" (1 Cor. 15:5). Even if there were only eleven remaining, Judas having killed himself, the group was still the symbolic twelve. There can hardly be any doubt about what the Twelve represented. The patriarch Jacob had twelve sons from whom came the twelve tribes that constituted Israel, God's elect nation. The gospel writers did not spell out explicitly the meaning of Jesus' calling exactly twelve disciples. But as Freyne points out, in the Gospel of Matthew, "as the Twelve they evoke for the reader the original Israel as a twelve-tribe people (Matt. 19:28)."[12]

---

12. Freyne, *Galilee, Jesus*, 87.

Questions remain: If Jesus intended the Twelve to signal something about the twelve-tribe Israel, what might that have been? Did the Twelve know what they represented? If so, did they act accordingly?

Twelve-tribe Israel had been dislocated and dismantled many years earlier when the Assyrians carried off the northern tribes in 722 BCE. The two tribes to the south, Judah and Benjamin, had survived their captivity in Babylonia. A remnant of them had returned to the Land, and had rebuilt the Temple and the city of Jerusalem. But the people continued to be dominated by outside overlords. At the time of Jesus, Rome ruled over the Land and its people. Along comes Jesus leading twelve men, and also sending them out to towns and villages to proclaim the message of the kingdom of God. The whole enterprise echoes the oracles of prophets and poets of Israel's past, only now the time is fulfilled and the kingdom of God is at hand. *All* Israel is being restored, not as a political reality, not as a nation, but as *a people ruled by God alone*. Strange as it may seem, "all Israel" does not require every member of every tribe to be included. A *remnant* can constitute the whole, as prophets and poets of Israel had announced repeatedly. The great prophet of Jerusalem, Isaiah, envisioned a time when "the Lord will extend his hand . . . to recover *the remnant* that is left of his people . . . He will raise a signal for the nations, and will assemble the outcasts of Israel, and gather the dispersed of Judah from the four corners of the earth" (Isa. 11:11–12; see also Micah 2:12; Zeph. 3:11–13).

The gathering and the assembling of a remnant from both Israel and Judah speaks of *all* Israel, which the Twelve represent symbolically. But there is more going on in the call and commission of the Twelve than a symbolic gathering of a remnant of Israel. Jesus really did send the disciples out to heal and to announce the good news of the arrival of the kingdom of God. Fredriksen makes the point that "the number recalls the plenum of Israel. By Jesus' day, ten of those tribes had long since ceased to exist . . . The kingdom was coming soon; [the disciples'] unpreparedness embodied their conviction . . . To assemble the twelve tribes so many centuries after the Assyrian conquest would take a miracle. But that, I think, is what Jesus was expecting."[13] Her last opinion is debatable. It is not at all clear that Jesus envisioned a miraculous restoration of the twelve tribes symbolized by his call and commission of the Twelve. Israel, or the remnant thereof, could just as well be a reference to the people of God who respond to Jesus' ministry in the company of the Twelve in Galilee and Judea, and by extension to any who heed the good news of the rule of God enacted in the word and deed of Jesus and the Twelve. Paul called himself an Israelite by birth (Rom. 11:1; 2 Cor. 11:22), but that by itself did not make him a member of "the Israel of God" (Gal. 6:16). "Not all Israelites truly belong to Israel" (Rom. 9:6). For Paul, "the only thing that counts is faith working through love" (Gal. 5:6). I suggest that the Twelve symbolized the "Israel of God," active in bringing the rule of God to the lives of the people of the Land, and ultimately to people of the world who turn and believe the good news.

---

13. Fredriksen, *Jesus*, 98.

Part II: Jesus

Sanders has demonstrated that the hope for the restoration of the twelve tribes was expressed variously in post-biblical Jewish literature. And even when the number twelve was not given, "it is nevertheless true that the expectation of the reassembly of Israel was so widespread, and the memory of the twelve tribes remained so acute, that '*twelve*' *would necessarily mean* '*restoration*.'"[14] Given the evidence Sanders adduces, his conclusion is beyond dispute. The question is whether or not Jesus espoused precisely the same view of the restoration of Israel as his Jewish contemporaries. His call and commission of the Twelve disciples suggests not that he was expecting a literal restoration of the actual twelve tribes to the Land, but that he was *enacting the eschatological beginning* of "the Israel of God" under the rubric of "the kingdom of God."

Mission Instructions to the Twelve

I take the character of the mission instructions to the Twelve in the Synoptic Gospels to represent those of the historical Jesus. The reckless nature of the instructions speaks to their authenticity. Furthermore, a form of the instructions—living off the hospitality of others—is evident in the letters of Paul, where he bases his expectation of sustenance on a tradition of Jesus that says "laborers deserve their food" (1 Cor. 9:14; Matt. 10:10; Luke 10:7).

Mark's version is the most basic of the three found in the Synoptic Gospels:

> [Jesus] called the twelve and began to send them out two by two, and gave them authority over the unclean spirits. He ordered them to take nothing for their journey except a staff; no bread, no bag, no money in their belts; but to wear sandals and not to put on two tunics. He said to them, "Wherever you enter a house, stay there until you leave the place. If any place will not welcome you and they refuse to hear you, as you leave, shake off the dust that is on your feet as a testimony against them." (10:7–11).

Matthew restricts the scope of the mission. The Twelve are not to go to the nations or the Samaritans, but to the "lost sheep of the house of Israel" (Matt. 10:5–6). Presumably the Samaritans did not qualify for the lost sheep of Israel, at least not in Matthew's understanding. Who, then, might be the lost sheep? I suspect they would be those without proper standing according to the Law, otherwise called "sinners." The subject of the "sinners" will come up again later.

Both Matthew and Luke include the instruction to proclaim the good news of the kingdom of God (Luke 9:2; Matt. 10:7). What stands out in the instruction is that the proclamation of the rule of God is corroborated by *acts of healing, and casting out demons*. Noticeably absent from the list of instructions in any of the gospels is the instruction to elicit repentance for the forgiveness of sins accompanied by purification and sacrifice. Instead, the in-breaking rule of God is depicted as having restorative effects for suffering humanity, beginning with the Jewish villages of Galilee.

---

14. Sanders, *Jesus and Judaism*, 98.

A Question about the Seventy (or Seventy-two) Others in Luke

Only in the Gospel of Luke do we find Jesus sending out "seventy others" (Luke 10:1). Some important manuscripts give the number "seventy-two." Whether the round-figure seventy or seventy-two, the number had symbolic significance, just as Twelve had. The symbolism is related to the distinctive character of the Gospel of Luke in relation to the Acts of the Apostles.

There can hardly be any doubt that the author-redactor of the Gospel of Luke was the same person who produced the Acts of the Apostles. More than that the two volumes were in view from the inception of Luke.[15] In short, the narrative of Acts, about the development of the early post-Easter community, purports to be the logical (more properly "theo-logical") extension of the work and word of Jesus and the Twelve as represented in the Gospel of Luke. But the Twelve of Luke, centered in Jerusalem, play their part only in the first part of Acts (1–15). Another group in Acts, headed up by Paul, carry the gospel forward "to the ends of the earth" (Acts 1:8). One common factor pertains between the *preaching of Jesus and the Twelve* in Palestine and *the preaching of Paul and his colleagues* to "the ends of the earth." That factor is the Jewish Scriptures. Jesus preached his message of the kingdom of God in response to the prophetic intent of the Bible. But there were two forms of Jewish Scripture in the first century. One was the Hebrew Bible known and used in Palestine. The other was the translation of the Hebrew Bible into Greek to accommodate those outside Palestine.

The Alexandrian Jewish legend about the translation of the Hebrew Scriptures into Greek is key to understanding Luke's report of a separate commission of seventy-two others beyond the Twelve. The rather long narrative account about "the translation of the Pentateuch into Greek under Ptolemy II Philadelphus of Egypt (283–247 BCE),"[16] can be found in a document known as *The Letter of Aristeas*. Here it is in brief. The Jewish people in the Greek-speaking city of Alexandria in Egypt were no longer able to understand the Hebrew Scriptures being read in the synagogue. The leaders of the Jewish community appealed to the hierarchy in Jerusalem to support the project of translating the Hebrew text into Greek, the common language in Alexandria. The leaders in Jerusalem agreed, and appointed seventy-two able scribes to do the work. Each of the seventy-two went into a separate cell to translate. The work took seventy-two days. When each of the seventy-two translators emerged they each presented a parallel translation without collaboration between them.

The *Letter of Aristeas*, probably written in the mid-second century BCE, served as propaganda for the wide acceptance of this Greek version of the Jewish Scriptures, commonly known as the Septuagint (LXX). This version became popular in many synagogues outside Palestine, and was the Scripture text Paul and his colleagues used in their mission to the Greek-speaking world. The author of Luke and Acts was immersed in the LXX, and knew very well the value of this translation for the successful mission to the larger world beyond the Jewish mission represented by the

---

15. I have made this case in Shillington, *Luke-Acts*, 6–20.
16. Scott, "Epistemology," 202.

Part II: Jesus

Twelve. "Moreover, the two commissions in Luke 9 and 10—those of the Twelve and of the Seventy-two—correspond rather well to the two-phase mission in Acts. Peter's missionary preaching represents the Aramaic-speaking Twelve of Judea (Acts 1–13), while Paul's missionary preaching represents the Seventy-two in the larger Hellenistic world (Acts 14–28)."[17]

How does this insight speak to the question of Jesus' sending "seventy-two others," a narrative found only in the special section of Luke? It would seem that Luke saw a need to generate a base of disciples *other than the Twelve* to authentic the world mission with which Luke-Acts is all too familiar. The symbolic "seventy-two" in Luke, the number associated with the "world Bible," underwrites the mission of Paul and his associates in Acts. As far as Luke-Acts is concerned, Paul's world mission stands in the tradition of Jesus along with, yet subsequent to, the Twelve. Thus, the commission of the "seventy-two others" attributed to the historical Jesus, should probably be viewed as the creative work of the historical author of Luke-Acts. His rearview perspective on the development of the Jesus-movement from a Jerusalem-based Jewish mission to an Antioch-based mission to the non-Jewish world likely informed his inclusion of a second sending of a larger symbolic group of "others."

HEALINGS AND EXORCISMS

Of the many acts attributed to Jesus in the gospels, none is more pronounced and pervasive than his acts of healing the sick and casting out demons. Several questions surround this phenomenon reported in the gospels: Were the healing powers of Jesus unique to him? Did Jesus consider his acts of healing characteristic of the coming kingdom of God? If so, how did Jesus think of his own identity in relation to his acts?

Miracles

Nineteenth century hymn writer, William Hunter, called Jesus "The Great Physician." To some extent the title is true: Jesus healed the sick. But his healing power did not consist of medicines and surgery of some kind. Without exception, the many acts of healing attributed to Jesus in the four gospels were not on par with the medical tradition of Hippocrates (*ca.* 460–370 BCE), and, quite frankly, not reducible to a modern critical explanation. Modern research and experimentation into psycho-suggestive healing of the body, while laudatory, should not be pressed into the service of understanding Jesus' acts of healing in his time. Harold Remus moved in this direction in his otherwise useful book on *Jesus as Healer*.[18] Remus does not doubt that Jesus performed healings. His concern, in part at least, is with the process by which the healings were accomplished. He cites positively the judgment of Dr. Franz Ingelfinger, "that 85 percent of illnesses fall within the body's power to heal. That power is not exercised in isolation, however. The sick person's physician, family, and larger social group also play significant roles. There is, moreover, a long tradition of healers. Jesus

---

17. Shillington, *Context*, 93.
18. Remus, *Healer*, 104–18.

Enacting the Kingdom of God

stands in this tradition."[19] The problem with this analysis is that Jesus does *not* stand in the tradition of Ingelfinger, Freud, Levi-Strauss, or any other modern scholar or physician. He stood, rather, in the tradition of prophets such as Elijah and Elisha, who, in turn, lived within the tradition of Judaism. Remus—with the rest of us—should heed his own warning about *The Peril of Modernizing Jesus*.[20]

A healing miracle of Jesus narrated in the gospels was extraordinary, not in accordance with normal processes of physical recovery from illness. Many of the diseases Jesus healed were outside the possibility of physical restoration to health at the time: blindness, deafness, mental disorders, death. To explain by rational argument the unusual power of Jesus to heal the "many who were sick with various diseases" (Mark 1:34) would speak implicitly against his popularity with the people of Palestine. As it was, "the crowd was amazed when they saw the mute speaking, the maimed whole, the lame walking, and the blind seeing. And they praised the God of Israel" (Matt. 15:31).

But was this out-of-the-ordinary work of healing people a divine power with which Jesus was endowed? The Temple authorities, those who knew and mediated the gracious power of God, had not sanctioned the work of Jesus. Nor did he inform them before performing his healing power. His acts were those of a prophet, not a priest. As mentioned above, the background to his work may be found in the stories of the prophets Elijah and Elisha. Elijah brought life back to the lifeless body of a child (1 Kings 17:17–23); he caused rain to fall after a three-year drought (1 Kings 18:41–46). Elisha also raised a dead son to life (2 Kings 4:32–37), and cured an army general of his leprosy (2 Kings 5:15–19). Moses also preformed extraordinary deeds in Egypt, which the Egyptian hierarchy deemed to be magic.

Some New Testament scholars view the special powers of Jesus as magic. In 1978 Morton Smith wrote a whole volume under the title, *Jesus the Magician*. In it he maintains, "some of Jesus' admirers thought him a magician and admired him as such (Mark 9:38f). Lots of magic was practiced in the early churches,"[21] says Smith. Acts 19:19 points to the practice in Ephesus. The practice of supernatural acts was not unfamiliar to the Jewish people. Josephus cites a story of a righteous man named Honi (65 BCE, otherwise called Onias) who called down rain in the midst of a drought as Elijah had done many years before. But when asked by one group of Jews to put a curse on certain other Jews, Honi refused. His refusal led the group to stone him to death.[22] The story of Honi the circle-maker who brought down rain is told also in the Mishnah with some variation.[23] All of this to say that the Jewish people were familiar with stories of divinely endowed figures in their history.

Whether these special powers of Honi (and other Jewish "holy ones" on record) should be called "magic" is debatable. Clearly, both Josephus and the Mishnah attribute the powers of Honi to the power of God. Honi prayed to God and it rained.

19. Ibid., 112.
20. Cadbury, *Modernizing*, 1–224.
21. Smith, *Magician*, 94.
22. *Ant.* 14:22–24.
23. Mishnah, *Taanith*, 3:8.

Part II: Jesus

As the word "magic" is used in English, it conjures up slight of hand, clever tricks that surprise an audience. In Crossan's use of the English word for the healing acts of Jesus, magic is "religious banditry" that challenges the ultimate legitimacy of spiritual power. His choice of "magic" over "miracle" is deliberate:

> Because of magic's position as subversive, unofficial, unapproved, and often lower-class religion, I have deliberately used the word *magic* rather than some euphemism . . . Elijah and Elisha, Honi and Hanina, were magicians, and so was Jesus of Nazareth. It is endlessly fascinating to watch Christian theologians describe Jesus as miracle worker rather than magician and then attempt to define the substantive difference between these two. There is, it would seem from the tendentiousness of such arguments, an ideological need to protect religion and its miracles from magic and its effects.[24]

I do not wish to be lumped in with "Christian theologians" who "need to protect religion and its miracles." I do wish to know, however, *what Jesus of Nazareth thought* of his ability to perform the unofficial works of healing. Did he think of them as magic, as we commonly think of the works of a magician? Or did he consider them—in the words of the magicians of Pharaoh concerning the mighty works of Moses—as coming from "the finger of God" (Exod. 8:19; see also Luke 11:20)? I believe the gospels make the answer self-evident. The kingdom of God relies on no other power to make it effectual. The wonder-works of Jesus in healing the sick were those of the coming kingdom of God, in keeping with the vision of Isaiah 35:5: "Then the eyes of the blind shall be opened, and the ears of the deaf unstopped; then the lame shall leap like a deer, and the tongue of the speechless sing for joy."

It is difficult for me to see how the Jerusalem hierarchy could see the extraordinary acts of healing the diseases among the Jewish people of Galilee or Judea as "subversive." The recipients of this beneficence of God in Jesus would surely not have thought so. Granted, Jesus acted on his own behalf as the agent of the power of God, quite apart from the approval of the Temple priesthood. His unapproved super-power of healing could have been irritating to them, but I doubt if they would have seen it as subversive to their rule. Mark, for example, records the story of Jesus healing a leper, and then instructing him (1) to show himself to the priest, and (2) to present an offering for cleansing as prescribed by Moses, (3) to serve as a testimony to them (Mark 1:40–44; Matt 8:1–4; cf. Luke 17:11–17). Leprosy—a skin disease, e.g. eczema, pigment discoloration, inflammation, disfiguration—was not simply an illness like any other. It was considered socially unclean and in that sense contagious. A leprous person was an outcast, unable to earn a living, and not permitted to participate in the regular religious activities of the Jewish people. By sending the healed leper to the priest for approval and acceptance, Jesus was recognizing the social and religious requirements necessary to reinstate the person into the social-religious order. This was not the behavior of a rebel or a bandit.

---

24. Crossan, *Historical Jesus*, 305.

At the same time, it would not be complete to state that Jesus was merely compassionate towards people afflicted with diseases of one kind or anther, and thus healed them out of love. To be sure, he was compassionate, but his compassionate acts of healing were unusual, as coming from a power-source beyond the ones present in the Land. As such they were eschatological, announcing the coming rule of God in contrast to, but in the presence of, all existing human powers, whether political or religious.

Who Benefited?

The question is not as redundant as it may appear. Obviously the sick people whose bodies Jesus healed benefited. I have also hinted above that the restored persons were reintegrated into society. They could work for a living, care for their families, perform the religious rituals, all without fear of recrimination. In short, they moved from the margins to the middle of society. Sometimes the benefit to the individual extended to others. For example, the raising of the widow's only son in the village of Nain in Galilee (Luke 7:11–16) was beneficial to his mother. With her husband gone, she would have been dependent on her son for support. "The 'healing' in the story is focused not so much on the raising of the dead son, which in a way is incidental, but on the restoration of the mother, whose place in the community is reborn when the son rises . . . Jesus gave the young man back 'to his mother.' That is the moment of *her* resurrection."[25]

Most of Jesus' healing ministry was carried out in Galilee among his Jewish compatriots, and some also in Judea (e.g. Mark 10:46–51). There was no universal health care program. The ones most susceptible to illness were the poor. And it was to them especially that Jesus brought the power of God (Q 6:20 = Matt. 5:3). The Lukan parable about the rich man and Lazarus bears this out: the rich man "feasted sumptuously every day" while the poor man lay at the gate "covered with soars" with only crumbs to eat (Luke 16:19–29).

What about the non-Jewish people in the region? Did they reach out to Jesus for healing, or he to them? People outside Judaism did live in Galilee, a good number of them in the cities, but others in the smaller communities. Yet there is not much evidence in the gospels about Jesus interacting significantly with non-Jewish residents of Galilee or Judea. Sanders has made the point clearly, however, that the movement arising out of the ministry of Jesus, consisting of Palestinian Jewish believers, "*came to see the Gentile mission as a logical extension of itself.*"[26] Given that all of the gospels were written after non-Jewish people had entered into fellowship with Jewish believers in Jesus, one would expect to find stronger hints of the successful mission to the nations in the gospels than there is. Presumably the tradition of Jesus' preaching and healing in Galilee had little in it about reaching out to non-Jewish residents, and the Evangelists apparently were not about to fabricate a mission of Jesus to the nations that did not in fact occur.

---

25. Malina and Rohrbaugh, *Synoptic*, 330.
26. Sanders, *Jesus and Judaism*, 220.

Part II: Jesus

One wonders why Jesus did not make a more deliberate effort to include people outside Judaism. There is ample evidence that he announced in word and deed the imminent kingdom of God as prefigured in the works of healing that he performed. The eschatological prophets of Israel spoke positively of gathering the people of the nations into Jerusalem in the end time. The list of biblical references is long. A few examples must suffice: Isa. 45:14, 22; 49:6, 23; 56:6–8; 66:19; Zech. 2:11; 8:20–23; Micah 4:1, 13; Zeph. 2:9. Add to these similar statements in non-canonical Jewish sources (e.g., Tobit 14:6–7; 1QM 12:13–14; 1 Enoch 90:30–33). With all these prophetic images in both biblical and later Jewish sources about the eschatological gathering of the nations to observe the glory of the Lord, one would expect Jesus to have been more decidedly active in opening the door to non-Jewish people of Galilee to experience the healing power of the kingdom of God. According to Jeremias, Jesus made a *promise to the nations* in his words and deeds. His "announcement of salvation to Israel, just as much as his vicarious death, was at the same time an act of service to the Gentiles. Both took place *in order that* the incorporation of the Gentiles into the Kingdom of God might be possible."[27] This statement after the fact of the mission to the nations is palpable, but not probative concerning the aims of Jesus when and where he lived in the first third of the first century.

Since this chapter is focused mainly on the acts of Jesus—although word and act are rarely separate entities in the gospels—I should cite the two occasions when Jesus did heal people outside Israel, but without being in direct contact with the subjects. The first comes from Q (7:1–10 = Matt. 8:5–10, 13), although reported quite differently by Matthew and Luke. It happened in Capernaum. A Roman officer approached Jesus about his young slave who became paralyzed and was in pain. Jesus responded immediately: "Am I, by coming, to heal him?" The centurion replied: "Master, I am not worthy for you to come under my roof; but say a word and let my boy be healed." The narrator says the slave was healed the moment Jesus spoke the word. Noteworthy in this rendering of the story is that the non-Jewish Roman knows intuitively that Jesus is not supposed to enter a non-Jewish house. The problem was one of purity/impurity. As it turned out, Jesus had the power to heal from a distance and thus avoid ritual contamination.

Luke renders the story quite differently. The Roman officer had heard about Jesus, and then elicited the help of some Jewish elders as go-betweens. They, not the Roman, approached Jesus, pleading with him to act graciously toward the non-Jewish Roman. The reason given in Luke is that this centurion loved the Jewish nation and built a synagogue for them. Again, the distance between Jesus and the house of the Roman is maintained at the Centurion's behest. The slave was cured without Jesus having to enter the house.

The only other account of Jesus healing an outsider is found in Mark 7:24–30 (par. Matt. 15:21–28). Matthew adds his spin to Mark's simpler narrative. The story is set in the region of Tyre on the coastal fringe of Galilee. A Syrophoenician woman—a

---

27. Jeremias, *Promise*, 73

Canaanite in Matthew—had a little daughter with an "unclean spirit." Having heard about Jesus, she found him, and bowed down at his feet to beg for his healing power for her little daughter. In Matthew the woman calls Jesus "son of David," a messianic title characteristic of Matthew. The response from Jesus in both Mark and Matthew is harsh by any standard of good will. Mark states, "Let the children be fed first, for it is not fair to take the children's food and throw it to the dogs." This is tantamount to refusing the woman the goodness and mercy of God for her daughter because she is not Jewish. It is also insulting. Dogs were considered scavengers in the Mediterranean world.[28] However, the illustrative dogs seem to be house pets with which the children of the house play. I think it is not correct to suggest that Jesus called the non-Jewish woman a dog. Nor is it true that Jewish people viewed their non-Jewish neighbors as dogs.[29] The comparison is between children and their pets: the children come first.

Matthew elaborates: "I was sent only to the lost sheep of the house of Israel . . . It is not fair to take the children's food and throw it to the dogs." Matthew leaves no doubt about the identity of "the children." Undeterred, the woman replied to Jesus that even the pet dogs get crumbs from the table. "She wants him to heal her daughter whose suffering outweighs the social kinship boundaries that separate her and Jesus."[30] For saying that, Jesus cast out the unclean spirit, again without entering the house of the Canaanite woman.

There may be something of a *promise* to the nations in these two stories, but it is still a long way from the decisive mission of Paul and companions to cities and homes among the nations with the good news of God's salvation found in Jesus. It is possible that Jesus was conscious of a priority in the eschatological breakthrough of the kingdom of God. Apart from the renewal of the covenant with Israel *first*, the other nations would not share in the bounty of the coming kingdom of God. Paul echoed a similar notion in his "Jew first and also to the Greek" (Rom. 1:16), and also in his eschatological image of the non-Jewish believers as olive branches grafted into the cultured root (Rom. 11:17–24).

About Exorcism

It is difficult for most modern, scientifically informed people to read about demon possession as though it were a self-evident phenomenon. Modern people know about mental illness, schizophrenia for example. Such people can hurt themselves and others, so they are often committed to a psychiatric facility where they are treated with medication and/or therapy. The doctors do not treat the patients as demon possessed, nor do they perform incantations to cast the demons out.

Whether the human disorder is called demon possession or mental illness, the erratic, irrational, abusive condition is the same. At the time of Jesus, the power manifested in such an aberrant condition was considered to come from a source other than

---

28. Malina and Rohrbaugh, *Synoptic*, 225.
29. See Nanos, "Paul's Reversal," 448–82.
30. Love, "Jesus," 17.

Part II: Jesus

the good power of God. It was well within the realm of Jesus' inauguration of the eschatological kingdom of God, therefore, to eradicate the disorder from the human person and replace it with the good order of God. Some of the stories of the expulsion of demons are outlandish, but instructive concerning the horrors of those powers not of God. An example is the story in Mark 5:1–13 about the dangerous man in the country of the Gerasenes. He was a danger to himself and others around him. When the man saw Jesus, he—or the demon named Legion—addressed him as "Jesus, Son of the Most High God," as though he knew him from somewhere. The name of the demon is telling, as also the presence of so many pigs in the area. These together "may imply the local view of the intrusion of Hellenistic culture in the region and the demonic incursion of Rome."[31]

What is peculiar about the story is that Jesus grants the request of the demons to enter the herd of two thousand pigs nearby. Whereupon the pigs ran down the hill into the Sea of Galilee and were drowned. One is left guessing if the demons were drowned with the pigs. Or were they released to occupy and torment some other living creatures? There is also the problem of the contamination of the precious water of the Sea of Galilee. However bizarre the story sounds, the point remains. A human being, probably Jewish—considering the way he addresses Jesus—was restored to wholeness, able to leave the area of tombs and return to his community to live a normal social life. The story portrays the character of the eschatological kingdom of God in the action of Jesus.

But the action of casting out demons did not sit well with the religious leaders from Jerusalem, as illustrated in Mark 3:20–30. Even his family, as I pointed out earlier, distanced themselves from him because people had declared, "He has gone out of his mind." How the people would have come to that particular conclusion is not clear. It is possible, as I have said, that they viewed Jesus as moving outside the bounds of the everyday expectation of the community to which he once belonged. To do so would be to lose one's bearing. But there may be more to their verdict than that. Jesus may have performed some sympathetic actions with those possessed with unclean spirits. That is, he may have shouted and gesticulated as the possessed person did, appearing also to be possessed. The evidence is not explicit, so speculation has to stop here. The point is that Jesus, by his action, drew not only crowds, but also opponents.

In the same passage in Mark 3, scribes from Jerusalem accused him of being in league with Beelzebul, the prince of demons. One wonders what they observed to lead them to that conclusion. It is possible that his unorthodox and unauthorized action in healing the demented persons, led the authorities to think that the power must be from some other source. Traditional Judaism believed the power of God was resident in the Temple and administered by the priests of the Temple. Jesus had acted independently of the Temple, so his power over demons must have come from Beelzebul and not from the God of Israel. Hence Jesus was accused as a blasphemer.

---

31. Malina and Rohrbaugh, *Synoptic*, 208.

Enacting the Kingdom of God

This was a serious charge, which appears again in the trial narrative in the synoptic gospels. In Mark 3 Jesus replies with parables about a divided kingdom and a plundered house. "How can Satan cast out Satan"? Such a kingdom cannot stand. To plunder a strong man's house one has to be able to tie up the strong man, and then plunder his house. The logic of the parabolic arguments[32] may not have persuaded the accusers. But Jesus' verdict on the matter, given in Mark 3, turns the charge back on his opponents. They are the blasphemers in the extreme. They attribute the good work of God to the power of evil. They blaspheme "against the Holy Spirit," and are thus guilty of an eternal sin that can never be forgiven (Mark 3:28–30).

The Beelzebul controversy is not limited to Mark 3. The scope of this chapter does not permit examination of other passages in Matthew and Luke (Matt. 9:32–34; 12:22–24; Luke 11:14–15). I defer to Dwight Sheets' helpful discussion of these passages in *Who Do My Opponents Say That I Am?*[33]

CROWDS

Mention has been made more than once about the crowds Jesus attracted. His actions were out of the ordinary, but beneficial to many people of the Land who would otherwise have been left to languish in poverty, sickness, social exclusion, and destitution. The gospels speak repeatedly about the crowds that gathered around Jesus when he came to a village. Often a crowd would follow him to another place. From this attracting of crowds it may be assumed simply that Jesus became popular with ordinary Jewish people. Popularity can be benign, but it can also contain an element of subversion. I have noted earlier the popularity of Judas the Galilean whose action was explicitly revolutionary. Rome would not brook opposition to its supreme rule in the provinces of its realm, and thus squelched the uprising instigated by Judas.

It could be said immediately, Jesus was not acting in the same way as Judas, and therefore would not have drawn the attention of the Roman prefect or the High Priest of Jerusalem. Nevertheless, his charismatic activity drew crowds. His actions and words must have had something in them to draw the people from their day-to-day world to listen to Jesus and to have him heal them. The very fact of crowds would raise suspicion in the mind of rulers charged with keeping the *pax Romana* (Roman peace). It does not take much to turn a crowd into a mob, and a mob into a rebellion.

Ellis Rivkin's investigation of the question of what led to the trial and execution of Jesus in Roman occupied Palestine is one of the most responsible I have read. In his book he highlights the problem of crowds in a society where the politics of the ruling elite were not favorable towards the lower classes, where a charismatic leader can fuel a revolt. Rivkin pictures the problem in dramatic prose:

> If such a charismatic [as Jesus] were believed to be an Elijah when he healed the sick, raised the dead, and cast forth demons, his wonder working would have attracted crowds—and crowds, as we know, were dangerous and could

---

32. See Marcus, "Beelzebul," 247–77.
33. Sheets, "Demon-Possessed," 27–49.

Part II: Jesus

get out of hand. If he seemed to be a visionary and, like Isaiah, proclaimed that the kingdom of God was near at hand, his high hopes would have attracted crowds—and crowds, as we know, were dangerous and could get out of hand. If he bore a likeness to the Son of man, the king-Messiah, his likeness would have attracted crowds—and crowds, as we know, were dangerous and could get out of hand. And if his compassion and love lifted up the wretched, gave hope to the outcast, and reassurance to the faint of heart, such compassion and love would have attracted crowds—and crowds, as we know, were dangerous and could get out of hand.[34]

TABLE COMPANIONS

I dare to open this discussion of Jesus' choice of table companions with a true story of a banquet. It happened in Winnipeg, Canada, where a large number of marginalized aboriginal Canadians live. The banquet was by invitation only. The guests were people of means. The idea of the banquet was to raise money for the Christian college that sponsored the event. When one of the invited guests came to the door of the banquet hall, an aboriginal man was there, poorly dressed and hungry. He was gazing through the glass door to the bountiful tables inside. He inquired of the invited guest: "Could I go in for the meal?" The invited guest, an honorable, sensitive Christian man, had to tell the hungry inquirer: "The banquet is for invited guests only. There would not be a place for you at any of the tables."

The guest told this story in a class on the parables of Jesus, a tremor in his voice and tears welling up in his eyes. On the evening of that banquet he faced the challenge of overriding social convention involving the act of sharing a table and a meal with an unlikely participant. Crossan, in his attempt to understand what Jesus was doing in relation to the rule of God, rightly makes much of the social act of eating. Events like the banquet story, he says, "are not just ones of eating together, of simple table fellowship, but are what anthropologists call *commensality*—from *mensa*, the Latin word for "table." *It means the rules of tabling and eating as miniature models for the rules of association and socialization.* It means table fellowship as a map of economic discrimination, social hierarchy, and political differentiation."[35]

Feasting versus Fasting

According to a saying in Q 7:31–35 (= Matt. 11:16–19), Jesus was aware of criticism against him concerning his eating practice. The passage in Q reads:

> To what am I to compare this generation and what is it like? It is like children seated in the market-place, who, addressing the others, say: We fluted for you, but you would not dance; we wailed, but you would not cry. For John came, neither eating nor drinking, and you say: He has a demon! The son of humanity came, eating and drinking, and you say: Look! A person who is a glutton and

---

34. Rivkin, *Crucified?* 49.
35. Crossan, *Revolutionary*, 68.

drunkard, a chum of tax collectors and sinners! But Wisdom was vindicated by her children.

From this reckoning, Jesus depicted his audience ("this generation") as indifferent to any kind of prophetic overture. At one extreme were children who put on a happy show accompanied by music of the flute, and at the other extreme a dirge. The response to both was the same: noncompliance. Judging from the follow-up story, the dance was that of the Kingdom Jesus was bringing, and the wailing that of the call to repentance-before-judgment that John proclaimed.

As discussed in ch. 7, John's diet was meager. Beyond that, he probably fasted as a way of mourning the coming judgment of God on the Land and its people. By contrast, Jesus enjoyed eating, not merely for the sake of eating, but as a way of celebrating with others the joyful coming of the rule of God. The religious elite of Palestine would probably not have had a serious problem with Jesus enjoying a good meal. They surely must have fared sumptuously themselves, being elite. The problem, according to the text in Q, was with the company Jesus kept while he shared a meal. It was not just the kind of food a Jewish person ate that made them impure. Ritual purity or impurity came from the company around the table. The participants all drank from the same cup, and ate from the same loaf. Mixed company at a Jewish table had a contaminating effect.

The accusation against Jesus was not only that he was "a glutton and a drunkard," but also that he ate and drank with two unsavory groups: "tax collectors and sinners." Labeling people has always been a way of maintaining accepted social order, and nowhere more useful than in Palestinian Judaism. The Temple elite did not attack Jesus for *announcing* the rule of God, but for the way he *enacted* that rule among his fellow Israelites in the Land. I doubt, however, that the High Priest of the Temple would have called for his execution because of the promiscuous way he shared his table.[36] At the same time, his kind of table fellowship must be added to the list of unconventional activities that eventually culminated in his trial and death.

Tax Collectors

As we have seen already, tax collectors and sinners, while appearing as two groups, were equally bad company at the table of the righteous in the covenant of *Yahweh*, Israel's God. Separate treatment of the two may help focus the problem of their participation at the table of the righteous within Palestinian Judaism.

Jewish tax collectors were traitors to the covenant between God and Israel, a covenant that excludes all other affiliation, and encompasses all of Jewish life. A Jewish person who accepted a position that violated the redemptive covenant of God became a traitor to God and to the salvation that God provided through the covenant. A Jewish tax collector became such by collaborating with Rome *against his own covenant people* by collecting tolls from them for the support of an occupying power, and by taking a commission for himself. By their collaboration with Rome, tax collectors effectively

---

36. Modica, "Glutton," 50–73.

Part II: Jesus

excluded themselves from the salvation of Israel's God. For an observant Jewish person to eat with such persons could be seen as guilt by association.

One of the most damning stories against Jesus as a faithful Israelite is found in all three Synoptic Gospels: Mark 2:13–17; Matthew 9:9–13; and Luke 5:27–32. As Jesus was walking along the shore of the Sea of Galilee he saw a man named Levi sitting at a tax booth. He summoned him to follow him. And Levi did so. There was no elaborate call for repentance or contrition for the heinous collaboration with Rome. No judgment passed. Instead, Levi threw a dinner party for "many tax collectors and sinners," and Jesus joined in the meal without further ado. The story in the gospels tells of scribes taking offence, asking the disciples to explain the behavior of their leader. Imagine the situation: a table surrounded by traitors and Jesus in the middle of them. He asked not for their contrition, but only for their company. Any faithful Jewish person, including disciples of Jesus who appear not to have participated in the dinner, would question Jesus' behavior.

One wonders if Jesus knew the reason why tax collectors accepted a job so despised by the Jewish faithful. Had they lost their peasant plot of land, and with it their livelihood to rich creditors? Were they unable to find another way to earn daily bread *within the Law* for themselves and their families? Had circumstances pushed them to become "lost sheep of the house of Israel"? Whatever Jesus saw, he did not condemn the perceived traitors, nor did he ask them to repent of their sin and be forgiven. He simply ate with them.

Luke has another striking story about a tax collector named Zacchaeus. Even though it comes from the Lukan source alone, it has a ring of authenticity to it, in that it resembles the other story from Mark 2. The place is Jericho. Zacchaeus heard about Jesus, and wanted to see this man for himself. When Jesus saw him he invited himself to the home of this "chief tax collector" who was rich. Again, there is no hint from Jesus that Zacchaeus must first leave his traitorous business and live an upright life. Those who saw what happened—they are not identified—grumbled about Jesus going to the house of this rich traitor to the Jewish nation. Then all on his own in the presence of Jesus, Zacchaeus decided to give half of his possessions to the poor, and to repay fourfold anyone he defrauded. The core story, apart from possible Lukan contributions, describes the same open attitude of Jesus toward eating with tax collectors.

Sinners

The word "sinners" (*hamartōloi*) in the gospels is not a label for people who transgressed one or another of God's laws for which they later repented and found forgiveness. Sinners in the context of Judaism, and also in the gospels, were in the same category as tax collectors: their way of life stood in contradiction to the covenant of God with Israel. Whether their ongoing behavior was prostitution, usury, tax collecting or some other habitual violation of the Jewish Law, the label was "sinners."

Sanders points to the Hebrew word behind the Greek word for "sinners" in the gospels, which he then translates as "the wicked." The word referred to people of the covenant of Israel "who sinned willfully and heinously and who did not repent."[37] By their willful and persistent violation of the redemptive covenant, they thus renounced the covenant and the salvation that came from obedience to it. These were the sinners with whom Jesus ate, asking nothing from them beyond their acceptance of him and the rule of God that he announced and enacted. As with the tax collectors, so also with the sinners, the call of Jesus to them was not to repentance and righteous living, but to membership in the coming kingdom of God. Judaism had already the ritual avenues through which sinners could repent, offer sacrifices—especially on the Day of Atonement, and be reinstated into full membership with the people of God. If Jesus' table fellowship with sinners had required them first to repent and change their behavior, then he would have been doing precisely what the Jewish leaders were doing as a matter of course. Instead, Jesus sat at table with them without any conditions.

Rank-and-File Jewish People

The Jewish population of first century Palestine, while sharing a common religious heritage, did not all practice their religion in exactly the same way. Some, as noted above, were perceived as not practicing it at all. They were labeled "sinners" and "tax collectors." But pre-70 Judaism had a single unifying symbol through which all of the people could make their peace with God: the Temple in Jerusalem ruled by the high priest and his priestly assistants. Sinners could repent, make appropriate sacrifice at the Temple, be forgiven, and go out to live righteous lives thereafter.

On the opposite end of the Palestinian Jewish spectrum were the righteous ones, those committed to doing the will of God as prescribed in the Law. But these were not of one mind in their Jewish belief and practice. Josephus speaks of three schools of thought (*haireseis*) among the educated of the Land: Pharisees, Sadducees and Essenes. Pharisees studied the Law as interpreted through their forebears, and encouraged the Jewish people to obey it in faithful response to the covenant God had made with the people through Moses. Sadducees, according to Josephus, differed from the Pharisees in that "the Pharisees have delivered to the people a great many observances handed down from their forebears, which are not written in the law of Moses; and for that reason it is that the Sadducees reject them [the Pharisees] and say that we are to esteem those observances to be obligatory, which are in the written word, but are not to observe instructions derived from the tradition of our forebears."[38] The Sadducees appear to have been the more elite of the Jewish groups, from which came the priests of the Temple. Of the Essenes Josephus speaks respectfully about their virtuous life, noting also that Herod held them in high regard. The ascetic life-style of the Essenes is reflected in the scrolls of Qumran mentioned earlier.

In addition to the three schools, or sects, of Judaism were the Zealots. As the name implies, they saw their mission as guarding jealously the traditions of the Land

---

37. Sanders, *Jesus and Judaism*, 177.
38. *Ant.* 13.297.

Part II: Jesus

of Israel against any incursion from outside power brokers. They considered it their godly duty to fight for their nation and its religious symbols.

But these five groups of Jewish inhabitants of Palestine at the time of Jesus—sinners, Pharisees, Sadducees, Essenes, Zealots—did not comprise the whole population. All of them together would constitute a small fraction of the total Jewish population. The educated (especially from the Pharisees) and the ruling class (from the Sadducees) appear prominently in the sources. They held and exercised power among the people. But by far the majority of Jewish people at the time were peasants, day laborers, or craftspeople. The large social base of Palestinian Judaism in the first century was agrarian: *rank-and-file Jewish people* making a subsistence living from their plot of land or from the work of their hands, while trying to maintain their place within their traditional religion. Repeated reference is made in Rabbinic literature to the "people of the land" (*'amme ha-arets*). They were rank-and-file Jewish people, mostly uneducated, not wealthy, and not the most observant of purity regulations as practiced by the Pharisees and the priests. But neither Pharisees nor priests would have considered them sinners.

These were the "common people" who heard Jesus gladly (Mark 12:37). A few would have turned to banditry out of desperation. Others lost their land through debt. Still others became destitute through sickness or poverty. But none of them were "sinners" by the definition given above. Those able to work their land, or skilled enough to manufacture goods, supported the ruling class, both Jewish and Roman, through taxation arbitrarily imposed. At the same time they tried to keep the faith in relation to the neighbor, and also before God through sacrifices and pilgrimage to the Temple. Jesus knew well these people of the Land, having grown up among them in lower Galilee. He experienced their plight, and offered them a "pearl of great value" (Matt. 13:46), which they could not afford to buy if it had been for sale: *the kingdom of God*. Josephus— something of a Jewish aristocrat himself—looked favorably on the lower class of Jewish people. He considered the great Lawgiver, Moses, virtuous, because he "behaved himself like one of the common people (*dêmotikos*)."[39]

CONCLUSION

What picture emerges out of this perusal of the sources about Jesus? He proclaimed a message about the kingdom of God without defining precisely what he meant by his use of the term. This much we can presuppose: Jesus stood in the tradition of the great prophets of Israel recorded in the Jewish Scripture. Their message became his message in his own time and place and situation. The Land of Promise was occupied. The Jewish High Priest was an appointee of the Roman Prefect. The rank-and-file Jewish people were weighed down under the yoke of taxation imposed on them by a foreign power. The rule of God, in contrast to the current rule in the Land, symbolized justice and acceptance for those "carrying heavy burdens" (Matt. 11:28).

---

39. *Ant.* 3.212.

Enacting the Kingdom of God

Jesus not only *announced* the coming of the rule of God, but also *enacted* it. He called disciples to be with him, and used the number "twelve" symbolically to hail the renewal of the "Israel of God" in keeping with the twelve tribes of ancient Israel. The call of disciples was unconditional. They had to be willing to leave all other responsibilities behind, including family and possessions, to follow after Jesus. Jesus sent out these twelve, completely unencumbered, to bring the rule of God to bear in the lives and homes of Jewish people in Palestine. Neither Jesus nor his disciples went to the other nations deliberately. When one or another non-Jewish person asked for healing for a household member, Jesus did heal the person without entering the house.

The kingdom of God in Jesus was marked especially by his extraordinary acts of healing. People brought their sick to him, and he healed them. Crowds followed. Rulers cast a cold eye on large crowds of the people in an occupied territory. A crowd can become a rebellious mob, and can get out of hand.

Another way Jesus enacted the rule of God was through his table participation. Eating at table in Jewish society could cause the law-observant participant to become ritually impure. Table fellowship with the wrong people implied guilt by association. Jesus deliberately ate with tax collectors and sinners, those estranged from the company of the righteous on account of their wicked practice of breaking trust with the covenant of God. Not only did Jesus eat with tax collectors and sinners, but also called at least one of them to be in his group of Twelve. Nor did Jesus require repentance, sacrifice and forgiveness before eating with the "sinners." He simply joined them as they were. Jesus came "to call not the righteous but sinners" (Mark 2:17).

With such open commensality in practice, and such compassion lavished on the sick, the poor, and the heavy-laden, Jesus appealed to the common Jewish people of Palestine, who heard him gladly. Among them he enacted the kingdom of God.

9

Speaking of the Kingdom of God

ONE WOULD THINK THAT THE SAYINGS OF JESUS WOULD BE THE FIRST AND best place to turn to discover his self-understanding, his attitude towards his environment, his participation in his religion, and, above all, his vision of the rule of God. Among modern Christians, the sayings, especially those of the Sermon on the Mount, figure prominently as the multi-paned window through which to view the heart and mind of Jesus. The sayings, understood thus, provide an authoritative guide to ethical living for believers. True enough, the sayings material makes up a large part of the gospels. About 1,500 individual units have been tallied. But the sayings material is fraught with difficulty when it comes to historical reconstruction of the figure of Jesus.

Sanders in particular is skeptical about using the sayings to capture a sense of what Jesus thought of himself and his mission. He says, "Analysis of the sayings material does not succeed in giving us a picture of Jesus which is convincing and which answers historically important questions."[1] Many of the sayings, especially the parables, evoke polyvalent interpretation. It is therefore hard to pin down exactly from the sayings what Jesus envisioned about the kingdom of God. The symbol of "kingdom" itself is multifaceted, so it should come as no surprise that the sayings of Jesus emit multiple angles on the rule of God.

But the many angles projected in the sayings can enrich one's understanding of Jesus, adding color and texture to his activities in Galilee and Judea. The *actions* and *sayings* of Jesus recorded in the gospels stand together as coming from one mind. The variegated features of the sayings served a rhetorical purpose by which Jesus "charged language with meaning," as Ben F. Meyer observes. "Here was one who without training, without writing, so charged language with meaning as to elicit, generation after generation, the disarming protest, 'Lord, to whom shall we go? You have the words of eternal life' (John 6:68)."[2] With such a testimonial etched onto the papyri of the gospels, it behooves the interpreter to give attention to this witness to Jesus and the

---

1. Sanders, *Jesus and Judaism*, 133.
2. Meyer, "Language," 82.

Speaking of the Kingdom of God

kingdom of God he represented. Nor is it helpful to say of the parables that "in many of them ... there is 'a reversal of values.'"[3] In all of them, I submit, the first *hearers*, and also later *readers* encounter "the challenge of the historical Jesus."[4]

Unfortunately, a selective approach becomes necessary within the limits of this chapter. I intend to listen imaginatively to the selected sayings—with the help of others who have listened before me—consisting mostly of parables and aphorisms, under six broad topics related to the location and situation in which Jesus first uttered them: *Land and Temple, imminent kingdom assured, first-last scenario, economic factors, social relations, and justice issues*. Before proceeding with these, a brief comment about the character of the sayings as they stand in the gospels would be in order.

AUTHENTICATING FORM AND CONTENT

New Testament scholars have expended much energy and time authenticating the sayings material in the gospels. The need for the enterprise arose out of the awareness of the time frame of the gospels in which the sayings of Jesus were embedded. The earliest surviving gospel, as noted in ch. 4, was written about forty years after the death of Jesus; the other gospels ten to twenty years later. By the time the gospels were written the Jesus-movement had passed through significant changes that affected the outlook and self-understanding of the communities involved. Two major events had a penetrating effect both on Judaism and on the Jesus-movement: the successful launching of a mission to the non-Jewish world in the decade of the fifties CE, and the destruction of the Temple of Jerusalem at 70 CE. The gospels were written in the consciousness of these two momentous events among others.

In addition, the communities of faith in Jesus increasingly thought of their leader in theological categories beyond anything Jesus would have used about himself. One of the best examples of this phenomenon occurs in the prologue to the Fourth Gospel (John 1:1–18). In that passage Jesus came into being uniquely and directly from the eternal God. His human birth is not mentioned. The eternal Word (*logos*) mysteriously became Jesus in the flesh (1:14). When and how that happened is not given. The historical Jesus of the village of Nazareth would hardly have used such sophisticated language to identify himself.

In their own way, Matthew and Luke, written a decade or more after Mark, describe the human birth of Jesus as originating from the Spirit of the eternal God, not from an earthly father's semen (Matt. 1:1–2:23; Luke 1:26–38; 2:1–39; 3:23–38). (Strangely, however, the two genealogies link Jesus with Joseph named as Jesus' earthly father). Both birth narratives sprang from the post-Easter conviction that the unusual character of Jesus' work and word in the world had its source in the divine Spirit. But Jesus did not *define himself* in the gospels in such terms, nor did he give any hint in his sayings of an unusual human birth. Paul, writing only twenty to thirty years after Jesus, likewise did not elicit a Spirit-impregnation of the mother of Jesus to underwrite his

---

3. Sanders, *Jesus and Judaism*, 150.
4. Crossan, *In Parables*, iv.

Part II: Jesus

theology and mission. More on the subject of Paul's thought in the upcoming section devoted to his life and work.

The point to this discussion is that the form and content of a number of sayings attributed to Jesus in the gospels bear marks of the later communities of faith from *their* situations in life and thought. For example, the short Q saying takes a different turn in Matthew 5:6. Here is the saying in Q: "Blessed are you who hunger, for you will eat your fill." Luke represents Q closely.

Matthew 5:6	Luke 6:21
"Blessed are those who hunger and thirst for righteousness, for they will be filled."	"Blessed are you who are hungry now, for you will be filled."

Matthew's Jesus views hunger and thirst, not in a physical sense, but in a purely ethical sense. Luke's Jesus, by contrast, views the hunger as completely physical. In Luke the second-person hungry audience (you) will be filled with food. In Matthew the third-person people (they) will be filled with righteousness. Matthew's theological DNA comes through in his use of "righteousness" used variously throughout the Gospel (1:19; 3:15; 5:10, 20, 45; 6:33; 9:13; 10:41; 13:43; 21:32; 23:35, 37; 25:46; 27:19). The saying in the *Gospel of Thomas* adds yet another variation to the second part: "Blessed are those who go hungry, for the stomach of the one in want will be filled" (69).

The same observation could be made with respect to many other sayings throughout the gospels. An effort must be made, therefore, to detect as far as possible the form of the saying that reflects the vision and work of Jesus in his time and place. Keep in mind also the further limitation that the sayings were translated out of Aramaic into Greek, and beyond both of those languages into modern languages.

Scholars have also identified a number of sayings attributed to Jesus that probably originated in the post-Easter communities, or with the gospel writers themselves. These will not enter the present discussion.

A Word about the Parables

Two sorts of sayings figure prominently in the gospels: narrative parables and aphorisms. An *aphorism* is a short pithy saying easily remembered for use in everyday life. One that I remember from my mother was, "A stitch in time saves nine," and from my father, "Cleanliness is next to godliness." There are many aphorisms in the synoptic gospels, which undoubtedly go back to the Aramaic voice of Jesus. Many of them carry colorful imagery, making the saying vivid and memorable.

A *parable* is a fictional story serving as a metaphor "drawn from nature or common life, arresting the hearer by its vividness or strangeness and leaving the mind in sufficient doubt about its precise application to tease it into active thought."[5] This now classic definition by C. H. Dodd has yet to be surpassed. Several points in it should be highlighted. (1) The internal features of the parable stories of Jesus would have been familiar to Jesus' audience in Palestine; the elements were drawn from *that* land

---

5. Dodd, *Parables*, 5.

Speaking of the Kingdom of God

and *that* common Jewish life and thought. (2) The vividness and strangeness of the language of a parable captures the imagination of the hearer; the parable creates another world, another way of life beyond the ordinary. (3) A straightforward "moral of the story" eludes the hearer; the parable creates doubt about the common life from which the story is drawn; the mind is thus teased into considering alternatives to conventional life in Palestine. In short, the parables of Jesus were utterly disarming. Their effect was to break through the accepted norms of Palestinian Jewish life, ruled as it was by the Temple of Jerusalem and the Senate of Rome, and to open up a way to the just and merciful and powerful rule of God.

More than any other type of language in the New Testament, the parable has been subject to allegorical interpretation. And that is not surprising. An allegorical interpretation alleviates the "strangeness," making the presumed "meaning" of Jesus' parable generally accessible to everyone in every generation. But allegorizing a parable violates both its form and its function. An allegory is not a parable, nor a parable an allegory. A parable pushes the accepted boundaries of everyday thinking. An allegory ameliorates the stark realities of a narrative into a worthy spiritual principle. The ever-present temptation to allegorize the parables of Jesus in one way or another is very strong. I urge the reader to resist the temptation, and so to let the strange and vivid imagery of the parable have its way, however unrealistic it may feel. A parable is not, as my Sunday School teacher taught, a earthly story with a heavenly meaning. A parable of Jesus consists of *a Palestinian Jewish story with a kingdom-of-God overlay*.

Jeremias judged correctly: "The student of the parables of Jesus, as they have been transmitted to us in the first three Gospels, may be confident that he[/she] stands upon a particularly firm historical foundation. The parables are a fragment of the original rock of tradition."[6] Given that understanding, the parables, along with other sayings of Jesus, provide a highly valuable resource for drafting a portrait of Jesus as he saw himself inaugurating the rule of God in the setting of Roman occupied Palestine at about 30 CE.

Time now for a perusal of selected sayings material under the six headings outlined above: *Land and Temple, imminent kingdom assured, first-last scenario, economic factors, social relations,* and *justice issues*. Someone else might come up with a different set of headings. I have chosen these six from my understanding of the concerns echoed in both the actions and the sayings of Jesus.

LAND AND TEMPLE

Land and Temple belong together, not merely because the Temple building was located within the boundary of the Land, but because the Land of Promise in Israel's history was gift from Israel's God whose saving presence was symbolically represented in the Temple of Jerusalem. The Land was holy; the city of Jerusalem also holy; and the Temple on mount Zion holy too. This basic idea of the Land in Judaism seems to have garnered considerable unanimity, although "there was no one doctrine of the land,

---

6. Jeremias, *Parables*, 11.

Part II: Jesus

clearly defined and normative, but, as is usual in Judaism, a multiplicity of ideas and expectations variously and unsystematically entertained."[7]

The Land

The Greek word for "land" is *gē*, which is often translated "earth" in the gospels, unless the context clearly means land or soil. I suspect that when Jesus used the Aramaic word for "land" it often meant "the Land," not the whole planet earth.

Whatever idealism ancient Israel had attached to the Land of Promise, that Land had gone through turmoil after turmoil. At the time of Jesus' ministry it was occupied by a Roman super power, with soldiers marching up and down its roads and paths. Many of the people had lost their land to rich householders through debt and taxation. The parable of the landless, unemployed workers (Matt. 20:1–15) who were standing idle in the marketplace all day bears witness to the depressed situation in the Land considered "holy." When asked by the landowner in the parable why they were standing around in the market place all day, they answer, "Because no one hired us." Jesus drew the picture from what he saw happening in his rural setting in Galilee.

But he also saw the elite few rich farmers stockpiling their crops while the poor people in the marketplace went home at night hungry. One such person is portrayed in the parable in Luke 12:16–29. The rich farmer talks to himself in the story, unconcerned about the poor and the destitute in the Land "flowing with milk and honey" for all the people. The rich parable-farmer says to himself, "I will pull down my barns and build larger ones, and there I will store all my grain and my goods. And I will say to my self, 'Self, you have ample goods laid up for many years; relax, eat, drink, be merry.'" All the while Jesus watched people go hungry, watched a poor widow casting her last two coins into the Temple treasury in her feeble attempt to maintain her standing as an Israelite in the Holy Land. That little bit of money was "all she had to live on" (Mark 12:44).

The covenant gift of the God of Israel had become, at the time of Jesus, a land no longer poised to sustain the large lower class of Jewish working people. The life-treasure of the Land was in jeopardy. There are signs in his sayings that Jesus had abandoned the hope of salvation in the Land that promised life to Israel. "Do not store up for yourselves treasures on the Land, where moth and rust consume and where thieves break in and steal; but store up for yourselves treasures in heaven, where neither moth nor rust consumes and where thieves do not break in and steal. For where your treasure is, there your heart will be also" (Matt. 6:19–21). Yet one other saying suggests that the meek should be happy "for they will inherit the Land," as though the Land was really their inheritance as originally promised by God (Matt. 5:5).

The issue with the Land may well have been the lack of proper distribution of its produce among the people. An agrarian society, such as that of Palestine in the first century, was predominantly land-based. A multitude of peasants could eke out a living from a plot of ground, provided they did not end up indebted to an elite city person

---

7. Davies, *Land*, 157.

Speaking of the Kingdom of God

interested in amassing wealth from the Land. Indebtedness had become a blight on the Land, much like a sin; hence the line in the Lord's Prayer, "Cancel our debts (*opheilēma*) for us, as we too have cancelled for those in debt to us" (Q 11:4 = Matt. 6:12)

Nowhere is the problem of distribution more vividly set out than in the short parable in Q about the salt of the Land: "Land-salt is good, but if land-salt becomes ineffective, with what will it be renewed? It is fit neither for the land nor for the manure pile; it is cast aside"[8] (cf. Matt. 5:13). There are several problems with most modern translations: (1) they assume that the "salt" (*halas*) was table salt, sodium chloride. If that were true, then (2) table salt would not lose its "taste": not when it is dissolved, not when it hardens, not when it is frozen in water, and not when it is boiled in water. If the "salt" were sodium chloride, (3) how could that chemical ever be "fit for the land (*gē*) [or] for the manure pile"? Sodium is always bad for soil. The issue in the metaphor is that the substance becomes not tasteless, but ineffective (*mōrainein*). Taste has nothing to do with the "salt" becoming useless for land or manure pile. The substance in view is *fertilizer for the land*: nitrogen, potassium, phosphate. Material found in the region of the Dead Sea to this day; material that makes crops grow. Fertilizer loses its potency when it is left in a pile too long. The idea is to distribute the chemical material over the land directly or mixed with manure. Otherwise it would have to be thrown out. Distribution is the key, not only for the fertilizer for the Land, but for the produce of the Land that results from the practice of spreading the fertilizing agent. Consider again the parable of the rich farmer who hoarded his surplus of produce from the Land while others went hungry. He was a fool who implicitly lost his stockpile of produce along with his life.

One more example of a Land parable must suffice. It appears in all three synoptic gospels (Matt. 21:23–42; Mark 12:1–11; Luke 20:9–17), and also in the *Gospel of Thomas* (65:1–7). The version in the synoptic gospels exhibits allegorical elements coming out of the experience of the early Jesus-communities. The parable in the *Gospel of Thomas*, on the other hand, is simpler, without allegorical incursions, and probably closer to the original telling. It reads as follows:

> Someone owned a vineyard and rented it to some tenants, so they could work it and he could collect its crop from them. He sent his slave so the tenant farmers would give him the vineyard's crop. They grabbed him, beat him, and almost killed him, and the slave returned and told his master. His master said, "Perhaps he didn't know them." He sent another slave, and the farmers beat that one as well. Then the master sent his son and said, "Perhaps they will show my son some respect." Because the farmers knew that he was the heir to the vineyard, they grabbed him and killed him. Anyone here with two ears had better listen!

The three main characters in the parable are the *absentee landlord, the resident tenant farmers* and *the landlord's son*. The slaves are go-betweens, retainers. If the tenants were to harm them there would be more to follow. Slaves were expendable. The absentee landlord sent for the crop, which could mean the grapes for wine, or the

---

8. My translation in context.

vegetables the tenants would grow between the rows of vines, or both.[9] The wine from the vineyard proper was the really lucrative produce. The vegetables were the staple food for the tenants and their families. There is no provision in the parable for a portion of the crop to go to the tenants and the rest to the landowner. One wonders if the tenants had lost their land previously to the rich absentee landlord, and had since become tenants.

The tenants are usually seen as the bad characters in the story. They do, after all, abuse the slaves and kill the son-and-heir. This parable of Jesus mirrors the pitiful inequity in the Land of promise: that tenant farmers were driven to violence to secure their right to an equitable portion of the produce of the Land that God had given Israel in trust. What were listeners supposed to hear from the parable? That violence works? Not likely. More likely that violence begets violence in a never-ending spiral.[10] The kingdom of God in the gospel-witness to Jesus is a non-violent rule. The parable, in my "hearing" at least, implies the futility of violence among the people of the Land, while teasing the mind into embracing an alternate way of life.

The Temple

From a Jewish perspective the power over the people was lodged in the Temple of Jerusalem, with Rome as overseer. The Temple government taxed the Jewish adherents based on the Law related to the Levites: the tithe, various offerings, animal sacrifices, etc. In return, the priests of the Temple mediated forgiveness of transgressions with assurance of continued membership in the covenant of God. The question here has to do with Jesus' attitude toward the Temple of Judaism as reflected in some of his sayings. Was he fully supportive of the Temple service as he experienced it? Or did his vision of the kingdom of God in his sayings include a critique of the Temple?

Two parables in Luke speak directly to these questions: the Pharisee and the Tax Collector (Luke 18:19–14), and the Good Samaritan (Luke 10:30–37). The drama of the parable of the Pharisee and the tax collector is acted out within the Temple precincts. As Michael Farris has pointed out insightfully, "The Temple is a player too in the parable, with a role at least as important as the well-known figures of Pharisee and toll collector."[11] Both men in the parable were Jewish, the Pharisee devoutly so, and the tax collector traitorously so. The righteous Pharisee had close access to the saving power emanating from the inner sanctuary, while the unrighteous tax collector, "standing far off," had no such thing. Yet there "the sinner" stood *in the parable*, approaching the Temple in clear view of the Pharisee. In actual Jewish experience the tax collector would probably not have shown up at all. The shocking element in the parable is that the perceived traitor has the gall to appear before the holy precincts without sacrifice, without proper repentance, and all the while expecting the God of the Temple to accept him as he was.

9. Herzog, *Subversive*, 103.
10. See Horsley, *Spiral*, 20–58, 147–66.
11. Farris, "Tale," 23.

Speaking of the Kingdom of God

More than a few later Christian interpreters find genuine repentance in the parable-sinner, and a turning away from his sinful life. Why else would Jesus declare the sinner acquitted as he heads home, and the Pharisee not? Judaism also would require repentance and appropriate sacrifice offered at the Temple, together with restitution where necessary, with a promise from the penitent to obey the Law in the future. None of this was required by the visionary Temple that Jesus projected in the parable. The God of *that* Temple accepted the sinner as he was, acquitted him, and sent him on his way without any further religious ado. The question the parable evokes is whether the Temple as it stood in real time was so accommodating to tax collectors. The inference one can draw is that the actual Temple in Jesus' experience accepted righteous persons, such as the Pharisee, as members in good standing, while excluding unrepentant sinners. Ironically, the Pharisee in the parable is not put right by his prayer of thanksgiving. He is righteous already. Jesus, as God's viceroy, came "to call not the righteous but sinners" (Mark 2:17), otherwise called "the lost sheep of the house of Israel" (Matt. 15:24).

The second parable about the Temple in Luke 10:30–37 evokes an even greater sense of the ineffectual Temple service on behalf of the marginalized and afflicted. The parable of the Good Samaritan is perhaps the best known, but also the most provocative when interpreted with an eye to the characters and plot in the context of first century Jewish Palestine. Robert Funk's analysis of this parable as vivid metaphor of the rule of God in the ministry of Jesus is incisive. He says:

> As a parable the Samaritan is a very powerful instrument. It sets the message of Jesus in unequivocal terms for its audience. No one could mistake. It explains why [tax collectors] and prostitutes understand the kingdom, whereas theologians, Bible scholars, and professional pietists do not. It explains why a hated alien must be the instrument of grace. It makes pretense on the part of the listener impossible. There is no other parable in the Jesus tradition which carries a comparable punch. The Christian community moralizes it in order to be able to live with it, and that is inverted testimony to its power.[12]

That a fierce animosity existed between the Judeans and the Samaritans is well known (e.g., John 4:9). From the perspective of observant Judeans, Samaritans could be classed with tax collectors and sinners. They had all perverted the Law in one way or another. The parable asks implicitly concerning the true neighbor to the victim in the ditch. Jesus' audience would have been Jewish, and would have identified the victim as Jewish along with themselves. The lines of the metaphor are drawn boldly. The first two characters, priest and Levite, were well known functionaries in the Temple of Jerusalem. These were the figures responsible for the mediation of God's grace to the people. In the parable they pass by. They may have had their legitimate priestly reasons for doing so, as noted in ch. 5. Whatever their reasons might have been, the victim in the ditch has no hope of restoration from the two Temple figures. Shockingly, the hated outsider stops and pours out abundant compassion on the man in the ditch. Any

---

12. Funk, *Parables*, 65.

Part II: Jesus

Jewish person in the audience, especially the Temple servants, would find the alien character unbelievable, unacceptable, and offensive to their social conscience. But the hated Samaritan in the parable was neighbor to the victim, *the only neighbor willing to save the Jewish man.*

The implicit question put to the Jewish people listening to the parable was unmistakable: Who is ready to accept the life-giving rule of God from a traditional enemy? But another question would likely spring to Jewish minds: How does the Temple of Jerusalem, run by priests and Levites, serve the needs of the downtrodden Jewish people who support its religious system? The implications would have been inescapable: the rules of the Temple and its servants do not measure up to the rule of God represented in the Samaritan. Jesus, the one telling the parable, stood alongside the Samaritan hero, and would suffer for doing so.

A more direct saying of Jesus about the Temple of Jerusalem would be in place here also, even though it will surface again in the next chapter. Mark 13:1–2 (par. Matt. 24:1–2; Luke 21:5–6; cf. John 2:18–20) records that while Jesus and his disciples were leaving the Temple, one of the disciples drew attention to the large stones and great buildings. The context suggests the disciple was referring to the Temple precincts on the Temple mount, not sundry other buildings in Jerusalem. In response Jesus said: "Do you see these great buildings? Not one stone will be left here upon another; all will be thrown down" (Mark 13:2). Some scholars have suggested that this saying is a reflection coming out of the post-70 Christ-community. That view, however, fails to account for the false charge brought against Jesus at the trial cited in Mark 14:58 "We heard him say, 'I will destroy this temple that is made with hands, and in three days I will build another, not made with hands.'" The falsehood in the charge seems to have stemmed from the notion that Jesus would destroy the Temple made with hands and build another in three days without human power. A form of the saying as it stands in Mark 13:2 is likely what the disciples (and others) heard Jesus say in Aramaic, not the one in the mouth of the false witnesses.

Linking this saying about he destruction of the Temple with the two parables that implicitly criticize the servants of the Temple, one detects Jesus making a dangerous judgment upon the Temple: dangerous because the Temple was the symbolic heartbeat of the Jewish nation. "The temple was the center, not only of the sacrificial cult, but also of the banking system, the meat industry, and the seat of political power in Jesus' time. In view of Jesus' concern for the poor, it is likely that he would have had something to say about the temple, and that something is likely to have been critical."[13]

IMMINENT KINGDOM ASSURED

The parable of the bridesmaids in Matthew 25:1–12 (cf. Luke 13:24) depicts two features of the kingdom of God: (1) its imminence, and (2) the certainty of its coming. The bridegroom was already known to the bridesmaids, and already betrothed to his bride. His coming merely consummated the marriage. The five wise women lived in proper

---

13. Funk and Hoover, *Five Gospels*, 109.

Speaking of the Kingdom of God

anticipation of the coming of the bridegroom; they had enough oil for their lamps. The foolish women failed to live up to their expectation of the arrival of the bridegroom. They ran out of oil for their lamps. When they finally arrived on the scene, the door to the wedding party was closed, and the foolish ones were denied entrance. The reign of God is assured, the parable suggests, by its preliminary operation in the ministry of Jesus. Those in waiting should not take its coming lightly.

Assurance of the kingdom's arrival comes through in the parables of growth. A farmer sows seed broadband (Mark 4:3–8), with some seed falling on a path where the birds ate it, some on rocks, some among thorns, but some fell on good soil where it grew to harvest. The kingdom of God, like the seed, will come to fruition despite some failures along the way. The seed growing secretly tells a similar story (Mark 4:26–29; *Gos. Thom.* 21:9). A person sows a seed and sleeps and rises thereafter, while another unseen power produces germination through stages of growth: the stalk, the head, then the full grain in the head. The harvest at the end of the process bespeaks final reckoning. Again, the final outcome of the kingdom is assured. The parable of the mustard seed is equally telling in its guarantee of the kingdom's arrival. The saying is well preserved in the *Gospel of Thomas* 20:1–4 (cf. Mark 4:30–32; Luke 13:18–19). The kingdom of heaven "is like a mustard seed, the smallest of all seeds. But when it falls on tilled soil, it produces a great plant and becomes a shelter for birds of the sky." Not much can be expected from the insignificant seed, compared to some other great seeds that grow into trees. But the mustard seed in the parable grows into a hefty bush that provides shelter for birds. One hears an echo of Ezekiel 17:22–23: God will plant a sprig from a cedar on a mountain of Israel, and it will grow into a tall tree and birds of every kind will live under its shade. But the parable of Jesus is more comic. The tiny beginning of the kingdom might appear to be of no consequence, but it will, in its own incredible way, provide shade for the birds. It will not become the mighty cedar dominating the landscape. It will be a bush, more weed than welcome tree.

The budding fig tree (Mark 13:28–30) gives the same impression of assurance of the kingdom's arrival in due course. The symbol of the fig tree had deep roots in Israel's traditional memory. It was a symbol of life from God. The rule of God in Jesus will come as surely as the bud becomes the fig, and will give life and joy. The parable of the leaven (Q 13:20–21 = Matt. 13:33; cf. *Gos. Thom.* 96) gives yet another picture that builds confidence that the small and secret beginning will become full-blown in good time. The imagery is striking. A woman hid leaven in fifty pounds of flour and it leavened the whole. Leaven in Judaism carried a negative connotation. It was associated with evil. At Passover all leaven had to be cleared out of the house. But in this parable Jesus used leaven to depict the way the kingdom of God comes. It thus gives the image a provocative turn. And the strange image is compounded by the large amount of flour for the small piece of leaven to affect: fifty pounds. It is reminiscent of the fifty pounds of flour the matriarch, Sarah, prepared on the occasion of the heavenly promise of a son from her barren womb (Gen. 18:1–8). Like the rising of the flour under the influence of the leaven, so also shall the kingdom of God appear before the eyes of those able to see it.

Part II: Jesus

A saying of a different sort ties in with the metaphors cited above (Mark 9:1; Matt. 16:28; Luke 9:27). Matthew and Luke picked up the saying from Mark and interpreted it in their own way. I take Luke 9:27 to reflect the vision of Jesus about the imminent rule of God pictured in the parables and aphorisms about its assured arrival. "But truly I tell you, there are some standing here who will not taste death before they see the kingdom of God." The expectation in the saying is that at least some in the audience will live to see the kingdom of God. If the saying is truly from Jesus, not the work of Mark, then it may have been given early in Jesus' ministry. The kingdom began to show itself in the healings, especially in the exorcism of evil spirits, as the saying in Luke 11:20 affirms: "But if it is by the finger of God that I cast out the demons, then the kingdom of God has come to you." In this light, then, the rule of God was not only at the doorstep, but had even made its way inside already. "For, in fact, the kingdom of God is among you" (Luke 17:21).

FIRST-LAST SCENARIO

Reversal of conventional wisdom is present in many of Jesus' sayings, and in none more starkly than this: "The last will be first, and the first will be last" (Matt. 20:16). Matthew tacked this saying onto the end of the parable of the workers in the vineyard (20:1–15). As a closing line to that parable it does not capture the full force of the outlandish behavior of the landowner. But the line does connect with the closing scene where the last workers of the day were paid first, while the first workers of the day were paid last. Beyond this obvious terminological connection the principle reaches into the fabric of everyday human intentionality. Whether in an ancient society or a modern one, the person who reaches for the top to win the prize earns the applause. Losers are losers by common human judgment. Those who come in first cannot, must not, be treated as the last. Jesus' saying is completely out of the ordinary. It breaks the rule of human intentionality. But paradoxically it epitomizes the rule of God in the work and word of Jesus.

A weaker form of the saying appears also in Mark 10:31: "*Many* who are first will be last, and the last will be first." The addition of "many" effectively disavows the principle as such: some will be first and some last. The more disturbing form of the saying in Matthew 20:16 is likely closer to the Aramaic form first spoken by Jesus. The kingdom of God that Jesus projected in such sayings operates in a way contrary to the rule of human life commonly understood and experienced. At Mark 10:31 the saying comes after a longer saying in response to Peter's remark about leaving everything to follow Jesus. Those, like Peter, who have left everything are "the last" kind of people, but by becoming last they become first to receive the life of the "age to come" (Mark 10:30 par. Matt. 19:30).

In the same chapter 10 of Mark is the story of brothers James and John, two of the first disciples, who put forward a request to Jesus that they be given places of honor, one on his right hand and the other on his left, when he comes into his glory. That

Speaking of the Kingdom of God

scene in Mark gives rise to a longer saying of Jesus that further illustrates the principle of first-last/last-first.

> You know that among the Gentiles those whom they recognize as their rulers lord it over them, and their great ones are tyrants over them. But it is not so among you; but whoever wishes to become great among you must be your servant, and whoever wishes to be first among you must be slave of all. For the Son of Man came not to be served but to serve, and to give his life a ransom for many. (Mark 10:41–45)

This saying highlights the tyranny of being first by human standards. With the power to rule other humans comes an inherent propensity to take advantage of the human position of power. By contrast, the true "Son of Humanity" (discussed in the next chapter) seeks not to be served but to serve. Instead of taking advantage of a ruling position this figure gives his life up for ransom to release those oppressed by the ruling elite, "the first" ones. By human standards, such a figure is at the lowest level of human power. But by the rule of God that figure is first of all, because he is "the Man for others." As Ben F. Meyer states so well, "Jesus, it seems, is a man for all ages, and to an age that does recognize and honor the free spirit of the unselfish man, he is the Man for Others."[14]

The principle of first-last/last-first shows up in various narrative settings in the gospels where the saying itself is not present. In Mark 12:38–39 Jesus issues a warning to watch out for the highly educated leaders among the people. They parade around in long robes, expecting the common people to pay them honor; they seek out the first-class seats in the synagogue and at banquets. As with the rulers in the political realm, so too the ruling teachers occupy first place in the realm of acquired knowledge. That acquisition sets them above those with little or no education, people who could not read or write, of whom there were many in Palestinian Jewish society. A similar criticism of Jewish scholars appears in Matthew 23:5–7.

In keeping with the first-last/last-first scenario of the rule of God, a rich person would have a hard time living under that rule. "How hard it will be for those who have wealth to enter the kingdom of God!" Jesus said (Mark 10:23, 25). "It is easier for a camel to go through the eye of a needle than for someone who is rich to enter the kingdom of God." Any effort to open up this saying to allow the rich to enter the kingdom of God along with the poor diffuses the shock value of the saying of Jesus. Recall when Jesus sent the disciples out he required extreme poverty of them. And again, "Give to everyone who begs from you; and if anyone takes away your goods, do not ask for them again" (Luke 6:30). That saying resurfaces in the *Epistle of Barnabas* (19:11) and the *Didache* (1:5). "Anyone who is dependent on his possessions and as a result forgets his neighbour lives in this state of anxious egoistic self-assertion: he rejects God's commandment to love for the sake of the idol mammon."[15]

---

14. Meyer, *Others*, 145.
15. Hengel, *Property*, 30.

Part II: Jesus

The radical reversal of values comes across in terms of old and new. "No one puts new wine into old wineskins; otherwise, the wine will burst the skins, and the wine is lost, and so are the skins; but one puts new wine into fresh wineskins" (Mark 2:22; *Gos. Thom.* 47:3). One suspects this saying comes from common knowledge about the making of wine. In the mouth of Jesus, however, the saying probably tied in with his criticism of the Temple system in Jerusalem. It occupied first place (old) within Palestinian Jewish life, but could not contain the last (new) in-breaking kingdom of God. A variation on the saying in the *Gospel of Thomas* is still consistent with the saying in Mark. "New wine is not put into old wineskins, lest they burst; nor is old wine put into a new wineskin, lest it spoil."

ECONOMIC FACTORS

There is bound to be overlap from one topic to the next. The social network in which Jesus lived was by nature a complex of factors. Economic factors impinged on virtually every aspect of the society, and figured frequently and variously in the preaching of Jesus. The foregoing discussions under different headings illustrate the point. Still, the matter of economics in the sayings of Jesus calls for separate treatment.

Atop the list of Jesus' sayings about kingdom-economics is one from Q, also found in the *Gospel of Thomas* (Q 12:22–29 = Matt. 6:25–30; cf. *Gos. Thom.* 36).

> Therefore I tell you, do not be anxious about your life, what you are to eat, nor about your body, with what you are to clothe yourself. Is not life more than food, and the body than clothing? Consider the ravens: They neither sow nor reap nor gather into barns, and yet God feeds them. Are you not better than the birds? And who of you by being anxious is able to add to one's stature a .. cubit? And why are you anxious about clothing? Observe, the lilies, how they grow: They do not work nor do they spin. Yet I tell you: Not even Solomon in all his glory was arrayed like one of these. But if in the field the grass, there today and tomorrow thrown into the oven, God clothes thus, will he not much more clothe you, persons of petty faith!

This kind of talk belongs to some other world. It lacks the kind of responsibility every human society admires. The image of the carefree ravens and lilies is unforgettable, especially when it is contrasted with the glory of Solomon. This king of Israel was one of the richest. His distinctive achievement in building the magnificent first Temple of God for the nation of Israel is effectively cast aside in the saying in favor of an unencumbered life like that that of birds and lilies. Solomon's amassing of wealth, similar to that of the self-centered farmer in the parable, came at a heavy cost to the people of the Land. Taxes were high during Solomon's reign. People were enslaved, all in the name of earthly power and glory. The kingdom of Solomon, including his glorious Temple, did not reflect the kingdom of God with respect to this saying of Jesus. A world like that of Solomon is full of care, subject to invasion from outside power, and lacking

Speaking of the Kingdom of God

trust in God. As Robinson puts it, "What made one as carefree as the ravens and lilies was trust in the kingdom of God, God reigning, as a caring Father."[16]

The problem with wealth is one of slavish idolatry, according to Jesus: "No one can serve two masters; for a person will either hate the one and love the other, or be devoted to the one and despise the other. You cannot serve God and Mammon" (Q 16:13 = Matt. 6:24; *Gos. Thom.* 47:1–2). Someone is bound to ask, as I find myself asking: Can a person posses great wealth without serving it? Or is it in the very nature of wealth to protect it, add to it, and thus to serve it? The word translated "wealth" in the NRSV is "mammon," an Aramaic loan word carried over into the Greek text of Luke. It bristles with negative connotation. Mammon implies possessions that end up possessing the individual holding onto them. Hence the idea of *serving* mammon.

Consistent with the saying about carefree birds and lilies is another in Luke 6:20 and *Thomas* 54, already noted above: "Blessed are you poor, for yours is the kingdom of God." The contrast is not between wealthy people and poor people. Poor people could still have a subsistence living from some source. Day laborers, such as those in the parable of Matthew 20 (below), were poor. But some in the society—how many is not known exactly—were reduced to beggary. Beggars were totally dependent on the goodness of others to survive, powerless to support themselves. These are the subjects in the beatitude. The Greek word in Luke 6:20 (*ptōchos*) means *destitute*, not simply people on a subsistence income. Jesus "spoke, in shocking paradox, not about a Kingdom of the Poor but about a Kingdom of the Destitute . . . The beatitude of Jesus declared blessed, then, not the poor but the destitute, not poverty but beggary."[17] Again, the saying, while drawn from the common life of Palestine, did not correspond to a common way of thinking. How could the kingdom of God be given to the lowest in society? One suspects that the people without any possessions, the destitute, were declared blessed because they had absolutely no power in life to block their entrance into the alternate rule of God.

Attention should be drawn again to the parable about the workers in the vineyard, which is clearly a parable about the economy. Some of the workers in the parable were employed for a full day, and thus earned a full day's wage, a denarius. Many others were overlooked at the beginning of the day. The owner of the vineyard went himself to the marketplace and saw the situation first-hand. Usually a servant would do the hiring. By the end of the day everyone from the marketplace was in the vineyard, some only working for one hour. But everyone received a denarius at the end of the day. That meant that everyone went home with enough to buy food for the next day. At one level the parable endorses "barefaced injustice."[18] On another level it introduces the shocking justice of the kingdom of God in which everyone has equal share from the Land. The landowner of the parable breaks the bounds of the everyday rich farmer. This one ensures that everyone has daily bread, regardless of the hours of work. Which

---

16. Robinson, *Jesus*, 129.
17. Crossan, *Historical Jesus*, 273.
18. Jeremias, *Parables*, 37.

Part II: Jesus

was harder: to work all day in the field with assurance of a full days' pay? Or to stand idle all day in the marketplace *without hope of bread for the day following*?

Two other narrative parables speak to the uneasy economics of the rule of God, each one of them deserving fuller treatment than is possible here.[19] I refer to the puzzling parable of the shrewd manager (Luke 16:1–8), and the equally puzzling parable of entrusted money (Q 19:12–27 = Matt. 25:14–30).

The manager in the Lukan parable becomes shrewd after the rich master fired him for "squandering" the master's money. The word translated "squander" carries the idea of distributing, or scattering. The master followed the dictates of conventional wisdom, and dismissed the man for his apparent dishonesty. But the unemployed manager, unable to dig and too ashamed to beg, decided to make friends with the master's debtors by reducing their debts. That way he would have friends to take him in and give him food and shelter after his dismissal. The debtors were happy to pay the reduced amount, and the master, presumably, was glad to receive at least a portion of the outstanding debt. The manager was reinstated with high praise from his master for his shrewdness. A strange story indeed! The manager at the end of the story was doing what he had been doing all along: *distributing the rich man's resources and relieving the oppressed debtors*. A new form of justice was afoot, and the master caught on in the end. Or was he caught? The parable-jigsaw remains unfinished, always unfinished.

The parable of the money in trust from Q is equally troubling. Details of the original story were modified in the *retelling* over the years, and also in the *writings* of Matthew and Luke with respect to their life-experiences. The return of the absent businessman corresponded with their belief in the return of Jesus. Marks of that belief impinge upon the story, not least in the phrase "enter into the joy of your master." The parable in Matthew seems closest to the original, mainly by reason of the exaggeration, which is part of the parable form. The three slaves are given an enormous amount of money in trust: five talents, two, and one. (A talent is an amount of money, not a spiritual gift or an acquired ability). Funk and Hoover describe the enormity of the amounts in this way: "the sums given to the three slaves are incredible (thirty thousand and twelve thousand silver coins each amount to a fortune; even the six thousand silver coins given to the third slave comes to about twenty years' wages for the common laborer)."[20]

The first two slaves with the thirty thousand and twelve thousand silver coins turned one hundred percent profit for their master, while the third hid his six thousand coins safely in the ground and then returned them to his master intact. But the big surprise comes at the end. The master orders the six thousand coins to be taken from the third slave and given to the one who had the most. What ever happened to the distribution of wealth and the reduction of debt? One thing is certain: this ancient parable of Jesus should not be used as a template for modern capitalism. Consider a peasant audience perspective. How would they have responded to the ending in

---

19. See Wohlgemut, "Money," 103–120; Trudinger, "Oppression," 121–37.

20. Funk and Hoover, *Five Gospels*, 256.

which the one with the least is punished for returning the master's money honestly and honorably? How would they have responded to the first servant receiving more at the expense of the last? William Herzog, among others, has asked questions like these, and concluded that the real hero of the extravagant parable was the last one who handed the master's money back to him in full, without profit. He paid a price for doing so. Here is Herzog's take on the role of the last slave in relation to the first two, and to the aristocratic master:

> The praise offered by the oppressive aristocrat mystifies the ugly realities suppressed beneath the profit margin: 'Well done, good and trustworthy slave.' Both retainers are good in terms of the aristocrat's values because they have proven to be effective exploiters of the peasants, and they have been trustworthy because they have produced a level of increased wealth in line with the aristocrat's expectations. The sheer extent of the aristocrat's wealth comes through his follow-up: 'You have been trustworthy in a few things.' Five talents! Two talents! A few things! . . . The third servant's remarks serve a critical purpose. They expose the sham of what has transpired and place it under the unobstructed light of clear analysis and prophetic judgment . . . The hero of the parable is the third servant. By digging a hole and burying the aristocrat's talent in the ground, he has taken it out of circulation. It cannot be used to dispossess more peasants from their lands through its dispersion in the form of usurious loans.[21]

One of the economic issues facing people in an ancient imperial society was the payment of taxes and tolls. Who sets the fair amount to be paid? On whom are the taxes imposed? Besides questions such as these, there was in Palestinian Jewish society the tension between paying the Temple tax, not to mention animal sacrifices, and the payment of a poll tax to the emperor. On one occasion, some Jewish leaders put a question to Jesus about paying the poll tax to the emperor (Mark 12:13–17; Matt. 22:17–22; Luke 29:19–26; *Gos. Thom.* 100:1–4). Does paying that tax violate the Jewish Law? Jesus' reply to the inquiry was non-committal: he did not advise them to pay the tax or not to pay it. His saying is nonetheless memorable: "Give to the emperor the things that are the emperor's, and to God the things that are God's." It could mean stop using Roman coins with the emperor's head on them. The emperor is not God. Even the Temple of Jerusalem as such is not God. One thing is clear from the saying: what belongs to the emperor and what belongs to God are completely separate entities. The two are like the two masters that one slave cannot serve, because he will love the one and despise the other. The rule of God is not the rule of the emperor. Do not confuse one with the other, the enigmatic saying implies.

Jesus' sayings about making money and owning property were scandalous in his time and place. Attempts to remove the scandal from the sayings by spiritualizing them, only robs them of their provocative power. Hengel may have overstated the extent of their provocative power, but his point should at least to be noted: "[Jesus']

---

21. Herzog, *Subversive*, 163–67.

Part II: Jesus

scandalous 'social' preaching was certainly one reason why he was condemned and executed by the Romans as a messianic pretender and rebel."[22]

SOCIAL RELATIONSHIPS

The culture in which Jesus lived and taught operated by a social script, of which Jesus was well aware, and within which he announced the kingdom of God.

Marriage and Divorce

The ideal of marriage at the time of Jesus was monogamous and lifelong. Divorce was allowed according to Jewish Law: a man could divorce his wife if she did not please him; a wife's right to divorce her husband was not given in the Law (Deut. 24:1–4). Jesus, in line with at least one prophetic tradition (Mal. 2:13–16), spoke against divorce categorically. His saying on divorce comes from three sources: Mark 10:5–9, Q 16:18 = Matthew 5:32, and Paul at 1 Corinthians 7:10–11. The saying from Q is brief and unequivocal: "Everyone who divorces his wife and marries another, commits adultery, and the one who marries a divorcée commits adultery." The saying in Mark and Paul is also categorical in prohibiting divorce. Only Matthew adds an exception clause to the prohibition: "except on the ground of unchastity." Paul retained a form of the unqualified prohibition in the saying of Jesus, but then added his own variations in light of contingencies arising in the Corinthian community (1 Cor. 7:11–15).

Precondition for Forgiveness

Jesus taught that forgiveness of sins against God was possible only when the person praying for forgiveness had already forgiven the human offender: "forgive and you will be forgiven" (Luke 6:37b; Matt. 6:14–15; Mark 11:25). Similar thinking comes through in the Lord's prayer: "And cancel our debts for us, as we too have cancelled for those in debt to us" (Q 11:4 = Matt. 6:12). Implicit in the prayer-saying is the precondition for obtaining God's forgiveness: that forgiveness on the human level has already happened before asking God for the same. Forgiveness on the human level does not invariably result in reconciliation between the human parties. But forgiving an offender frees up both parties to move toward reconciliation. The parable of the Unforgiving Slave (Matt. 18:23–35) drives the point home: the flip side of being forgiven is to forgive.

About Loving the Enemy

The forgiving attitude assigned for human relations corresponds with the curt, radical saying: "Love your enemies" (Q 6:27, 32 = Matt. 5:43–44). Matthew sharpens the point of the saying with the antithetical construction: "You have heard that it was said, 'You shall love your neighbor and hate your enemy.' But I say to you, Love your enemies." There is no command in the Hebrew Scripture to hate the enemy. An echo of Psalm 139:19–22 may be present, or a precept from the Qumran community about loving

---

22. Hengel, *Property*, 30.

and hating (1QS 9:21–24). The saying from the mouth of the historical Jesus, however, is the outrageous one: "love your enemies." This goes well beyond the love for the neighbor. The radical demand of the aphorism calls for treating the enemy first and foremost as a fellow human being with hopes and dreams not unlike one's own. The saying does *not* contain the notion that loving enemies will transform them into good friends. The act of loving the enemy is unconditional. "If you love those who love you, what credit is that to you? For even sinners love those who love them" (Luke 6:32). The parable of the Good Samaritan comes back to mind. The Samaritan was enemy to the Jewish man half-dead on the side of the road, and the Jewish man enemy to him. The rule of God about loving the enemy was at work in that parable-world.

Along the same line, and from the same Q (Q 6:34–35 = Matt. 5:39–42; cf. *Gos. Thom.* 95:1–2), are three case-parodies about non-retaliation against evil. (Luke omits the third about going the second mile, probably because Luke aims at easing tensions between the Jesus-community and the Roman officials). A case-parody sets up a scenario in such a way as to make it ridiculously comic. The case is clearly connected to a real life, but is then exaggerated to the point of being laughable, but possible nonetheless. Here are the three case-parodies: (1) *when someone strikes you on the right cheek, turn the other also;* (2) *when someone wants to sue you and take your coat, give your cloak as well;* (3) *when someone forces you to go one mile, go also the second mile.* While the reaction clause to each situation is possible, it is usually not performed. (1) Only a slap on the right cheek is set up, not the left cheek, or any other part of the body. Tit-for-tat justice is replaced with an offer of a double measure of injustice. The parody is not merely a lesson in non-retaliation, no striking back, but an uncharacteristic reaction that puts the striker in a position of *shameful injustice*. (2) In a society where people wear two garments, the offer of the second garment along with the first would make the person naked. The person bearing such shame in turn shames the one making it happen. (3) The "someone" conscripting a person to go one mile could be a Roman soldier. The offer to go two miles exposes the unjust power of the one doing the conscripting. Again, the parody reaction to evil is beyond simple non-retaliation. It exposes the shameful practice of injustice by a completely unlikely response. (See further on honor/shame below under "Family and Community Dynamics").

Unlikely Dinner Guests

One thing is reasonably sure about Jesus: he enjoyed eating with people. His opponents accused him of being "a glutton and a drunkard" (Luke 7:33). As a statement from opponents, the words were doubtless tinged with polemic for rhetorical effect. He enjoyed his meals with different sorts of people. One wonders how he was able to eat and drink as he did, having given up working for a living. But hospitality was an expected norm in that society. I suspect Jesus made many friends who shared their food with him along the way. Sharing a meal was a highly social event. It is not surprising, then, to find sayings in the repertoire that reflect Jesus' attitude towards table fellowship, and especially towards the list of invited guests.

Part II: Jesus

The narrative parable of the Great Supper (Q 14:16–24 = Matt. 22:1–10; *Gos. Thom.* 64:1–12) is a shocking example of uninvited guests at the dinner table. Matthew and Luke record the story from Q differently, and both of them at odds with the *Gospel of Thomas*. Matthew allegorizes the details out of the memory of the destruction of Jerusalem, and the increasing separation of the Jesus-community from the Jewish community. Luke's rendition echoes the success of the mission to the nations. Inside all three renditions lie the parameters of the parable Jesus told. A man prepared a great dinner, and invited his friends. When they received the invitation through the man's slave, they gave excuses for declining the invitation. All of them had important events that needed their attention: a property purchase, an animal purchase, a business deal, a marriage. Their type seems to have been well-to-do, quite busy, and certainly not hungry. Upon hearing the excuses from his invited guests, the man issued another invitation to people of the streets and alleys of the town. Luke describes them as "the poor, the crippled, the blind, and the lame": most unlikely dinner guests. They accepted because they had no other pressing engagements to hinder them. "The invited guests were left out of the feast by their own act, and their places taken by rag-tag-and-bobtail."[23] What comes through is the exclusion of the elite for the inclusion of the street people. The parable-scene begs the question: Had the proper dinner guests accepted the invitation, would they have been comfortable taking their places alongside the motley group? This saying of Jesus, like so many others in the collection, upsets the accepted rules of social behavior to allow the rule of God to break through.

Family and Community Dynamics

One of the best known parables of Jesus, on par with the Good Samaritan, is the parable of the Prodigal Son found only in Luke 15:11–32. Behind the standard—and not so standard—ways of allegorizing this long narrative, stands a powerful metaphor about family relationships in the context of a Jewish village community. Richard Rohrbaugh wrote a very insightful chapter on this parable under the title, "A Dysfunctional Family and its Neighbours."[24] His social science analysis focused on the family dynamics that Jesus set in motion in the parable against the accepted rule of Jewish village life. The younger son who asks for his inheritance prematurely becomes the lost son of the household. His dalliance with a non-Jewish lifestyle—in a far country feeding pigs—left him alienated from his home and village life, and ceremonially impure. By returning to his Jewish village environment he would risk expulsion and destitution; hence his well-prepared return-speech. His impure presence in the community would jeopardize the good standing of the other members. His only hope, he thinks to himself, would be utter penitence toward his father, and removal from his standing as family member to that of hired hand.

While he was still some distance from his Jewish village his father saw him and *ran* to meet him. Running was not considered proper behavior in that society,

---

23. Dodd, *Parables*, 93.
24. Rohrbaugh, "Dysfunctional," 141-64.

especially for an older man. The father threw his arms around his lost son, perhaps to protect him from painful censure from the watching community. The young son had no chance to give his penitent speech, nor did his father ask him to perform ritual cleansing and offer sacrifice. Instead, his father threw a banquet to celebrate the son's return. The older brother's voice at the end of the parable speaks for the status quo, the conventional wisdom of the Jewish family and community. He refuses to enter the celebration in honor of his profligate brother's return. By so doing, this upsetting parable of Jesus seems to say, the conventional older brother excludes himself from *the radical rule of God for Jewish families and communities.*

Unlike modern industrial societies, the ancient society in which Jesus lived operated very much on the basis of honor and shame. The parable of the prodigal son exhibits elements of this thinking. The younger son lost his honor, evident in his speech about being reduced from son to servant. The parable challenged the honor-shame system by which the community operated.

In the same vein, Luke offers another story—more anecdote than parable—that likely goes back to Jesus (Luke 11:5–8). Luke sets it in the context of prayer, following the Lord's prayer. Originally the story Jesus told probably called to account two very important features of his society: hospitality and honor/shame. Here is the gist of the story. Someone in the neighborhood had a friend drop in to the house in the middle of the night after a journey. The host's obligation was to offer his guest some food, but the host had no bread. The host then went to his neighbor, who was in bed with his family, and called to him to lend him three loaves. The neighbor at first refused because it was the middle of the night, but then yielded to the request, not because of the persistence of the neighbor-friend, but because his honor would be threatened. His refusal would mean that his neighbor would be shamed by his inability to offer hospitality, and the sleeping neighbor would also be shamed for refusing to help his neighbor live up to the hospitality code that applied to both of them. This story of Jesus called into question the honor/shame social code in light of the code-breaking kingdom of God.

JUSTICE ISSUES

In many of the parables, discussed above, where human action was involved, justice issues came to the fore variously: the Friend at Midnight, the Vineyard Tenants, the Workers in the Vineyard, the Rich Fool, among others. One more will illustrate Jesus' concern for justice for all in the Land: the parable of the Heartless Judge (Luke 18:2–5).

> In a certain city there was a judge who neither feared God nor had respect for people. In that city there was a widow who kept coming to him and saying, "Grant me justice against my opponent." For a while he refused; but later he said to himself, "Though I have no fear of God and no respect for anyone, yet because this widow keeps bothering me, I will grant her justice, so that she may not wear me out by continually coming."

It is hard to know what to make of this parable. I see two characters pitted against each other, one an important figure assigned to the administration of justice and the other a widow systemically in need of justice. The first listeners to this tale might have thought the widow's boldness in appearing before such a judge a precarious move on her part. Widows were usually left to the mercy of their immediate family or community for survival. This widow made her appeal to an appointed judge, and the judge refused to hear her case at first. Eventually, because she kept bothering him, he granted her justice, not because he found her cause to be just, but because he wanted to get rid of her. The judge's motives, like those of the friend at midnight, are questionable: the widow shamelessly shames the judge into acting on her behalf. It appears that the parable has the effect of exploding the social code of honor-and-shame, and the instrument in this cause is none other than a powerless widow. There are signs here, as elsewhere in the sayings of Jesus, of the other rule of God eroding the current system of injustice.

CONCLUSION

Without doubt, the rule of God figured prominently in the ministry of Jesus, and nowhere more prominently than in the sayings material preserved in the gospels. For that reason a candid discussion of the sayings became necessary. That said, Jesus wrapped the sayings in social codes within which the hearers were expected to grasp the meaning of the rule of God. Like any code, the code-language that Jesus used is not easy for a modern interpreter to decipher. It may have been more immediate to the first hearers, but even first readers living within the same code-world as Jesus would still find their everyday thought world challenged beyond usual bounds: A hated Samaritan saving the life of a Jewish man, and the Jewish man having to accept such alien salvation; all day-workers finding work to do, and all of them receiving the same wage without discrimination; a deviant son welcomed home after becoming impure, and given a banquet without repentance or sacrifice. The list of exaggerated, and sometimes comic, images is long. Their function in the context of Jesus' ministry in occupied Palestinian Judaism was to explode conventional codes that held some members of his society captive: honor-shame, deviance, labeling, etc.

The very presence of this provocative story-telling Jesus within his world meant that the kingdom of God was at hand: present in his actions and present in his words. At the same time, Jesus taught his disciples to pray not only for forgiveness of debts and provision of daily bread, but also for the kingdom of God to come. Its activity in the healings and exorcisms and provocative sayings of Jesus was paradigmatic of even greater manifestation of the extraordinary ruling power of God to come. The mustard seed would become a large and beneficial shrub. The small amount of leaven would bring about noticeable change for good. Anyone wanting to enter that good kingdom would have to remove obstacles, such as mammon, and trust God alone to provide the necessities of life, as the birds of the air and the lilies of the field do.

10

The Last Days in Jerusalem

EVENTS LEADING UP TO JESUS' DEATH IN JERUSALEM HAPPENED WITHIN A week. However true this statement may be, it is not the whole truth. What happened in that short time frame had plenty of precursors in the activities and sayings of Jesus, as evidenced in the previous two chapters. Implicit in and through his every deed and word on record was *the kingdom of God*. The term, however it may be translated, implied an alternate domain transcendent to but impinging upon every other domain whether religious or political. Two powers existed in Palestine at the time of Jesus: the Jewish Temple and Imperial Rome. Jesus challenged both by introducing the breakthrough of the reign of God. Events in which Jesus participated in the last days of his life merely brought to a head what had been brewing for some time during his charismatic ministry.

In Chapter 5 I dealt with the coherence between the crucifixion of Jesus and his earlier acts and words, and also with the impact of the crucifixion on the preaching of the surviving disciples. In the ensuing discussion I shall try to reconstruct (as many have done before me in their own way) events that culminated in the sentence of death by crucifixion of "the man for others," using the following lines of thought: sources of information, titles ascribed to Jesus, symbolic entrance into the holy city, provocative demonstration in the Temple, the last meal, betrayal, execution with inscription, burial, and, as a conclusion, the disciples' experience of the risen Jesus.

SOURCES OF INFORMATION

Little more needs to be stated about sources of information concerning the last days of Jesus' earthly life beyond that which has already appeared in ch. 4. Historical information about the momentous events of those days is wrapped up particularly in the Passion narratives of the four gospels of the New Testament. Neither the *Gospel of Thomas* nor the Q document pays any attention to the events surrounding the execution of Jesus in Jerusalem. Those two sources are sayings gospels and are therefore not very useful in reconstructing what happened in the last week. The *Gospel*

Part II: Jesus

of Peter, on the other hand, is a narrative gospel, a surviving parchment of which was discovered in 1886 on the east bank of the Nile over two hundred miles south of Cairo. While excavating in Akhmîm (ancient Panopolis), members of the French Archaeological Mission in Cairo discovered the tomb of a monk. Buried with the monk's remains was a little book of sacred texts in fragmentary form. Scholars determined from the handwriting that the manuscript came from the early Middle Ages, but concluded also that the copy represents the ancient *Gospel of Peter*. A late second century bishop of Antioch made reference to this gospel, as did Origen (253 CE), and Eusebius, bishop of Caesarea (300 CE). But the *Gospel of Peter* itself was lost for almost nineteen centuries.

Its particular relevance to the present discussion comes from the fact that the surviving fragment is *a passion narrative* in line with the Passion narratives of the four gospels of the New Testament, but differing from them at several points. For example, Herod Antipas, not Pilate, plays a leading role in bringing about Jesus' death. Let me emphasize, the *Gospel of Peter* was not written by Simon Peter, disciple of Jesus. That would be rather much to expect. It was written under Peter's name after his death, a custom not uncommon in ancient Jewish society. When the gospel was written is not certain. Crossan maintains that the core of the *Gospel of Peter*, what he calls the Cross Gospel, circulated earlier than the gospels of the New Testament, and that the latter were dependent on the Cross Gospel embedded in the *Gospel of Peter*.[1] That hypothesis cannot be proven, nor is it necessarily a good working model.

The priority of Mark's passion narrative to that of Matthew, Luke, and John in the New Testament, and probably also to the *Gospel of Peter*, remains a viable option. Each of the gospel writers following Mark added pieces from their own tradition, and/or from their creative imagination as believers in the efficacy of the crucifixion of Jesus for salvation. Complete and satisfactory harmonization between all four or five passion narratives is not possible. Each gospel writer wrote out of a particular situation in life, and each writer selected texts from prophetic Scripture to validate each part of their Passion narratives. Keep in mind also that the primitive community of Jewish believers in Jesus after his death was at odds with their fellow Jewish religionists who did not so believe. Thus one finds an internal religious polemic at work in the gospels' narration of the events surrounding Jesus' execution. The Jewish leaders in the narrative, and the Jewish people in league with them, bear most of the blame for the sentence of death on Jesus. The Romans, represented by the appointed prefect, Pilate, appear less culpable, to the point of being innocent of any wrongdoing whatsoever with respect to Jesus. Such initial internal polemic—a sectarian Jewish group against another Jewish community—evident in the Passion narratives eventually became anti-Jewish slander when the later Christian Church became the preferred religion of the Roman Empire. That irresponsible racial-religious slander reached its dastardly high point in the twentieth century during the Nazi regime in Europe when millions of Jewish people were put to painful death simply for being Jewish.

---

1. Crossan, *Who Killed Jesus?* 24–25.

The Last Days in Jerusalem

Modern interpreters of the passion narratives should be aware of two factors bearing on the interpretation of those texts: (1) the early history of the Jesus-movement encoded in the Passion narratives, and (2) the history following the ascendency of Christianity over Judaism. Modern interpreters live in the shadow of the second. The challenge is to understand the narratives in light of the first, and then get behind that stage to what was really happening during the last days of Jesus in Jerusalem.

Outside sources, not from the post-Easter faith communities, are sparse. Late first-century Jewish historian, Josephus, gives a few lines that have some bearing on the present reconstruction:

> Now, there was about this time Jesus, a wise man . . . for he was a doer of wonderful works—a teacher of such men as receive the truth with pleasure. He drew over to him both many of the Jews, and many of the Gentiles . . . When Pilate, at the suggestion of the principal men amongst us, had condemned him to the cross, those that loved him at the first did not forsake him, . . . and the tribe of Christians, so named after him, are not extinct at this day.[2]

Notice that Josephus claims that Jesus' followers did not forsake him in his hour of suffering. Mark (14:50) and Matthew (26:56) both say "*all* the disciples deserted him and fled." Luke (23:49) holds that "*all* his acquaintances, including the women who had followed him from Galilee, stood at a distance." John (19:25–27), on the other hand, has the mother of Jesus and three other women, together with the beloved disciple, "standing near the cross of Jesus." The *Gospel of Peter* explains why the disciples deserted Jesus: "I [Peter] with my companions was grieved, and being wounded in mind, we hid ourselves because we were being sought for by [the elders and priests] as malefactors who wished to set fire to the temple."[3]

From all of this an interesting scenario emerges: (1) all of the Synoptic Gospels agree that *all* the disciples and friends deserted Jesus at the time of his death; (2) the Gospel of Peter plays out a similar theme with reasons given; and (3) John did not follow any of the other gospels, but is more in line with Josephus in asserting that Jesus had friends close by during his death on the cross. Now to the question about these sources of information. Which one (or ones) of these should be used in reconstructing what happened during the Passion of Jesus? The data of the sources cannot be harmonized on this point. Either *all* the disciples and friends left Jesus to die alone or they did not *all* do so. The point to this exercise is that each of the available sources narrates the story of the events of Jesus' last days in Jerusalem with creative imagination and specific confessional conviction characteristic of ancient narrative writing. Out of that complex an historical picture emerges of what was happening and why.

The only other outside source related to the passion narratives of the gospels can be found in the *Annals* of a Roman historian, Tacitus (56–117 CE). The text was written in 116 CE and reads as follows:

---

2. *Ant.* 18.63.
3. *Gos. Pet.* 7.

Part II: Jesus

> Christus, from whom the name [Christian] had its origin, suffered the extreme penalty during the reign of Tiberius at the hands of one of our procurators, Pontius Pilatus, and a most mischievous superstition, thus checked for the moment, again broke out not only in Judaea, the first source of the evil, but even in Rome, where all things hideous and shameful from every part of the world find their center and become popular.[4]

Neither Tacitus nor Josephus had ready access to the gospels. The two men wrote their works before the gospels were in wide circulation. And neither of them belonged to a faith-community where the gospels were at home. Yet somehow the two writers had information about the death of Jesus without the help of the gospels. Josephus and Tacitus lived in different places and adhered to different cultural convictions: Josephus was from a Jewish priestly family and Tacitus a Roman historian. Yet the two brief accounts of Jesus' death agree on three significant points: (1) *Jesus suffered the extreme penalty, crucifixion; (2) Pontius Pilate, the procurator of Judea, was the one responsible for the sentence; and (3) the followers of Jesus continued his work after his death.*

TITLES ASCRIBED TO JESUS

I have left the titles ascribed to Jesus to this point, because they surface in the Passion narratives in the gospels as having something to do with the sentence of death passed upon him. By specifying that the titles were *ascribed* to Jesus I mean that he did not apply the titles to himself directly during his ministry, except for "Son of Humanity."

Messiah/Christ

It is common practice in popular Christian culture to use "Jesus" and "Christ" interchangeably or together, "Jesus Christ," as though the person in view had been given these two names at birth. The fact of the matter is that "Jesus" was the single given name of the man who appeared before Pilate. "Christ" was *a title* the disciples deemed appropriate for Jesus, especially after his crucifixion and vindication by the resurrection. In the early communities of believers in Jesus, the title became more important than the given name. As a title, it carried a wealth of meaning for the post-Easter Jewish followers, much more so for them than for later non-Jewish believers up to the present time.

In English, "Christ" is a loan word from the Greek, *Christos*. It means "one who is anointed"—literally smeared with oil—and thus appointed to an important leadership task. But the antecedent of the Greek word *Christos* ("Christ") is the Aramaic/Hebrew word transliterated "Messiah." The essential meaning is the same. Someone with authority in Israel performed the anointing, and the anointed one was thus granted the right to carry out a high-ranking assignment on behalf of the people. Anointing was done to kings and priests of Israel, and possibly prophets. Their life and work thereafter carried weight among the people for whom the anointing was intended to serve. Samuel, a faithful judge in Israel, anointed both Saul (1 Sam. 10:1)

---

4. Tacitus, *Annals* 15.44.

The Last Days in Jerusalem

and David (1 Sam. 16:12–13) to kingship over Israel under the divine sanction of Israel's God, the king supreme.

Messianic aspirations existed in Judaism before and during the time of Jesus. When the people were without their own king, suffering under the yoke of a foreign power, they longed for a deliverer to restore their fortunes in the Land. In the scrolls of the Qumran covenanters two messiahs come to the fore. The *War Scroll* anticipates a prophetic Messiah who will *not* engage in battle between the "children of light" and "the children of darkness." At other places the Messiah is a war hero (4Q*Florilegium*; 4Q458).

Another document written shortly before the time of Jesus under the title name, *Psalms of Solomon*, pictures the Messiah as a wise teacher of righteousness. The scroll may have originated in the Qumran community, where an enigmatic figure called Teacher of Righteousness was admired. Here is an excerpt from the *Psalms of Solomon* to illustrate:

> And Messiah shall be a righteous king, taught of God, over the nations, and there shall be no unrighteousness in his days, for all shall be holy and their king the Messiah of the Lord. For he shall not put his trust in horse and rider and bow, nor shall he multiply for himself gold and silver for war, nor shall he gather confidence from a multitude for the day of battle. The Lord Himself is his king, the hope of him that is mighty through his hope in God. All nations shall fear before him, for he will smite the earth with the word of his mouth forever. He will bless the people of the Lord with wisdom and gladness, and he himself will be pure from sin, so that he may rule a great people. He will rebuke rulers, and remove sinners by the might of his word (*Ps. Sol.* 17.32–36).

With this background of various visions of Messiah/Christ circulating in Judaism it is not difficult to understand the Jewish followers of Jesus ascribing the title to him. They longed for deliverance from oppression, coupled with the institution of divine justice. On two occasions the title was ascribed to Jesus, once by Peter at Caesarea Philippi (Mark 8:27–30) and by Caiaphas the high priest in the form of a question in the trial (Mark 14:61–62; Matt. 26:63). Whether Jesus accepted the title as given in each case is not clear. In Mark 8:30, after Peter had ascribed "Messiah" to him, Jesus "sternly ordered" the disciples not to tell anyone about him. If Jesus actually accepted their title for him, he did *not* accept Peter's understanding of the Messiah. Peter rejected the notion of a *suffering* Messiah, at which point the Markan Jesus rebuked him as an instrument of Satan (Mark 8:31–33). When Caiaphas, in Mark, inquires if he is Messiah, Jesus answers, "I am," but then elaborates with echoes from Psalm 110:1 and Daniel 7:13–14 about the Son of Humanity seated at the right hand of power, and coming in the clouds of heaven. In the parallel text in Matthew 26:63, Jesus does not answer the high priest with a clear affirmative. Instead he says, "you have said so," as though not prepared to accept the title as understood by the high priest.

There is some question about the authenticity of the ascription of Messiah to Jesus in both instances. Christology developed in the communities soon after the Easter experience, which may account for the ascription of the title to Jesus at the two

Part II: Jesus

critical moments in the synoptic narratives, cited above. Evidence of this developed Christology bursts onto the canvas at the opening of the Gospel of Mark in the form of a bold confession minted in a faith-community many years after Jesus' death: "The beginning of the good news of Jesus *Messiah*, the Son of God" (Mark 1:1). Right away the stage is set for the unfolding of Mark's drama aimed at anchoring that post-Easter confession in the ministry of the historical Jesus. At the same time, Mark and his synoptic partners exercised restraint by not having Jesus *declare himself* Messiah. In any case, when the title was boldly ascribed to Jesus *after* Easter, the meaning(s) of the Jewish Messiah had gone through another change in light of Jesus crucified and risen.

Son of God

The concept "Son of God" was well known in the first century, both in Judaism and in Hellenism. In the Hebrew Scriptures the earthly king of Israel was described as God's son (2 Sam. 7:14; Ps. 2:7; 89:27–28). He reigned as God's viceroy. But the prophet Hosea has God declare Israel the "son" that God called out of Egypt (Hos. 11:1). Jeremiah hails the tribe of Ephraim as God's "dear son" (31:9, 20). In Jewish literature of the Second Temple period, the righteous person was considered a "child of God" (e.g. *Wisdom* 2:17–18). The metaphor in Judaism spoke to the question of a special relationship with God: Israel's son-king ruled in God's stead; Israel as a son-people observed the law of God; the righteous son received help from God, as from a father.

The chief god in ancient Egypt was Ra, the sun god. Ra was creator of all life, and the Pharaohs who ruled Egypt viewed themselves as the life-giving sons of Ra. Alexander the Great is said to have thought of himself as a son of the Greek god, Zeus. The Roman Emperor, Caesar Augustus, was named "divine son" (Lat. *divi filius*), which, translated into Greek, becomes "son of god" (*huios theou*).

With this background in mind, the title "son of God" as attributed to Jesus variously in the gospels is completely understandable. He healed the sick, promised the kingdom of God to the poor, opposed injustice, stood up to the elite powers as one ordained of God, and faced death on behalf of others. In his vision and work and word he was standing in for God, and was thus related to God as son to father who acts in this way. Remarkably, the earliest narrative gospel, Mark, attributes the title to Jesus only a few times. As noted already, it occurs in the opening confessional statement from the author. After that, the unclean spirits recognize Jesus as "son of God" (3:11). And finally, Caiaphas the high priest combines Messiah with "Son of the Blessed One" in his question to Jesus (14:61).

Matthew and Luke (following Q) put the title in the mouth of the tempter in the wilderness in the form of a condition: "If you are the Son of God . . ." (Matt. 4:3, 6; Luke 4:3, 9). They also follow Mark in having the demons call Jesus "Son of God" (Matt. 8:29; Luke 4:41). Still following Mark, Matthew (26:63) has Caiaphas address Jesus in a trial scene: "tell us if you are the Messiah, the Son of God." Luke (22:69) has the whole council of chief priests and elders ask Jesus: "Are you, then, the Son of God?" Jesus' answer in both Matthew and Luke simply turns the question back at them: "You have

The Last Days in Jerusalem

said so," implying that he had not used the title of himself. In all three accounts in the Passion narratives in the Synoptic Gospels Jesus was viewed as a messianic pretender. That is, he was acting as God's righteous deliverer of the people. Jesus' accusers may have deduced from his actions and words that he considered himself God's agent for justice. As such, he would have stood in opposition to the established powers of the Temple and the Roman prefect. If that was in fact the understanding of the rulers in Jerusalem, then the ascribed titles of "Messiah" and "Son of God" would have cast Jesus in the role of subversive radical, an intolerable role to play in the presence of the coalition government in Jerusalem.

As a matter of interest, the genealogy of Jesus in Luke traces his ancestors back to Adam, who is then said to be "son of God" (Luke 3:38). By logical extension then everyone born of Adam is a son/daughter of God, and subject to the redeeming blessing of Creator-God. The appellation arises from the human being (Adam) created in the image of the invisible God (Gen. 1:26–27; cf. 2 Cor. 4:4; Col. 1:15).

Son of Humanity

While Jesus did not use the titles "Christ" and "Son of God" to describe his own identity, he did employ the "Son of Humanity" (*huios anthrōpou*) as a self-designation. However, he did not coin the phrase. The prophecies of Ezekiel, with which Jesus would have been familiar, have the Hebrew equivalent term strewn throughout the oracles. God addresses the prophet as "Son of Adam" repeatedly. The NRSV translates the phrase acutely with the English word "mortal." For example: "He said to me: 'O *mortal*, stand up on your feet, and I will speak with you'" (2:3); "and you, O *mortal*, do not be afraid of them, and do not be afraid of their words" (2:6); "but you, *mortal*, hear what I say to you; do not be rebellious like that rebellious house" (2:8); so you, *mortal*, I have made a sentinel for the house of Israel (33:7). In each case the Hebrew attribution is literally "Son of Adam," traditionally translated "Son of Man."

God addressed the prophet Daniel also as "Son of Adam" (8:17). But in recalling his own night visions Daniel reports that in them he "saw one like a *human being* coming with the clouds of heaven" (7:13). The NRSV rightly translates the title in 7:13 "human being," because the Hebrew word used there communicates the more general idea of "human being," without the specific notion that the human descendent of Adam is mortal.

Jesus may have drawn on either or both of these prophetic sources, or even Psalm 8:4: "What are the human beings that you are mindful of them, or the *son of Adam* that you care for him." Many New Testament scholars believe that Jesus had in mind the apocalyptic figure of Daniel 7:13, and applied it to himself in response to the question from the high priest (Mark 14:62; cf. 13:26). Some have suggested that Mark, writing out of a post-resurrection experience, supplemented Jesus' answer to the high priest with the allusion to Daniel's vision of a human being "coming with the clouds of heaven." Those who continued to trust in Jesus after his death and resurrection looked

Part II: Jesus

forward to heavenly justice and salvation, which, for them, could only come through Jesus, victorious "in the clouds of heaven."

However that may be, Jesus used "Son of Humanity" as a personal self-definition during his ministry, i.e., a third person prophetic figure in place of the first person, "I" (cf. 2 Cor. 12:2). Jesus addressed four crucial topics recorded in Mark (and parallels) under the title, "Son of Humanity" instead of "I": "the Son of Humanity has *authority* on earth to forgive sins" (2:10); "the Son of Humanity is lord even of the *Sabbath*" (2:28); the Son of Humanity must undergo great *suffering* (8:31); and "the Son of Humanity came not to be served but *to serve*, and to give his life *a ransom* for many" (10:45). In the apocalyptic sections of Matthew and Luke (Matt. 24–25; Luke 17) the coming of the Son of Humanity in power and glory and judgment is pronounced, doubtless drawing on the vision of Daniel 7.

Whatever may be said of Jesus' use of the title "Son of Humanity," this much is evident from the gospels: it caused no serious concern to either the Jewish or the Roman authorities in Jerusalem. On the other hand, "Christ" and "Son of God" could generate certain anxiety in the minds of the elite rulers of the Temple and of the Roman court. But the next title was the most provocative of all.

King of the Judeans

As demonstrated already, during his ministry Jesus did not mute the central feature of his teaching and acting: *the kingdom of God*. Even though Jesus did not broadcast that he was the ruler of the kingdom he announced, it would have been an easy step for the disciples and others to take. Three of the four canonical gospels reserve the title "king of the Judeans" for their passion narratives. The Gospel of Peter uses "king of Israel." Only the writer of Matthew sequesters the title to the birth narrative in the voice of the *magi* inquiring: "Where is the child who has been born *king of the Judeans*?" (2:2). Herod the Great was king of the Judeans at the time, and was not at all impressed by the inquiry. That story at the beginning of Matthew serves as a foreshadowing of the question from Pilate to Jesus in the passion narrative: "Are you the King of the Judeans?" (Matt. 27:11; Mark 15:2; Luke 23:3; John 18:33). If Jesus' answer affirmed as much, then the case was closed. I will discuss later the sentence Pilate passed on Jesus.

As for Jesus' own self-understanding with respect to the kingdom of God, there is not a hint that he considered himself the supreme ruler of the kingdom he announced. It was *God's* kingdom. Jesus probably thought of himself as the one given the responsibility for carrying out the plan of the sovereign God for the people. Israel's God was the only king with final authority to execute justice and create peace on the earth. In the Lord's Prayer Jesus directed the disciples to address Father-God as the arbiter of all things good and just in heaven and on earth. Yet Jesus did engage in bringing God's will to bear in human affairs, especially among the people living in the Land of promise.

The Last Days in Jerusalem

There are a few instances in the gospels where the kingdom seems to belong to Jesus. For example, in his response to a request from the mother of the two sons of Zebedee, that they should have places of prominence in Jesus' coming kingdom, Jesus refers the matter to his Father-God: "to sit at my right hand and at my left, this is *not mine to grant*, but it is for those for whom it has been prepared by my Father" (Matt. 20:20–23; cf. Mark 10:35–40). In the Gospel of John, however, during the trial before Pilate Jesus explicitly states that he has a kingdom, except that it is "not of this world" (John 18:36). This saying is consistent with the theology that informs the entire Fourth Gospel: the kingdom of Jesus is eternal, spiritual, peaceful, non-political, "not of this world." Sanders believes that the first disciples, being Jewish, would have understood the relationship between Jesus and the kingdom to have been "the kingdom of God with Jesus as his viceroy."[5]

SYMBOLIC ENTRANCE INTO THE HOLY CITY

The story of Jesus' entrance into the city of Jerusalem on the back of a donkey is reported in all four gospels. A number of scholars question the authenticity of the account, especially the highly provocative cries of the people "Hosanna! Blessed is the one who comes in the name of the Lord! Blessed is the coming kingdom of our ancestor David! Hosanna in the highest heaven!" (Mark 11:9–10). The refrains echo the words of Psalm 118:25–26 and 148:1. In his influential book on *The Historical Jesus*, Crossan does not list in his index—much less discuss—Mark's report about Jesus' entrance into Jerusalem. In a subsequent publication, however, Crossan does mention the story, but then concludes: "I do not think . . . that it ever actually happened, except as later symbolic retrojection."[6] For Crossan the account in the four gospels is "prophecy historicized" not "history remembered."[7] Yet all four gospels carry the account as though it were well embedded in the collective memory of the post-Easter community as having happened. With all due respect to Crossan's scholarly suspicion, I find no good reason to discount *the event* as having happened (history remembered), and the evangelists' later citing prophecy to endorse its symbolic significance.

Matthew's invoking of Zechariah 9:9 to complement his use of Mark (11:1–10) muddies the water. In Matthew 21:2–11 Jesus sends the disciples to find a donkey and her colt. They are to bring both animals to Jesus for him to ride *both of them* into Jerusalem in fulfillment of the prophecy: "Lo, your king comes to you; triumphant and victorious is he, humble and riding on a donkey, on a colt, the foal of a donkey." What Matthew seems to have misconstrued from Zechariah 9:9 is the Hebrew parallelism in the two poetic lines of the oracle: there was only one animal refracted onto the two lines. Mark, Luke (19:29–38), and John (12:12–15) all have Jesus riding on one donkey. I take *the event* to be historical, including the strewing of clothes on the roadway. Jesus would have known the prophecy, and may have acted it out. His humble ride on

---

5. Sanders, *Jesus and Judaism*, 308.
6. Crossan, *Revolutionary*, 129.
7. Crossan, *Who Killed Jesus?* 1–38.

Part II: Jesus

a donkey signaled the kind of kingdom he had been enacting and announcing to this point: *a kingdom of peace and non-violence that brings the justice of God*. Pontius Pilate would hardly have used such a humble steed for his ride into Jerusalem for the festival.

Quite apart from its connection with a prophetic word, the event attracted a crowd beyond the number of Jesus' disciples. And, as Rivkin points out, "crowds were dangerous and could get out of hand,"[8] especially so if they were chanting some words of honor to the one riding the donkey. Fredriksen rightly points to the "crowd" of pilgrims attracted to Jesus on the occasion of this particular Passover. This act of Jesus, and the crowd's enthusiastic response, could quickly have come to the attention of the powers, both Jewish and Roman. But Pilate did not send the police to arrest Jesus for his action. He posed no real threat to Pilate's rule. He had no army. His humble entrance was powerless by Roman standards. But the holiday crowd of pilgrims was another matter. Fredriksen writes:

> The excitement of the crowds around Jesus that Passover might easily have spilled over into riot, or been perceived as about to do so by the Roman troops staring down at them from the roof of the Temple stoa. The priests were perfectly positioned both to know their mood and the likely Roman response. If this is what Caiaphas feared, then as the highest Jewish leader responsible for preserving the peace, he would have alerted Pilate . . . Working in conjunction with the high priest's Temple guard . . . he [Pilate] would move swiftly, arresting Jesus by stealth, at night, to keep these noisy enthusiasts quiet as long as possible. Let them wake up to their messiah already on a cross by the next morning. Killing Jesus publicly, by crucifixion, would go a long way toward disabusing the crowd. Let him hang indicted by their own belief: KING OF THE JEWS. A nice touch an insult to the idea itself as well as to their convictions[9] . . . . His death warrant had already been signed by the very crowd that had clamored around him, responding to his message of impending redemption. Pilate's soldiers had their orders, and they knew what to do.[10]

PROVOCATIVE DEMONSTRATION IN THE TEMPLE

As with Jesus' entrance into Jerusalem for Passover, all four gospels record his demonstration in the Temple shortly after he had entered the city. The Gospel of John, for reasons known only to its author, has the incident happen at the beginning of Jesus' ministry (2:13–22). According to the chronology of John, that would put the demonstration about three years prior to the one recorded in the Synoptic Gospels. To suggest that there were two such demonstrations violates the integrity of both John and the Synoptics. The plot of the whole Gospel of John concerning Jesus unfolds out of that event in the Temple that prepares the reader for the new Temple of his body "after he was raised from the dead" (2:22). The time of the event in the Synoptic Gospels is historically more likely (Mark 11:15–18//Matt. 21:12–16//Luke 19:45–47).

---

8. Rivkin, *Crucified?* 49.
9. Fredriksen, *Jesus*, 254
10. Ibid., 258.

The Last Days in Jerusalem

It was precipitous, provocative and conspicuous. The saying of Jesus that accompanied his action alludes to two texts from the Hebrew prophets: "My house shall be called a house of prayer for all the nations (Isa. 56:7). But you have made it a den of robbers (Jer. 7:1–11)." Mark, or his source, may have underwritten the event with these two prophetic words, as some suggest. It was the thing to do in the post-Easter community to provide Scriptural warrant for a meaningfully charged event.

Be that as it may, the act of Jesus was in itself prophetic, symbolically so. What exactly did he do? All of the gospels agree on one important point: there was exchange of money going on somewhere in the Temple precincts. One body of opinion suggests that it was happening on the southern side of the outer court where non-Jewish worshippers were permitted. But the trading posts at that Passover had not always been located within the precincts of the Temple. The collection of the half shekel and the purchase of unblemished animals for sacrifice happened across the Kidron Valley on the Mount of Olives. "Around 30 CE, Caiaphas expelled the Sanhedrin and introduced the traders into the Temple, in both ways centralizing power in his own hands."[11] The outer porticos were traditionally used for teaching the people, a function of the Pharisees and others thus gifted. The installation of tables for the exchange of money and the sale of unblemished animals was practical: the worshipper did not have to risk the animal becoming imperfect during travel. In this respect the priests who served at the tables were performing a service for the people.

Apparently Jesus did not see it that way. Chilton prefers to call the action of Jesus in the outer court of the Temple an "occupation" rather than a "demonstration." The overturning of the tables of the traders constituted, symbolically at least, a take-over of the precincts for purposes other than the proper presentation of animals for sacrifice. According to Chilton, again, Jesus was not engaging in any symbolic act other than "an attempt to insist that the offerer's actual ownership of what is offered is a vital aspect of sacrifice."[12] Purity of worship within the Temple may have concerned Jesus to a point. But his act of overturning the tables of the buyers and sellers appears to have signaled something more in line with his saying about the coming destruction of the Temple. The saying *in Mark* is not likely to have come from that Evangelist's knowledge of the Temple's destruction in 70 CE, although it is possible. Mark even includes a perverted form of the saying in the mouths of the false witnesses at the trial of Jesus (Mark 14:57–58). At any rate, the overturning of the tables in the Temple was bound to come to the attention of Caiaphas. He would have seen it as a threatening act against the system as it stood. Implicitly, Jesus was calling the priestly performance in the Temple to account as a misrepresentation of the God of Israel. If that was how Caiaphas perceived Jesus' demonstration, it would not sit well with him. It may not have been sufficient cause in itself to condemn Jesus to death, but it could have been enough to induce Caiaphas to go to Pilate with accusations about Jesus as a disturber of the peace, not merely of the Temple, but also of Rome. Pilate would not have cared

---

11. Chilton, *Pure*, 122.
12. Ibid., 119.

Part II: Jesus

one way or the other about the purity of the sacrifices in the Temple. But a precipitous disturbance anywhere in Jerusalem, one that could result in a riot, would certainly arouse Pilate's ire against the perpetrator. And if the "crowd" happened to be sympathetic toward the person, so much the worse for the one creating the uproar.

THE LAST MEAL

Jesus seems to have enjoyed eating with people. Recall that he had been accused of being a glutton and a drunkard, not very flattering labels (Q 7:34 = Matt. 11:19).[13] Yet Jesus seems not to have eaten merely for the sake of consuming food and drink, but for fellowship with people of various types. Table fellowship united the group thus gathered in a bond of friendship and common concern. Meals often celebrated some good memory, or some saving event in the history of the people. The Passover Seder was such a meal. During the dinner the story of the Exodus of the Hebrews from slavery in Egypt was told in ritual fashion generation after generation.

The Synoptic Gospels agree that the last meal Jesus had with his disciples—and the last meal in his earthly life—was a Jewish Seder. (The Fourth Gospel places the meal before Passover, without any Eucharistic words, John 13:1–30). But Jesus inserted a new feature into the usual words of the Seder ritual. Referring to the bread and wine he said: "Take; this is my body. This is my blood of the covenant" (Mark 14:22–24). It was this unusual insertion of act and word into the traditional Seder that made it memorable within the post-Easter community of faith in Jesus. How the first participants around the table would have understood the new feature has been a matter of some debate. They would almost certainly *not* have understood it in the same way the post-Easter community came to appreciate it.

Chilton places Jesus' new feature squarely within the sacrificial setting of Judaism. Remember, the meal was being observed in Jerusalem. The Temple, with its sacrifices and offerings, was just down the street. Worshippers were there, dutifully presenting their unblemished animals to the priests for sacrifice. The body of the animal represented the body of the one presenting. Chilton's insight into the unusual character of Jesus' last meal with his disciples is illuminating:

> In Jesus' context . . . of his confrontation with the authorities of the Temple, his words can have had only one meaning. He cannot have meant 'Here are my personal body and blood;' that is an interpretation that only makes sense at a later stage in the development of Christianity. Jesus' point was rather that, in the absence of a temple that permitted his view of purity to be practiced, wine was his blood of sacrifice and bread was his flesh of sacrifice . . .
>
> The meaning of "the last supper," then, actually evolved over a series of meals after Jesus' occupation of the Temple. During the period, Jesus claimed that wine and bread were a better sacrifice than what was offered in the Temple, a foretaste of the new wine in the kingdom of God. At least wine and bread were Israel's own, not tokens of priestly dominance. No wonder the opposition to him, even

---

13. Modica, "Glutton," 50–73.

among the Twelve (in the shape of Judas, according to the Gospels), became deadly. In essence, Jesus made his meals into a rival altar.[14]

The Temple authorities would not have heard him say the strange new words uttered in the context of a meal with his followers, so they could not have taken offense. At the same time, the rival words in the last meal bespeak Jesus' vision that came to expression variously during his itinerant charismatic ministry, and came to a head in the Temple precincts with the overturning of the tables of the moneychangers, and the driving out of the buyers and sellers. The scene in the Temple could not have gone unnoticed by the priests, despite Fredriksen's argument to the contrary. According to her assessment of the situation in the Temple on a high holiday, "The effect of Jesus' gesture at eye-level—where everyone else was—would have been muffled, swallowed up by the sheer press of pilgrims. How worried, then, need the priests have been"?[15] I submit that the action of Jesus in the Temple exhibited a subversive element, not merely a "gesture." The action attacked the traditional system of sacrifice performed in the Temple. The priestly attendants at the tables would surely have noticed what happened. Suddenly their tables were upended, and the money scattered throughout the crowd at "eye-level." To suggest that the priests would have paid little attention to Jesus' action is hard to believe. Instead, as Sander's puts it in military metaphor, "the gun may already have been cocked, but it was the temple demonstration that pulled the trigger."[16]

I draw attention, as I did above, to the subversive nature of Jesus' overturning the tables in the Temple to make connection with his unusual introduction of bread and wine as a new sacrificial body. The disciples remembered the meal, not because it was the same as all the other meals they shared with Jesus, but because it instituted a new, memorable element quite unlike anything they had experienced before with Jesus. They remembered the moment, and celebrated it in a new way within their new community of faith in the crucified-resurrected Jesus.

BETRAYAL

One of the most infamous traitors in Christian collective memory was a disciple of Jesus named Judas Iscariot. The story is well known from the accounts in the four gospels. The Jewish leaders in Jerusalem wanted to arrest Jesus, the Galilean, during Passover week, but needed someone to identify him. Judas put himself forward as a reliable accomplice with the leaders. They paid him thirty pieces of silver for his service. He led them to the place where he knew Jesus and the disciples would be together. The plan was to identify Jesus to the police by kissing him. After Jesus was crucified, Judas, filled with remorse, went out and hanged himself (Mark 14:43–45; Matt. 26:47–27:5; Luke 22:47–49; John 18:1–6; Acts 1:15–23).

---

14. Chilton, *Pure*, 125.
15. Fredriksen, *Jesus*, 232.
16. Sanders, *Jesus and Judaism*, 305.

Part II: Jesus

That account, harmonized from texts in the four gospels and Acts, has been the traditional story in mainline Christianity to the present time. But there was another trajectory of the Judas-tradition that cast his character in a more positive light. Irenaeus, a second-century mainline apologist, wrote about a group that represented that trajectory. He spoke against such "heretical" groups of Gnostic persuasion (*gnōsis* is a Greek word meaning "knowledge"). Gnostics—there were a number of variations—believed in secret knowledge of the divine mind by which the true human being could attain salvation. Human flesh, as the bulwark of evil, would not be saved, but the human spirit would. Irenaeus was aware of a group of Gnostics who viewed Judas as an instrument in the divine plan to liberate the true Son of God from his body of flesh, and thus lead the followers of Jesus into similar salvation of spirit. In his writings, Irenaeus referred to a Gospel of Judas. He condemned it, of course, as heretical.

The Gospel of Judas disappeared from the Christian landscape until recently. A Coptic version of the ancient document, said to be the testimony of Judas in conversation with Jesus, has recently come to light.[17] The Coptic text of the surviving manuscript is a translation of an earlier Greek text. The historical Judas did not write the document, but a group, trying to understand his action in relation to redemption through Jesus, composed the short treatise as testimony to the divinely planned destiny of Judas to be the one to bring about the death of Jesus for the salvation of the world.

A modern Christian scholar, William Klassen, not so far afield from the stance of the Gospel of Judas, views Judas' act of handing Jesus over to the authorities to be his defining deed. It was not betrayal in the classical sense, but a "handing over." "[Judas] served as a go between and brought about a meeting between the Temple authorities and Jesus. . . . We have no reason to believe that Jesus considered the act of Judas sinful or wrong. I consider it possible that Jesus did express woe, a commiseration towards the one who had been selected to do the task . . . The lexical base for a classical 'betrayal' does not exist."[18]

Whether it is called "betrayal" or "handing over," the earliest sources treat the deed of Judas as an act of treachery, carried out without the sanction of Jesus. That Judas was a member of the Twelve whom Jesus called to be with him in his ministry is troubling, to be sure. But Judas, unlike Simon Peter who shrouded himself in denial (Mark 14:66–71 par.) actively put Jesus in front of the death squad. He, like Peter, probably did not understand the nature of Jesus' peaceful kingdom, and may have been trying to force his hand to act with conventional kingly power over his enemies. The texts do not say one way or another, only that Judas handed over his teacher and friend to his accusers. That tradition was passed on to Paul, who then passed it on to the Corinthian congregations as context for their celebration of the Eucharistic meal: "the Lord Jesus *on the night when he was betrayed* took a loaf of bread" (1 Cor. 11:23). Paul does not name Judas as the betrayer, only that betrayal was part of the complex

---

17. Kasser et al., *The Gospel of Judas*.
18. Klassen, "Judas," 409–10.

of Jesus' suffering, and thus belongs with the ongoing memorial of his selfless death on behalf of others.

The betrayal by Judas and the denial by Peter are both manifestations of the human urge to survive, and of failure to understand the kingdom of God whose viceroy goes willingly to an ignominious death at the hands of his enemies.

EXECUTION AND INSCRIPTION

Living as they did under the shadow of imperial Rome, the writers of the gospels, together with their communities, did all they could within the bounds of good conscience to prevail within the Roman world as a minority religious group, without sanction from Rome or from emerging Rabbinic Judaism. They argued back and forth with their Jewish incumbents about the viability of their new vision of the Jewish Scriptures with respect to the death and resurrection of Jesus. But they dared not antagonize Rome, on whose political benefaction they depended for survival. Consequently, the key role the Roman prefect of Judea played in the execution of Jesus is muted in the gospel narratives, to a point where Pilate borders on a compassionate governor who would gladly have released Jesus were it not for Jewish pressure to crucify him. At worst, Pilate is pictured as a weak ruler. At best he is favorably disposed to saving Jesus' life, but had to abide by the wish of the Jewish authorities. Caiaphas, by comparison, accuses Jesus of blasphemy and hands him over to Pilate for Roman execution without hesitation (Mark 14:53–65; 15:1–15 par.).

In the Gospel of John the single issue that concerns Pilate is the kingship of Jesus (John 18:28–19:16).[19] Is this Galilean really the king of the Judeans? Jesus in John defended his kingship before Pilate, qualifying it boldly as a kingship from a realm other than Rome or Israel. Pilate knew full well that there was no political threat from this peasant Galilean man. He flogged Jesus anyway, and his soldiers mocked him, crowned him with thorns, dressed him in a purple robe, and ridiculed him, "King of the Judeans." Pilate topped the callous treatment by presenting the bleeding figure of Jesus in his mock robe and thorny crown to the Jewish leaders. "Here is your king," he said to them. Pilate succeeded in wringing from their Jewish minds a confession that violated their covenant with God: "We have no king but the emperor" (John 19:16). What ever happened to their allegiance to the Lord Yahweh, their God? Their daily prayer in the Temple hailed Yahweh God as their ruler, the Lord alone (Deut. 6:4). Now caught in Pilate's political maneuvering they effectively deny their holy allegiance in favor of the emperor.

Pilate handed Jesus over to the soldiers for execution by crucifixion. But Pilate was not satisfied to crucify Jesus. He had an inscription printed up to be fastened to the cross above Jesus' head. All of the gospels agree on this point (Mark 15:26; Matt. 27:37; Luke 23:38; John 19:19). It reads in John: "Jesus of Nazareth, the King of the Judeans." This was not a sign of Pilate's change of heart, a confession, after all, that Jesus was the true king of the Judeans. No. This was Pilate's deliberate affront to the

---

19. Rensberger's insights inform this analysis, *Johannine Faith*, 87–106.

Part II: Jesus

Jewish people, as much as to say, "This is what happens to anyone who comes forward as king of the Judeans over whom I rule." The Gospel of John reports that the Jewish leaders asked Pilate to change the wording to read, "This man said, 'I am the king of the Judeans.'" Pilate refused to change a word. This crucified, bleeding, helpless, figure is the only kind of king the Judeans can ever hope to have. Pilate snuffed out the pretentious rule of Jesus one festival morning by the word of his mouth. That was how it appeared at the moment.

BURIAL

The practice of crucifixion in the Roman Empire continued until Emperor Constantine ruled it out of existence in the fourth century. Archaeological artifacts pointing to widespread crucifixions in the first century are sparse, not surprisingly. Nothing could be more shameful to family and friends than to have one of their number hung on a wooden cross-bar in public, and left there to die. Even if a family member asked for the body to give the remains an honorable burial in the family tomb, the authorities were not usually disposed to allow it. Bodies of crucified criminals were usually left on the crosses for animals and birds to devour the flesh. The bones were eventually thrown into an unmarked grave, or cave.

The remains of one crucified man were discovered in 1968 in a burial cave northeast of Jerusalem, a rare find indeed![20] The caves, excavated by Vassilios Tzaferis, were part of a necropolis containing rock-hewn tombs of Jewish families. The necropolis dates from the Second Temple period. Five ossuaries (boxes containing the bones and artifacts of family members) were found, two of them dated in the first century CE. In one of the ossuaries were the remains of three individuals: two men and one young child. Careful analysis of the human remains found that one male was in his mid twenties, about five feet six inches in height, and died by crucifixion. His Aramaic name was *Yehochanan*, "John" in English. His right heel bone was attached to a piece of wood by a 4.5-inch nail, which was then attached to the upright piece of the cross. The purpose of the small board was to prevent the man from wriggling his foot out of the grip of the small-headed nail. The board, the nail, and the man's foot were then hammered onto the upright piece. The head of the nail in this case bent as it was being driven into the hard olive wood. When the man was taken down from the cross, the nail and the wood could not be separated, so both were buried together. His arms were tied, not nailed, to the upper crossbar.

This is the single piece of hard evidence of a family member claiming the body of a crucified member, and then burying the bones with those of other members. There is nothing on record of any member of Jesus' family claiming his body after his crucifixion. It may have been futile to ask the authorities for the body. Or the shame may have been too great. Honor was highly valued in ancient Mediterranean society. The family members of Jesus were no exception. "Honour means the perception someone has of his or her own worth and an appreciation of how he or she is rated by a relevant

---

20. Crossan and Reed, *Excavating*, 3–4; Rousseau and Arav, *Jesus*, 75–76.

social group."[21] The passion narratives in the gospels imply that Jesus had an honorable burial, not in the usual sense of being placed in a family tomb by a member of the family, but in a new tomb by a member of the Jewish hierarchy, a man named Joseph, "a respected member of the council" (Mark 15:43). The Fourth Gospel brings in Nicodemus, also a member of the Jewish council, to assist Joseph with the burial. But was such a burial truly honorable?

Byron McCane argues otherwise. There was no family member present at the burial to mourn his death, no eulogia, no funeral procession. The tomb was empty, and thus not associated with any honorable tradition. Jesus was buried in that tomb in disgrace equal to the disgrace of his death by crucifixion. "One or more members of the Sanhedrin must have obtained the body of Jesus from Pilate and arranged for a dishonorable interment."[22] An honorable burial would have contradicted the verdict Pilate had just passed on the man, Jesus. The best that a council member could do was to put the body in an *unused* tomb reserved for Jewish criminals. "By sunset on the day of his death," says McCane, "the body of Jesus lay within a burial cave reserved for criminals condemned by Jewish courts. No one mourned."[23]

Whatever merit McCane's analysis might have regarding the dishonorable burial of Jesus, it falls short in accounting for the role of *Pilate* in scourging Jesus, and allowing his soldiers to mock him and persecute him before passing the sentence of death by crucifixion. The likelihood of a full-fledged Jewish court assembling in the middle of the night during a holy day of the High Holiday is slim. The high priest did have the responsibility of reporting to Pilate any disturbance in the city. Jesus had created a scene in the Temple, had drawn crowds, and had talked of another kingdom. All of this had to be brought to Pilate. It was Pilate who condemned Jesus to death by crucifixion. He needed no Jewish court to approve of his action.

A better scenario would be that one (or more) of the members of Jewish hierarchy in Jerusalem found Jesus' message hopeful, and sought a way to preserve the memory of his person from the despicable spectacle of hanging on a cross until wild animals and carrion birds had mutilated his crucified flesh. Jesus' body may not have received an honorable burial in the usual way, but it was, by all accounts, saved by at least one Jewish leader from the ghastly disgrace of most crucified criminals of the day.

CONCLUSION: THE DISCIPLES' EXPERIENCE OF THE RISEN JESUS

The crucifixion and burial of Jesus were not the end of the story. Even though the twelve disciples and other believers in Jesus had deserted him in his hour of suffering and death, they reconnected with each other in Jerusalem a short time after the burial. As they were remembering his life among them, the risen Jesus *appeared* to them.

The earliest surviving text about the appearances is found in 1 Corinthians 15:3–5. Its origin in the tradition pre-dates Paul's letter, as the formula indicates: "I *handed*

---

21. Esler, *First Christians*, 25.
22. McCane, "'Where No One Had Yet Been Laid,'" 432.
23. Ibid., 452.

Part II: Jesus

on to you . . . what I in turn *had received*." What Paul had received and handed on was an early faith formulation, which included word about appearances of Jesus after his crucifixion: "he *appeared* to Cephas, [Peter] then to the twelve. Then he *appeared* to more than five hundred brothers and sisters at one time . . . Then he *appeared* to James, then to all the apostles. Last of all, as to one untimely born, he *appeared* also to me" (1 Cor. 15:5–8). Four times the word "appeared" (*ōphthē*) occurs in this short text. The word implies that the risen Jesus revealed himself to his disciples and friends in a new form. The same holds for the gospel narratives: he *appeared* to the ones who knew and loved him before his crucifixion. Several points can be made from this observation.

Experience over Event

None of the disciples witnessed the resurrection of Jesus as an event. Instead, they experienced the person of Jesus alive among them. His form had changed, but his being and character had returned to them with comfort and encouragement. Here is a sampling of their encounters with the risen Jesus according to the gospels:

- "*Suddenly* Jesus met them and said, 'Greetings!' And they came to him, took hold of his feet, and worshiped him" (Matt. 28:9).

- "Now the eleven disciples went to Galilee, to the mountain to which Jesus had directed them. When they saw him, they worshiped him; but *some doubted*" (Matt. 28:16–17).

- "While [two disciples] were talking and discussing, Jesus himself came near and went with them, but *their eyes were kept from recognizing him* . . . When he was at the table with them, he took bread, blessed and broke it, and gave it to them. Then *their eyes were opened*, and they recognized him; and he *vanished* from their sight" (Luke 24:15–16, 30–31).

- "When it was evening on that day, the first day of the week, and *the doors of the house where the disciples had met were locked* for fear of the Jews, Jesus came and stood among them and said, 'Peace be with you.' After he said this, he showed them his hands and his side. Then the disciples rejoiced when they saw the Lord" (John 20:19–20).

- "A week later his disciples were again in the house, and Thomas was with them. Although *the doors were shut*, Jesus came and stood among them and said, 'Peace be with you' . . . Thomas answered him, 'My Lord and my God!' Jesus said to him, 'Have you believed because you have seen me? Blessed are those who have not seen and yet have come to believe'" (John 20:26–29).

I have emphasized some phrases in the above statements to indicate the unusual form of the appearances of the risen Jesus: the person of Jesus had returned to his people, but no longer in a finite, mortal body.

The disciples' experience of Jesus, now vindicated and present with them again in a new form, was all they needed to move forward in his name. "Some doubted" their experience of the risen Jesus, but sufficient numbers trusted their experience for the new movement to take hold. The risen Jesus would appear "suddenly," and vanish just a quickly. He could enter a "locked" room, show himself to his disciples, and disappear again.

Spiritual Rather than Physical

It is difficult to know what to call the new form of being in the risen Jesus. "Spiritual" seems not quite appropriate. Yet that is precisely the term Paul used to identify both the resurrected body of Jesus, as well as the future resurrected state of those related to Jesus by faith. 1 Corinthians 15 again: "What is sown is perishable, what is raised is imperishable. It is sown in dishonor, it is raised in glory. It is sown in weakness, it is raised in power. It is sown a *physical body*, it is raised a *spiritual body*. If there is a physical body, there is also a spiritual body." For Paul, "body" signifies a recognizable person, the self, or being. From the gospel texts cited above, it is clear that the "body" of the risen Jesus was not physical, as it was before his death. The physical is mortal, subject to death and decay. The spiritual is not.

What the disciples experienced was Jesus in a new form, appearing and disappearing as only a spiritual body could do. To suggest that the risen Jesus came back to *physical* life, as he had been before the crucifixion, is to propose that his resurrected body would be subject to the same realities as before, including death by crucifixion. Nothing in the sources gives any ground for that conclusion. The risen Jesus appeared vindicated; he was alive again in a new and powerful way, and worthy of honor.

Some make much of "the empty tomb" with respect to the risen Jesus. A theology of the "empty tomb" is empty theology. Mark—and the other gospel writers who follow him—puts forward an account of the empty tomb to underwrite the reality of the risen Jesus, present to those who had believed in him. The focus finally falls, and remains, on *the person and presence of the risen Jesus* for ongoing life and work in the world, not on an empty tomb.

Reality Beyond Hallucination

It was not that the disciples were seeing things. True, their heart-wrenching experience of dashed hopes and dreams after the crucifixion of Jesus may have set their minds in a dither. But the fact of the upturn in their confidence and courage to carry on the ministry of Jesus against overwhelming odds requires more than hallucination. Something real happened to the remnant of believers after Jesus' death. A dynamic presence filled their hearts and minds, which can only be described as the spirit and power of the Jesus they once knew and loved.

It was their new experience of the risen Jesus that led to their heightened understanding of who he was for them. As Paul attests in Romans 1:4 (probably drawing on an earlier tradition), the risen Jesus "was declared to be Son of God with power according to the spirit of holiness by resurrection from the dead, Jesus Christ our Lord." Notice the presence of titles in this declaration: "Son of God," "Christ," "Lord." These

Part II: Jesus

are now boundless titles, universally used in the post-Easter proclamation of the good news emerging from the crucified Jesus, now vindicated before a watching world.

Empowering but Not Intimidating

The risen Jesus in the experience of his followers was not completely other than Jesus of Nazareth. His character and message remained unchanged. Jesus thus revealed alive from the dead energized the remnant of disciples: he had returned to them in a new form. The pierced hands, head, and side of Jesus they could not forget. Paradoxically these signs of shame became badges of honor that the apostles wore as they forged ahead in the hostile Roman world with the good news of God's salvation. The risen Jesus was still the historical Jesus insofar as he had returned to them in spirit and power. Just as Jesus had announced and enacted the kingdom of God, so his apostles will carry forward the same vision.

The risen Jesus empowered the believing remnant lovingly, not now as a triumphalist Jesus, intimidating his enemies and running roughshod over the weak. His power was still the nonviolent, healing, freeing power of God at work in the world as it had been in Jesus of Nazareth. As the centuries rolled on, however, the church transformed the risen Jesus into a triumphalist figure, enshrined in cathedrals and invoked in military battles as conquering hero over enemies, as in the Christian Crusades of the Middle Ages (*ca.* 1096–1272 CE).

It remains now to explore the missionary career of an outstanding apostle of the risen Jesus who received a call from God to bring the vision of Jesus to life in a non-Jewish environment. I refer, of course, to Paul the Apostle, whose proclamation to the nations was sharpened to a point: "Jesus Christ, and him crucified" (1 Cor. 2:2).

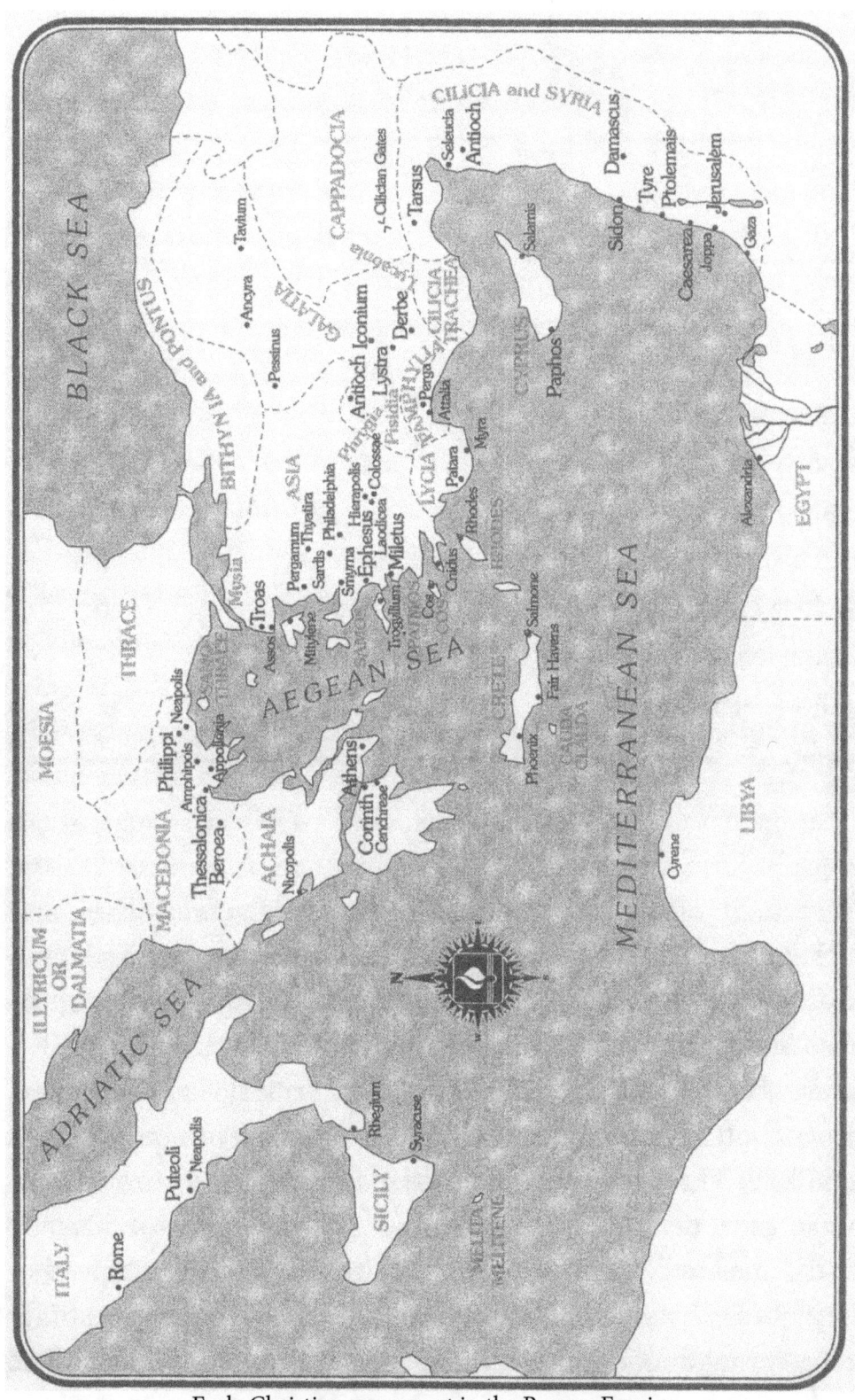

Early Christian movement in the Roman Empire

Part III
Paul

"Crucified with Christ"
(Gal. 2:19)

11

Interface

Between Jesus and Paul

PAUL, MESSIANIC THEOLOGIAN, ESCHATOLOGICAL PREACHER AND COMMUNity builder, energetic letter writer, and persecuted apostle entered center stage of the Jesus-movement *in the middle of the first century*. Unlike the original disciples, he had not known Jesus in the flesh. Rather, he encountered the risen Jesus in the interval between 30 and 50 CE through a revelation, and thereby accepted a divine call to bring the gospel of Jesus Messiah to the non-Jewish world (Gal. 1:16). That twenty-year interval between Jesus and Paul—if it should be called an interval—was one of ferment and fervor among the groups of believers in Jesus. They were living in anticipation of the kingdom of God as announced by Jesus prior to his crucifixion, and were themselves proclaiming the same message in the name of Jesus Messiah.

Yet events and developments of that critical twenty-year period suffer from a shortage of *primary* evidence from that time. If the people involved wrote anything of their experience, their documents have not survived. We are left, instead, with the remnants of tradition—stories and beliefs passed down orally—together with possible literary pieces embedded in later writings. Fortunately, a number of modern scholars have carried out critical analyses of the available material, thus opening windows onto the various configurations of the Jesus-movement in those formative years following the death and resurrection of Jesus.

Outstanding among those scholars is the person of Martin Hengel, who spent about twenty years (*ca.* 1970–1990) investigating as many sources as he could find, from the obvious ones in the New Testament to the tiniest inscriptions on cave walls and archaeological artifacts, and everything in between. His book, to which the subtitle of this chapter is indebted, is testimony to the brilliant erudition that professor Hengel brought to his extended project: *Between Jesus and Paul*.[1]

---

1. See also Hengel, *The Pre-Christian Paul*.

Part III: Paul

WORKING WITH THE SOURCES OF INFORMATION

The two principal sources from which to draw conclusions about the development of the earliest messianic movement in the name of Jesus are the genuine letters of Paul and the Acts of the Apostles, both in the New Testament. Both were written after the fact, but the first, the letters of Paul, out of personal memory of some of the developments. Paul's letters were written between 50 and 58 CE; the Acts of the Apostles (hereafter Acts) about forty years later by someone not personally acquainted with the events. Each of the two sources reflects its author's current concerns while recounting the earlier period. A brief comment about the two sources of information might be in order before using them to reconstruct an image, or images, of the emerging communities of faith in Jesus Messiah.

The Letters of Paul

It is generally acknowledged among biblical scholars today that the thirteen letters under Paul's name in the New Testament fall into three categories: seven definitely written by the historical Paul during his mission in the fifties CE (1 Thessalonians, 1 and 2 Corinthians, Galatians, Philippians, Philemon, Romans); three disputed, possibly composed by Paul's devotees between 70 and 90 CE (2 Thessalonians, Colossians, Ephesians); and three written to update (or correct) Paul's counsel to fit the situation of the Christ-communities at the beginning of the second century CE (1 and 2 Timothy and Titus, called "pastorals"). Borg and Crossan have characterized these three "Pauls" as follows: "We call the Paul of the seven genuine letters the *radical Paul*. We call the Paul of the three pastoral letters the *reactionary Paul,* for the author of these letters is not simply developing Paul's message, but countering it at important points . . . In comparison to the radical Paul, we name the Paul of the disputed letters as the *conservative Paul*."[2]

For the present purpose the undisputed letters, written in the fifties by Paul himself, constitute a vital source for understanding the forward movement of the communities of believers in Jesus following his death and resurrection. Vital as the seven letters are, they were not written as memoirs, much less critical historiography. Paul was writing to non-Jewish communities struggling to redefine themselves in relation to their new understanding of Jesus, Messiah of Israel. Moreover, his letters are charged with rhetoric aimed at persuading his readers to follow a particular course of thought and life. Within the rhetoric, however, Paul incorporated memorabilia from his Jewish background, from his rocky encounter with a growing community of Jewish believers in Jesus Messiah, and from experiences following his personal encounter with the risen Jesus. Let me repeat, Paul incorporated into his letters only selected snapshots from the critical period (30–50 CE), and that illustratively and rhetorically, not as a running commentary on each and every phase or each and every group of believers. Still, his snapshots serve to counterbalance (or correct) the narrative commentary in Acts.

2. Borg and Crossan, *First Paul*, 14–15.

Interface

The Acts of the Apostles

Because of its dramatic narrative quality, Acts is a favorite book of the New Testament for many people interested in the origins of Christianity. For those of us engaged in reconstructing a picture of the forward movement of the new community of Jewish adherents to Jesus Messiah after his death by crucifixion, however, Acts requires a careful, critical reading in keeping with the relevant material in the letters of Paul from the fifties. As stated above, the author of Acts had an agenda for his own time and his own community in a later situation in life. The narrative about the early period is meant to speak poignantly to the later communities in a place far removed from the earlier fledgling Jewish messianic communities.

Having advanced that qualifier for Acts, it needs to be said unequivocally that the book of Acts contains within its rhetorical structure traditions and sources about the twenty year period between Jesus and Paul that date back to a time before the composition of Acts, and also before the letters of Paul. But Acts is not a tightly woven tapestry, detailing consistently the chronology and circumstances and thought patterns. For example, the idyllic communal life of the early Jerusalem communities described in Acts 4:32–34, where "everything they owned was held in common" and "there was not a needy person among them," suddenly gives way to complaints from one group in 6:1, "because their widows were being neglected in the daily distribution of food." Nothing is said of any time span separating the two circumstances, except that it was "during those days"—not a very helpful phrase for determining chronology. Nor is there any explanation given for the breakdown in the system of community of goods.

Nevertheless, the author of Acts has drawn on valuable sources of information for the creation of his dramatic narrative, without revealing the identity of the sources (or traditions). Ignoring Acts is not an option. A completely skeptical reading hardly works either. Only a careful, critical reading of the relevant texts will do, and sometimes also an informed reading between the lines. This latter is often called conjecture, inescapable at points, but subject always to revision in light of new evidence.

CENTERED IN JERUSALEM

The disciples of Jesus, for whatever reason, escaped judgment and death following the crucifixion of their leader. Neither the Jewish high priest nor the Roman prefect brought any charge against them. According to Luke and Acts, both works composed by the same author, the apostles remained in Jerusalem after the crucifixion, just as Jesus had instructed them (Acts 1:4). The risen Jesus appeared to the apostles in the environs of the city, and ascended to a seat of heavenly power from that location as well.

Mark and Matthew, by contrast, give no such account. In those gospels the risen Jesus instructed the Eleven to go north to Galilee to a designated mountain. The disciples did so, and Jesus appeared to them at the appointed place (Mark 16:7; Matt. 28:7, 16–17). Neither Mark nor Matthew makes any provision for the disciples to return

Part III: Paul

to Jerusalem and remain there. But there can be no doubt that the apostles lived in Jerusalem, not Galilee, after the death of Jesus.

Paul was well aware of the presence of the apostles in Jerusalem from an early time, especially the three "pillars," Peter, James (Jesus' brother), and John (Gal. 2:6–10). Paul also spoke of a visit he had with the apostle Peter in Jerusalem three years after his sojourn in Arabia, about 35/36 CE (Gal. 1:18—2:1). Paul's account in Galatians 1 and 2 assumes that Peter and the other original apostles had taken up residence in the city of Jerusalem after the crucifixion of Jesus in that city. On this point Paul and Acts agree, against Mark and Matthew. But why settle in Jerusalem, the seat of political and religious power that brought Jesus to trial and execution? The answer almost certainly may be found on three fronts: Jewish religious conviction about the sacred site, eschatological preaching and action of Jesus with respect to the city and Temple, and the death of Jesus in the city as "a ransom for the many" (Mark 10:45).

Jerusalem was the city of David, messianic king of Israel. As compared to other cities in the land, Jerusalem was holy. On its sacred Mount Zion stood the Temple of the living God, the place where sacrifices were offered and sins forgiven. Thousands of pilgrims travelled for miles to attend the high festivals centered in the Holy City. Jesus and his disciples were such pilgrims. On his last Passover in the city Jesus uttered eschatological words against the existing Temple system, overturned its tables, and predicted its demise in preparation for a new temple (Mark 13:1–2; 14:58; cf. John 2:16–22). The original disciples apparently felt the urge to make the Holy City of Jerusalem their center as they waited for the coming breakthrough of the rule of God for the restoration of Israel and the redemption of the world.

The Spirit-empowered word of the apostles spread to the synagogues throughout Jerusalem. More and more members of the synagogues accepted their word about Jesus, and in turn spread the word to others. Jerusalem was a magnet for Jewish people from all over the Mediterranean world (Acts 2:5). Many who had lived in other parts of the world came to Jerusalem out of reverence for the Holy City and its Temple, some of them hoping to be buried in the sacred earth where the remains of holy ancestors likewise lay. These Jewish expatriates from the Diaspora brought their language and culture with them to Jerusalem, and doubtless worshipped together in their own synagogues using the language most familiar to them. The first seven chapters of Acts bear witness to this character of the city of Jerusalem at the time.

Two Groups of Jewish Believers Identified in Acts 6 and 7

In both the letters of Paul and Acts two labels are used to designate the two classes of humanity in the Greco-Roman world of the first century: Judeans (*Ioudaioi*) and Greeks (*Hellēnai*), or the singular inclusive form of the words in each case (Rom. 1:16; 2:9; 3:9; 10:12; 1 Cor. 1:24; Gal. 3:28; Acts 14:1; 18:4; 19:10, 17; 20:21). Paul at one point defines a non-Jewish enclave as "barbarians" in distinction from Greeks (Rom. 1:14). Neither of the two broad labels implies specifically geographic identity, Judea and Greece. One might think of "Judeans" as people living specifically in the Holy

Interface

Land of Judea. But that is not the case. Many Judeans lived in communities outside the land of Judea in what is generally called the Diaspora. Paul would have considered himself such a Judean of the Diaspora. These people honored the Holy Land of Judea, its Law and its Temple. But they lived and worked in countries such as Egypt, Syria, Cilicia, Asia Minor, Greece and Italy. Even those who lived in the country of Greece considered themselves Judeans (*Ioudaioi*) at heart, not Greeks. Their orientation, which included their religious belief and practice, esteemed the rich heritage associated with the land of Judea, its Scriptures, symbols, rituals, and festivals.

But Judeans of the Diaspora lived in a Greek-speaking environment and culture, and were by force of circumstance completely at home in the Greek language. In their synagogues they would have used the Greek translation of the Hebrew Scriptures for worship and instruction. Those of the Diaspora who sought a Jewish education would find it offered in Greek, not Hebrew or Aramaic, the traditional languages of Judea. The Greek translation of Scripture first appeared in Alexandria in Egypt in the third century BCE, but soon took hold throughout the Greek-speaking Diaspora. Nevertheless, in their religious hearts the Judeans of the Diaspora supported the leaders in the land of Judea, especially the priests who performed services in the Temple on behalf of Jewish people everywhere.

With this broad description of the Jewish people in the Greco-Roman world in place, we come now to the two denominational labels, one might say, in Acts 6:1. The two terms are meant to identify two distinct groups of Jewish believers in Jesus who lived and worshipped the God of Israel in Jerusalem in the early days of the new movement. The author of Acts seems to have had in hand a source from which to name the two groups, but did not attach a meaning to the names to help his readers understand. The context within which the two terms of reference sit provides some clues about the composition of the groups and the clash that occurred between the participants. I will use the original Greek spelling of the group names in an effort to locate as nearly as possible the implications involved in their use in Acts 6:1.

Hebraioi

"Now during those days, when the disciples were increasing in number, the *Hellenistai* complained against the *Hebraioi* because their widows were being neglected in the daily distribution of food" (Acts 6:1). The NRSV translates (or transliterates) the two terms as "Hellenists" and "Hebrews." The problem with this rendering of the group names is that it effectively identifies native Judean believers by the more archaic name "Hebrews," leaving "Hellenists" ambiguous: they could be Greek-speaking Judeans, or simply anybody who spoke Greek.

The issue is particularly one of language, not ethnic or religious identity. And lest we think of language of little consequence for group definition and pattern of religious thought, we should take the word of Hengel to heart regarding "the fundamental significance of language for theology."[3] The group of believers in Jesus called *Hebraioi* in Acts 6:1 spoke Aramaic among themselves, and used the Hebrew Scriptures in their

3. Hengel, *Between*, 26.

Part III: Paul

synagogues in Jerusalem. The word has a similar linguistic meaning in Acts 21:40; 22:2, and in John 19:13, 17, 20.

Of course, the term has ethnic connections as well. Paul, a Jewish resident in the Diaspora, cites as one of his Jewish credentials that he is "a Hebrew born of Hebrews" (*Hebraioi*, Phil. 3:5; cf. 2 Cor. 11:22). The sense is not that his home language was Hebrew (or Aramaic), but that he could claim unmixed descent from one of the ancient clans delivered out of Egypt. He may have known some Aramaic, but his letters demonstrate his complete familiarity with the Greek language, including also his intimate and comprehensive knowledge of the Greek translation of the Hebrew Bible used in the synagogues of the Diaspora.

In the context of Acts 6:1, however, language, more than ethnicity, was at issue. The *Hebraioi* had lived in the Land of Promise for all, or most of their lives. They spoke and worshipped freely and easily in the language of their Jewish ancestors. Their synagogues operated according to the idiomatic thought patterns expressed in the Aramaic/Hebrew words and phrases. Their language, in short, was the basis of their religion and culture. They probably knew enough Greek to get by in society, but their native tongue at home and synagogue shaped their theology and way of life.

The original disciples of Jesus belonged to this group of *Hebraioi* in Jerusalem. They, like their Master, grew up in the Land where the native Jewish Aramaic language marked them off from their Greek-speaking non-Jewish neighbors. In Acts 6:1-6 the Twelve, probably led by Peter, spoke on behalf of the *Hebraioi* in response to the complaint that the widows of the other group were being neglected in the distribution of food. A note of superiority comes through implicitly from the Twelve representing the synagogues of the *Hebraioi*. "It is not right that *we* should neglect the word of God in order to wait on tables" (6:2). One could infer that the tables in question were those in the meeting places of the Greek-speaking synagogues. Implicitly, the widows of the *Hebraioi* were not neglected. The Twelve representing the *Hebraioi* gave instruction to the group of complainants: "Select from among yourselves seven men of good standing, full of the Spirit and of wisdom, whom we may appoint to this task, while *we*, for *our* part, will devote ourselves to prayer and to serving the word" (6:3-4). At this point in the narrative, the power of appointment rests with the representatives of the *Hebraioi*: the complaining group can select, but the Twelve approve and appoint.

Hellenistai

Who were these people in Jerusalem known by this label, *Hellenistai*? Some have suggested simply non-Jewish believers living in Jerusalem whose language from birth was Greek (*Hellēn*). That view has all but vanished. Instead, the *Hellenistai* in Acts 6:1 and 9:29 were Jewish people whose native language was Greek, not Aramaic. They had come to Jerusalem out of loyalty to the longstanding Jewish traditions related to the Land, the Law, and the Temple. They would have come to Jerusalem to live and worship there, perhaps hoping to be laid to rest in the land of their ancestors. Apparently some had already died, leaving behind widows who were being neglected. Some members of this group of Greek-speaking Jewish people from the Diaspora, now living in Jerusalem, had heard the message about Jesus and adapted it to their Hellenistic Jewish faith nurtured initially in the Diaspora. As Hengel has observed, "for the Greek-speaking Diaspora the use of [the term] *Hellenistai* would be meaningless, as here [in the Diaspora] the use of Greek as a mother tongue was taken for granted."[4] Not so in Jerusalem. The Greek-speaking Jewish loyalists would have stood out from the majority of Jerusalemites who spoke Aramaic. The *Hellenistai* would have understood little of the synagogue services conducted in Aramaic. Consequently, the *Hellenistai* would have created their own synagogues in Jerusalem, used their Greek translation of Scripture, and instructed the members using the Greek language.

Out of this Greek-speaking Jewish synagogue context in Jerusalem came believers in Jesus crucified and risen, whose vision of the coming rule of God would have captured their imagination. Of note also are the names of the seven men appointed to the task of distributing food to the widows: all seven had Greek names. In double quick time, judging from the compressed narrative in Acts 6:6–15, two of the appointed *Hellenistai* began proclaiming the word about Jesus. The most provocative was a man named Stephen; the other man, Philip, less so.

Stephen

The narrative about Stephen in Acts moves very quickly; his speech to his accusers, by contrast, is circuitous. Stephen functions in Acts as a model for all those outspoken Jewish followers of Jesus who suffer for their testimony. Paul, as a believer, is especially portrayed in Acts as the antitype of Stephen. He too had to answer his accusers, and suffered for his behavior that *appeared* to encourage Jewish people to abandon the Law and the traditions of Moses, and thus to become no better than uncircumcised people of the nations. Some from Asia Minor even accused him of defiling the Temple (Acts 21:21–28).

But the narrative episode about Stephen and the *Hellenistai* deserves to be examined for what it conveys about the history of this Greek-speaking group of Jewish believers in Jesus located in Jerusalem, represented in the figure of Stephen. The description of the key players bringing the accusation against him is mixed. The mixture could have come from the author's use of a source (or sources) to which he adds his own slant about the identity of the perpetrators. Stephen had attracted attention by performing "great wonders and signs among the people" (6:8). But that was not the offence that incited the people against him.

The accusers are said to have belonged to the synagogue of the Freedmen (*Libertinoi*). At least three conjectures have been made to understand the meaning of this label: (1) the Freedmen were non-Jewish Roman slaves who gained their freedom, embraced Judaism, and set up their synagogue in Jerusalem; (2) they were migrant Libertines from the Jewish community in Libertum in Africa; (3) they were Jewish people enslaved during Pompey's military crusade, brought to Rome, released some time later, and then moved from Rome to Jerusalem to live. The last scenario is a live possibility, although not supported by hard evidence. The account in Acts claims

---

4. Hengel, *Between*, 8.

Part III: Paul

that they originated in different parts of the empire: Cyrene, Alexandria in Egypt, Cilicia, and Asia Minor. That they were Jewish is beyond dispute. Their argument with Stephen—who seems to have had some connection with their synagogue—attacked his open view of the Jewish heritage.

Elders and scribes became involved. Hengel believes the mention of scribes points to "a Pharisaic rather than a Sadduceean coloring, even if Luke gives no such expression to it."[5] Since no such expression is given, I suggest that both elders and scribes may simply refer to educated teachers from within the Greek-speaking, sectarian synagogue of the Freedmen. Elders were those considered wise and experienced enough to teach and correct false teaching. Scribes were expert in their ability to interpret the sacred texts and write their findings for future generations. It is doubtful if the official Sanhedrin of Jerusalem was involved in the uprising against Stephen. The trial seems to have been a local matter tied in with the Greek-speaking synagogue, not with the high court of Judaism. The synagogues had certain powers to pass judgment on their members, and inflict appropriate punishment. More on this point below. The high priest enters the dramatic proceedings only once in what appears to be an afterthought. The ones who question Stephen, and instigate others to offer testimony, are from the Hellenistic synagogue of the Freedmen, not the Sanhedrin. Then suddenly the high priest appears on the scene and asks a single, short question: "Are these things true?" (7:1). The high priest is not heard from again! His appearance in the narrative seems contrived.

Now come two crucial questions: (1) What was so offensive in Stephen's preaching to lead members of the synagogue to persecute him to death? (2) Why did the leaders of the *Hebraioi*, especially the original apostles, not come to his defense?

In answer to the first question we can enlist some help from the stated charges brought against him. Acts promptly serves notice that the accusations from the witnesses were false. The problem with that idea is that the words in the mouth of the witnesses are the sole evidence on record against Stephen, apart from his own speech in his defense (7:2–53). Ironically, the line of thought in Stephen's speech confirms the central elements in the testimony against him. The first group of witnesses lays out the charge in one broad brush-stroke: "We have heard him speak blasphemous words against Moses and God" (6:11). Words believed to be against Moses would be tantamount to words against God. Nothing is stated precisely about the nature of the blasphemy. When the second set of witnesses add their voice the offense begins to appear more boldly: "This man never stops saying things against this holy place and the law; for we have heard him say that Jesus of Nazareth will destroy this place and change the customs that Moses handed on to us" (6:13–14).

Three issues come into focus. Stephen is said to have spoken against the "holy place," which can only mean the Temple with all the symbolism it embodied. They said also that he spoke against the Law. Of course, if he spoke against the Temple then he also called the Law of Moses into question. The primary model of the Temple was

---

5. Hengel, *Between*, 19.

the Tent of Meeting that Moses set up in the wilderness. God met the people of Israel at the Tent of Meeting (Ex. 27–30). Rituals of purification and sacrifice for Temple service were prescribed by God through Moses and thus became sacred Law. To speak against the Temple was to speak against Moses, against the Law, and ultimately against God who gave the Law.

The third issue concerned Jesus of Nazareth. Stephen purportedly cited Jesus positively as the one to bring the Temple and its service to an end in preparation for something new. Jesus had recently been tried and found guilty of subversion by the Roman prefect, supported by the high priest. Loyalist *Hellenistai*, having returned to the Holy Land from various places in the Diaspora, did not take kindly to a fellow *Hellenistēs* undermining the very fabric of their Jewish conviction that brought them to the Holy Land, the Holy Temple, and the divine Law. Stephen represents a group of eschatological charismatics from within the Greek-speaking synagogues of Jerusalem, inspired by the word and work of Jesus concerning the in-breaking rule of God that would bring to an end the current Temple and its priestly functions.

The historical Stephen did not prepare his speech in advance. And it is also rather unlikely that a stenographer recorded the speech with quill and papyrus on the spot for the evening news in Jerusalem. This was a heated uprising against a radical member of the *Hellenistai*. Stephen's community of faith in Jesus remembered *the episode*—not the exact wording of the speech—and handed the story on to succeeding generations. The author of Acts wrote the speech on behalf of Stephen many years after the event. Even though the speech embodies elements of the vision and interests characteristic of Acts, the content and texture of this speech is distinct from all the other speeches in Acts. The author shaped it in a way that captured the spirit of Stephen and the *Hellenistai*.

Too long to discuss in detail, the speech accents elements that appear to fit the offence that Stephen caused. A selection of the highlights must suffice to illustrate the nature of the offence from the perspective of Acts.

(1) The glory of God appeared to Abraham in Mesopotamia, not in the land of Israel or the Temple of Jerusalem (7:2). A large settlement of expatriate Judeans lived in Mesopotamia at the time of Stephen. (2) The patriarchs of Israel sold Joseph into Egypt, where he distinguished himself in Pharaoh's house. Egypt, not Israel, sustained the patriarchs and their families during a famine (7:10–16). As with Mesopotamia, so with Egypt, a large Jewish settlement lived in Alexandria in the first century, and nurtured their community there without the language and ritual of Temple worship. (3) Moses was raised and educated in the house of the Pharaoh of Egypt, not in a Jewish household in Israel. He was forced to flee to Midian in Arabia to escape the anger of his Hebrew kinsfolk (7:23–30). The inference the hearers could draw was that Moses, reared in the court of the Egyptian Pharaoh, was God's choice to deliver the Hebrew people. (4) After spending forty years in the Sinai Peninsula, Moses received a revelation from God, who spoke out of a burning bush, not a Temple court. God told Moses to remove his sandals because that place in the wilderness, many miles from Israel, was "holy land" (7:30–33). At the time of Stephen the only land that loyal

Part III: Paul

Judeans would call "holy" was the land of Israel. (5) The ancestors had a portable tent of testimony that moved with them wherever they moved (7:44–45). God was present and powerful anywhere the covenant people lived, not exclusively in the fixed stone Temple of Jerusalem. This reflects the attitude of a member of the *Hellenistai* inspired by the prophetic word of Jesus who likewise passed judgment on the large stone Temple (Mark 13:1–2). Finally (6), Stephen launched a direct attack on his accusers, calling them "stiff-necked" opponents of the Holy Spirit, disobedient to the Law they claimed to uphold (7:51–53). I imagine Stephen's accusers were able to draw these inferences from such a speech, as I was able to do in this paragraph. Their belligerent reaction, as we shall see in a moment, affirms as much.

An answer to the second question will necessarily be short: it is an answer from silence. But the silence is deafening. Why would the leading apostles from the *Hebraioi*, the original disciples of Jesus, not come to Stephen's defense at some point in the narrative? They do not. The tentative conclusion I draw from their absence is that they did not see eye to eye with Stephen's open interpretation of the Scripture, which echoed much of the thinking of the community of Greek-speaking Jewish believers in Jesus. As we shall see shortly, a bitter persecution fell on the *Hellenistai*, not on the apostles from the *Hebraioi* (Act 8:1).

Philip

Philip, one of the chosen seven, came from the same synagogue of the *Hellenistai*, and preached a similarly open, inclusive message to that of Stephen. But Philip fled Jerusalem, and preached his inspired word in Samaria instead, where it found a ready response (Acts 8:4–8). He kept on the move, however, heading south along the Gaza road where he met a man from Ethiopia. He baptized the Ethiopian in the available water near the old territory of the Philistines, ancient Israel's dreaded enemies (8:26–40). Far away from Jerusalem, Philip operated on his own, beyond the authoritative oversight of the apostles of Jerusalem, which had followed him earlier in Samaria (8:14–25). Without checking with the original apostles, Philip interpreted the Scripture text of Isaiah for the Ethiopian with respect to "the good news about Jesus" (8:35).

PERSECUTION AND SCATTERING

It is not altogether clear what led one group within a Jewish synagogue to persecute another Jewish group, the Stephen episode in Acts notwithstanding. The author of Acts tends to implicate the Jerusalem hierarchy in all persecution of believers in Jesus, including the execution of Stephen by stoning. As indicated above, the high priest (ruler of the Sanhedrin) appears only once in the narrative, utters a few words, and then falls silent thereafter. It is more probable that Stephen "fell victim to lynch law.... Stoning remains possible as the manner of his death, as lynch law often made use of it."[6] But the law of the synagogue, by contrast, did not include the authority to pass the

---

6. Lüdemann, *Traditions*, 92.

death sentence on any of its members. Paul bears personal testimony to the synagogue law regarding punishment: "Five times I have received from the Jews the forty lashes minus one" (2 Cor. 11:24). Based on the injunction of Deuteronomy 25:3 forty lashes and no more could be applied to a wrongdoer. To avoid breaking that law—by going over the limit— the rule was one lash short of forty as "the maximum number allowed by synagogue courts."[7] The synagogue could apply fewer than thirty-nine depending on the severity of the infraction, but not more than thirty-nine.

Both Acts and the letters of Paul agree that a branch of the emerging Jewish community of Jesus-followers suffered persecution at the hands of other Jewish loyalists. That fact raises several questions: Who were the persecuted? Who were the persecutors? And what engendered the persecution? We shall consider these three in order.

If Stephen in Acts 6 and 7 is the paradigm of the persecuted members of the new movement, as the evidence suggests, then clearly the persecuted group came initially from the Greek-speaking synagogues in Jerusalem. Immediately after Stephen's death, to which Saul/Paul is said to have approved, "a severe persecution began against the [Christ-community (*ekklēsia*)] in Jerusalem, and all except the apostles were scattered throughout the countryside of Judea and Samaria" (Acts 8:1). Why not the apostles? They, of all the believers, were the principals behind the new movement after Jesus' death and resurrection. This exception phrase points beyond itself. The apostles, and presumably those of the same mind in the same believing community, seem to have escaped the early persecution and scattering. Recall the name of the synagogue(s) with which they were affiliated: the *Hebraioi*. The apostles were Aramaic-speaking, native Judeans. Their interpretation of the Law, the Temple and the vision of Jesus seem not to have carried the same radical train of thought and action as that of the Greek-speaking group. They were allowed to remain in Jerusalem without censure or punishment, at least not from their fellow Aramaic-speaking Jerusalemites. The target of the persecution, rather, was Christ-believers from the Greek-speaking synagogues.

Something about their message and way of living brought down the fury of their fellow Greek-speaking Jewish loyalists upon them. And one of the chief perpetrators was a man named Saul (Hebrew), better known as Paul (Greek). He too came from the Diaspora, spoke and wrote Greek fluently, as his letters attest. In his letters he admits to his persecution of the Jewish Christ-believers before his own encounter with the risen Jesus (ca. 30–33 CE). He considered his fellow Jewish believers in Jesus to be promoting dangerous doctrine and practice. Here is how he describes his punitive action against them: "I was persecuting the church of God [to the fullest] and was trying to destroy it" (Gal. 1:13); "I am the least of the apostles, unfit to be called an apostle, because I persecuted [the community (*ekklēsia*)] of God" (1 Cor. 15:9); "as to zeal, [I was] a persecutor of the [Christ-community]" (Phil. 3:6). The city center of Paul's persecuting activity was most likely Damascus, not Jerusalem. He seems to have made Damascus his home base (2 Cor. 11:32; Gal 1:17). The narrative in Acts is confusing on this point

---

7. Fredriksen, *Jesus to Christ*, 143.

Part III: Paul

(9:1–2). Paul did not need authorization from the high priest to punish recalcitrant members of the Diaspora synagogues. Synagogue law was sufficient.

But why the persecution of one Jewish group by other Jewish people such as Paul? How was Jewish belief and way of life threatened by this group advancing the message of the Jewish Jesus? These questions have puzzled New Testament scholars for some time. For the sake of space, I will merely list the prevailing answers.

1. In their mission the early Jewish believers of the Diaspora proclaimed a crucified Messiah. Based on the text of Deuteronomy 21:23 crucifixion could be viewed as a curse. A crucified messiah would thus be contrary to the law in Deuteronomy. Paul called the crucifixion of the Christ "a scandal to Jews" (1 Cor. 1:23; cf. Gal. 3:13). But the Romans had crucified many Jewish people, as they did Jesus, yet the crucified victims were not thereby considered cursed in the eyes their Jewish compatriots. The curse in Deuteronomy does not refer to the manner of execution, but to the public display of an executed criminal on a tree.

2. The new movement had relaxed some of the regulations of the Law, to the point of allowing non-Judeans to worship with them without becoming observant members. But synagogues allowed sympathetic outsiders to join in the synagogue service. Acts refers to them as "worshipers of God" (Acts 16:14; 18:7).

3. The Greek-speaking Jewish believers did not require circumcision for full membership in their community of faith in Jesus Messiah. But circumcision did not become an issue until some years later (*ca.* 40–50) when non-Judeans were being incorporated into community with full member status. Some of the observant Jewish believers in Judea went to Antioch to teach the new members: "Unless you are circumcised according to the custom of Moses, you cannot be saved." This was an issue within the believing community of Jesus at this later time when people from the nations were given equal status with believing Judeans.

4. Table fellowship may have been an issue. If non-Jewish believers were in fact part of the new Jewish missionary activity, their presence at the same table with Jewish believers could have been offensive. Yet, as Fredriksen proves, "Jews could and did eat with Gentiles. The discussions preserved in the Mishnah that detail the correct procedure on such occasions attest to the frequency with which they occurred."[8]

5. Fredriksen makes a broader point that the early Jewish community of Jesus extended the message of Jesus about the coming of the kingdom of God, and they did so in three ways: "(1) it saw itself as continuing his work to prepare Israel for the Kingdom; (2) it was motivated by the same excited conviction that the Kingdom was at hand; and (3) the message of Jesus . . . ('the Kingdom of is at hand') necessarily became the message of Jesus . . . ('the Son of Man [i.e., Jesus himself] is coming in power to establish the Kingdom')."[9]

---

8. Ibid., 151.
9. Ibid., 154.

Interface

Fredriksen's view is worth quoting at length, and will serve to conclude this section on the persecution and scattering of the early community of Greek-speaking Jewish followers of Jesus:

> The synagogue court had no jurisdiction over its Gentile sympathizers. But it could discipline those Jews who, seemingly oblivious to the politically sensitive nature of declaring a coming *christos*, endangered the well-being of the entire community. The form that discipline would take was makkot mardut—lashing. Were Paul an officer of the court, he would be responsible for the administration of its decisions, perhaps executing its orders [to the fullest] (Gal. 1:13), to the maximum thirty-nine lashes allowed by the law.[10]

A NEW CENTER: ANTIOCH ON THE ORONTES

The ancient city of Antioch, located on the east side of the Orontes River, became one of the influential Greek-speaking cities of the Greco-Roman period. Alexander the Great is said to have camped on the site during his crusade around the Mediterranean basin, and consecrated an altar there to the god Zeus Bottiaeus. But it remained for one of Alexander's generals, Seleucus I Nicator, to create a city on the site. The city grew during the Greek period, rivaled only by Alexandria in Egypt. When the Romans occupied Antioch its population was about half a million people. It was the third largest city of the Roman world, after Rome and Alexandria. Eventually the Romans put their imprint on the city. Julius Caesar visited it in 47 BCE and proclaimed the city's freedom. The city increasingly took on Roman symbols of power and religion, including a temple to Jupiter Capitolinus, a Roman forum, and a large theatre. Today the site of ancient Antioch falls inside the boundary of modern Turkey, near the city of Antakya.

Among its population in the mid-first century was a large community of Greek-speaking Jewish people. Both Acts and Paul's letters affirm that a significant contingency of the persecuted *Hellenistai* migrated to Antioch. Here is how Acts describes the situation: "Now those who were scattered because of the persecution that took place over Stephen traveled as far as Phoenicia, Cyprus, and Antioch, and they spoke the word to no one except Jews. But among them were some men of Cyprus and Cyrene who, on coming to Antioch, spoke [even] to the *Hellenistai*, proclaiming the Lord Jesus" (Acts 11;19–20). Recall, the *Hellenistai* of Acts 6 were Greek-speaking Jewish people who had moved to Jerusalem out of loyalty to the deep tradition associated with the Holy City. One of their number, Stephen, a follower of Jesus, was persecuted to death by his fellow *Hellenistai*. Hence the tone of hesitation on the part of the missionaries to speak to this particular group: they spoke even to them.

Paul recalls a personal experience that happened at Antioch during the growth of the messianic community of Jesus there (Gal. 2:11–14). Barnabas and Paul were the key leaders of the Jesus-communities in Antioch, Barnabas first and then Paul. These two did not found the new community, however. Jewish believers in Jesus had

---

10. Ibid., 155.

Part III: Paul

already gathered there before the two teachers came on the scene. The openness of the Antiochan group to non-Jewish outsiders (Acts 13:1—14:28) came to the attention of some conservative Jewish believers in Judea. Their specific identity is not given in Acts 15:1, only that they were sufficiently concerned about the carte blanche inclusion of non-Judeans without the stipulated mark of inclusion in the covenant between God and Israel (Gen. 17:9–14). Whether these individuals had the backing of the original apostles of Jesus is not stated. It is quite possible that they did. The upshot in any case, according to Acts 15, required Paul and Barnabas to appear before the apostles in Jerusalem to plead their case for the full inclusion of people from the nations without requiring the mark of circumcision.

Paul gives his own account of the meeting and its result, which, from his memory, was a rather casual meeting (Gal. 2:1–2). He met with the "acknowledged leaders" and some others that were brought in secretly, but "did not submit to them even for a moment." The outcome, from Paul's perspective, was a division of missionary labor: Paul "had been entrusted with the gospel for the uncircumcised, just as Peter had been entrusted with the gospel for the circumcised. . . . [The Jerusalem apostles] asked only one thing, that we remember the poor, which was actually what I was eager to do" (Gal. 2:1–10).

The account in Acts 15 reads more like a court trial. At the end of the trial the judge (James) handed down a verdict. There was nothing in it about remembering the poor, nothing about circumcision one way or the other, but something of a requirement regarding kosher regulation: non-Judeans in the new community of Jesus were "to abstain only from things polluted by idols and from fornication and from whatever has been strangled and from blood" (15:20). If Paul actually knew about such a kosher requirement coming out of the Jerusalem apostolate, he did not cite it or enforce it in the new communities of believers in Jesus, as First Corinthians 8 and 10 attest.

The interchange between the leaders in Jerusalem and the leaders in Antioch illustrates a shift of authority between two groups and two city centers. The figure of Jesus remained central to the preaching of both groups, but an understanding of the significance of Jesus for the life of the two groups of believers developed according to their place, composition, and experience. Jerusalem had had a long history of being the center of authority for the united kingdom of Israel, and later for the kingdom of Judah. Upon their return from Babylonia to Judea, the repatriated Jewish exiles reconstituted the city of Jerusalem as the sacred center for the religion of Judaism worldwide. The original apostles of Jerusalem, moreover, considered themselves the rightful custodians of the new messianic movement in the name of Jesus. Peter was their chief spokesperson. But Antioch became the safe city-haven for the persecuted ones, and became also the launching pad for the mission to the non-Jewish world, with Paul at the helm. Tension between the two centers and the two eschatological visions comes through in one of Paul's narrative recollections. He recalls a rather testy visit from Peter to Antioch. Whether the visit happened before Paul's meeting in Jerusalem or after is not clear. Here is how Paul writes about the rather heated exchange between him and Peter:

Interface

> But when Cephas [Aramaic for Peter] came to Antioch, I opposed him to his face, because he stood self-condemned; for until certain people came from James [leader of the Jerusalem community], he used to eat with the Gentiles. But after they came, he drew back and kept himself separate for fear of the circumcision faction. And the other Jews joined him in this hypocrisy, so that even Barnabas was led astray by their hypocrisy. But when I saw that they were not acting consistently with the truth of the gospel, I said to Cephas before them all, "If you, though a Jew, live like a Gentile and not like a Jew, how can you compel the Gentiles to live like Jews?" (Gal. 2:11–14).

One thing is reasonably certain from our two principal sources of information: the dynamic community of Jesus at Antioch originated not from the efforts of the Jerusalem apostles, but from the mission-minded *Hellenistai*. Their forced scattering became the catalyst for preaching the good news of the coming rule of God for the restoration of Israel and the inclusion of the nations of the world. Their radical dynamism attracted non-Jewish people. Their openness welcomed them fully into the community without insisting that they adopt the distinguishing marks of Judaism. Such a bold move grated on the traditional Jewish sensibilities of the apostolate in Jerusalem. Concessions were made, and confessions of faith formulated.

Early Messianic Faith Formulations

My purpose in drawing attention to the early confessional formulas, embedded especially in Paul's letters, is simply to flag the thoughtfully structured expressions of faith arising out of the memory of the death and resurrection of Jesus. The time and place and composers of these lapidary statements cannot be determined with certainty. Some may have come from the Jerusalem community, and others from Antioch or elsewhere. All of them are prior to Paul's letter-writing (ca. 50–58 CE), and in some instances may go back to the first few years after Easter. Meyer rightly affirms that the "lapidary form functioned as a preservative with the result that numerous expressions of primitive christological faith are still accessible to us."[11]

The forms can be detected within the literary texture of Paul's arguments. The most obvious are those where Paul introduces the form using technical terminology that points back to early Jesus-tradition: "I *handed on* (*paradidōmi*) . . . what I *received* (*paralambanō*)." This terminological feature occurs at two places in particular, First Corinthians 11:23 and 15:3.

1 Corinthians 11:23–25

> For I received from the Lord what I also handed on to you, that the Lord Jesus on the night when he was betrayed took a loaf of bread, and when he had given thanks, he broke it and said, "This is my body that is for you. Do this in remembrance of me." In the same way he took the cup also, after supper, saying, "This cup is the new covenant in my blood. Do this, as often as you drink it, in remembrance of me."

---

11. Meyer, *Aims*, 60–61.

Part III: Paul

Paul was not present at the Last Supper, and almost certainly not present either at the crucifixion of Jesus. He received this tradition, which he accepted as coming from the Lord. Received tradition makes the past events present for liturgical use in fostering faith. This form in First Corinthians 11 recalls the night, the betrayal, the bloody crucifixion, and the body of Jesus, and grounds the interpretation of these in Jesus himself. Repetition of the memorable Eucharistic form, accompanied by the communal eating the bread and drinking the wine, keeps the word and work of Jesus alive and intact within the community of faith.

1 Corinthians 15:3–5

Paul had received the form in these verses, handed it on to the Corinthians, and now incorporates it into the opening of his argument concerning the resurrection of the dead:

> that Christ died for our sins in accordance with the scriptures, and that he was buried, and that he was raised on the third day in accordance with the scriptures, and that he appeared to Cephas, then to the twelve.

Meyer describes this form as a "handsomely sculpted kerygmatic formula, probably first composed in Aramaic, dating at least from the forties of the first century."[12] There is no way of knowing for certain that the lines were first composed in Aramaic. If they were, then this faith statement would have originated in Jerusalem. Reference to Cephas and the Twelve hints at a Jerusalem origin, but not necessarily: the tradition about Cephas and the Twelve would have travelled with the *Hellenistai* outside Jerusalem. The only form available to us was written in Greek, and may just as readily have originated in the Greek-speaking messianic community at Antioch.

The four lines affirm the two principal components of early convictions about Jesus as the Messiah of God: his death "for our sins" and his resurrection as vindication of his righteous life. The reality of the death is affirmed by line 2, "that he was buried," and the reality of the resurrection is affirmed by line 4, "that he appeared. . ." Scripture—not merely proof-texts—undergirds the statement of faith. What happened to Jesus was in accord with the plan of God for Israel and the world: "in accordance with the scriptures."

Similar Forms in Romans

The two main messianic themes, the death of the Messiah and his resurrection/vindication, found boldly in 1 Corinthians 15:3–5, were formulated variously during the twenty years following Easter. Several of these variations appear in Romans, but without the technical introduction: received/handed on.

---

12. Ibid., 61, relying on Jeremias, *Eucharistic*, 101–3.

Interface

Romans 1:3–4

"The view has increasingly gained ground that we have in [Rom. 1:3b–4] a pre-Pauline liturgical fragment,"[13] so stated Käsemann in 1980. That view is now widely recognized by New Testament scholars.[14] Poetic parallelism is evident:

| the gospel concerning his Son, who was descended from David according to the flesh, | and was declared to be Son of God with power according to the spirit of holiness by resurrection from the dead |

Jesus Christ our Lord

Without going into detail about the likelihood of this confessional formula coming out of a setting that predates Paul's mission, suffice it to point out that Paul nowhere else in his letters identifies Jesus as "descended from David," nowhere else states that Jesus was "declared to be Son of God . . . by the resurrection from the dead," and nowhere else uses the term "the spirit of holiness." Its original setting may have been in Jerusalem, and its language Aramaic. The Greek-speaking Jewish believers could easily have translated it into their own language and liturgical life. In that locale Paul would have heard it used, remembered it, and used it to introduce himself and his message to the Jewish and non-Jewish believers in Rome.

The accent falls on the side of resurrection power. The death of the Messiah/Son is absent in this formula; only that he was a descendent of David "according to the flesh." In this confession believers in "Jesus Christ our Lord" can be assured of sharing in resurrection power that comes from the same "spirit of holiness" responsible for the eschatological breakthrough in the person of Jesus Messiah.

Romans 4:25 and 8:34

| who was handed over to death for our trespasses and was raised for our justification (4:25). | who died, yes, who was raised, who is at the right hand of God, who indeed intercedes for us (8:34) |

Both of these likely fragments from earlier confessions again proclaim the two-part gospel: the death of Jesus Messiah and his vindication by resurrection. Both parts together guarantee the salvation of those who belong to this eschatological figure, Jesus Messiah. His death "for our trespasses" renders the Temple service unnecessary, a major function of which was the removal of trespasses from the people of Israel.

Philippians 2:6–11, Hymn of Christ

> who being in the form of God did not clutch equality with God but emptied himself taking the form of a slave. Having become like human beings and being known as a human person he humbled himself becoming obedient to death.

---

13. Käsemann, *Romans*, 10.
14. See Jewett, *Romans*, 98–103.

Part III: Paul

> For this reason God raised him up to the highest and gave to him a name over every name that in the name of Jesus every knew should bend and every language confess that Jesus Christ is Lord.[15]

In the mid-1930's Ernst Lohmeyer made a convincing case for the non-Pauline origin of this hymn. Thirty years later R. P. Martin refined and expanded Lohmeyer's seminal work. Today Martin's *Carmen Christi*[16] (hymn of Christ) has become a standard reference work for all modern studies of this richly textured hymn within Paul's letter of encouragement to the community of Jesus Messiah at Philippi. It is "another precious testimony of early [messianic] faith."[17] Because of its distinctive literary, terminological and theological features within the Pauline corpus, the hymn can reasonably be taken as a composition that Paul encountered in his early days inside the primitive community, in places such as Antioch or Damascus. He may have heard it chanted antiphonally in one of the services, perhaps even at his own baptism.

The hymn celebrates the same two-fold christological confession present in the more compressed faith formulations examined above. The content of the hymn is the product of contemplative thinking about Jesus Messiah; it opens in eternity in the form of divinity, giving cosmic scope to the Messiah in relation to God. The two antiphonal parts are easily identified: the descent of the pre-temporal Messiah to temporal humanity, slavery and death (vv. 6–8), resulting in God raising the self-emptied Messiah to the highest status in the universe (vv. 9–11). Echoes of the Servant of Second Isaiah are audible here, especially Isaiah 53. One can imagine a whole company of believers, including Paul, in a meeting singing the last line of confession in unison: *Jesus Christ is Lord!*

CONCLUSION

Some years ago I was invited to enter into public dialogue with a Muslim scholar on the question, "Was Paul the founder of Christianity"? Implicit in the question is the notion that Jesus and Paul occupied two quite different worlds of thought and belief; that Jesus would not have sanctioned Paul's Christology; that Paul created a religion (Christianity) that Jesus did not envision.

My contribution to the debate consisted essentially of the content of the foregoing discussion of this chapter. The historical Paul did not come to his messianic faith-convictions in isolation. A religious-theological interface existed between Jesus and Paul, embodied in a community of trust in Jesus crucified and vindicated by God. The interface was well under construction prior to Paul's revelation of the risen Jesus. Shortly after Easter, Paul, by his own admission, persecuted the vibrant group of Greek-speaking Jewish enthusiasts who were carrying forward the vision of Jesus about the rule of God for Israel and the world. Their eschatological message about imminent judgment and salvation threatened the established traditions of Judaism,

---

15. My translation.
16. Martin, *Carmen Christi*, vii.
17. Meyer, *Aims*, 64.

especially so if Roman authorities got wind of it. The scattered Jewish group, nevertheless, pressed forward beyond the borders of Jerusalem, carrying their messianic mission about Jesus crucified and risen to other cities. Antioch of Syria became a key center for the Greek-speaking group. After his revelation and call, Paul connected with the community at Antioch, and from there launched a mission to the nations of the world in the name of the Jewish Jesus Messiah.

The mission was eschatological, as was the mission of Jesus. The kingdom of God, announced and enacted by Jesus, was already under way with cosmic potential as contemplated in the hearts of post-Easter believers. They formed concise confessions of this faith for use within their communities, and passed them on to succeeding generations of believers. Paul received the forms, including at least one christological hymn, handed them on to his congregations, embedded them in his letters, and bequeathed them thus to the world of humankind. But Paul did not found a new religion known today as "Christianity."

12

Prophetic Call in Jewish Context

ONE OF THE MOST WIDESPREAD MYTHS AMONG CHRISTIANS TO THIS DAY has been that the Apostle Paul converted from his old religion of Judaism to a new non-Jewish faith in Jesus Christ. His conversion involved a radical new direction in life and thought, from a defective religion based on "Jewish legalism" to a new divinely approved religion based on faith in Christ apart from works of the Jewish Law. This supposed conversion of Paul then became the model for all kinds of "sinners" to turn to Jesus, leaving behind their shady lifestyle.

By "myth" I mean *an unexamined belief* adopted by a religious group, then repeated categorically from generation to generation without further investigation or qualification. If someone from within the group should explode the myth, they are viewed with suspicion (if not contempt) by other members. Such a belief about Paul's "conversion experience," however, casts a dark shadow over the religion of Judaism—ancient and modern—and over the Jewish people who practice it. As a result, anti-Jewish sentiment has run the gamut, as history attests all too graphically.

Recently a number of reputable Jewish scholars have been re-reading the sources related to the towering figure of the *historical* Paul (vis-à-vis Paul of Church tradition). The fruit of their work has become for me—as for others in the field—a breath of fresh air. I refer especially to the works of Daniel Boyarin, Pamela Eisenbaum, Paula Fredriksen, and Mark Nanos, whose publications are listed in the bibliography. Traces of their interpretive work on Paul inform my own in this and subsequent chapters. It must be said as well that a number of non-Jewish scholars have also re-examined variously the traditional interpretation of "Paul the convert from Judaism to Christianity," among them William Campbell, Terrence Donaldson, Neill Elliott, John Gager, Lloyd Gaston, Krister Stendahl, and Stanley Stowers. Representative works of these scholars likewise appear in the bibliography.

DAMASCUS REVELATION

Something momentous must have happened to the Jewish persecutor of the Jewish Jesus-followers. His punitive discipline directed at them suddenly came to a halt. Many have inferred from Paul's radical change of heart that he thereafter abandoned his loyalty to Judaism to follow a new path in the name of Jesus Messiah apart from Judaism. But does Paul state clearly in his letters that his mind-changing experience in favor of Jesus crucified and raised pushed him away from his Jewish heritage, away from observing the Law, and into the development of a new movement apart from the Israelite history of salvation as expressed in Second Temple Judaism?

In response to such a question as this, Nanos is unequivocal: "The Paul I meet in these texts [of his letters] remained a Jew who practiced Judaism, and the communities he formed were Jewish subgroups, Judaisms—not the Jewish-free and Torah-free communities usually attributed to him."[1] To say the least, this is nothing short of a radical overturning of the traditional interpretation of Paul as apostate from Judaism, the proponent of a Law-free gospel, and creator of new groups of "Christians," called "churches," made up mostly of non-Jewish members. Nanos's re-reading of the Pauline texts goes well beyond "The New Perspective on Paul"[2]: he has laid bare a feature of Paul's thought, behavior, and mission that unravels the tapestry of traditional Christian interpretation of Paul, pre- and post-Reformation. And I find his exegesis and arguments persuasive, to the point of having had to go through something of a conversion experience myself!

There are, again, two sources from which to glean information about the transformation that took place in Paul's mind and behavior: his own letters and Acts.

The Acts account is the more popular one, not surprisingly. It is a highly charged dramatic telling of the story, related on three occasions throughout the book, with some inconsistency from one place to the other (9:3–19; 22:6–16; 26:12–18). The main features of the story in Acts remain constant from one context to the next:

1. while Paul was entering Damascus on a mission to discipline Jewish followers of Jesus for their disturbing way of speaking and acting,

2. a light shone around him so that he fell to the ground;

3. he heard a voice of someone asking why he was persecuting him;

4. the voice was that of Jesus, commissioning him to go to the nations to bring them to God.

A few observations about the three narratives in Acts should be made before turning to Paul's own account of his experience.

Ironically, this Jewish man zealously committed to upholding the Jewish way of life and thought is the very one found worthy of an encounter with the risen Jesus of Judaism. Paul was not a "Gentile sinner" (Gal. 2:15) in need of repentance and faith toward the God of Israel. His concern in imposing severe discipline on the radical

---

1. Nanos, "Torah-Observant?" 6.
2. Attributed to Stendahl, Sanders, Dunn, Hays, and Wright.

Part III: Paul

members of his Jewish religion was to maintain covenant loyalty and pure worship in the synagogues. Those of his Jewish people now preaching a resurrection as having *happened already* he considered in violation of Jewish teaching. Some Pharisees, perhaps even Paul himself, believed in resurrection, but only so in terms of the windup of the present age and the beginning of the age to come. "Resurrection language is end-time language and unintelligible apart from the apocalyptic thought world to which resurrection language belongs."[3] Paul had only the word of the Jesus-followers that a resurrection had *occurred already*. He was interested in maintaining the precarious peace of Israel in the volatile Roman world. Talk about the resurrection of a crucified Messiah could jeopardize the covenant life of the Jewish people, which they had managed to negotiate with their Roman overlords. For Paul's part, he had no first-hand insight about a resurrected Messiah, not until his extraordinary encounter in the environs of the city of Damascus in Syria. Jesus resurrected was *revealed* to Paul, not by persuasive argument made by the followers of Jesus, but by a bright light and a mysterious voice, according to Acts.

The Acts narratives also give the purpose of the epiphany: to go to the nations "so that they may turn from darkness to light and from the power of Satan to God" (Acts 26:18). Which God? There were many gods in the Greco-Roman world of Paul's day. It hardly needs to be stated: the God to whom the nations outside Israel should turn is the God of Israel. As a faithful member of the covenant of Israel, Paul would not have considered any other option possible. He knew the *Shema Israel*, and doubtless repeated it every day of his Jewish life: "Hear, O Israel: The LORD (Yahweh) is God, the LORD (Yahweh) alone" (Deut. 6: 4). Here is the question: Did Paul disown this Israelite confession of covenant faith after his Damascus epiphany? The answer is an unequivocal NO. However one might describe Paul's experience, it can hardly be called a conversion from one religion to another, from one God to another, or even from one Jewish sect to another. "Whatever it was, he never felt that he had left Judaism."[4] That there was a transformation in his Jewish thinking about his role in carrying forward a mission in the name of Jesus to the non-Jewish world is beyond dispute. But he did not leave behind his Israelite confession of the one God of Israel to fulfill his call.

I have dwelt on the narratives in Acts about Paul's Damascus experience mainly to show points of correspondence between the Pauline traditions reported in Acts and Paul's own reporting of his experience.

RECOLLECTION AND LANGUAGE IN GALATIANS 1:13–17

Credit goes to Krister Stendahl for drawing attention to Paul's language of "call rather than conversion."[5] The nuance is worth pondering. Having had family connection with a Wesleyan Methodist tradition, I have some personal memory of the meaning of "conversion" in that context. It could mean simply coming to a personal faith in

---

3. Beker, *Paul*, 152.
4. Segal, *Paul*, 284.
5. Stendahl, *Paul*, 7–23.

Jesus Christ, even if the person was reared in a Methodist Christian home and church. Or conversion could involve turning from a life of wrongdoing and faithlessness to an upright life of faith in Jesus Christ. Or it could mean leaving one religion, deemed inferior or untrue, to join the true faith embodied in a particular group of believers.

But that story is not on par with Paul's story. He did not convert from Judaism to Christianity, nor from a lawless life of crime to an exemplary moral life. The Christian religion was not yet conceived when Paul received his call, nor did Paul mastermind a plan to create Christianity as a world religion separate from, and consequently opposed to, Judaism. That development came years after Paul's mission to the nations and his corresponding letter writing.

Of course, Paul did go through a radical re-orientation *within* his Jewish faith tradition. His punitive discipline against Jewish radical believers in Jesus resurrected ceased when he became a Jewish radical believer himself. Should that be called "conversion" as commonly understood? I think not, although "there has been a renewed willingness recently to view Paul as a convert, and to construct, with aid from the social sciences, a more satisfactory model of conversion within which his experience can be described."[6] Yet because of the baggage commonly associated with the English word "conversion" I would urge alternative terms to describe Paul's new orientation within his Jewish faith tradition. If Paul uses *call language* to explain the new direction in his life, then I see no good reason to persist in using "conversion" language to understand his call to be a Jewish apostle of Jesus Messiah for the ingathering of the nations (*ethnē*) to join "the Israel of God" (Gal. 6:16). More on the subject of the ingathering of the nations in the next chapter.

Paul did not inscribe an elaborate narrative about his call in the manner of Acts. His written recollection in Galatians 1:13–17 about his call is rhetorically tailored to convince his non-Jewish believers in Jesus Christ at Galatia to maintain their present posture and practice as members of the new community of Jesus Messiah. Keeping the audience/readership in mind plays a vital part in the interpretation, as Eisenbaum has driven home forcefully: "Paul is speaking (*sic*) to Gentiles. One must always keep this in mind: Gentiles, Gentiles, Gentiles!"[7] The importance of so-doing, I submit, is twofold: (1) to observe Paul's shaping of his arguments to persuade *specifically non-Jewish* members of the community of Jesus Christ of their full membership in the Abrahamic covenant between God and Israel without becoming proselytes to Judaism, and (2) to recognize Paul's concern to have the non-Jewish members in the covenant remain faithful to the God of Abraham, who made their full membership effective through the death and resurrection of Christ. In short, reading targeted rhetoric requires diligence in sorting out underlying convictions from the literary elements used to make an argument achieve a particular goal.

Returning now to Paul's version of his call in Galatians 1:13–17: his few sentences on the subject provide insight into his self-definition *before and after his call*. This key

---

6. Donaldson, *Gentiles*, 302.
7. Eisenbaum, *Paul*, 244.

Part III: Paul

text warrants full quotation. (I offer my own translation aimed at a literal rendering in English).

> For you have heard about my way of life *at one time in Judaism*, that I persecuted the congregation of God to the extreme and was destroying it. I also pressed forward in the Jewish [religion] beyond many of my age among my own people, being even more enthusiastic for the traditions of my forebears. Then when God who *set me apart from my mother's womb*, and having *called me* through his grace, was pleased to *reveal his son in me*, so that I might proclaim him *among the nations*, I did not immediately seek advice for myself from flesh and blood, neither did I go up to Jerusalem to the apostles before me. But I went to Arabia and again returned to Damascus.

I have highlighted some phrases in the text that speak pointedly to Paul's change of heart and direction in life. Paul's way of life "at one time in Judaism" should *not* be taken to mean that he has now abandoned his Jewish heritage for a new religion. Commenting on this text, H. D. Betz suggests that Paul "converted from one Jewish movement, the Pharisees, to another, the Christians."[8] To his credit, Betz recognizes that the early believers in Jesus were a "Jewish movement." But his easy use of the anachronistic "Christians" is unfortunate. More to the point, this text makes no mention of Paul's affiliation with the Jewish group called Pharisees. Paul's earlier activity in Judaism was that of a virulent disciplinarian, bringing what he considered a radical Jewish element in line with conventional Jewish thought and life. The comparison between his "before" and "now" is *not* between Judaism and Christianity, but between (1) his former forceful resistance to the incorporation of non-Jewish believers in a resurrected Messiah into full membership in the Abrahamic covenant, and (2) his present practice of doing that very thing himself.

The prophetic nature of Paul's call to be an ambassador to the nations comes through in his reflective image: "God who set me apart from my mother's womb." From this kind of statement it is hard to determine exactly what happened to Paul historically to bring about the change: What earthly power influenced him? Still his statement about his experience affirms that the God of Israel initiated it, not at a whim, but when he was in the womb of his Jewish mother. His prenatal consecration echoes two pieces of prophetic tradition, Isaiah 49:1–6 and Jeremiah 1:5. The Jeremiah text is particularly germane to Paul's expression in Galatians 1:15: "Before I formed you in the womb I knew you, and before you were born I consecrated you; I appointed you a prophet to the nations." Moreover, like Jeremiah's prophetic call, Paul's call was entirely by God's grace, not by human choice, his or anyone else's.

God "called me by his grace," states Paul, and then determined when "to reveal his son in me." The description has a ring of ecstasy about it, not unlike that of 2 Corinthians 12:1–4, "whether in the body of out of the body I do not know; God knows." In Galatians 1:15, however, the accent falls on the content and purpose of the revelation. The Greek word translated "to reveal" is *apocaluptō*, from which come the English words "apocalyptic" and "apocalypse." This was more than a "mystical

---

8. Betz, *Galatians*, 69.

experience of Jesus Christ as Lord."[9] Prophetic tradition springs to mind at the sound of such words. Paul understood the revelation of the Son of God, together with the purpose of his call, as belonging to end-time experience and activity in line with the vision of Israel's prophets. Without any explanation Paul introduces the term "son of God" as though his non-Jewish audience will understand. And they will. The Greco-Roman pantheon was populated with gods and their sons. The terminology would have been familiar to them. But the Jewish Paul did not have in mind a son of Zeus or Jupiter, much less a son of Caesar Augustus. Israel's one-and-only God revealed the "son" to Paul.

In Paul's Jewish context, the idea of God having a Son is metaphor, for God is One (Deut. 6:4). Jewish philosopher, Philo of Alexandria, wrote about the *divine Logos* ("word," "reason," "generative power" of God) as the Son of God. For example, in discussing Zechariah 6:12, ("Behold the one whose name is the Rising" [*anatolē* = sunrise]), Philo describes the creative power of the uncreated God as God's first-born son. "For the Father of the universe has caused this one to *rise up* as the eldest son, . . . the first-born, . . . imitating the ways of his father."[10] But neither Philo nor Paul considered the metaphoric son to be a second god generated by seminal impregnation or otherwise. At the same time, Paul conceives of Christ Jesus being "in the form of God" (Phil. 2:6), not as flesh and blood, but as creative mind beyond time and space. Paul's experience of the revelation of the Son of God was not a sensory, external, physical experience. The phrasing in Galatians 1:15 rules out common human experience: "God was pleased to reveal his son *in me*" (*en emoi*), not "to me" as in the NRSV. There can be no doubt concerning the identity of the "son" whom God revealed: the risen Jesus Christ; so also in First Corinthians 15:8 (cf. 9:1).

The purpose of God's revelation of the "Son" was not to deliver Paul from a life of sin, but to grant him a life-long vocation: "to proclaim *him* among the nations." The pronoun "him" could refer to God, but more likely to the closer antecedent, "son." Either way, the intent of the call is the same. People of the nations will encounter the God of Israel through the proclamation of the son-revelation of God in Jesus Messiah crucified and raised.

POST-REVELATION IDENTITY

There are other indications in Paul's letters that he maintained his Jewish identity, while vigorously gathering non-Jewish people into communities in the name of Jesus Christ. During that endeavor Paul faced opposition from two fronts: from the Jewish synagogue, and from Jewish believers in Jesus who challenged his apostleship among his non-Jewish converts to Christ, especially at Corinth.

The first should be expected. Paul was creating congregations of believers in Jesus Messiah and calling them children of Abraham (Gal. 3:16, 29; Rom. 4) with full membership status (Gal. 6:16), but without becoming proselyte members of the synagogue.

---

9. Borg and Crossan, *First Paul*, 27.
10. Philo, *Confusion of Tongues*, 63.

Part III: Paul

He recalls receiving the thirty-nine lashes on five occasions for his belief and practice among the non-Jewish people (2 Cor. 11:24). As Acts suggests, he may have preached his gospel among non-Jewish worshipers at the synagogue, and then called them out from that setting to meet together with like-minded believers in Jesus. Hence the name *ekklēsia*, "a called-out group." We now have proof "from numerous sources that Gentiles frequented synagogues throughout the Greco-Roman world. In this case, we may presume that Paul preached to Gentiles in synagogues because he knew that they would already be somewhat attuned to the biblical language and content of his message as he conceived it."[11] This scenario would explain his repeated punishment from the synagogue authorities. For such a punishment to be carried out, Paul would have had to show up at the synagogue. By this account, then, Paul continued to identify himself as a member in the covenant of Israel as practiced in Second Temple Judaism. Otherwise he would not be subject to the discipline of the synagogue?

The more painful opposition came from within his own Christ-believing circle. It is difficult to identify the opponents on their terms. All we have is the highly charged rhetoric of the letters in which Paul characterizes the opponents. The rhetoric directed at opponents in Second Corinthians speaks tellingly to the question of Paul's Jewish identify *after* his revelation and call. Apparently some "ministers of Christ" (11:23) had entered the community at Corinth, waving their Jewish credentials before the congregations, claiming that their ministry was superior to Paul's (2 Cor. 11:5; 12:11). A full investigation into the character of Paul's opponents at Corinth is beyond the scope and purpose of this discussion. (I have dealt with the issue elsewhere[12]). My interest here is simply to locate Paul's self-identity encoded in his polemical defense of his call and mission in the name of Jesus Messiah.

In Second Corinthians 11:22–23 Paul puts forward a series of four rhetorical questions to the congregation, and gives four corresponding answers. He couches his boast in the voice of a fool, a rhetorical conceit to avoid "real" boasting.

> Are they Hebrews? So am I.
> Are they Israelites? So am I.
> Are they the seed of Abraham? So am I.
> Are they ministers of Christ? I am talking like a madman—I am a better one.

The questions imply the opponents' claim to hold these identity markers in a way that undermines Paul's stature at Corinth. Consider each of the labels in turn.

As I mentioned in the previous chapter, "Hebrews" in this context is an ethnic designation. The term could refer to one's ability to use the Hebrew (or Aramaic) language, as in the context of Acts 6:1. But that is not the case here. A "Hebrew" can boast of membership in the Jewish faith by *birth from full-blooded Jewish parents*, as compared to proselytes to Judaism. This ethnic use of the term "Hebrews" is confirmed by

---

11. Gager, *Reinventing*, 51.
12. Shillington, *2 Corinthians*, 269–74.

Prophetic Call in Jewish Context

excavations at Corinth that revealed "a lintel inscribed with the words . . . '*Synagogue of the Hebrews.*'"[13] Paul claims the same for himself in the present tense.

An "Israelite" is not exactly the same as a "Hebrew." An Israelite is a member of the covenant people of God. "Hebrew" is ethnic; Israelite is religious, social, and nationalistic. One could become an Israelite by repentance, and by accepting the Jewish religion: its laws and social norms, and its worship. One could not become a Hebrew except by birth. Paul claims to be an Israelite with every attendant connotation that the name carries.

To be a descendent of Abraham, literally Abraham's seed (*sperma*), was to be an heir to the covenant promise of God for blessing and salvation made to Abraham (Gen. 17:7-8). "It may thus be said to describe the [Jewish people] from a theological point of view." To be of Abraham's "seed," however, "connotes the people of God in a collective sense, as those who come into existence as a body on the basis of God's call and promise."[14] Paul carries this credential too. The point is that Paul lays claim to all of these Jewish characteristics in *his present experience* as an apostle of Christ.

Traditional interpretation mutes that judgment, with unwarranted anti-Jewish consequences. Fallon, for example, imagines that Paul's opponents at Corinth thought "the aeon and the dispensation of Abraham, Moses, and the Scriptures were still in force. For Paul the old aeon and old dispensation had passed: the promises had been fulfilled in Christ."[15] This is nothing short of a misreading of the text. Paul claims for himself precisely what his opponents tout about themselves: he continued to be thoroughly Jewish after his revelation and call. Why Fallon would bring Moses and the Scriptures into his assessment of Paul's position is puzzling. These terms are not in Paul's text. Paul did *not* think the Scriptures of the Jewish people had run their course: he quotes from those Scriptures extensively in his letters in support of his mission and his argumentation. The Jewish Scriptures were therefore current for Paul, not "old" and outmoded.

Paul's description of his change of heart in Philippians 3:5-9 is said to clinch the case for Paul's conversion from Judaism to the new Christ-faith. His loyalty to the covenant of God in Judaism was exemplary: "circumcised on the eighth day, a member of the people of Israel, of the tribe of Benjamin, a Hebrew born of Hebrews; as to the law, a Pharisee; as to zeal, a persecutor of the church; as to righteousness under the law, blameless" (3:5-6). There is hardly any need to explain each element in this description: together they paint a picture of an ardent member of Israel as practiced within Second Temple Judaism. Majority Christian opinion about this text is that Paul was looking back at his Jewish past from the superior vantage point of his relationship to Jesus Christ. That which he considered valuable in his past Jewish affiliation he now considers "nothing more than 'crap [*skubala*]'"[16] (3:8). For many scholars, especially those influenced by the Protestant Reformation, this can only mean he had given up

13. Murphy-O'Connor, *Corinth*, 78.
14. Barrett, *Second Epistle*, 294.
15. Fallon, *2 Corinthians*, 100.
16. Nanos, "Paul's Judaism?" 124.

Part III: Paul

on Judaism as a works-righteousness religion in favor of a faith-based relationship to Jesus Christ. And from that Reformation perspective Paul criticizes Judaism as inferior.

But this way of reading Paul's description of himself—from the history of Christian interpretation—minimizes the rhetorical force of his argument in writing to the Christ-community at Philippi. Keep in mind, his readers are non-Jewish people who have been included in the Abrahamic covenant without becoming proselytes to Judaism. Were it a strictly Jewish audience, one wonders how Paul would have described his experience of being "in Christ" to them. At the very least he would *not* have derided the Law, which he believed to be the gift of God through Moses to the people of Israel for their good (Rom. 7:7–12). Gaston has this to say about the two states that Paul describes in Philippians 3:5–9: "It seems that it is possible to have a status of righteousness from either of two sources, from the law (in the sense of covenant) or from the faithfulness of Christ. Paul once had the former (cf. v. 6) and has shifted to the latter . . . . but he does not deny at all the validity of life in Torah."[17]

Commendable as this reading is, I find the notion of Paul's "former" and "latter" status somewhat questionable. Did Paul remove the marks of circumcision after his call (cf. 1 Cor. 7:18)? Did he now deny that he was an Israelite from the respected tribe of Benjamin? Did he now reject his covenant birthright and his Hebrew parents through whom he had received it? Was he now violating the Law that he once observed blamelessly? Did his revelation and call to bring Messiah to the nations, and the nations to Messiah, make him unrighteous, or less righteous than before? I submit that the answer to all of these questions is an emphatic NO! The single item in the list that Paul no longer practices, the one he regrets, is his persecution of the Jewish believers in Christ. His revelation and call gave him *a new vision of the time*: the end of the ages had begun with the resurrection of Jesus. Non-Jewish people of the world were now offered an open door into a Christ-relationship with Israel through the faithfulness of Jesus Christ: they could become full members without becoming proselytes to Judaism. Paul did not give up his standing in Judaism, nor his participation in synagogue life, when he accepted his new role as ambassador of Christ among the nations. No longer will he treat non-Jewish people of faith in Jesus Christ, such as those at Philippi, as outside observers of the covenant people of Israel. They have become full and equal members with Law-observant Jewish people through the faithfulness of Jesus Christ. I will deal with the incorporation of the nations into covenant relationship with God in Jesus Christ in more detail in the next chapter.

Before bringing this chapter to a close, there remains one more observation to make about Paul's self-identity, written by him near the end of his mission in the north-Mediterranean territory (ca. 57/58 CE). I refer to Romans 9:1–5 and 11:1–2.

> 9:1–5: I am speaking the truth in Christ—I am not lying; my conscience confirms it by the Holy Spirit—I have great sorrow and unceasing anguish in my heart. For I could wish that I myself were accursed and cut off from Christ for

---

17. Gaston, *Torah*, 136.

> the sake of my own people, my kindred according to the flesh. They are Israelites, and to them belong the adoption, the glory, the covenants, the giving of the law, the worship [in the Temple], and the promises; to them belong the patriarchs, and from them, according to the flesh, comes the Messiah, who is over all, God blessed forever. Amen.
>
> 11:1–2: I ask, then, has God rejected his people? By no means! I myself am an Israelite, a descendant of Abraham, a member of the tribe of Benjamin. God has not rejected his people whom he foreknew.

A reminder again, Paul's target audience in Romans is non-Jewish believers in Jesus Messiah located in Rome. A number (probably a smaller number) of Jewish believers lived and worshipped among the non-Jewish group, or perhaps were meeting in another quarter of the city. The problem Paul addresses explicitly in Romans 9–11 is an arrogant attitude among the non-Jewish Christ-believers toward their Jewish counterparts. His corrective rhetoric leads him to adopt his Jewish persona through which he speaks personally and powerfully in a Jewish voice to the arrogance of his non-Jewish audience of Christ-believers.

Stowers imagines the impression this rhetorical measure would have made:

> "Yes, I, the apostle to the gentiles, am truly as a gentile in Christ and have shared their experience but you must understand that *the irreducible core of my identity* making my apostleship a reality *is that I am a Jew*, a member of God's people Israel."
>
> Paul impersonally joins gentile believers in the first person plural in chapters 5–8, but here [in 9–11] a bold and forceful ego appears. That ego remains at the core Jewish. His words leave no doubt about his ultimate commitment to the Jewish people and his confidence in their future.[18]

Suffice it to say, by way of conclusion, that Paul at no time abandoned his Jewish heritage and religious conviction as a member of Israel to join, or create, another religious movement in the name of a non-Jewish Jesus. He, like Jesus, was Jewish to the end. The time had changed: God's eschatological clock had struck with the resurrection of Jesus as the Messiah for all creation. The non-Jewish people of the world had become the beneficiaries of the grace of God through faithful Israel represented in the Jewish figure of Jesus of Nazareth crucified and raised. Paul's revelation and call were part of the eschatological plan of God for the world, a plan aimed at including both Jewish and non-Jewish people equally yet distinctively in covenant relationship with God.

---

18. Stowers, *Rereading*, 293, emphasis added.

13

Gathering the Nations into Jesus Messiah

WE NEED TO ASK NOW: WHAT WERE THE CONVICTIONS THAT ACCOMPANIED Paul's call to go to the non-Jewish nations with the gospel of Jesus Messiah? However we may answer that question —and there are multiple facets—one thing is certain: Paul labored under the compulsion of his call. "For an obligation is laid on me," he says, "and woe to me if I do not proclaim the gospel!" (1 Cor. 9:16). The ensuing discussion aims at unveiling how Paul executed the call together with the results.

URBAN UPBRINGING AND ORIENTATION

It helps to know something of a person's background before passing judgment on their thought and action. Paul says little about his birth, education, economic status, and cultural orientation. He may have told his newly formed congregations about himself, and therefore did not need to cover the same ground again in his personal letters to them. His letters were "conversations in context,"[1] as Roetzel detects wisely. The contexts of the conversations, however, are more implicit than explicit. So we are driven to enquire elsewhere about the formative years of Paul's life, which would surely have had a bearing on the shaping of his convictions under the "obligation" of his call. Acts is the best source available—apart from the genuine letters—for some helpful background information. Still, the author of Acts wrote many years after Paul's death, and relied on traditions that had circulated in various Christ-communities over the years.

Paul was born about twelve to fourteen years after Jesus (ca. 6–8 CE). Compared to Jesus from the village of Nazareth in Galilee, Paul was born and reared in the "important city" of Tarsus in the province of Cilicia (Acts 21:39; 22:3). Tarsus was the capital of Cilicia. When a group of us Canadians visited the modern Tarsus in 1995 we could easily imagine how Tarsus would become "important." We saw the fertile land surrounding the city, and the majestic Taurus Mountain range to the north. A

---

1. Roetzel, *Letters*, 3.

well-preserved piece of a Roman road sits inside the city, and an even larger section of a Roman highway lies fifteen kilometers away. Our group walked on that solid Roman road that connected east and west, between Syria and Greece, and imagined Paul walking with us on a mission. Tarsus was not very far north of the great Mediterranean Sea with which Paul was very well acquainted.

Tarsus was a city in which people could learn a trade and put it to good use. Paul became a tent-maker, according to Acts, and used this skill when necessary to support himself in fulfilling his call (18:1–4). Tents in Paul's time were made of cloth and goats hair sown together. They could be rolled up and taken on trips to places where other forms of overnight accommodation were not available. But Paul was also an educated man of his time: he could read and write and argue a case, as his letters illustrate. Tarsus was just the city for such an education in Greek and Roman thought and rhetoric. Philosophers delighted in setting themselves up in cities such as Tarsus for the publication of their thought, and the education of the citizens.

But Paul was also Jewish by birth, as noted earlier, and committed himself diligently to learning his Jewish heritage. Whether he went to Jerusalem, as Acts maintains, to learn Torah in the Hebrew language is open to question. If he did so, he also learned his Scripture from the Greek version of the Hebrew Bible. He quotes nothing else in his letters. Tarsus being a thoroughly Hellenized center, the synagogue-schools there would have used the Greek Bible for services and for the education of the young Jewish men. Paul had memorized sections of Scripture and recalled them strategically in support of pertinent points in his arguments in the letters. Memorization in the ancient world was not merely a pastime for fun. Scrolls were scarce. Important ones were kept in key locations, such as synagogues, for reference at any time. If a bundle of scrolls of Scripture were to become available to Paul, they would be awkward to carry from place to place. (The book—codex form—was a great invention!). The only sensible way to carry Scripture scrolls on a journey was to memorize as much as possible. Memorization was part of the education in the first century. Here is what geographer, Strabo (ca. 64 BCE–25 CE), has to say about the citizens of Tarsus:

> The people at Tarsus have devoted themselves so eagerly, not only to philosophy, but also to the whole round of education in general, that they have surpassed Athens, Alexandria, or any other place that can be named where there have been schools and lectures of philosophers. But it is so different from other cities that [in Tarsus] the men who are fond of learning, are all natives . . . ; neither do these natives stay there, but they complete their education abroad; and when they have completed it they are pleased to live abroad, and few go back home.[2]

I have often wondered why Paul did not set his sights on his own important Tarsus for the proclamation of Jesus Messiah. There may be a clue in Strabo's assessment of the educated citizens of Tarsus: *they travel abroad and few return home*. That could explain Paul's behavior, although Acts reports that some believers in Jerusalem sent him back to Tarsus (Acts 9:30). One thing is clear: Paul's upbringing in the city fitted

---

2. Strabo, *Geography* 14.5.13.

Part III: Paul

him well for his missionary forays into the cities of the north Mediterranean territory. His urban orientation is so blatantly evident in the stated destinations of his letters that it requires no further proof. He had to pass through small hamlets going from one city to the other, but neither the letters nor Acts makes any mention of a stop-over in the small villages for the proclamation of Jesus and the formation of groups of Christ-followers. While Jesus went from village to village, including his own little Nazareth, Paul brought the good news to city people of the larger world.

An urban center such as Corinth, or Ephesus, or Philippi, or Rome had what sociologists call a hierarchal social and political structure: a small ruling elite class at the top, a merchant elite class one step down, and a large working class making up the majority of the population. The lower classes supported the elite classes. Borg and Crossan provide a helpful list of the types of workers in an urban center: "drivers, drovers, porters, cleaners, custodians of public buildings, bathhouse attendants; construction workers, bricklayers, masons, carpenters; tanners, butchers, bakers, spinners, weavers; artisans in workshops working in cloth, leather, pottery, gold, silver, wood, and stone; small entrepreneurs and shopkeepers selling various goods; day laborers looking for work, and sometimes not finding any."[3] Paul seems to have targeted the working class, including slaves. These working class city folks were probably more inclined to pay attention to the good news about a new rule of life already under way in the world. As Paul affirms, "not many of you [Corinthians] were wise by human standards, not many were powerful, not many were of noble birth" (1 Cor. 1:26). Not many, but presumably there were some wise, powerful, and noble in the fellowship meetings (cf. 1 Cor. 11:20–22).

Even though a city environment was the place to acquire an education, not many working class people managed to do so. They were too busy working for a living. Education, especially the ability to read and write, was the bailiwick of the elite class. They also had secretaries and ambassadors who were granted the privilege of an education in the service of their patrons. Paul was privileged to acquire an education, and so also persons alongside him to serve as secretaries. Tertius, for example, was such a secretary to Paul for the composition of his weighty letter to the Roman congregations of Christ-believers (Rom. 16:22). Paul may have written part (or all?) of Galatians and Philemon in his own hand (Gal. 6:11; Phlm. 19).

Acts informs us, not once but seven times, that Paul was a citizen of the important city of Tarsus (21:39; 22:25–29; 23:27). This set of texts points to the significance of Roman citizenship: a free citizen of a well-endowed city meant privileged status; was not subject to whimsical punishment; citizenship by birth was indisputable; was subject to the protection of Rome. Remarkably, Paul not once mentions this privilege in any of his letters to congregations in the cities. As shown in the previous chapter, he did recite his status as an observant Judean in comparison to his highly valued new relationship to Jesus Messiah. Why he would not do the same for his Roman citizenship is hard to understand. Did he not count his citizenship as rubbish compared to knowing Jesus

---

3. Borg and Crossan, *First Paul*, 82.

Gathering the Nations into Jesus Messiah

Christ as Lord (Phil. 3:7–10)? Roman citizens valued their privileged status. Did Paul? It could be argued, rather, that he valued a higher citizenship: "our citizenship is in heaven," he writes, "and it is from *there* that we are expecting a Savior, the Lord Jesus Christ" (Phil. 3:20 emphasis added). Roman authorities would not take kindly to such a proposition. Roman government under the "divine" Caesar was the savior and Lord of the world. Augustus had prevailed in battle and brought the imperial "peace of Rome" to the world. Philippi was the scene of such battle. The city of Philippi became a colony of Rome. Paul's announcement of another savior and Lord of the world was courting an accusation of subversion, especially so if announced in the city of Philippi.

On the other hand, Paul may not have held Roman citizenship after all. The punishments he lists in 2 Corinthians 11 includes "imprisonments," "countless floggings," "three times beaten with rods," and once "a stoning" (2 Cor. 11:24–26). These all came from the hands of non-Jewish authorities, all under Roman sanction. If Paul was a Roman citizen by birth, it offered little protection to his person. The author of Acts, in making Paul the hero of his book, may have granted him the honor of literary citizenship posthumously. There is another explanation, however. Paul's public proclamation of another kingdom, another ruler and savior of the world would have been grounds for punishments and imprisonments from imperial Rome. Beyond proclamation, he called non-Jewish people away from their religions, including the state religion, to meet and worship in a new way (cf. 1 Thess. 2:14). This too would raise the ire of local authorities, resulting in the kind of punishments and imprisonments Paul lists, whether citizen or not. More on the formation of the new Christ-communities shortly.

To conclude these comments about Paul's urban upbringing and orientation, let me reiterate that Paul *adopted the great city of Damascus in Syria*, leaving behind his birth city of Tarsus. He freely mentions Damascus in his letters, but not once his famous home city of Tarsus in Cilicia that gave him a rich urban environment and an enviable education. Permit me a personal example related to the puzzling silence of Paul about Tarsus. I grew up on the outskirts of the city of Armagh in Northern Ireland. St. Patrick worked out of that city center. Today Armagh is called "the ecclesiastical capital of Ireland," boasting two great cathedrals. As you enter the city from its various sides you will see a sign which reads: "ARMAGH: City of Saints and Scholars." As you can see, I am not the least reluctant in letting the world know that I was reared and educated in Armagh. I appreciate my home city so much that I return there as often as I can. Why on earth would Paul not give a hint in his letters that he hailed from the important city of Tarsus? And why would he not bring the good news of Jesus Messiah to that great urban center? I have no final answers. Here is a conjecture. Paul of Tarsus, like Jesus of Nazareth, may not have received a warm welcome in his home city, if the maxim is true that "prophets are not without honor, except in their hometown, and among their own kin, and in their own house" (Mark 6:4).

Part III: Paul

ONE IMPARTIAL GOD FOR ALL

In the previous chapter I mentioned the central confession of Israelite-Jewish faith that *God the Lord alone is one*. Paul inherited this creed, rooted in Deuteronomy 6:4, and operated under its influence in his life and mission. The implications of that confession relate significantly to Paul's drive to fulfill his Damascus call.

Universal Scope

A group of people may acknowledge only one God. They may give that god a name, agree on the way that god operates in their personal and communal lives, and then serve and worship that one god. But that notion is not Jewish monotheism to which Paul subscribed. Confessing only one God, not merely *our* one God, disavows the reality of all other gods of the world. This monotheistic confession and outlook was bound to result in casting aspersion on the gods and their devotees among the other nations of the world: their gods are all false, or worse, demons (1 Cor. 10:20). From a Jewish perspective, therefore, the core problem with the other nations of the world is that they do not acknowledge the one God of the universe revealed to Israel. This oneness and universality of Israel's God comes through strongly in Paul's words in 1 Corinthians 8:6: "For us there is one God, the Father, from whom are all things and for whom we exist, and one Lord, Jesus Christ, through whom are all things and through whom we exist."

Oneness and universality are clearly coordinates. The implication is far reaching. While Israel can claim to be the chosen nation of people under the one God, they are but one group of people among the many created in the image of the one God (Gen. 1:27). Israel's election came with a purpose and program, as Isaiah declares vividly:

> I am the LORD, I have called you in righteousness, I have taken you by the hand and kept you; I have given you as a covenant to the people, a light to the nations (Isa. 42:6). It is too light a thing that you should be my servant to raise up the tribes of Jacob and to restore the survivors of Israel; I will give you as a light to the nations, that my salvation may reach to the end of the earth (Isa. 49:6). .

Paul's convictions that undergirded his world mission were born of these three long-standing bedrock beliefs in Judaism: that God is one over all, that God chose Israel as a special possession among the nations, and that Israel was to bring the light of God's covenant grace to the whole inhabited world that God created. With respect to his Damascus revelation of Christ and his corresponding call, Paul operated as one compelled to carry out the divine plan for the world, especially for the nations outside Jewish Israel. They too belong to creator God, and are subject to the grace of God embodied in the person of Jesus Christ.

Impartial and Just

If God is one, and God's created humanity one, then the salvation of God should come to all humanity, however differentiated it may be. And it was differentiated in Paul's time, as it is still: different languages, different cultural mores, different skin color, different genders, etc. But Paul's understanding of God and world is that both Jewish and non-Jewish people are inherently one, and that God is just and justifies anyone who accepts the faithfulness of Jesus Messiah (Rom. 3:26). Moreover, God is not partial to one human group over another. Here is how Paul states the case: "There will be anguish and distress for everyone who does evil, the Jew first and also the Greek, but glory and honor and peace for everyone who does good, the Jew first and also the Greek. *For God shows no partiality*" (Rom. 2:9–11, emphasis added).

Even in a more restricted human situation than "Jew first and also Greek," Paul makes the same point about the divine mind. The text is Galatians 2:6, and the situation is a meeting between Paul and the Jerusalem apostles. Paul appeared before the original group in Jerusalem to give an account of his work in the world in the name of Jesus. In his letter to the Galatians he reports that he did not have to change his preaching or his program of incorporating non-Jewish people into community. Here is how he puts it: "And from those who were supposed to be acknowledged leaders (what they actually were makes no difference to me; God shows no partiality)—those leaders contributed nothing to me." Even within the group of apostles, the latecomer Paul (1 Cor. 15:8f) is included: *God shows no partiality.*

There are two sides to divine impartiality. One is that all people, regardless of ethnic origin, can count on the grace of God in Jesus Christ to be received by faith. Another is that the one impartial God will judge evildoers, regardless of ethnic origin, "since all have sinned" (Rom. 3:23). Donaldson states the matter thus: "God's impartiality is . . . firmly rooted in the Hebrew Scriptures and widespread in postbiblical Jewish literature . . . Paul moves [in Romans 1:18—3:20] from the notion of divine impartiality to that of Gentile salvation."[4]

THE CHRIST-EVENT AND THE TURN OF THE AGES

Following his Damascus experience, Paul was no longer operating out of his long-time knowledge and practice of Judaism. He had not abandoned Judaism, but his revelation of Jesus Messiah crucified and raised by God transformed his concept of time. That may seem strange. By time I do not mean the counting of minutes, months, and years, but time in terms of ages or eras. Judaism was an historic religion. The people of Israel intended another age beyond the present routine. Events were always moving the people forward toward a destination, an outcome, and Israel's God was the prime mover of events along the way toward a *dénouement*. The Israelite prophets are testimony to this world-view. Jewish thinkers, following in the prophetic tradition, envisioned two ages, the present age and the age to come. The age to come is the goal of the present, the final resolution of human bungling that happens along the present course of events. God alone brings about the turn of the ages, from first to last, from old to new.

In 1980 an insightful article by C. J. A. Hickling argues that Paul was highly aware of a cosmic time-change in which he was involved, following his Damascus

---

4. Donaldson, *Gentiles*, 88.

Part III: Paul

revelation and call. God had enacted the change by vindicating the crucified Jesus. Here is Hickling's understanding of Paul's thought in mission:

> God has already brought about in Christ a decisive and final transformation of time . . . In Paul's imagination of this *Aeonewende* [change of ages] it always bore the predominantly dualistic colour provided by the world-view of apocalyptic . . . Here is the center of Paul's thought, and indeed of his religion: not simply, or even principally, in the content of his assertions about God and Jesus and his own calling, but in the sense of a fundamental and paradoxical contrast, as of one standing at a cosmic frontier, with which this content was perceived.[5]

The urgency that comes through in many of Paul's statements in his letters may be attributed to this change of the ages: he was "as one standing at a cosmic frontier." A new creation was under way. This pattern of thought is called "eschatological": understanding the way God ushers in the "last" (*eschatos*) age. One of the features of the turn of the ages—from first to final, from old to new—was the gathering of the nations into a relationship with Jesus Christ crucified and raised. The Christ-event was the catalyst for the arrival of the new day of salvation and judgment in Paul's thinking in his letters. Here is a list of statements from his letters illustrating his vision of the *imminent end of the present age and the beginning of the age to come*:

- "the appointed time has grown short" (1 Cor. 7:29);
- "the present form of this world is passing away" (1 Cor. 7:31);
- "salvation is nearer to us now than when we became believers" (Rom. 13:11);
- "the night is far gone, the day is near" (Rom. 13:12);
- "The Lord is near" (Phil. 4:5);
- "[examples from Israel's past] were written down to instruct us, on whom the ends of the ages have come" (1 Cor. 10:11);
- " if anyone is in Christ, there is a new creation: everything old has passed away; see, everything has become new!" (2 Cor. 5:17);
- "neither circumcision nor uncircumcision is anything; but a new creation is everything! (Gal. 6:15);
- "the creation waits with eager longing for the revealing of the children of God" (Rom. 8:19);
- "we ourselves, who have the first fruits of the Spirit, groan inwardly while we wait for adoption, the redemption of our bodies" (Rom. 8:23);
- "We will not all die, but we will all be changed, in a moment, in the twinkling of an eye, at the last trumpet" (1 Cor. 15:51–2).

Paul connected his call to proclaim the good news to the non-Jewish people of the world with this end-time vision. Hence the urgency of getting on with the job.

---

5. Hickling, "Centre," 208–9.

Gathering the Nations into Jesus Messiah

One resurrection had happened already, and the full and final one was just around the corner, when "the full number of the Gentiles has come in" and "all Israel will be saved" (Rom. 11:25–26). The resurrection of Jesus Messiah was the "first fruits" of the final harvest.

GATHERING THE NATIONS INTO END-TIME COMMUNITIES OF CHRIST

Paul captured the prophetic vision about gathering the nations into Zion, into God's salvation provided through Jesus Christ crucified and raised (Isa. 11:10; 66:18; Jer. 3:17; 50:2; Joel 3:2; Ps. 17:50; 117:1. Cf. Rom. 15:9–18). This goes to the heart of what mattered to Paul in the middle of the first century CE: his mission to the non-Jewish nations was "promised beforehand through [God's] prophets in the holy scriptures" (Rom. 1:1–2).

A Mysterious Start in Arabia

A precise chronology of Paul's career is notoriously hard to pin down, as Gerd Lüdemann's 300-page volume on the subject attests. The uncertainty begins with "two possible dates for the death of Jesus,"[6] 27 CE or 30 CE. Assuming the traditional date of Jesus' crucifixion at 30 CE, Paul received the revelation and call about three years later (33 CE) after the Jewish believers in Jesus had scattered south and north, as far away as Damascus in Syria.

Damascus was the center of Paul's persecution of the Greek-speaking Jewish believers in Jesus, and also the place of his revelation and call. The question now is, What did he do immediately after this call? He tells us cryptically in Galatians 1:17: "I did not go up to Jerusalem to those who were already apostles before me, but I went away at once into Arabia, and afterwards I returned to Damascus." There was no waiting period between call and mission. Why he did not elaborate on his activity in Arabia for about three years (Gal. 1:18) remains a mystery. The conjecture has been made repeatedly over the years that Paul went to Arabia to ponder his new commission, to get used to his new experience, and/or to draw up a strategy for carrying out the mandate that God had laid upon him to bring the good news to the nations. This period of three years in Arabia is a mystery for several reasons: (1) Paul is completely silent about what he was doing there, (2) Acts does not mention a three-year period in Arabia, and (3) Paul does not mention any convert-friends he made while he was there.

But the mysterious silence has not deterred scholars from filling in the three-year blank in Paul's career. By far the most prevalent view over the years, till recently, has been that Paul went all the way south to the region of Sinai to contemplate his call in the geographical area of the giving of the Law to Israel. Qualifiers have been added: he went to Arabia to be far away from the setting of his persecution of Jewish believers in Jesus; he hoped the time away would heal the wounds he caused in his pre-call life, and so open the door into the Jerusalem group. All of these are conjectures from silence.

---

6. Lüdemann, *Gentiles*, 262.

Part III: Paul

A much more likely scenario is that Paul went into Arabia immediately after his Damascus experience to engage in the mission to which he had been called. Arabia at the time of Paul's call in the early thirties was not restricted to the Sinai region. The whole territory east of the Jordan and south to the Negev had come under the political control of the Nabataean ruler, Aretas IV, who ruled from the impressive capital city of Petra in modern Jordan. Paul knew of this king and his governor first hand, as he states in Second Corinthians 11:32–33: "the governor under King Aretas guarded the city of Damascus in order to seize me, but I was let down in a basket through a window in the wall, and escaped from his hands." This is the only place in his letters where Paul makes any mention of a direct confrontation with a civil authority. The story about the escape from Damascus is also told in Acts 9, but the persecutors there are from the Jewish synagogue of Damascus, not from the governor of the Nabataean King of Arabia as Paul himself remembers.

A question arises from the brief mention of the governor's pursuit of Paul: What was he doing in the Nabataean territory to engender such antagonism from the governor? He was hardly sitting serenely in some desert place contemplating his call and his future work. He must have been active, and in such a way as to incur the anger of the governor of the territory. Hengel has argued that Paul was visiting Jewish synagogues in the Nabataean area to meet up with Arab God-worshippers in an effort to convert them to Jesus Messiah crucified and raised. His efforts would have come to the attention of the governor who determined to bring his missionary activity to an end. There was already bad blood between king Aretas and Herod Antipas of Galilee and Perea. Antipas divorced his wife, daughter of Aretas IV, to marry Herodias a few years before Paul's call. By 36 CE king Aretas waged war against Antipas and defeated him. Notice 36 CE, the approximate date of Paul's expulsion from Arabia. The conflict between Antipas and Aretas may have had something to do with the swift removal of the radical Jewish missionary who talked about a Jewish Messiah from Nazareth of Galilee.

There is no record of a Christ-community in the Nabataean region in Paul's time, so the thought is that Paul's three-year mission in the area was unsuccessful. One might suspect that Paul initially required circumcision from his non-Jewish male audience, which they would have refused with disgust. In Galatians 5:11 he admits that he did preach circumcision of males at one time: "why am I still being persecuted if I am still preaching circumcision?" The reference is more likely to his pre-call practice in Judaism. In any case, the Arab males to whom Paul preached the gospel of Jesus crucified and raised would have been circumcised already. They, along with their Jewish counterparts, traced their heritage to Abraham to whom God gave the covenant mark of circumcision for males, and enjoined the same to his seed, even though the Arab seed came through the slave-woman, Hagar (Gen. 17:18-23).

Whatever Paul was doing in the Nabataean territory during the first three years of his career it is evident that his efforts did not yield much fruit. If he had formed new messianic communities (*ekklēsiai*) in the area, surely he would have alluded to them in his letters. Outside sources show no record of such communities in Arabia from the period of Paul's sojourn there. Acts is completely silent about the three years.

Gathering the Nations into Jesus Messiah

Since there is no apparent result of Paul's mission, a number of scholars believe Paul's mission in Arabia was "such a disaster."[7] Hengel is not so convinced about Paul's lack of success in Arabia:

> We do not know whether Paul's missionary activity in "Arabia" was unsuccessful. One should not jump to hasty conclusions based on his silence on this issue, since he is equally silent concerning his entire work of fourteen years in Syria and Cilicia following his visit to Jerusalem . . . Without anticipating this himself, he lit a blaze that developed into a continually growing wildfire that finally reached the Orient and Europe and that influenced the particular course of our European history.[8]

However eloquent and poetic this statement is, Paul's work in Nabataea hardly "lit a blaze" that became a "wildfire" there. There may not have been as many Jewish synagogues in Arabia as Hengel suggests, and thus not as many Arab God-worshippers at Jewish synagogues for Paul to convert. My own tentative opinion is that Paul presented himself as a Jewish Messianic preacher of salvation through the Jewish Jesus crucified and raised. Arabs would not have taken kindly to such Jewish overtures, as though the Arab religion from Abraham-Hagar were inferior to the Jewish-Jesus counterpart. Paul thereafter turned to the other nations of the world where he gained a more receptive audience.

Basis of Inclusion: The Faithfulness of Jesus Christ

Inclusion in the new community of the end-time was not on the basis of works of law (Gal. 2:16; 3:2, 5, 10, 12; Rom. 3:27). That was also true of ancient Israel. God did not choose the Hebrew people because they kept the law: they were chosen before the law was given. Israel became the covenant people by their acceptance of God's grace. The same principle holds also for the non-Jewish people of Paul's mission: they are called to accept the grace of God revealed in *the faithfulness of Jesus Christ*.

The last phrase needs explanation. To do so, a simple lesson in Greek grammar is required: Greek because that was the language Paul used; required because most modern translations of the phrase, including the NRSV, are influenced by later theology. (The other day when I corrected the grammar of my ten-year-old grandson he replied: "I'm not into grammar." But every speaker/writer is "into grammar," consciously or not!). Our job now is to set aside the nudging of later Christianity, especially the Reformation kind, so as to capture Paul's grammar, which carries his meaning.

One of Paul's most famous Greek words is *pistis* (noun) *pisteuō* (verb) and *pistos* (adjective). You can see the same root, *pist*, in all three. The noun is usually translated "faith," the verb, "to believe," or "to exercise faith," and the adjective, "faithful." Martin Luther made this word-group famous with his emphasis on a person's "faith alone" in Jesus Christ for salvation. This emphasis has led, quite frankly, to a mistranslation of a very significant phrase for Paul. I invite you now to take a short tour to every one

---

7. Borg and Crossan, *First Paul*, 75.
8. Hengel, "Arabia," 65–66.

Part III: Paul

of those mistranslations, beginning with Romans 3:21–22, and watch what happens when the English follows literally the Greek grammar that Paul purposely put on the page. I will use the NRSV as the baseline.

Romans 3:21–22: "But now, apart from law, the righteousness of God has been disclosed . . . through *faith in Jesus Christ* for all who believe." The highlighted phrase implies that the righteousness/justice of God is revealed by personal faith in Jesus Christ. Now for the grammar of the Greek phrase: *dia pisteōs Iēsou Christou*. The last two words end with "*ou*," called a genitive case ending. A genitive case describes what precedes it, as in "peace *of God*," "book *of prayer*," "type *of fruit*," etc. In each instance the highlighted genitive phrase acts as subject of the noun that precedes it. Here, now, is the literal translation of Paul's telling phrase: "through (*dia*) faith (*pisteōs*) of Jesus Christ (*Iēsou Christou*)." There is no "in" (*en*) in Paul's text. If there were, the ending of the words following would be *Iēsou Christō*. If Paul had intended a human person's "faith in Jesus Christ," he could have written that phrase in Greek easily. Instead, he wrote that the justice of God is revealed "through the faithfulness of Jesus Christ." The word *pistis* is about loyalty, trustworthiness, faithfulness, reliability, confidence.

The same word, *pistis*, occurs along with a genitive construction at Romans 3:3, and there the NRSV translates correctly: "What if some were unfaithful? Will their faithlessness nullify the *faithfulness of God (pistiv tou theou)*"? It would make no sense to translate "faith in God" in this case. The point here is that God keeps promise, keeps faith, hence "the faithfulness of God." Why would it be otherwise with the same grammar in relation to Jesus Christ? He is the faithful representative of the justice of God for the sake of those who exercise their faith in him. Here is a literal translation of Romans 3:21–22: "But now, apart from law, the justice of God has been revealed, being affirmed by the law and the prophets, the justice of God through *the faithfulness of Jesus Christ* on behalf of all who exercise faith."

The phrase was important for Paul. He repeats it a number of times at key points in his arguments. We would do well to get it right. Here is a list of places where the phrase calls for the re-translation recommended above:

- Galatians 2:16. "We know that a person is not put right by works of law but through *the faithfulness of Jesus Christ*."

- Galatians 2:19–20. "The life I now live in the flesh I live by *the faithfulness of the Son of God*, who loved me and handed himself over for me."

- Galatians 3:22. "But the scripture has imprisoned all things under the power of sin, so that what was promised through *the faithfulness of Jesus Christ* might be given to those who exercise faith."

- Philippians 3:9. "That I may gain Christ and be found in him, not having my own justice that comes from the law, but one that comes through *the faithfulness of Christ*, the justice from God based on faithfulness.

What result does this exercise in retranslating offer? Just this: that the basis on which people of the world are included in the covenant God made with Abraham is

Gathering the Nations into Jesus Messiah

not human faith, but the faithfulness of Jesus Christ in making the saving justice of God accessible to all humankind. To be sure, human persons gain access to the saving grace of God in Jesus Christ through an exercise of their faith, or trust. But their faith is not the sum and substance of their salvation. Jesus Messiah is. Being "in Christ," the faithful one, is the ground on which end-time salvation rests for all who trust in him.

Transferring into Christ-communities

Not many matters of history can be stated with complete certainty. That is as true of Paul's life, thought, and career as it is for any other figure or movement of the ancient world. For Paul, one matter can be stated with certainty: his message about Jesus Messiah crucified and risen could not be added onto the existing religions of the nations. His preaching was a call to his non-Jewish audience to come out from their present religious belief and practice into a new and separate fellowship in the name of the Jewish Jesus Messiah.

Social-Religious Location of the Non-Jewish Audience

I have noted briefly already, something of the social structure of the cities in which Paul preached his good news. Much more could be given. Whatever the social levels of people in the audience, we can be reasonably sure that they belonged to a community in which non-Jewish rituals of religion were conducted. Ritual "is itself a kind of speech."[9] It speaks symbolically of the beliefs that govern a way of thinking and living. Rituals in the ancient world included offering sacrifices to the chosen gods of the group, chanting mantras, dancing, praying, washing the body, eating sacred meals, etc. Society at the time was not as modern Euro-American society is: largely secular, with religion as a personal option. Societies at the time of Paul were decidedly religious. Opting out of religious community was hardly an option for the mass of people. Even those who achieved a higher social status were drawn to powers beyond the mundane. Communities formed around common gods and common rituals. Meeting times were set for carrying out the necessary rituals in honor of the deities, and for fellowship with like-minded worshippers.

Part of the ritual in a non-Jewish community meeting involved adulation directed to a god represented in a material object, called an idol. The idea of paying homage and sacrifice to the idol-god was to gain favor with the god. Life for many in the first century, especially for those of low status, was hard. Sickness was rampant. Many children died before the age of six. Day laborers were always at the mercy of rich employers. There was little or no government-sponsored social service to provide for those in need. The ritual expression of religion was for many a way of expressing their deepest longing for a better life, for salvation.

When Paul extended an invitation within his proclamation of Christ crucified and raised, it was a call to cross over *into Christ*, which meant participation in the community of Jesus Messiah. Being "in Christ"—Paul's vintage phrase—was not a solitary

---

9. Meeks, *First Urban*, 141.

Part III: Paul

experience. It was relational through and through. Relationship to Christ presupposed relationship with a community of like-minded people of Christ. Paul uses familial language for the relationship. To the Galatians he writes that "all the members of God's family" are with him in sending greetings (Gal. 1:2; cf. 6:10). Repeatedly he refers to the members of the new Christ-communities as his siblings, brothers and sisters. So when Paul calls non-Jewish people to separate themselves from their communal celebrations he offers them an alternative community. They cannot be members in both at the same time. Inclusion in the Christ-community excludes all other non-Jewish religious affiliation.

No Other Gods and No Icons

The top two of the Ten Commandments defined Israel's distinctive theology and worship throughout the nation's history: "You shall have no other gods before me. You shall not make for yourself an idol" (Ex. 20:3–4). This defining character of Israelite and Jewish religion is what Eisenbaum calls "aniconic monotheism": the belief in and worship of one God without sensory representation of the deity. "Aniconic monotheism is the signature mark of Judaism in the Hellenistic and Roman world, especially from the perspective of Jews themselves, though it is remarked on by Greek and Roman writers as well, sometimes with admiration."[10] And it was also Paul's "signature mark" for incorporating non-Jewish converts into communities of Jesus Messiah.

Iconic religion was common in the cities of the world of Paul's time. A visit to the site of ancient Ephesus in Turkey today will illustrate the iconic nature of religions of the time. A major challenge of Paul's mission to the non-Jewish people of the cities was in persuading his converts to "flee from the worship of idols" (1 Cor. 10:14). Idols, whatever their form, are human creations born out of the need for sensory connection with the divine. But the idol, or icon, is lifeless. Jewish religion celebrated *the living God*, visible only in *God's* created universe and in the human imagination, which is ever open to fresh insight. Paul is glad to report to the congregation at Thessalonica what people are saying about them: "how you turned to God from idols, to serve a living and true God" (1 Thess. 1:9). The implication of Paul's complement is that the idols from which the Christ-believers turned were lifeless and false. The worship of such representations of a deity devalues the living, and life-giving, character of the true God, the God of Israel.

More than that, from a Jewish perspective the worship of inanimate forms made by human hands is connected with human sexuality, or more precisely with sexual promiscuity. Paul expresses this view in the opening of his letter to the Christ-believers in Rome. In characterizing non-Jewish religious people he says:

> They exchanged the glory of the immortal God for images (*eikonos*) resembling a mortal human being or birds or four-footed animals or reptiles. Therefore God gave them up in the lusts of their hearts to impurity, to the degrading of their bodies among themselves, because they exchanged the truth about God for a lie and worshiped and served the creature rather than the Creator, who is blessed

---

10. Eisenbaum, *Paul*, 68; cf. Van Kooten, *Anthropology*, 343, 352; Davies, *Scribes*, 104.

Gathering the Nations into Jesus Messiah

> forever! Amen. For this reason God gave them up to degrading passions. Their women exchanged natural intercourse for unnatural, and in the same way also the men, giving up natural intercourse with women, were consumed with passion for one another. Men committed shameless acts with men and received in their own persons the due penalty for their error. (Rom. 1:23–24)

Paul is expressing here a view common in Judaism, that sensory idolatry and sexual immorality are inherently intertwined. And he will have none of it in the body of Christ—as we shall see focused in the next chapter—because "what [non-Jewish people] sacrifice, they sacrifice to demons and not to God . . . You cannot drink the cup of the Lord and the cup of demons" (1 Cor. 10:20–21).

Entrance Requirement

Transferring into the Christ-community entails both negative and positive factors for non-Jewish converts. I have identified the negative ones already: giving up the worship of idols, thus also leaving the community in which such worship is conducted, and abandoning all sexual impropriety. But there is also a positive side to the transfer.

When non-Jewish listeners to Paul's proclamation of Jesus Messiah crucified and raised respond positively, they thereby signal their heart's desire to move into a new community of faith in the faithful representative of God's covenant with Abraham, Jesus Messiah. Faith is the principal requirement for the transfer to take place. But faith (*pistis*) in Paul's vocabulary is more than an act of believing, of giving mental assent to a statement, even Paul's statement about Jesus. It involves, rather, heartfelt trust in *the subject* of the proclamation, namely, Jesus Christ crucified and raised on behalf of the world. Faith in this faithful representative of God's grace is saving faith. This faith brings God's righteousness/justice to bear in personal experience and in communal relationship, as it did for Abraham with whom God made the covenant in the first place. "Faith was reckoned to Abraham as righteousness," not by means of circumcision, but by trusting the faithfulness of God to bring righteousness/justice to bear in Abraham's life (Rom. 4:9–10; cf. Gal. 3:6–9).

This is "justification," being put right with the one righteous God of the universe. Non-Jewish people of the end-time have access to this same right relationship with God that father Abraham had. And they have it on the same basis: *faith apart from circumcision*, i.e., works of the law (Gal. 2:16; Rom. 3:28; 4:6). Heart-faith in Christ, like that of Abraham toward God, entitles non-Jewish Christ-believers to the status of Abraham's children. For Paul, Christ was Abraham's "seed" (*sperma*, Gal. 3:16–29). Trusting in Christ is first and foremost how non-Jewish people transfer into Christ, which means also transferring into the communal-body of Christ. "For in the one Spirit we were all baptized into one body—Jews or Greeks, slaves or free—and we were all made to drink of one Spirit" (1 Cor. 12:13; cf. Rom. 12:4–8).

Baptism was also part of the transfer, an initiation ritual one might say. Paul would probably not have viewed baptism as a sacrament, but the water ritual did carry strong symbolic meaning for him. To the Christ-followers in Rome he writes: "Therefore we have been buried with him by baptism into death, so that, just as Christ was raised from the dead by the glory of the Father, so we too might walk in newness of life" (6:4). According to this account, baptism involved immersion in water, not for ritual purification or for the washing away of sins, but for full identification with the death and resurrection of Christ. For the initiate the "burial" in the water meant the end to the old life in the old community of idol-worship, and the coming out of the water meant taking on a new way of living and thinking in the community of Jesus Messiah. One needs to be careful here. Paul does not invoke resurrection language for the "newness of life" in view. He reserves the resurrection of believers in Jesus for the future wind-up of the present age. Their present experience is that of the Spirit of Christ, which "guarantees" the future and final resurrection at the coming of Christ in glory (*parousia*). "He who has prepared us for this very thing is God," he says, "who has given us the Spirit as a guarantee" (2 Cor. 5:5; also 1:22; Rom. 8:23).

Paul is confident that the crossover into Christ requires no waiting period for learning rules for living in community and in society. The Spirit is sufficient. Like the air we breathe for physical life, so the Spirit of life in Christ is sufficient law for living. But note well: "the law of the Spirit of life in Christ Jesus" does not contradict, or contravene, the Law of God prescribed in the Jewish Torah (Rom. 8:2). "For we know that the law is spiritual" (Rom. 7:14). Paul also calls the Spirit-life in community "the law of Christ" (Gal. 6:2). I will take this discussion further in the next chapter. One more point still needs to be brought to light here.

The Synagogue and its Counterpart

Today Jewish synagogues and Christian churches exist in the major cities of North America, and beyond. Members in one or the other do not consider the two religions—Judaism and Christianity—related in any meaningful way. Put more starkly, they may view each other as opposite, wrong, misguided, etc. Modern interpreters of the historical Paul and historical Judaism(s) of Paul's time can hardly resist the two-millennia of consciousness of "synagogue" and "church" as being mutually exclusive entities. I am now convinced that it was not so at all for Paul.

In his book, *The First Urban Christians*, Meeks explores "models from the environment"[11] on which Paul may have organized his *ekklēsiai*, groups of believers in Jesus Messiah. He describes the household, voluntary association, synagogue, philosophical or rhetorical school models, all of them operating in the society of the time, but decided on none of the four specifically as *the* model of the fellowship group that Paul formed. "The fact is," Meeks concludes, "that none of the four models we have surveyed captures the whole of the Pauline *ekklēsia*, although all offer significant analogies."[12] Distinctive features must be so, of course, by virtue of the innovative features of groups that believe in a crucified and resurrected Messiah who is about to usher in the end of the age. Still, the end-time Christ-group under Paul's influence would be more likely to follow the model of the aniconic monotheistic Diaspora synagogue in which Paul had been a member for most of his life. And, as I have argued

---

11. Meeks, *Urban*, 75–84; cf. Adams, "Models," 60–78.
12. Meeks, *Urban*, 84.

Gathering the Nations into Jesus Messiah

already, Paul continued to be Jewish while he engaged in an end-time mission to the non-Jewish world. To be sure, his experience of the resurrected Jesus transformed his thinking about the fullness of God's time (Gal. 4:4), and about his discipline of Jewish Christ-believers. But Paul continued to "uphold the Law" of Judaism (Rom. 3:31), and continued to identify himself with Judaism centered in Jerusalem. Why else would he recognize so positively the Jewish festival of Pentecost that celebrated the giving of the Law? (1 Cor. 16:8). And as we have seen, he must have visited synagogues periodically to receive the prescribed discipline from the synagogue authorities.

But Paul does not call his new communities of Christ-believers "synagogues." That term was taken already, defined by a rather long history of usage within Second Temple Judaism. A *synagōgē* was not a designation for a building, but for a group of Jewish people gathered together for worship, teaching, and the celebration of God's election and the gift of Torah. Jewish synagogues of the Diaspora would accept non-Jewish worshippers as guests. To become full and equal members with their ethnic Jewish counterparts they would have to adopt the requirements for inclusion, particularly repentance and obedience to Torah, which included circumcision of males, together with kosher and Sabbath observance for all. One can only imagine how non-Jewish adult males would have resisted the requirement of removing the foreskin. But some submitted. These were then proselytes to Judaism, members in good standing with ethnic Jewish worshippers.

Called as he was to gather the nations to join with "the Israel of God" of the end-time, Paul was not prepared to treat his non-Jewish converts to Christ as second-rate members of the family of Abraham, as guests merely. He created a new group-identity for them, one in which they could consider themselves full and equal partners with their Jewish counterparts. The Greek term Paul applied to the new Christ-groups was *ekklēsia*, a group called out from their old religion and way of life into a new one. The new groups could consider themselves put right with the one God of Israel through their faith in the faithfulness of Jesus Christ. Mark Nanos calls these new groups collectively a Jewish subgroup. "Paul spoke for a Jewish subgroup that upheld faith in Christ, to be sure, but this was not a new religion, nor did he imagine that it would be one. He was a reformer, involved in the restoration of Israel, and the gathering of the nations initiated thereby."[13]

I appreciate the point Nanos makes for the full inclusion of non-Jewish believers in Jesus on par with their Jewish counterparts. The new communities were Jewish "subgroups," but not Jewish substandard. Jewish believers in Jesus Messiah could join with the non-Jewish believers without denying their ethnic Jewish identity or their Jewish practice, any more than Jesus denied his. The same was not the case for non-Jewish members. They had to surrender their old religious identity, especially polytheism and idolatry, to become part of the family of Abraham through Jesus Christ. When Paul admonishes the mixed membership in the *ekklēsia* at Corinth to remain as they were at the time of their call, he surely was not admonishing the non-Jewish members

---

13. Nanos, "Jewish Tradition," 5.

Part III: Paul

to maintain their former religious identity and practice. The specific issue was the circumcision—versus uncircumcision—of males for full inclusion. Proselytes to Judaism had to submit to circumcision for full inclusion. Paul admonishes the circumcised members to remain as they are, and the uncircumcised to do likewise. The passage is worth quoting in full:

> Was anyone at the time of his call already circumcised? Let him not seek to remove the marks of circumcision. Was anyone at the time of his call uncircumcised? Let him not seek circumcision. Circumcision is nothing, and uncircumcision is nothing; but obeying the commandments of God is everything. Let each of you remain in the condition in which you were called. (1 Cor. 7:18–20)

Two observations may be made. The first is that the new Christ-communities are Jewish in orientation and practice, the Jewish members with the mark of physical circumcision and the non-Jewish members without it. Why mention circumcision at all if the new community of Christ is non-Jewish? The second observation relates to "obeying the commandments of God." Does Paul mean commandments of God other than those expressed in the Jewish Scriptures? That can hardly be the case. If the commandments are those of the Jewish Torah, then circumcision was one of the commandments given to Abraham and his household, including also aliens and slaves within his circle (Gen. 17:9–14). In a Jewish context Paul's instruction would sound strange. Why would he not require non-Jewish converts to obey that command of God given to Abraham? The answer probably lies in Paul's understanding of end-time salvation now upon him and the world of humankind. In this cosmic time-change, inaugurated by the resurrection of Jesus Messiah, non-Jewish converts are included without that particular commandment of God. The focus is on the inclusion of non-Jewish people. For them "the just requirement of the law" does not include circumcision (Rom. 8:4).

The formation of new communities of Christ opened the door for full membership of non-Jewish people with the covenant people of God that would not have been possible had Paul tried to bring his converts into the synagogues. In that context they would have been guests. In the new counterpart, the *ekklēsia*, they are full and equal members. As Nanos puts it, "non-Jews were being identified not merely as guests, however welcome and celebrated, as in other Jewish groups. They were instead being treated as members in full standing, on the same terms as proselytes, children of Abraham, and yet at the same time not proselytes, not members of Israel, but representatives of the other nations bearing witness to the proposition that the end of the ages had dawned in Christ."[14]

To conclude, Paul had encountered the resurrected Jesus as the Jewish Messiah who had called him to bring the end-time news about the faithfulness of Jesus to the nations. When the non-Jewish people of the cities accepted the message of Christ crucified and raised, they were called out from their non-Jewish religious worship, marked by idolatry, into a new community of Jesus Christ, there to be regarded as full

---

14. Nanos, "Paul and Judaism," 145.

members of the covenant people of God, children of Abraham, by virtue of the faithfulness of Jesus Christ. The new *ekklēsiai*, far from being opposed to Judaism, were Jewish counterparts to the synagogues. The difference between the two bodies had to do primarily with the requirement(s) for incorporation into full membership. The synagogue required circumcision of males, together with kosher and Sabbath observance for all; the *ekklēsia* required only the explicit confession of faith in Jesus Messiah for all, which, for non-Jewish converts, meant leaving behind their idolatrous religion (Rom. 10:9). Baptism was the rite of passage, a crossing over from an old allegiance to the new one, a dying with Christ followed by walking "in newness of life" (Rom. 6:4). Whether Paul would have required baptism for Jewish believers in Christ is debatable. He probably did. They too confessed their allegiance to Jesus Messiah for membership, but they did not have to leave behind their Jewish faith in the one God of Israel.

It is one thing for non-Jewish believers to *enter* the end-time community of Christ, it is another to *maintain* membership after incorporation. That will be the subject of the next chapter.

14

Life Together in the Fellowship of Jesus Messiah

NON-JEWISH PEOPLE THAT PAUL CALLED TO JOIN WITH OTHERS OF LIKE FAITH and like mind in relation to Jesus Messiah came from all walks of Greco-Roman life, and from a variety of associations or clubs. But the new faith-orientation of the believers in Christ required a new association, a new group identity, new ritual, and an all-round "newness of life" (Rom. 6:4). Life in the ancient world was one of association, not the individualism of the post-industrial world. When someone accepted the call of God in the name of Jesus, their old association was thereby put in jeopardy. That was especially so if the association was religious, as most were, directly or indirectly Paul's new groups "in Christ" were exclusive, just as the synagogues were. Full membership in a synagogue excluded membership in other non-Jewish religious clubs or associations. The same was true for the Pauline *ekklēsiai*, the groups of believers in Jesus Messiah.

There were certain features of the new Christ-associations by which the members defined themselves, and by which outsiders recognized them. There was a "coming together" at regular meeting times, no doubt, perhaps on "the first day of every week" (1 Cor. 11:17; 16:2), but at others times as the need arose or as the Spirit moved. The groups probably met in homes, if the homes were large enough. Some members may have been shopkeepers and opened their shops for meetings. The size of the groups is not known. Group numbers probably varied in relation to the space available in a given area. What interests us here, however, is the character of the meetings that took place at the designated times. How did the symbols, rituals, and teachings shape identity for both the individual members and the called-out group? And as an adjunct question, to what extent did the form and meaning of the meetings move into the ebb and flow of daily life in the society?

IN ACCORDANCE WITH WHICH SCRIPTURE?

Group identity in relation to Jesus Messiah was, for Paul, "in accordance with Scripture" (e.g., 2 Cor. 4:13; 1 Cor. 15:3–4; Gal. 4:30; Rom 15:4). My purpose here is not to discuss the way in which Paul interpreted Scripture. Richard Hays has blazed a trail already on that issue so as to require no further comment here.[1] Two points are at issue here: the particular Scripture Paul used in establishing the identity of the new communities, and the degree to which Paul believed Scripture to be indispensable and authoritative for the life and thought of the communities of Jesus Christ.

On the first point, Paul had only one body of Scriptures in mind when he cited and echoed texts in support of various points in his arguments: the Scriptures of Judaism with which he was completely familiar. He appears to have used the Greek translation of the Hebrew Scriptures, as he had done in the Diaspora synagogues for all of his adult life. There were no new *texts* from the original Apostles, or from anyone else in the new Jesus-movement. Even traditional material from or about Jesus, such as sayings of Jesus, are few and far between in Paul's letters. His own letters were the first writings of the new Jesus-movement, and he did not consider them "Scripture" on par with the scrolls of the Jewish Bible that he quotes and echoes frequently in his letters—too frequently to list! The Jewish Scriptures, including the five scrolls of the Law, helped define the new non-Jewish members of the Christ-groups. Whether the groups had actual scrolls of the Jewish Scriptures in hand is not the point. Paul had them in mind, ready at a moment's notice to deploy in support of a point of theology or behavior.

Nor did Paul wrest the Jewish Scriptures from the Jewish people for his exclusive use in his new communities of Christ-followers. To be sure, he interpreted the Scriptures in light of his experience of the risen Jesus, and used them to underwrite his directives to the non-Jewish communities of believers in Jesus Messiah. But they were the Scriptures of the Jewish people of God still. Paul's regret, it seems, was that the Jewish people were not able to see the redemptive figure of Jesus Messiah in those Scriptures (2 Cor. 3:15–18). Nevertheless, Paul's Scriptures were the same Scriptures of the synagogue and Temple. William Campbell confirms the point: "It is clear that in his use of scripture, Paul does not claim the scriptures for Christ-followers alone. He argues as a Jew of his own era, with the patterns and models of scriptural interpretation which he shares with those who do not share his view of the Christ."[2]

We are already broaching the second point, the degree to which Paul viewed his Jewish Scripture as indispensable and authoritative in the formation of thought and ethical behavior in relation to life in Christ Jesus. It is possible, but unlikely, that Paul carried a bundle of scrolls of Scripture with him on his travels; possible also that he read from them during the meetings of the communities. Whether he did or not, he had the Scripture texts in mind and cited them as the word of God. That much we can infer from the abundant use he makes of Scriptures in his letters. He assumes his

---

1. Hays, *Echoes*.
2. Campbell, *Identity*, 48.

Part III: Paul

readers are aware of the sacred literature he cites. Their awareness may have come from their previous guest-attendance at synagogue services where the Jewish Scriptures were read. But it is just as likely that Paul himself instructed his new converts from the same synagogue Scriptures he viewed as authoritative.

Marcion of the second century thought he understood Paul, while denying the Jewish Scriptures from which Paul drew spiritual and theological insight. Marcion missed—or misunderstood—the defining role the Jewish Scriptures played in shaping Paul's Christ-communities. The Paul that Marcion claimed to admire never tired of quoting the Jewish Scripture to make a point, and to direct the life and thought of his new communities "in Christ." For Paul, those writings were not an "old testament" about another God now defunct, as Marcion thought. They were current for Paul, and relevant for his communities as they were for the synagogues. An understanding of God, and of God's righteousness on behalf of the human family, comes from the Jewish Scriptures that testify to God's faithful Messiah, Jesus.

LED BY THE SPIRIT

Even so, Paul did not expect the new Christ-groups to follow the written text of the Jewish Bible literally. He interpreted Scripture tradition in the freedom of the Spirit, and expected his congregations to do the same. Beker put his finger firmly on this point. He writes:

> Paul's hermeneutical skill exhibits a creative freedom that allows the gospel tradition to become living speech within the exigencies of the daily life of his churches. The 'core' is for Paul not simply a fixed, frozen message that must either be accommodated to more or less adaptable occasions or simply imposed upon them as immutable doctrine. For Paul, tradition is always interpreted tradition that is executed in the freedom of the Spirit.[3] .

Take, for example, the Scripture tradition about the rock that gave the Israelites water in the wilderness. Paul calls it a "spiritual rock" from which the Israelites drank: "and the rock was Christ" (1 Cor. 10:4). This is freedom in earnest! He interprets the ancient story from his present experience of the Spirit of Christ. This method of reading Scripture texts corresponds with his dictum: "the letter kills, but the Spirit gives life" (2 Cor. 3:6).

Paul believed in the reality of the Spirit of God in the life of the community of Christ. The Spirit was not merely a doctrine to be recited, or talked about, but a life-experience to be lived. Thus he employs such phrases as "life of the Spirit" (Rom 7:6), "the law of the Spirit" (Rom. 8:2), "led by the Spirit" (Rom. 8:14), "sharing in the Spirit" (Phil. 2:1), "live by the Spirit," "guided by the Spirit" (Gal. 5:25), "walk according to the Spirit" (Rom. 8:4), "the fruit of the Spirit" (Gal. 5:22). There are many more. The Spirit in view, of course, is the "Spirit of the living God" (2 Cor. 3:3), and interchangeably "the Spirit of Christ" (Rom. 8:9).

---

3. Beker, *Paul*, 334.

Mind and Spirit go together. Paul believed that the Spirit of God occupied the minds of the members of the community of Christ (cf. Phil. 2:5). Community was possible, not by a well-crafted constitution against which everyone was held accountable, but by the dynamism of the Spirit of Christ. Paul saw no contradiction between the Scripture and the Spirit. Scripture sprang to newness of life through the illumination of the Spirit. Moral understanding came to expression through the work of the Spirit. People of Jesus Messiah could live together in harmony, as one differentiated body, by virtue of the unifying Spirit of Christ at work in the communities, "enabling [them] both to will and to work for God's good pleasure" (Phil. 2:13).

But here comes the crucial point. The Spirit of God in Christ is communal in character, not a private, personal property. Personal insights and questions are tested in the climate of community where the Spirit operates to create a people, an elect people of God in Christ. There is no such thing in Paul's letters as private ownership of the Spirit, one member following one way of thought and life and another following a different one. First Corinthians 12 and 14 bear witness to the unifying role of the Spirit. The Spirit of God is one, not many. The members of the community are one with different gifts. Community in Christ is the home of the Spirit of God in the world. Division in the community of the Spirit is unthinkable for Paul. "Has Christ been divided?" he asks the Corinthians rhetorically (1 Cor. 1:13). Inside the Christ-fellowship is the family of God, brothers and sisters all born from one womb, whether Judean or Greek, and all bound together under one name and one nature. This is the work of the Spirit of the living God through the faithfulness of Jesus Messiah, according to Paul.

THE JUST REQUIREMENT OF THE LAW

Paul wrote many diverse statements about the Jewish Law. Here is a list from the letters to illustrate the diversity—if not contradiction:

- "For it is not the hearers of the law who are righteous in God's sight, but the doers of the law who will be justified" (Rom. 2:13).
- "For we hold that a person is justified by faith apart from works prescribed by the law" (Rom. 3:28).
- "For all who rely on the works of the law are under a curse" (Gal. 3:10).
- "So the law is holy, and the commandment is holy and just and good" (Rom. 7:12).
- "For we know that the law is spiritual" (Rom. 7:14).
- "For if a law had been given that could make alive, then righteousness would indeed come through the law" (Gal. 3:21).
- "The law was our disciplinarian until Christ came, so that we might be justified by faith" (Gal. 3:24).
- "For Christ is the end of the law so that there may be righteousness for everyone who believes" (Rom. 10:4).

Part III: Paul

- "We uphold the law" (Rom. 3:13).
- "For the whole law is summed up in a single commandment, 'You shall love your neighbor as yourself.'" (Gal. 5:14; Rom 13:9).
- ". . . so that the just requirement of the law might be fulfilled in us" (Rom 8:4).

Many have taken in hand to explain Paul's view of the Law from his vantage point in relation to Jesus Messiah, and in mission to the non-Jewish world. In this space I wish to focus on the phrase in the last entry on my list above: "the just requirement of the law." What is the just requirement? And to whom does the just requirement apply?

Justified and Just (or Righteoused and Righteous)

For Paul the supreme source of justice, or righteousness, is God. In Jesus Christ the "the righteousness of God is revealed" for the purpose of end-time salvation: "the righteousness of God through the faithfulness of Jesus Christ for all who believe" (Rom. 1:17; 3:22). Participation in Christ means being put right with God, also known as "justified by faith in Christ" (Gal. 2:16). This word "justified" needs some explanation. It occurs twenty-three times in Galatians and Romans, and elsewhere in Paul's letters only at First Corinthians 6:11. The verb (*dikaioō*) and its corresponding participle appear in the *passive voice*: the action happens to the subject. In short, the act of being "righteoused," to use Sanders coinage,[4] is God's doing, not human action in keeping the Law.

But this was not new with Paul. It was already at the heart of Israel's theology. God elected the people of Israel, not by anything good they had done, but solely by the grace of God. Membership in the community of Israel, as in Judaism, was given, not earned. Paul knew that, and applied the same principle of election to his non-Jewish converts. To the Corinthians he writes, "you were washed, you were sanctified, you were justified in the name of the Lord Jesus Christ and in the Spirit of our God" (1 Cor. 6:11). Notice all the passive verbs, all of them implying the same *divine* action for incorporating them into the new community: were washed, were sanctified, were justified. This is how the non-Jewish members entered into relationship with the Messiah of God, "not by doing the works of the law, because no one will be justified by the works of the law" (Gal. 2:16). "No one" includes Jewish and non-Jewish people alike. God reveals divine righteousness for the purpose of creating a right relationship with God through the faithfulness of Jesus Messiah. Entrance into Christ, and into the community of Christ, moreover, is by the justifying grace of God in Christ. "The topic is how one transfers from the state of sin and condemnation to the state which is the pre-condition of end-time salvation,"[5] that latter state being "the righteousness of God."

So much for the entrance requirement: the transfer happens through the faithfulness of God's righteous Son, Jesus Messiah, to be received by faith apart from any work

---

4. Sanders, *Paul, the Law*, 6, and note 18.
5. Ibid., 45.

Life Together in the Fellowship of Jesus Messiah

of any law, including the Law of Judaism. Questions arise: What does it mean to be "in Christ," and in the community of Christ? Is the new status of being righteoused simply theological language? Is it merely "the *status* of the person which is transformed by the action of 'justification, not the *character*"?[6] Does God only *declare* the sinner righteous, as a judge in a courtroom would find in favor of the accused, without any change in identity and character accruing from the declaration? From my reading of Paul, to be righteoused means more than a *declaration* about status. It has to do with life lived in relationship with Christ. Esler's treatment of the righteous language in Galatians has merit. Paul "drew out the significance of righteousness as descriptive of a privileged identity, as essentially equivalent to life and blessing, but with faith in the crucified Christ as the source of that life and the experience of the Spirit as the primary content of that blessing."[7]

I now appeal to the text that triggered this discussion, Romans 8:3-4: "For God has done what the law, weakened by the flesh, could not do: by sending his own Son in the likeness of sinful flesh, and to deal with sin, he condemned sin in the flesh, so that *the just requirement of the law might be fulfilled in us*, who walk not according to the flesh but according to the Spirit."

Two movements appear to be at work in this text. The first has to do with how an unrighteous person becomes "right" with God, and thus be incorporated into the people of God in Christ. It is not by human effort ("flesh") in keeping the requirements of the Law. God and God alone takes care of the transfer: by sending God's son to deal with sin, and thus to justify—or to righteous—the one-time sinner without his/her human help.

But now the second movement in the text needs to be exploited. What happens after God has justified the unjust—or righteoused the unrighteous? What does the transfer into Christ and his community mean in life and thought? Does the sinner remain a sinner? The answer comes from Paul's pen in this text (not from Martin Luther and company). God has done all of this in Christ "so that (*hina*) the just requirement of the law might be fulfilled in us, who walk not according to the flesh but according to the Spirit." That little Greek *hina* is important. It introduces a purpose clause. God went to such great lengths to bring end-time salvation to the world, *so that* the transferred people might reflect the righteousness of God in their personal and communal lives. That feat is accomplished when "the just requirement of the Law is fulfilled." Once in the community of God's faithful Messiah, Jesus, the members are to live by "the law of Christ," which agrees completely with the Law God gave to Israel and to the Jewish people thereafter. Of course, the Spirit empowers for the fulfilling of the just requirement of the Law. But the just requirement is to be lived, observed, and fulfilled.

What might that "just/right" requirement mean in real terms? Paul does not spell out the answer in detail. One thing is certain for Paul: it does not include circumcision of non-Jewish males, and probably not kosher diet or Sabbath observance for either

---

6. See Wright, *Justification*, 91.
7. See Esler, *Galatians*, 76.

gender. But there is in God's law, as represented in Israel's Law, a right way of living life in the fellowship of Messiah and his people. The just requirement of God's law is not impossible to keep. That would make God's Law unjust! Paul sums up the just requirement in one word: *love* (*agapē*). That is the single most important ingredient of communal life in relation to Christ. "Love is patient; love is kind; love is not envious or boastful or arrogant or rude. It does not insist on its own way; it is not irritable or resentful; it does not rejoice in wrongdoing, but rejoices in the truth. It bears all things, believes all things, hopes all things, endures all things. Love never ends" (1 Cor. 13:4-8). This is how the just requirement of God's law is fulfilled in the Christ-communities in the world: "'Love your neighbor as yourself.' Love does no wrong to a neighbor; therefore, *love is the fulfilling of the law*" (Rom. 13:9-10; Gal. 5:14; emphasis added).

No End to the Law of God (Romans 10:4)

On the matter of "fulfilling the law," Romans 10:4 springs to mind: "For Christ is the end of the law so that there may be righteousness for everyone who believes." This is one of the most debated texts from Paul's letters. Has the Jewish Scripture, the Law, come to a temporal end in Christ? The critical term is "the end of the law" (*telos nomou*). Paul quotes the Jewish Scriptures copiously as authoritative. In this respect, at least, the Law has not come to a temporal end with the coming of Christ: Paul continues to use it. The spotlight falls on "end" (*telos*). It can mean a temporal end, as in termination (e.g. 1 Cor. 1:8, 13; Matt. 13:39; 24:13). But "end" can imply purpose, goal, outcome, or fulfillment. It is sometimes used in this way in English: "to this *end* it would be expedient for us to complete the project."

Badenas argues wisely that Romans 10:4 in context does not support the idea that "Christ has abrogated, or terminated, the law . . . The meaning of Romans 10:4, then, would be that the way contemplated in the law for receiving God's righteousness is through Christ."[8] So, the "end of the law" points to its fulfillment, goal, purpose, high point, with the result that "in Christ 'righteousness' is granted not just to a particular in-group, not just to those whose zeal for the law is aggressively advanced, but simply to 'all who believe' in the gospel."[9] Christ as the "fulfillment" of the Law could be construed, at one level, as Christ the replacement of the Law. But that cannot be the case, for the simple reason, let me repeat, that Paul continues to use the Law to guide his churches in thought and behavior. Jesus Messiah embodies the Law in his person and work of redemption, and transmits "the just requirement of the law" through the Spirit to be received by faith.

God's Law cannot be terminated, any more than God can. Christ brings out the fullness of God's Law for the benefit of the whole of human family, Judean and Greek, slave and free, male and female. Paul demonstrates by his persistent use of the Jewish Scriptures that there is no temporal end to God's Law. Nor does he propose that the

---

8. Badenas, *End*, 143.
9. Jewett, *Romans*, 620; see also Toews, *Romans*, 262.

Jewish people set the Law of God aside, whether they are believers in Jesus Messiah or not. In fine rhetorical style, Paul asks his readers in Rome, "Do we then overthrow the law by this faith?" Then answers swiftly and categorically, "By no means! On the contrary, we uphold the law" (Rom. 3:31).

All Things to All People?

If Romans 10:4 presents a Pauline puzzle, then 1 Corinthians 9:19-23 is no less puzzling. The text needs to be set out in plain view:

> For though I am free with respect to all, I have made myself a slave to all, so that I might win more of them. To the Jews I became as a Jew, in order to win Jews. To those under the law I became as one under the law (though I myself am not under the law) so that I might win those under the law. To those outside the law I became as one outside the law (though I am not free from God's law but am under Christ's law) so that I might win those outside the law. To the weak I became weak, so that I might win the weak. I have become all things to all people, that I might by all means save some. I do it all for the sake of the gospel, so that I may share in its blessings.

As we read this text, five problems present themselves: (1) If Paul is Jewish himself, why would he have to become as a Judean to win Judeans? (2) Why the distinction between being Jewish and being under the Law? (3) How is it possible for Paul to become as a lawless (*anomos*) person yet remain faithful to "God's law" and "Christ's law"? (4) Is Paul being deceitful, or ethically inconsistent, to accomplish his goal of gaining more converts to the fellowship of Christ? And (5) how would such behavior—if "behavior" is intended—appear to the different groups when they come together under one roof? I shall try to address these pieces of the puzzle, but in no particular sequence.

Conzelmann suggests that Paul's "statement of the aim of his conduct has an opportunistic sound, as if it were determined by tactical considerations."[10] Is "conduct" the appropriate term? Is Paul really talking about actual practice? Or is he, rather, implying a rhetorical stance? Paul can argue from various perspectives to arrive at the conclusion that he wants in the end. Ethical behavior may not be in view at all. Take, for example, the last category on his list of *apparent* compromises: the weak. There is no obvious clue to the identity of the weak in the text. In the context of 1 Corinthians 8–10 the "weak" could refer to those of "weak" conscience about eating food that had been offered to an idol (e.g., 1 Cor. 8:7). But the weak in that context are already won to the fellowship of Christ. The weak in the immediate context appear to be outside the Christ-community, along with the lawless ones and the Law-observant Judeans. I cannot imagine Paul admitting to having a lawless group on the inside, "in Christ!" If the weak are outside, as I believe, Paul may be implying those of little education, of low status, perhaps slaves. This seems likely. He has made himself "a slave to all." Then he is implying that he takes on that posture in his conversation with them, which is not

---

10. Conzelmann, *1 Corinthians*, 159.

Part III: Paul

an easy posture for a sophisticated thinker to take. In short, becoming weak may not mean *doing* what the "weak" outsider does.

I think we should opt on the side of caution in having Paul *practice* "all things to all people." In my opinion, Hays opens the practice-door too wide when he states: "Everything that Paul does is aimed at winning as many people as possible to the gospel. He will adapt his behavior (not his message!) in whatever way necessary to achieve that end . . . Paul's slavery to Christ is expressed in the form of submitting himself in various ways to the cultural structures and limitations of the people he hopes to reach with the gospel."[11] Really? Adapt his behavior in whatever way necessary? Will Paul, in good faith, submit to the "cultural structures" of the people he hopes to gain for Christ? Greco-Roman culture was religious, polytheistic, idolatrous, violent, and to some degree sexually immoral. To be sure Paul hoped to reach these people with the gospel. But did he "adapt his behavior" to their behavior in order to win as many as possible? If that were true, then the converts would be in for a big surprise when they entered the Christ-community! Paul did not tolerate a hint of any such behavior in the fellowship of Christ. Thus, becoming "all things to all people" must mean something other than *doing* as "all people" *do*.

For Paul to become as a Judean would be easy. He was one already. As for keeping Jewish Torah, as loyal Jewish people did, that would not be a compromise for him. He knew the Jewish Law, saw no contradiction between the Law from Sinai and the Law of Christ, so it would have been a breeze for Paul to be Jewish and Law-observant among the Jewish people while he proclaimed the new end-time way of keeping God's law through faith in the faithful Jesus Messiah. In the end, however, practice is not the issue, even when the practice of Jewish Torah would not compromise his commitment to Christ. I believe the "all things to all people" implies rhetorical engagement with all kinds of people, from the Law-observant to the outright lawless. Such engagement involves empathic understanding, not practice. Friendly association with people is possible without compromising one's convictions and ethical practice. Otherwise, as Paul states elsewhere in the same letter, "you would then need to go out of the world" (1 Cor. 5:10).

In line with what I call Paul's way of friendship and empathetic understanding, Nanos rightly appeals to the way Jesus associated with various kinds of people. Paul probably did not draft a policy of behaving like "lawless" or "sinful" people in order to gain them for Christ. "That would be no more likely than it would have been for Jesus. He [Jesus] is presented in the Gospels as engaging in a similar policy of fraternizing with Jewish "sinners" and even tax collectors and non-Jews, yet it is not generally held that Jesus behaved sinfully or Gentilely or collected taxes to do so!"[12] The point I want to make from wrestling with this Pauline puzzle is this: Paul did not incorporate lawless, immoral, idolatrous, polytheists into the fellowship of Christ without calling for change in allegiance, which resulted in change in behavior. When non-Jewish people

---

11. Hays, *First Corinthians*, 153.
12. Nanos, "Torah-Observant," 36.

accepted the call to enter into the fellowship of Christ, which included relationship with the people of Christ, they accepted also the law of Christ. The law of Christ, like the Law of Judaism, was "holy and just and good" (Rom. 7:12).

The great challenge for Paul was in bringing the two very different groups together into one fellowship of Jesus Messiah. Fully observant Jewish believers in Jesus were expected to join with uncircumcised, non-kosher, non-Jewish believers in the same Jesus Messiah without one group claiming superiority over the other. Both groups, with their differences, were obliged to accept each other as equals by their faith in the faithful end-time Messiah, Jesus crucified and vindicated. Ethnic, gender and cultural differences remained in the Christ-communities, even though Christ had made all members one body (Gal. 3:28; 1 Cor. 12:12–13). The challenge may have been less steep had Paul, in principle (if not policy), insisted that Jewish Christ-followers congregate on their own, and non-Jewish converts do likewise. One can only imagine the pressure on a minority group within the whole group, either to conform to the practice of the majority or to leave the Christ-community and go back to their former social-religious setting.

Within these few paragraphs I hope I have moved the five pieces of the puzzle into position without forcing them. (I have often wondered what Paul would think of our management of his texts).

PURIFYING A DEFILED COMMUNITY (1 COR. 5)

One of the sternest passages in the Pauline corpus is found in 1 Corinthians 5, especially at v. 5: "you are to hand this man over to Satan for the destruction of the flesh, so that his spirit may be saved in the day of the Lord." The principle of "all things to all people" in order to gain some seems to have gone by the wayside with respect to this immoral man. The problem for Paul is that the man brought his "lawless" attitude and practice into the community of Christ under false pretenses, and the community did nothing about it. The man was having sexual intercourse with "his father's wife"—probably his stepmother (5:1). And the congregation accepted him without censure, sat with him at the Lord's table, and thus defiled the community of the Spirit of Christ.

A detailed discussion of this text would take us too far afield here. (I have discussed this text at length elsewhere[13]). A few key points should be made to illustrate Paul's view of membership in the new *ekklēsia* on its way to end-time salvation.

The sin is one of incest, strongly forbidden in the Jewish Law (Lev. 18:2–17; 20:11; Deut. 27:20). Punishment for both offenders, according to the Torah regulation, was drastic: "The man who lies with his father's wife has uncovered his father's nakedness; both of them shall be put to death; their blood is upon them" (Lev. 20–11). When the community of Israel, or the community of Jesus Messiah, allows such immorality to persist, the sin of the one contaminates the many. Paul's rebuke is directed to the community at Corinth, not to the immoral man per se. The purity code of the Torah comes into play in Paul's argument. When sin enters the elect community the community

---

13. Shillington, "Atonement Texture," 29–50.

needs to take action to remove it. Otherwise the people of God come under divine judgment.

In ancient Israel and in Second Temple Judaism there was recourse for removing sin from the elect people. That recourse happened on the Day of Atonement, described in Leviticus 16. An important part of the ritual involved the priest laying the sins of the people on the head of a goat. The goat was then led ceremoniously out of the community into the desert where it was "handed over" to a desert demon under the name of Azazel. Symbolically and ritually the goat carried the sin of the congregation on itself, and thus purged the holy congregation. I submit that this background from the Torah of Judaism informs Paul's censure of the congregation (vv. 1–4) and the sentence passed on the immoral man at v. 5.

A number of modern interpreters are keen to see in this text not merely Paul's call for the excommunication of the sinful member who had contaminated the Christ-community, but redemptive action for the sake of the sinful *individual*. But the community as a whole is clearly the subject. Typical of modern individualism, however, the immoral man has become the focus. For Paul, however, it was the Christ-life of the *community* that was at stake. All of the second-person pronouns (you) in the text are plural. The corporate community of Jesus Messiah is the temple of God, and "if anyone destroys God's temple, God will destroy that person" (1 Cor. 3:17).

Consider the wording of verse 5 quoted above from the NRSV. The *community* is to hand the man over to Satan. The ritual is not described. It may simply be Paul's pungent way of instructing the community to take the man physically out of the sphere of the Spirit-filled community into a domain where evil abounds for the time being. The second part of the sentence of verse 5 is baffling. The removal is not a simple expulsion out of the community circle. The handing over to Satan is "for the destruction of the flesh." Does this mean the death of the man's physical body? Most interpreters think of "the flesh" as the sinful nature of the man, the sensual side of the human person. True enough, Paul does use "flesh" in this way at points (e.g., Gal. 5:19; Rom. 8:4). But he uses the word also to denote simply the physical person (e.g., Rom. 1:3; 9:5). If the man's sinful propensity is in view, then the man's sin is purged from his flesh by handing him over to Satan. How strange that sounds! This mythical figure, opposed to God, carries out a positive redemptive process on a human being. On the contrary, the figure of Satan in Jewish Scripture and tradition is a destroyer of the good. Satan's assault on Job, for example, was to make this *righteous man* curse God. The destruction of *the* flesh quite plainly implies the death of the man's physical being in the deadly domain of Satan, and concomitantly the removal of the fleshly disposition of the community in which the man had spread his immoral contagion.

Then comes the second part of the sentence, the purpose clause: "so that his spirit may be saved in the day of the Lord." This is the NRSV rendering. But the literal wording from the Greek text is otherwise: "so that *the* spirit may be saved in the day of the Lord." Why replace the article, "the," with a pronoun, "his"? If a pronoun should be supplied in the second part of the sentence then it should be supplied in the first part as well: "hand this man over to Satan for the destruction of *his* flesh." But I have not seen such a translation. The two phrases are literary coordinates: *the* flesh/*the* spirit. If one should be understood as a pronoun then so should the other. I suggest, rather, that both be translated literally: the destruction of *the flesh*, so that *the spirit* may be saved. That raises the question of the identity of "the spirit." Is the individual spirit of the man intended, or the Spirit of Christ present in the corporate mind of the community, the temple of God? Paul's concern is for the ongoing life of the community on its way to day of the Lord. The whole focus is on community life, community Spirit. The course of action is not to save the man's spirit from its sin with Satan's redemptive help, but to save the Spirit-endowed community by the removal of the one immoral man from the company of the many. I have not found a single case where Satan is responsible for saving any part of the human family.

After the sentence in passed at v. 5, Paul shifts from Day-of-Atonement echoes to Passover symbolism and ritual. Compared to the penitent attitude required for the Day of Atonement, the Passover was occasion for rejoicing in God's deliverance from oppression. In the new Christ-community, "our paschal lamb, Christ, has been sacrificed" (5:7). This is the only place in Paul's letters where Christ is described as the Passover Lamb. Here also, in his Passover imagery in verses 6 to 8, Paul insists that purity must be maintained in community life. The presence of the immoral man has defiled the Spirit resident in the minds of the members. The man must be removed, as leaven is removed from the house, in preparation for the Passover celebration. One piece of leaven corrupts "the whole bath of dough" (5:6). The community's acceptance of such a person as "brother" was not a cause for celebration. They should, rather, have "mourned" the sinful situation (5:2), as the Jewish people did on the Day of Atonement until the sin was taken away.

However harsh it may sound, this re-reading of Paul's text is in line with his conviction about the new community living under the law of Christ by the power of the Spirit. As far as Paul is concerned the immoral man "names himself a brother" (middle voice), but his life contradicted that self-claim. The true Christ-community is here instructed "not to associate with anyone who bears the name of brother or sister who is sexually immoral or greedy, or is an idolater, reviler, drunkard, or robber" (5:11). In other words, members in the community of the Spirit of Christ follow the law of Christ, which is consonant with the Law of Judaism. Vices such as those on the list are excluded in the presence of the Spirit, which is the guarantee of salvation on the day of the Lord (2 Cor. 5:5).

MEMORIAL TO CHRIST (1 COR. 11:17–26)

Paul was not present at the last meal Jesus shared with his disciples, or at any other meal in the presence of Jesus. Yet Paul knows about the last meal, knows its significance, knows the highly charged words Jesus uttered during the last meal, and hands down the tradition of the meal and the words to his congregation(s) at Corinth:

> For I received from the Lord what I also handed on to you, that the Lord Jesus on the night when he was betrayed took a loaf of bread, and when he had given

Part III: Paul

> thanks, he broke it and said, 'This is my body that is for you. Do this in remembrance of me.' In the same way he took the cup also, after supper, saying, 'This cup is the new covenant in my blood. Do this, as often as you drink it, in remembrance of me.' For as often as you eat this bread and drink the cup, you proclaim the Lord's death until he comes. (1 Cor. 11:23-26)

Whereas baptism was an initiation ritual, a once-for-all experience of inclusion in the *ekklēsia* of Jesus Messiah, the Eucharistic meal of bread and wine was a repeated ritual in which the gathered group participated as one body, and by which they maintained the memory of Jesus crucified in self-sacrifice on behalf of others. The memorial meal was not in celebration of the resurrected Christ, but in memory of the crucified figure of Jesus. That image can easily be forgotten in favor of a victorious Lord *apart from the crucified One.* The reason for the repeated observance of the memorial meal is to "proclaim the Lord's death until he comes."

With respect to the immoral condition in the community of Christ depicted in 1 Corinthians 5, discussed above, genuine participation in the death of Jesus rules out such self-centered passions. Hence Paul's pointed judgment of the community complicit in the immoral man's sin. The memorial ritual of ingesting the bread and wine evokes participation in the saving grace of God in Jesus Messiah crucified, thus uniting the community of Christ in one heart and one mind. Communal remembering has the effect of bringing the redeeming character of the bloody death of Jesus to life in the "body of Christ" on its way to the day of the Lord (1 Cor. 12:27).

Paul also expects the memorial meal of Jesus crucified to eliminate any sign of special privilege in the *ekklēsia*. But privilege and inequality emerged anyway, much to Paul's chagrin. Some members were well-to-do, and ate sumptuously, perhaps separately, while the poorer members fared meagerly. Here is Paul's vivid description of the situation, wrapped in corrective rhetoric:

> For when the time comes to eat, each of you goes ahead with your own supper, and one goes hungry and another becomes drunk. What! Do you not have homes to eat and drink in? Or do you show contempt for the *ekklēsia* of God and humiliate those who have nothing? What should I say to you? Should I commend you? In this matter I do not commend you! (1 Cor. 11:21-22)

Ethnic, social, and gender differences, which Paul recognizes in the Christ-community, can easily threaten the equalizing unity of the Spirit when the image of Jesus Christ crucified is diminished. One effect of the memorial meal of one bread and one wine for all is to eliminate privileged status. Ritual for ritual's sake is worthless. The ritual of eating and drinking in memory of the crucified Jesus, coupled with hearing his word in community, renders the differences inoperative.

Esler correctly highlights "the problem with mixed table fellowship": both Jewish and non-Jewish members eating from the same loaf and drinking from the same cup.[14] "It risked the commission of idolatry in breach of biblical commandments,"[15] even

---

14. Esler, *Galatians*, 93-116.
15. Ibid., 116.

Life Together in the Fellowship of Jesus Messiah

though Paul insisted that his non-Jewish converts in every place separate themselves completely from idolatry when joining the new community of Christ. If Jewish members happened to be present at the celebration of the Eucharist at Corinth, they may have felt the need to eat at separate tables, or even in separate rooms. Yet Paul's corrective language in the Corinthian context aims, not at Judean and non-Judean in the community of Christ, but at socially privileged members in relation to less privileged. The audience at Corinth appears to have been made up of people from the nations, not from the Judeans.

To the point of the memorial meal, the impact of the self-sacrificial death of Jesus is not substitutionary for Paul—making believers exempt from sacrifice—but participatory. Paul speaks in the rhetorical first person on behalf of all participants in Christ: "I have been crucified with Christ" (Gal. 2:19). That mind-set is the way he lives in relation to Christ regardless of his social station, ethnic identity, or geographical location. He calls on all the believers in Rome, for example, to present themselves "as a living sacrifice, holy and acceptable to God," and thus be transformed for the better "by the renewing of [their] minds" (Rom. 12:1–2). "Sacrifice" echoes the practice—current at the time in Judaism—of offering an unblemished commodity that represents the attitude of the worshipper. To offer sacrifice meant allegiance to the holy Other, giving oneself to the cause of the Other, and thus to participate in the good and acceptable and perfect will of God. Paul transposes the well-known practice of sacrifice in the Temple into a self-sacrificial way of living in relation to the crucified Jesus. Repeating the ritual of eating bread and drinking wine and hearing the word of Jesus brings to mind and life that sacrificial attitude and behavior epitomized in the death of Jesus.

EQUAL YET DIFFERENT

At three points in three letters the equal-yet-different scenario comes to the fore. There are other passages, of course, but these three will illustrate Paul's view: Galatians 3:26–29; 1 Corinthians 11:3–16; and 2 Corinthians 8:8–15.

The Equalizing Effect of Baptism (Galatians 3:26–29)

A number of scholars and preachers, eager to promote unity between people, will quote Galatians 3:28: "There is no longer Jew or Greek, there is no longer slave or free, there is no longer male and female; for all of you are one in Christ Jesus." But these few lines belong to the unit that runs from v. 26 to v. 29. As Betz has noted, in this unit of text "we have before us a form of a saying, made up of a number of components, which must have had its place and function in early Christian baptismal liturgy."[16] A bold clue to the baptismal setting appears in one of the lines of the formula at v. 27: "As many of you as were baptized into Christ have clothed yourselves with Christ." Baptism applied to every Christ-believer equally. Everyone entered the new end-time community on the same footing, taking on the same Spirit of the one Jesus Christ from the one God, Israel's God. Paul's comment on the formula leaves no doubt about the connection

---

16. Betz, *Galatians*, 181.

of the new non-Jewish *ekklēsia* with Israel's God and with the Jewish people: "if you belong to Christ, then you are Abraham's offspring, heirs according to the promise" (3:29). That makes the new people of Messiah equal with their Jewish counterparts who are also Abraham's "heirs according to promise."

We come now to the much-quoted v. 28 (above). The text depicts differences in the human family along three main lines. The first is ethnic, Judean or Greek, or the Jewish people and all others. Within each of the two broad categories are smaller groupings. From Paul's Jewish perspective the two categories were real. The second is social-cultural, slave or free. Again, this was an overarching social reality of the time. Within each category further differences could be cited. For example, not all free people were rich, and not all slaves were necessarily poor. The third duality is gender, male and female. This difference was not simply biological; it was socially conditioned as well. Males were considered the socially dominant gender in the two-gendered society. The book of Genesis in the Jewish Torah, underwrites the socio-cultural difference attached to gender difference. God tells the primordial woman, "your desire shall be for your husband, and he shall rule over you" (Gen. 3:16). Unfortunately for women who followed, men took over that word of God and used it too freely and too often to dominate women, particularly their wives. The word of Paul to people of Christ is a liberating word, a life-giving and equalizing word. Differences remain in the *ekklēsia* of Christ, to be sure. But the ethnic, social, and gender differences no longer carry advantage for one member over another, because "all . . . are one in Christ Jesus."

Equal Opportunity to Lead in Worship (1 Cor. 11:3–16)

The full passage of 1 Corinthians 11:3–16 is too long to quote here. Its subject and argument focus on head covering for women-prophets, as compared to no head covering for men-prophets. Textured into the argument is the assumption that both women and men in the community of Jesus Messiah prophesy and pray equally; that is, lead in worship and teaching. The question Paul presses in his complex rhetoric has to do with how the women and men *appear* within the worshipping community. While the two pray and prophesy equally, their gender identity has to be maintained, so the argument implies. There is no suggestion that the women-prophets should consult with the men-prophets before they speak in the worship setting (cf. 1 Cor. 14:34–35 and the discussion below). Head covering is the issue. And it appears that the women prophets in Corinth are the ones in default.

Antoinette Wire's analysis and insight on this passage are worth noting.[17] One question, difficult to answer adequately, is why the women prophets chose to pray and prophesy with their heads uncovered? Wire suggests that the "theological weight of Paul's argument makes it likely that the women who prophesied uncovered chose to do so for some purpose with social consequences and theological justification."[18] The

---

17. Wire, *Women Prophets*, 116–34.
18. Ibid., 123.

women may have developed a new self-understanding growing out of their baptismal confession: "no longer male and female . . . all one in Christ Jesus" (Gal. 3:28).

Wire's judgment that "the baptismal confession developed from Genesis as a new creation story," and that the women prophets' "confession of a new creation indicates a concern to state how male and female are related in the same way to Christ as God's image" has some merit. But she speaks too confidently on behalf of the charismatic women whose historic voice is scarcely audible within Paul's rhetoric. He is not trying to silence them in the worship setting, but to instruct them to lead as authentic women prophets. True enough, Paul echoes parts of Genesis 1 and 2 in his argument—especially about the "image of God" and "man was not made from woman, but woman from man," but that does not mean that the women prophets at Corinth were also interpreting the Genesis story from a different premise and with a different result. Whatever their reasons for their uncovered heads, the women prophets earned a place in Paul's corrective rhetoric, but only on the matter of head covering while carrying out their spiritual leadership in the congregation. Paul does not instruct them to hand over the leadership to the men. Both the women and the men pray and prophesy equally, but their gender identity remains as a matter of course for the present time.

Surrounding Paul's plea in this passage for women and men to lead honorably in worship are his instructions about eating food offered to idols, with the possibility of becoming idolatrous, on one side (1 Cor. 10), and eating and drinking at the Lord's table "in an unworthy manner" on the other (1 Cor. 11:17–33). All three arguments are about conduct related to worship. Some parts of Paul's argument about the proper way for men and women to pray and prophesy in worship are nothing short of weird to modern thinking: by covering her head a woman honors the man; by covering his head the man dishonors Christ; if a woman does not wear a head covering she might as well shave off her hair; a woman ought to have "authority" on her head "because of the angels;" nature itself teaches a man not to have long hair. Behind all of the overreaching rhetoric is the simple plea for the two human-gendered leader-groups to dress appropriately when they lead in worship.

As noted above, Paul alludes to Genesis 1:27 where he finds the man in the "image of God," except that he sells the Genesis text rather short in favor of his argument. In Genesis 1:27 the "image of God" applies to both male and female inclusively, not the man exclusively. Paul also argues in this passage from a notion of a hierarchy of headship: God is the head of Christ, Christ is the head of a man, and the man is the head of the woman. All of this headship language is to ensure that women wear a head covering when they pray and prophesy, and that men do not. This is when I call to mind a handy guideline that E. P. Sanders taught us students in a graduate seminar: *distinguish between the parts of Paul's argument and his reason for making the argument*. The two may not correspond logically. I believe Paul's bottom line supports equal opportunity for women and men to lead in worship, provided both conform to an accepted social norm of the time. Neither the men prophets nor the women prophets are privileged in the end.

Part III: Paul

Remarkably, at the end of his argument about headship hierarchy in favor of head covering for women prophets and not for men, Paul suddenly reinstates his equality theme: "Nevertheless, in the Lord woman is not independent of man or man independent of woman. For just as woman came from man, so man comes through woman; but all things come from God" (11:11–12). He ultimately passes the baton to the prophets themselves, men and women, to judge concerning head covering from their knowledge of an assumed social practice (11:13–16).

Someone should be asking by now, What about Paul's prohibitive word at First Corinthians 14:34–35 against women speaking in the community of Christ?

> Women should be silent in the churches. For they are not permitted to speak, but should be subordinate, as the law also says. If there is anything they desire to know, let them ask their husbands at home. For it is shameful for a woman to speak in church.

To my mind, there are only two possible explanations for such an obtrusive boulder in the middle of an otherwise level pathway: (1) someone other than Paul wrote this command under Paul's name years after his death and inserted it into a copy of First Corinthians, or (2) Paul is completely inconsistent in his thought and letter writing. In the same letter he equalized the conjugal rights between husband and wife, 7:2–5, permitted either the husband or wife to separate, 7:14–15, and sanctioned the equal right of women and men to speak publicly in the congregation, 11:3–16. Then suddenly at chapter 14 he admonishes women to be silent in the congregation, and to ask their husbands questions at home. Wire believes the historical Paul wrote this text, effectively "silencing [women's] voices in the community."[19] I, rather, share the view of Neil Elliott that this restrictive command to the congregation at Corinth is "an interpolation made by someone sharing the views of the author of 1 Timothy,"[20] who enjoins women to "learn in silence with full submission" in a worship setting (1 Tim. 2:11–15). First Timothy was written at least a generation or more after the historical Paul, at a time when the Christ-communities were building conservative walls around themselves to keep out "heresy."

Even though there is no direct manuscript evidence supporting the view that 1 Corinthians 14:34–35 was added by a later copyist, the internal evidence points strongly in that direction. Furthermore, that text appears at different places in some manuscripts of First Corinthians. This fact is at least one piece of external evidence. I suggest, moreover, that this restrictive text was inserted into a manuscript in the second century, and persisted in the manuscript tradition to the present time, to the detriment of women, and of the historical Paul.

A Fair Balance in the Eschatological Economy of the Faithful (2 Corinthians 8–9)

Paul did not accept money from his Corinthian congregation for his own support in mission. Why he refused is a bit of a mystery. When the Corinthian believers (or their

---

19. Ibid., 17.
20. Elliott, *Liberating*, 52.

Life Together in the Fellowship of Jesus Messiah

leaders) criticized Paul for his refusal, he replied: it could become "an obstacle in the way of the gospel of Christ" (1 Cor. 9:12); "I will not be a burden" (2 Cor. 12:14); "I love you more" (2 Cor. 12:15). But when it comes to collecting money for others, Paul urges his congregations to give up some of their financial resources to help the poor.

But the collection for the poor is designated for a particular group of poor people. The poor are not those down the street. Presumably there were poor in the cities where Paul preached, and poor members in the congregations he formed in the name of Christ. But the poor Paul has in mind are "the poor among the saints at Jerusalem" (Rom. 15:25). His double argument in 2 Corinthians 8 and 9 pleads with the non-Jewish believers in Jesus Messiah to share their resources with their Jewish counterparts in the Holy City, so that there will be "a fair balance between your present abundance and their need, so that their abundance may be for your need, in order that there may be a fair balance" (2 Cor. 8:14).

Ironically, the Corinthians probably had greater financial resources than their neighbors to the north in Macedonia, yet the Macedonian believers had already contributed liberally without Paul's strong persuasion (2 Cor. 8:1-2). According to Strabo, "Corinth is called 'wealthy' because of its commerce, since it is situated on the Isthmus and is master of two harbors, of which the one leads straight to Asia, and the other to Italy; and it makes easy the exchange of merchandise from both countries that are so far distant from each other."[21]

Why the "saints" in Jerusalem were poor is not known exactly. They may have lost their jobs because of their new confession of Jesus as the Messiah crucified. Paul's concern, however, goes beyond providing for their need: they are Judeans located in the Holy City. Paul's determination to bring together a collection of money from the non-Jewish congregations for the Jewish congregation in Jerusalem has an unmistakable ring to it. When he and his colleagues eventually travel to Jerusalem with the "generous undertaking" (*charis* = grace) from the nations of the world they are bringing the nations symbolically into Zion in fulfillment of prophecy (Isa. 66:18; cf. 2:2; Hag. 2:6-9). "Moreover, the collected money was not merely pragmatic relief for the impoverished of Jerusalem, but was as well an offering representing the [nations] who believed the word of the gospel of Jesus Christ, God's agent of salvation whom Paul preached."[22]

Nowhere in Paul's letters is this eschatological ministry of bringing an offering from the nations to Jerusalem so pronounced as in Romans 15. Paul describes himself and his mission to Jerusalem as:

> a minister of Christ Jesus to the Gentiles in the priestly service of the gospel of God, so that the offering of the Gentiles may be acceptable, sanctified by the Holy Spirit. At present, however, I am going to Jerusalem in a ministry to the saints; for Macedonia and Achaia have been pleased to share their resources with the poor among the saints at Jerusalem . . . Join me in earnest prayer . . . that I

---

21. Strabo, *Geography* 8:6.20.
22. Shillington, *2 Corinthians*, 262.

may be rescued from the unbelievers in Judea, and that my ministry to Jerusalem may be acceptable to the saints. (Rom. 15:16–31)

So, the "fair balance" is not merely an equalizing of material resources between rich and poor. That factor is in play, of course, as Paul affirms by his appeal to the story of the Israelites gathering manna in the wilderness: "the one who had much did not have too much, and the one who had little did not have too little." (2 Cor. 8:15; cf. Ex. 16:18). The "fair balance" is also between Judean and non-Judean believers in Jesus Messiah. Paul took a great risk in going to Jerusalem. His radical message and practice among the nations had reached the ears of the Jewish religious elite in Jerusalem. Undeterred by the prospect of recrimination, Paul delivered the "offering of the nations" to the heart of Judaism, and by so doing gathered his non-Jewish congregations into the covenant people of God in the name of Jesus Messiah. This is further evidence that Paul sought to ensure his non-Jewish congregations had equal status with the Judean congregations worshipping in the Temple-city of Jerusalem.

To sum up, Paul the Apostle of Jesus Messiah was a liberator and an equalizer at heart. Yet he expected members of the new communities of Jesus Christ to join him in being "crucified with Christ" (Gal. 2:19), in becoming "slaves of righteousness" (Rom. 6:18), not "slaves of impurity" (Rom 6:19) or "slaves of sin" (Rom. 6:20). He appealed to his Jewish Scriptures to guide the called-out groups to right living, and trusted the Spirit of Jesus Messiah to empower the members to live upright lives. When a sexually immoral person entered the community, thus making the whole group impure, Paul drew on his Jewish tradition, especially the Atonement and Passover rituals, to pass sentence on the immoral man in a bid to save the community for the "day of the Lord."

Far from having come to a temporal end with the coming of Jesus Christ, the Law of God was renewed in Christ, fulfilled and embodied in him, and summarized in the command to love one's neighbor as one's self. In so doing the community fulfils the "just requirement of the law" (Rom. 8:4), having been justified (or righteoused) by faith in the faithful self-sacrifice of Jesus Christ crucified.

Effectively, the Spirit of the crucified Jesus eliminates privileged status from among the members of the new community. By virtue of eating the consecrated bread and drinking the consecrated wine together in memory of Jesus' death until he comes, the community-life in the Spirit of Christ is renewed and maintained. "Whoever, therefore, eats the bread or drinks the cup of the Lord in an unworthy manner will be answerable for the body and blood of the Lord" (1 Cor. 11:27).

Paul recognized ethnic, social, and gender differences among the members, but promoted equality and unity in relation to Christ Jesus in the midst of the diversity. Women could lead in prayer and preaching as women, and equally so the men as men. Similarly, Paul brought the equalizing gospel to its zenith by bringing the offering of the nations into the Holy City, thus uniting Judean believers with non-Judeans, rich Corinthians with "the poor among the saints at Jerusalem" (Rom 15:26), and all in the name of Jesus Messiah: "that there may be a fair balance" (2 Cor. 8:14).

15

Universal Restoration

God, Israel, and the Nations

ONE MORE PAULINE PUZZLE REMAINS TO BE RESOLVED. THE FINAL WORD HAS not yet been spoken to everyone's satisfaction, after numerous attempts. Nor do I expect to reach such finality in this chapter. Perhaps more than any of the other puzzles of Paul, this one presents a formidable challenge. I refer to the "mystery" that Paul names as such in Romans 11:25, and tries to unveil in his three distinctive chapters of Romans 9–11. The mystery, in brief, concerns God's plan for gathering the nations into end-time salvation in concert with historic Israel through whom God's promised restoration reaches the world.

Here are some key questions that Paul's rhetoric in 9–11 raises: Are there two Israels, remnant-Israel that believes in Jesus as Messiah, and the rest of Israel that does not? Will God unite believers from the nations with remnant Israel to make one Israel from the two? To what extent do the gifts and election promises of God to ancient Israel remain in effect in relation to historic Israel? What is meant by "the fullness of the nations" and "all Israel" (11:25–26)?

THE RHETORICAL LANDSCAPE OF PAUL'S LETTER TO THE CONGREGATIONS IN ROME

Jacob Jervell proposed that the purpose of Romans should be explored with reference to Jerusalem. Paul makes plain at the end of Romans that he is preparing to go to Jerusalem with the collection of money from the non-Jewish congregations of Achaia and Macedonia before going to Rome and Spain (Rom. 15:24–25, 28). "The impending trip to Jerusalem and his relationship to the church there are forcing Paul to devote full attention to matters which he only hinted at in earlier letters."[1] In particular, he faces the prospect in Jerusalem of having to account for his attitude to the Torah, his incorporation of non-Jewish people into covenant relationship with Abraham without

---

1. Jervell, "Jerusalem," 59.

Part III: Paul

becoming proselytes to Judaism in the usual way, his view of historic Israel in relation to faith in Jesus Messiah, among other matters. In a sense, then, his letter to the Romans is a way of preparing himself for his defense in Jerusalem, if he should be called to account there.

Up front, though, the letter is addressed to "all God's beloved in Rome" (1:7). One does not have to look far in the letter to find Paul's understanding of his intended readership, otherwise called the implied readers, or rhetorical readers. His stated aim is "to bring about the obedience of faith among all the Gentiles for the sake of [Christ's] name, including yourselves" (1:5–6; also 11:13, 17–18, 21). Paul had not visited Rome before writing his long letter, yet he seems to know about a boastful attitude among the non-Jewish Christ-followers over their Jewish counterparts in the city. Using the analogy of the cultured olive tree as representative of historic Israel, Paul warns his imagined non-Jewish audience: "If you do boast, remember that it is not you that support the root, but the root that supports you" (11:18). With respect to the priority of Israel in God's plan for the world, Campbell's observation that chapter 3 is "the structural center of the letter"[2] as a whole is well founded. The proposition, argument and intertexture of that chapter "is none other than the good news of the fulfillment of God's promises to Israel. Paul's gospel did not originate in a vacuum, it has a pre-history."[3] The center of gravity in Romans 3, around which the rhetorical texture of that chapter takes shape, reads as follows:

> But now, apart from law, the righteousness of God has been disclosed, and is attested by the law and the prophets, the righteousness of God through [the faithfulness of][4] Jesus Christ for all who believe. For there is no distinction, since all have sinned and fall short of the glory of God; they are now justified by his grace as a gift, through the redemption that is in Christ Jesus, whom God put forward as a sacrifice of atonement by his blood, effective through faith. He did this to show his righteousness, because in his divine forbearance he had passed over the sins previously committed; it was to prove at the present time that he himself is righteous and that he justifies the one who has faith in Jesus. (Rom. 3:21–26)

"The justice of God" is the driving force behind and within the operation of restoring the whole human family, all of it "attested by the law and the prophets" of Israel.

Of the three large blocks of rhetorical and theological material in Romans that carry this major theme of God's righteous restoration (chapters 1–8, 9–11, and 12–16), the argument in Romans 9–11 brings the theme into sharp focus for the congregations in Rome—especially the boastful non-Jewish groups—and prospectively also before the Jewish leaders in Jerusalem when he delivers the "offering of the nations" there (15:16). Those three chapters unveil the mystery of God's plan, with Israel being the agent through whom, and to whom, God's end-time restoration comes.

The first eight chapters pave the way for the difficult questions raised in 9–11, and the last four chapters (12–16) work out the implications for life in the multi-cultural

---

2. Campbell, "Romans 3," 257.
3. Ibid., 254.
4. See chapter 13 regarding "the faithfulness of Jesus Christ."

community of Christ before the restoration project is complete. Meanwhile, "the whole creation has been groaning in labor pains until now; and not only the creation, but we ourselves, who have the first fruits of the Spirit, groan inwardly while we wait for adoption, the redemption of our bodies" (8:22–23). It would be worthwhile to focus other principal features of the first eight chapters before attempting to sort out Paul's complex argumentation in chs. 9–11.

Perhaps the best place to begin is with the formula Paul elicits for carrying out the divine plan for the world: *the Judean first and also the Greek*. Stated only in Romans (1:16; 2:9), the formula appears first at 1:16–17: "For I am not ashamed of the gospel; it is the power of God for salvation to everyone who has faith, to the Jew first and also to the Greek. For in it the righteousness of God is revealed through faith for faith; as it is written, 'The one who is righteous will live by faith.'"

Using the schema of Acts—written many years after Romans—Nanos views the formula as Paul's two-step pattern of bringing the gospel of Jesus Christ to the cities of the Greco-Roman world. "Paul's apostolic ministry maintained the continuity of salvation history: the gospel brings Israel's restoration first, only then as a representative of restored Israel did Paul turn fully to bring light to the gentiles."[5] Acts does indeed have Paul go to the synagogues first when he enters a city, except that the members of the synagogues in Acts reject Paul's message. Their rejection moves Paul of Acts to go to the nations instead. Here are examples of the pattern in Acts (emphases added):

- Acts 13:46: "Paul and Barnabas spoke out boldly, saying, 'It was necessary that the word of God should be spoken first to you [Judeans]. Since you reject it and judge yourselves to be unworthy of eternal life, *we are now turning to the Gentiles.*'"

- Acts 18:6 "When they [the Judeans] opposed and reviled him [Paul], in protest he shook the dust from his clothes and said to them, 'Your blood be on your own heads! I am innocent. *From now on I will go to the Gentiles.*'"

- Acts 22:21: [Paul, in a trance in Jerusalem, heard Jesus say to him]: 'They [the Judeans] will not accept your testimony of me . . . Go, for *I will send you far away to the Gentiles.*'"

- Acts 28:28: "Let it be known to you [Judeans in Rome] then that *this salvation of God has been sent to the Gentiles; they will listen.*"

To my mind, Acts of late first-century composition, is not the place to turn to understand Paul's use of "Judean first and also Greek" in Romans. Paul's abiding conviction is that Israel has priority in the plan of salvation, that Jesus crucified and raised was God's faithful Israelite, that the first witnesses after Jesus were all Israelites preaching to Israelites, that Paul as an Israelite brings the gospel to the nations, and that "all Israel will be saved." I doubt that the author of Acts held the same conviction in the same way at the end of the first century when the Jesus-movement had become largely non-Jewish. I submit, rather, that Paul of Romans uses the Jew-first-and-also-Greek

---

5. Nanos, *Mystery*, 272.

Part III: Paul

formula in the broad salvation-historical sense, and also in the plainly historical sense noted above, all in an effort to persuade his non-Jewish audience in Rome to welcome their Jewish counterparts as members of the elect people of Israel through whom God plans to save the world: "Welcome one another, therefore, just as Christ has welcomed you, for the glory of God" (Rom. 15:7). Within the plan, thus formulated, Paul understands the aim of his specific call to be the proclamation of the gospel about Jesus to the non-Jewish nations: "Inasmuch then as I am an apostle to the Gentiles, I glorify my ministry" (Rom. 11:13). Paul was "entrusted with the gospel for the uncircumcised, just as Peter had been entrusted with the gospel for the circumcised" (Gal. 2:7). The eschatological priority thus pertains, "Judean first and also the Greek." Peter and his fellow apostles were the first to proclaim the gospel of Jesus to their fellow Judeans; Paul and his colleagues took the good news to the nations thereafter.

Oddly enough, immediately after setting forth his Judean-first-and-also-Greek formula, Paul presents God's case against the people of the nations *first* (1:18-32), and *then* also the case against the Judeans (2:1-29). Both groups stand indicted by divine decree. Strikingly, Paul creates an imaginary Jewish interlocutor, presumably because the case against the Jewish people is rather more complicated. Paul is aware of their status as the elect people of God. So, he asks, "Then what advantage has the Jew? Or what is the value of circumcision?" Answer: "Much, in every way." They were "entrusted with the oracles of God," and even if they are found unfaithful, God remains faithful to the promise made to them (Rom 3:1-3). Even so, Paul still renders his verdict "that all, both Jews and Greeks, are under the power of sin" (3:9). The human plight is universal, but God's restoration project is also universal, as the remaining chapters of Romans explain variously. Note, it is "God's restoration project," so that no one can boast of privileged status in the end, neither Israel nor the other nations. Even though Israel was entrusted with the oracles of God, "it is God who justifies," not the oracles (Rom. 8:33).

Chapter 4 illustrates the point by presenting the patriarch Abraham as the paradigmatic type of the ungodly person from the nations who exercises faith in God, and is thereby reckoned righteous by God as a gift. Paul's conviction that guides his argument in chapter 4 is that righteousness before God is attained apart from circumcision. Arguing from the chronology in Genesis, he adduces that Abraham was already justified *before* he was circumcised. Circumcision was merely a seal of the righteousness reckoned by faith prior to, and apart from circumcision (Rom. 4:9-12).

Chapter 5 continues to emphasize the gift of God's righteousness through the death of Christ "for the ungodly," thus proving God's "love for us in that while we yet sinners Christ died for us" (5:1-11). Then the figure of Adam enters as a "type of the coming one" (5:14-21; cf. 1 Cor. 15:20-27). "The coming one" is an eschatological label, implying another Adam to undo sin, condemnation, and death brought into the human family by the first Adam. The one essential characteristic that the two Adams share is their humanness (*anthrōpos*), God's creation in God's image (Gen. 1:27). The second Adam, Jesus Messiah, restores the image by his righteous act through which sin and death are cancelled by the justifying grace of God in Christ. Again, the whole operation is God's doing, apart from the works of the Law. That does not make the works of the Law invalid for Paul. It simply means that the Law does not give life to sin-bound humanity. "For if a law had been given that could make alive, then righteousness would indeed come through the law" (Gal. 3:21). The structure of the sentence implies that no such law exists. God gives life through the justifying grace of God in Jesus Christ.

Chapters 6 and 7 continue the same line of thought. Human beings all, both Judeans and Greeks, are slaves of sin, unable to free themselves. Even the "holy and just and good" Law is not the redeemer-savior. God is. To make his point, especially for his non-Jewish readers, Paul takes on the persona of a human being striving in his/her own way to live an upright life. By his pervasive use of "I" (*egō*) in 7:7–24 Paul draws himself rhetorically into the struggle of every human being related to the first Adam to obtain righteousness before God. The futility running throughout the passage is not the last word, and certainly not a description of Paul's personal experience of faith in the faithful Jesus Christ. Far from being a picture of "life in Christ Jesus," Romans 7:7–24 is yet another rhetorical picture of the human predicament. The solution, by comparison, is made abundantly visible in chapter 8.

Chapter 8 describes three aspects of the work of God in Christ for the sake of the human family: the present experience of life in the Spirit of Christ awaiting God's finale (vv. 1–17); a vision of a bright future not only for the human family but also for the whole ruptured creation (vv. 18–30); and an encouraging reminder of the boundless love of God in Christ Jesus on behalf of the elect (vv. 31–39). A word about the first part must suffice to bring the present discussion to a close.

The language of Romans 8:1–17 is assuring and promising, and places the Torah in its rightful place in relation to Christ in the life of believers, especially those from the nations. Rather than risk muffling Paul's poignant language with my discourse, I think it best to lift out leading lines of thought to accent Paul's vision of the solution to the human condition in preparation for God's great dénouement on behalf of the world:

- "there is therefore now no condemnation for those who are in Christ Jesus" (v. 1);
- "the law of the Spirit of life in Christ Jesus has set you free from the law of sin and of death" (v. 2);
- "you are not in the flesh; you are in the Spirit, since the Spirit of God dwells in you" (v. 9);
- "he who raised Christ from the dead will give life to your mortal bodies also through his Spirit that dwells in you" (v. 11);
- "all who are led by the Spirit of God are children of God" (v. 14);
- "you have received a spirit of adoption" (v. 15);
- "we suffer with [Christ] so that we may also be glorified with him" (v. 17).

Part III: Paul

THE DESTINY OF ISRAEL AND THE NATIONS IN THE MYSTERIOUS PLAN OF GOD

I cannot think of a more promising passage in Paul's letters than Romans 9–11, and at the same time a more problematic one. The problem, as usual, is one of interpretation. A scan of the secondary sources attests to a lack of consensus on the precise meaning of Paul's terms of reference. Traditional Christian interpretation has held that Paul envisions a "new Israel," or "true Israel," that includes believers in Jesus from both historic Israel and the other nations. This "new Israel" then becomes "the church" to be saved at the end of the present age. A variation on this interpretation has "all Israel" saved by faith in Jesus Christ at the end of the age, without necessarily joining the Christ-community consisting of people from the nations. Toews attempts to nuance the traditional reading of 11:25–26: "The Gentiles first and then the Jews for Paul represents universality, the fulfillment of God's plan to reconcile Jew and Gentile into a single Israel."[6] But this reading casts the name "Israel" in a mold unfamiliar to Paul, or any other Jewish thinker of the time. Such a "spiritual interpretation associated with 'covenant theology' which takes 'all Israel' to be the full complement of the church of Jews and Gentiles can be dismissed."[7]

In 1976 Stendhal broke from this traditional Christian interpretation by proposing that Paul envisioned, in Romans 9–11, a separate path for the salvation of Israel. "It should be noted," he states, "that Paul does not say that when the time of God's kingdom, the consummation, comes Israel will accept Jesus as the Messiah. He says only that the time will come when 'all Israel will be saved.'"[8] Since 1976 a number of interpreters have developed, and modified, Stendhal's perspective.[9]

A comprehensive debate of the secondary sources on the topic and texts would not serve a worthwhile purpose here. That is not to suggest that my reading of the pertinent texts of Romans 9–11 will be final and absolute. Far from it. It will still be an interpretation, but one that grows out of the discussions in the preceding chapters concerning Paul's thought and activity in world mission. My approach will be to engage relevant, and often difficult, terms of reference *leading up to* the critical text of 11:25–26 and others *growing out of* it.

A Lament over Historic Israel (9:1–5)

The opening of chapter 9 is clearly a lament over Israel's refusal to recognize Jesus Messiah crucified and raised. But it is more than that. It is an expression of Paul's personal anguish over the increasing number of non-Jewish believers compared to the relatively limited response from the Jewish people. "I have great sorrow and unceasing anguish in my heart," he says. "For I could wish that I myself were accursed (*anathema*) and cut off from Christ for the sake of my own people, my kindred according

---

6. Toews, *Romans*, 282.
7. Zerbe, "Jews and Gentiles," 26.
8. Stendhal, *Paul*, 4.
9. E.g., Campbell, *Paul's Gospel*; Nanos, *Mystery*; Jewett, *Romans*; Eisenbaum, *Paul*.

to the flesh" (9:3-4). One hears an echo of Moses' cry of lament to God on behalf of the Israelites, that God would forgive their sin (Ex. 32:32). Two matters are beyond dispute in Paul's text: he identifies himself as an Israelite, and as a believer in Jesus, Messiah of Israel. His quandary, related to his angst, casts his own call and mission in a strange light. Why are people of the nations coming to faith in the faithful Israelite, Jesus Messiah, and the Jewish people largely passing up God's offer to save the world through Israel's faithful representative, Jesus? Quandary and anguish or not, one conviction remains firm for Paul: "the irreducible core of my identity making my apostleship a reality is that I am a Jew, a member of God's people Israel."[10]

The rest of the argument to the end of chapter 11 takes the reader along a circuitous route to the climax at 11:25-26: "I want you to understand this mystery: a hardening has come upon part of Israel, until the full number of the Gentiles has come in. And so all Israel will be saved." A few important stops should be made along the way before arriving at that destination.

What to Make of the Remnant (9:27; 11:5, 15:16)

Paul did not invent the idea of remnant. The concept is deeply embedded in Israelite prophetic tradition, made evident by Paul's incorporation of Isaiah 10:22-23 to make his point: "Though the number of the children of Israel were like the sand of the sea, only a remnant of them will be saved" (9:27). But what is his point? Does he imply that Jewish believers in Jesus are the remnant of Israel, the group that now constitutes Israel? Given Paul's complete commitment to the justice of God in the death and resurrection of Jesus he doubtless believes the remnant of Israel to be Jewish believers in Jesus. But one must ask Paul then, are the others no longer Israel? Judging from the language of 9:1-5 Paul continues to view the Jewish people as "Israel." If that is so it raises the question for him about the justice of God who made a promise to that people above all other nations. "Is there injustice on God's part?" Paul asks. He answers with his strong denial formula: "By no means!" (9:14).

Furthermore, Paul must have known other texts of his prophetic scriptures where the remnant is representative of Israel: because there is a remnant, Israel as Israel is preserved; the divine promise to Israel as a people is kept, and divine justice maintained. Take Jeremiah's jubilant remnant song, for example: "Sing aloud with gladness for Jacob, and raise shouts for the chief of the nations; proclaim, give praise, and say, "Save, O LORD, your people, the remnant of Israel." The line-up of terms here is significant: "Jacob," patriarch after whom the nation was called; "chief of the nations," namely the elect nation of Israel; "your people," a corporate designation of the members of Israel; and "remnant of Israel." All of the terms in the string point to the same entity, the same people, Israel. Surely Paul knows such texts as this one in Jeremiah.

This remnant-on-behalf-of-the-whole idea comes to its sharpest expression at Romans 11:15-16: "For if their rejection is the reconciliation of the world, what will their acceptance be but life from the dead! If the part of the dough offered as first fruits

---

10. Stowers, *Rereading*, 293.

is holy, then the whole batch is holy; and if the root is holy, then the branches also are holy."

"Their rejection" does not mean God's rejection of his people, but *their* rejection of something, the identity of which Paul takes as a given among his non-Jewish readers. It is probably safe to assume Paul implies the rejection of the message of Jesus Messiah that Paul and colleagues preach. What is striking is Paul's belief that "their rejection" facilitates "the reconciliation of the world." If that is the role of their rejection, Paul argues, imagine what their acceptance will be: "life from the dead!" Their acceptance is not in doubt here. In case his readers might think so, Paul uses two metaphors to prove otherwise: the holy character of the first fruits guarantees the same for the whole; the holy character of the root of a tree guarantees the same for the branches. Given this idea of the remnant, Paul envisions end-time salvation, not for a portion of the people of Israel, but for the whole of Israel, and that because of the remnant.

Yet he does have anguish in his heart for his people. I suggest that his anguish for those Jewish people who have not accepted Jesus comes from his own experience of knowing Jesus Messiah. Why can they not see as he sees, understand as he does? Still, his anguish does not stop him from citing the divine favor bestowed on the people of Israel, represented in Second Temple Judaism: "They are Israelites, and to them belong the adoption, the glory, the covenants, the giving of the law, the worship, and the promises; to them belong the patriarchs, and from them, according to the flesh, comes the Messiah, who is over all, God blessed forever. Amen." This is no trifling statement. It is a benediction, a eulogy to God for all the good wrapped up in one people, Israel, for the sake of the world. What he states as the status of Israel in the divine economy he believes to be true under God. Hence the Amen, the Yes of God. Paul is glad for the remnant "chosen by grace" (11:5), of which he is a member, for through the remnant God works out the divine plan to save the world, including especially Israel.

Stumbling and Hardening

Paul uses these two images to describe Israel's present state within the divine plan. First the stumbling. At two points in his exposition of the mystery Paul describes Israel's condition as a misstep, or tripping on the path toward the final salvation. As with all imaginative language, the image of stumbling could conjure up a picture of a person falling flat on their face, thus disqualifying them from the race. It is likely that Paul has a marathon in view as he writes. The question the image poses regarding Israel is this: Has their stumbling disqualified God's people from the race toward their full and final restoration? Paul's strong negative reply again is unequivocal: "By no means" (*mē genoito*, 11:11); "Perish the thought!"

The strong negative at 11:11 is not so strong at 9:32–33 where Paul cites a prophecy from Isaiah (28:16; 8:14): "See, I am laying in Zion a stone that will make people stumble, a rock that will make them fall, and whoever believes in him will not be put to shame." According to this translation Israel's stumbling will result in a fall that will eliminate Israel from the race toward the prize. But is the NRSV true to the Greek text in Paul's quotation? It appears not! The "rock that will make them fall" comes from only two Greek words, *petran* (rock) *skandalou* (of offense). How the NRSV translators came up with the notion of a stumbling that will make Israel fall is a mystery—another mystery! God is responsible for putting the rock in the way. Was the divine aim to make Israel fall? That would make God unjust, but Paul has ruled out that possibility absolutely! (9:14).

The word *skandalon*, from which comes the English "scandal," appears also at 1 Corinthians 1:23: "we proclaim Christ crucified, a stumbling block (*skandalon*) to Jews." There is nothing here about stumbling "that will make them fall." The sense of the word in 1 Corinthians 1:23 is "offense." The same sense should come through at Romans 9:33, as it does in a number of major translations: "rock of offense" (KJV, ASV, NASB), "a rock that offends people" (CEB), "a rock to stumble against" (NEB). One of the most revered lexicons of the Greek New Testament gives three possible meanings of the word from the literature of the period: (1) a trap, (2) temptation or enticement, (3) that which gives offense or causes revulsion.[11] There is nothing at all in the lexicon about falling. It makes one wonder, then, what would lead some translators to view the rock on the path as leading inevitably to a fall.

They may have taken their cue from Paul's "note" at 11:22: "Note then the kindness and the severity of God: severity toward those who have fallen, but God's kindness toward you, provided you continue in his kindness." How strange this sounds! A few paragraphs earlier Paul rules out Israel's fall categorically. Observe that "severity" and "kindness" are juxtaposed, as in God's judgment and mercy. At the moment Israel has "fallen" under God's judgment. That does not make Israel extinct, never to be restored to God's favor. Nor does it imply that Israel has become apostate, fallen away from their historic faith in their Redeemer-God. Remember, "all Israel will be saved." What, then, can Paul mean by his turn of phrase, "those who have fallen"? Recalling the strong negation of Israel's fall at 11:11, "the phrase means 'those who have not believed.'"[12]

Consider more closely the text of 11:11. "So I ask, have they stumbled so as to fall? *By no means!* But through their stumbling salvation has come to the Gentiles, so as to make Israel jealous." Jealousy is hardly the purist motive for gaining salvation. Apparently Paul thinks "Israel's stumbling would arouse in [them] a jealousy of the Gentiles, who were attaining the uprightness before God that Israel had been pursuing."[13] A variation on the motivation appears at 11:13-14. As an apostle to the nations, Paul states, "I glorify my ministry in order to make my own people jealous, and thus save some of them." So, it is his ministry—presumably successful ministry—that will lead to Israel's jealousy. The goal in this instance is limited: to save "some of them," but not "all Israel" as in 11:26. The difference between the limited and the inclusive view could be between the interim and the end. In the interim, while Paul's

---

11. Arndt and Gingrich, *Lexicon*, 760.
12. Fitzmyer, *Romans*, 616.
13. Ibid., 611.

Part III: Paul

mission to the nations is still ongoing, some of Paul's own people will be saved along with the people from the nations, and then at the end when the mission is complete "all Israel will be saved."

Far from making Israel fall—and thus fail to gain God's salvation—their stumbling opens the way for the people of the nations to accept God's gift of salvation. Their acceptance, in turn, will cause part of Israel to want to catch up and receive the same salvation of God. In all of Paul's theologizing about the way Israel will be saved, the figure of Jesus Christ is very much behind the scenes. However, "the God and Father of our Lord Jesus Christ" (15:6) is the principal actor in the grand eschatological drama with respect to Israel's destiny. That same "God and Father" is Israel's God, and takes responsibility for bringing the elect people to final salvation. "For Paul, Israel's salvation was never in doubt."[14]

Now, what about the "hardening" that "has come upon part of Israel" (11:25)? It cannot mean a petrifying effect. The traditional interpretation of the metaphor believes it to be Israel's hardness of heart, a pejorative reading echoing a displacement theology: the Church has displaced Israel. But that phrase is not in the text, and should therefore not be imposed upon Paul's one Greek word (*pōrōsis*). Nanos argues for a more therapeutic English word, given the context of the "healing" of the broken/damaged branches of the olive tree. "If Paul meant 'callus,' . . . it would offer a more positive and arguably more salient choice that has to do with the healing and protecting process that takes place after an injury has occurred."[15] Keeping this positive possibility in mind, it is noteworthy that God is credited with the hardening process. "Israel failed to obtain what it was seeking. The elect obtained it, but the rest were hardened, as it is written, 'God gave them a sluggish spirit, eyes that would not see and ears that would not hear, down to this very day'" (11:7–8). Again, the justice of God is not in question: there is a holy and just purpose for the hardening.

Paul has already elicited the "hardening" of the Pharaoh of Egypt, recorded in Torah, leading up to the freeing of the Hebrew slaves. "For the scripture says to Pharaoh, 'I have raised you up for the very purpose of showing my power in you, so that my name may be proclaimed in all the earth.' So then he [God] has mercy on whomever he chooses, and he hardens . . . whomever he chooses" (9:17–18; cf. Ex. 9:16). Just as the hardening of Pharaoh served to save Israel at that time from their bondage in Egypt, and thus have the name of Israel's God proclaimed in all the earth, so in Paul's time the hardening of "part of Israel" serves to save "all Israel" when the "fullness of the nations" enters in (11:25–26).

In case the non-Jewish Christ-followers in Rome continue to think they are the replacement of Israel, Paul asks a pointed rhetorical question: "Has God rejected his people?" Then answers with his usual catchphrase, *mē genoito*, "may it never be," "perish the thought." He then points to himself as an example of one member of Israel, "descendant of Abraham, a member of the tribe of Benjamin," to prove that "God

---

14. Gager, *Reinventing*, 146.
15. Nanos, "Callused," 63.

has not rejected his people whom he foreknew" (11:1–2). "What [Paul] taught and preached was instead a special path, a *Sonderweg*, for Gentiles:"[16] they did not have to become proselytes to Judaism in the usual way.

Imagine Such an Olive Tree (Rom. 11:17–24)

Paul knows his metaphor of the olive tree is "contrary to nature." Any horticulturalist, then or now, would consider Paul's figure of speech absurd, to say the least. Good horticultural practice is to graft a cultivated shoot into a hardy wild root. The fact that Paul's horticultural scenario is completely unconventional does not bother him. On the contrary, the unconventional aspect may be the very idea he wants to project as the way God executes the divine plan: it is not according to human convention or imagination.

Perhaps this is as close as Paul comes to a parable in the manner of Jesus' parables. Puzzling as it is, Paul's metaphor of the olive tree serves his purpose. Broken branches of the cultivated olive tree will be grafted in again, just as the wild branches were grafted in "against nature." The metaphor serves not only as a plea to the readers to acknowledge the primary status of Israel in God's plan (cf. "Judean first and also Greek"), but also as a warning to the non-Jewish Christ-followers not to "become proud," but to "stand in awe" of Israel as chosen by God. Here, I believe, is the sense of Paul's puzzling parable of grafting wild branches and broken natural branches into the cultivated olive root: if God in grace and power is able to perform totally unconventional action to save the ungodly nations of the world, "how much more" will God do so for the elect nation of Israel to whom God promised salvation in the covenant made with Abraham. Twice in Romans 11 Paul uses the how-much-more argument: the lesser proves the greater (11:12, 24).

It is tempting to treat the image of the olive root and branches as a new Israel, comprised of converts from the nations along with historic Judeans as one and the same covenant community under God. The one root provides life-giving nutrients for all the branches equally. But that reading is not quite true to the image Paul has constructed. The root was present already before the grafting, and the wild branches are still wild branches after being grafted into the cultivated root. They gain life from the same root, but they do not become identical with the cultivated olive branches. Moving out of the metaphor, then, converts from the nations do not become proselytes to Judaism. True enough, they have gained the redemptive benefit that comes from the faithful Israelite of Judaism, Jesus Messiah, but they have not thereby become Judeans. On the other hand, Paul's non-Jewish readers should not consider themselves independent of Israel, replacing the "old" Israel with a new identity altogether. "There is nothing clearer from Romans 11 than that Paul is entirely in opposition to a gentile Christ-movement that prides itself on its independence of Israel."[17]

---

16. Gager, *Reinventing*, 146.
17. Campbell, *Identity*, 79.

Part III: Paul

The Mystery Unfurled (Rom. 11:25-32)

We come now to the climax of the whole circuitous argument: Paul's revelation of the "mystery" of Israel's ultimate salvation. "Mystery" in this context is a "secret" within the divine mind, to which Paul claims access. The unfurling of this "secret" reveals a feature of God's good news, seemingly in creative tension with the gospel of Messiah Jesus that Paul had been preaching among the nations. The latter was not a mystery any more. The question facing Paul at the end of his north Mediterranean mission, before taking the offering of the nations to Jerusalem, before going to Rome and to Spain to complete his commission, at a time when the non-Jewish Christ-followers in Rome claimed privilege for themselves, is this: *What will be the fate of God's elect people, Israel, when the mission to the nations of the world is complete at the end of the age?*

Paul's answer is no longer circuitous, no longer this way and that, but straight to the point: *When the fullness of the nations has entered in, then all Israel will be saved* (11:25b-26a). Some interpreters have drawn attention to the switch in priority. What once was "Judean first and also Greek" has become the nations first and then Israel. I doubt that Paul changed his mind during the writing of this long letter. The priority is still as it was, Israel first and also the nations. But the time-frame has changed in the context of Romans 9-11, and with it also the topic. Israel had received the gospel of Christ first, to be sure. Some responded positively, some did not. Meanwhile, people of the nations had accepted the message of Messiah in significant numbers. At Romans 11:25-26, however, the time frame in Paul's vision of the race toward salvation is at the finish line. At that time, when the fullness—or full number—of people from the nations have accepted God's offer of salvation in Christ, then "all Israel will be saved."

"It is beyond dispute that Paul means the statement seriously: it is not a vague hope, but a concrete prediction communicated as an eschatological mystery."[18] Granting the seriousness of Paul's prediction, interpreters through the centuries have wondered *how* "all Israel" will be saved. There are essentially two positions in present-day discussions. One is that Israel *en mass* will turn to Christ in faith just before the end, and thus be saved. This view is said to be in harmony with Paul's prevailing conviction that the only way for anyone, or any people, to be saved is through faith in God's faithful Messiah, Jesus. A variation on this view is that Paul has in mind the glorious return of Christ, who will miraculously bring "all Israel" to believe in him and thus be saved.

A second view is that Paul in Romans 11:25-32 believes God to be the prime mover in the salvation of Israel at the end of the age. It was "the God and Father of our Lord Jesus Christ" who made a covenant with the people of Israel, which cannot be broken. Israel was to be a light to the nations. Paul and his companions have represented Israel in bringing the light of God's Messiah Jesus to the nations. When that work is completed, when the fullness of the nations has come in, and the end of the age is in sight, then Israel's hardening will cease, God will keep the covenant promise made with Abraham, and will save "all Israel," even though some of them did not accept Jesus as Messiah.

---

18. Sanders, "Paul's Attitude," 183.

What lends support to the second position is not merely the absence of any mention of Jesus in Paul's argument from Romans 10:17—11:36, but the distinctive way in which Paul confirms his prediction of the salvation of "all Israel" in the argument that follows. Paul first calls upon the authority of Scripture for support, specifically the prophecy of Isaiah 59:20-21: "'Out of Zion will come the Deliverer; he will banish ungodliness from Jacob.' 'And this is my covenant with them, when I take away their sins'" (Rom. 11:26b-27). Without explaining precisely the identity of the "Deliverer," whether the one God of Israel or Jesus Messiah of God, Paul implies this much: God's covenant once made with the chosen people cannot be broken, and the Deliverer is the sole agent in banishing ungodliness from the people, not the people themselves.

As emphasized in an earlier chapter, the covenant of salvation made with Abraham was for Israel first, and through Israel for the nations also. Paul does not promote two covenants, one for Israel and another for the people of the nations. Mention of a "new covenant" elsewhere in Paul's letters (2 Cor. 3:6; 11:25) should not be taken to mean that the one God has two plans for the salvation of the world. The covenant with Israel was *renewed* in ways appropriate for the time. Paul saw himself living in the end-time when the renewed covenant with Israel in the person of Jesus Messiah was being extended to the nations of the world.

Still, the question remains: What does Paul imply by "all Israel"? Does he imply that believers in Jesus from the nations and believers from Judaism will constitute "all Israel"? If so, then the age-old displacement interpretation easily falls into place: The Church is the one "true Israel," thus removing historic Israel from the plan of God and from the covenant God made with the patriarchs. This cannot be sustained. "On the contrary, Israel has a special eschatological destiny for Paul, for it will enter the kingdom of God as a people at the time when the mission . . . to the [nations] has been fulfilled . . . Israel's priority, then, rests in God's faithfulness to his promises."[19] Nor can one maintain that Paul's "all" allows exceptions. Nothing in Paul's text at 11:25-26 suggests a truncated "all." Jewett cautiously acknowledges that "all" means all: "it seems most likely that Paul's 'mystery' was believed to include all members of the house of Israel, who, without exception, would be saved."[20]

In addition to his proof from the prophecy of Isaiah that "all Israel will be saved," Paul appeals to the character of the covenant-making God of Israel. This is Paul's linchpin that makes his argument: "As regards election they are beloved, for the sake of their ancestors; for the gifts and the calling of God are irrevocable" (11:28-29). They are irrevocable because they come from the divine will, not from changeable human intention and ambition. Even though Paul does not call the people of Israel "Judeans" throughout Romans 11, he no doubt has his fellow Judeans in mind. They have criticized Paul and his mission, inflicted severe discipline on him for his preaching and practice, and in that sense are "enemies" of the gospel Paul preaches. But they are not

---

19. Beker, *Paul*, 335-36.
20. Jewett, *Romans*, 702.

Part III: Paul

enemies of God, as the NRSV wrongly proposes.[21] As a people they are "beloved," and will be saved when the time comes, "for the gifts and the calling of God are irrevocable" (11:29).

Seldom does Paul introduce a benediction in the middle of a letter, but he does so at the end of this very important revelation of the "mystery" about Israel's destiny. Even in the benediction he does not invoke the name of Jesus Christ, which is unusual for him. God is all in all, and the ways of God in their fullness are beyond the grasp of human minds, including Paul's:

> "O the depth of the riches and wisdom and knowledge of God!
> How unsearchable are his judgments and how inscrutable his ways!
> 'For who has known the mind of the Lord?
> Or who has been his counselor?'
> 'Or who has given a gift to him, to receive a gift in return?'
> For from him and through him and to him are all things.
> To him be the glory forever. Amen." (11:33–36)

IN THE MEANTIME: THE POWERS THAT BE (ROM. 13:1–7)

Paul leaves his disclosure of the mystery of Israel's eschatological salvation at the end of chapter 11, and moves forward to ethical and practical matters facing the Christ-communities in Rome in the meantime. He spends four chapters (12–15) on such issues. All of the concerns Paul cites there deserve full treatment, but the limited scope of this book does not allow it. One issue, however, has haunted the interpretation of Paul through the centuries: his view of the Christ-community's relationship to the civic authorities in Rome (Rom. 13:1–7). That issue should be touched upon, at least, before drawing this chapter to a close.

Some key statements from the seven verses should be highlighted to focus the discussion.

- "Let every person be subject to the governing authorities; for there is no authority except from God, and those authorities that exist have been instituted by God" (v.1);

- "Do what is good, and you will receive [the authority's] approval; for it is God's servant for your good" (vv. 3–4);

- "Therefore one must be subject, not only because of wrath but also because of conscience" (v. 5);

- "You also pay taxes, for the authorities are God's servants, busy with this very thing" (v. 6).

If the governing authorities Paul is referring to are those of imperial Rome, then this instruction is somewhat bewildering. Paul knows well enough that the Roman authority in Jerusalem tried Jesus in a Roman court and executed him for subversion. I doubt

---

21. The phrase "of God" is not in Paul's Greek text (11:28), and should not be supplied.

that Paul would say Jesus went about doing evil, and thus incurred the penalty from the Roman authority in Jerusalem. Paul must have known also who the Caesar was at the time: Nero. It is said, however, that in the early years of Nero's rule as emperor, he did not behave recklessly and wickedly. Paul wrote Romans in Nero's early years.

Or we could read this passage as Paul's rhetoric of expediency in the short time before the end of the present age of Roman rule. That is, live ordered lives within the temporary Roman society, and pay taxes to avoid reprisal from the civic authorities. While there is rhetoric in the passage, as one would expect, recognition of it does not fully account for the conviction that seems to inform the rhetoric: that the civic authorities are ordained by God, are for the good of society, and should be respected and given their due.

Is it possible that Paul is not referring to the civic authorities appointed by imperial Rome? Nanos, in a rather elaborate argument, believes Paul is still addressing the relationship of the new communities of Christ to the synagogue authorities.[22] He suggests the context of the surrounding discussion in Romans, especially the ethical counsel of chapters 12–15, leads to the insight that Paul is pleading for the subordination of the Christ-followers to the authority of the synagogue, especially in matters of behavior. The problem is that the "righteous Gentiles" in Rome have begun to distance themselves from the synagogue, perhaps to the point of replacing the synagogue, so Paul urges them to keep faith with the synagogue authorities. Their newly constituted community stands in the tradition of the synagogue, and should be subordinate to the authorities there. According to Nanos, subordination of the Christ-community to the Jewish synagogue includes "the payment of the two-drachma Temple tax."[23] (13:6–7).

Much as I appreciate Nanos's well-crafted argument, I am not convinced that Paul intended *only* the synagogue authorities. Roman civic authorities were an ever-present reality, especially in Rome, authorities under whom both synagogue and Christ-community had to live, and to whom both groups were expected to pay taxes. For Paul to ignore those authorities in his instruction to Christ-followers living in Rome seems unreasonable. Furthermore, if Paul intended synagogue authorities exclusively, surely he would have given a hint as to the identity of that particular institution. The Roman one was by far the more pervasive in the capital city, and by far the more powerful.

The difficulty with Paul's advice about "the powers that be" (KJV) remains. Perhaps a key to understanding lies in Paul's comparison of powers: the power of the Roman government, against the power of God. Jewett makes a telling assessment of this factor in Paul's rhetoric of subordination to civic authority. I yield the last word on the subject to Jewett:

> The God who grants authority to governmental agencies in Paul's argument is not Mars or Jupiter, as in the Roman civic cult; nor is he represented by the pantheon of Greco-Roman deities that had been assimilated into the civic cult since the time of Augustus . . . ; it is the God embodied in the crucified Christ that is in view here, which turns this passage into a massive act of political co-

22. Nanos, *Mystery*, 289–336.
23. Ibid., 293.

Part III: Paul

optation. If the Roman authorities had understood this argument, it would have been viewed as thoroughly subversive.[24]

To conclude, Paul envisions the restoration of the whole human family, with all its diversity, to a complete and right relationship with God. God provided the means and agency through which that feat will be accomplished: by creating a covenant people to bring the blessing of God to he nations of the world. Paul believed Jesus crucified and raised to be the Messiah through whom the sin problem of the world was removed. Jesus was God's faithful Israelite in whom the people of the nations could put their trust and thus be saved in the Day of the Lord.

The offer of salvation through faith in Jesus was offered first to Israel, represented in the Jewish people. A number of them accepted the offer, including Paul. These constituted a faithful remnant of Israel. That still seemed to leave the fate of Israel as an elect people of God in doubt. Not according to Paul. In his challenging three chapters of Romans 9–11 he takes his reader hither and yon to his concise unveiling of the mystery: "a hardening has come upon part of Israel, until the full number of the Gentiles has come in. And so all Israel will be saved" (11:25-26). The reason for his confidence about the destiny of Israel is that God has made a covenant-promise to deliver the people of Israel from sin and lead them into salvation. God is the sole actor in keeping covenant with Israel, "for the gifts and the calling of God are irrevocable" (11:29).

While Israel and the faithful members of Christ await their final deliverance, Paul gives instruction for the waiting period. In particular, he calls on them to recognize the supreme authority of God under whom all other authorities take their position for the time being. They are temporary instruments under God, adjudicated in relation to the crucified Messiah of God, for the welfare of society. Paul does not address the problem of a corrupt institution, corrupt because of corrupt people in power. It is hard to imagine Paul, for example, hailing Nero's abuse of his authority in the latter part of his reign as representative of God's authority, and therefore worthy of respect.

One cannot construct a theology of the state from Paul's few verses in Romans 13. An extended period of civic and political rule was not in Paul's horizon. For him the time before the end was short. Instructions for a long term, say 2000 years, did not occur to him. That task remained—and remains—for his successors to mastermind.

---

24. Jewett, *Romans*, 789-90.

16

Conclusion

Jesus First and also Paul

TAKING MY CUE FROM PAUL'S PRIORITY-FORMULA IN ROMANS, *JUDEAN FIRST and also Greek*, I propose a corollary formula as a way of concluding the exploration of the word and work of the two principal figures of the New Testament: *Jesus first and also Paul*. I mean this priority not merely in the obvious historical sense, but especially in a theological way. Jesus probably was born before Paul, by about six to eight years. But that chronological priority by itself is of little consequence. Their historical paths did not cross, as far as we know. Yet Paul, within thirty years after Jesus' death, became an outstanding spokesperson and letter-writer on behalf of the Jesus he never knew in the flesh.

Paul's missionary efforts in the name of Jesus did not happen in a vacuum. Apart from the extraordinary influence of the historical Jesus on his followers in Galilee and Judea, Paul would have remained a nameless Pharisee among the many others of his time, and his eschatological mission to the non-Jewish world a pipe-dream. His knowledge of Jesus began with his discipline of some Jewish followers of Jesus—not the original apostles (Acts 8:1–3). He had heard their confession of Jesus as Lord, heard them speak of him as Israel's Messiah, listened to them hail his crucifixion as the supreme sacrifice for sins, and witnessed them bear the pain of punishment without relenting.

I do not see the earthly lives of Jesus and Paul as parallel, apart from the fact that they both lived in the first half of the first century in a Jewish context. Instead, their respective lives and ministries can be compared constructively and comprehensively, which means not picking and choosing bits of information from the sources and then piecing the bits together to ensure some connection between them. My approach throughout was to respect the integrity of the two figures, working with their terms, in their time frames, in their places, and thereby to appreciate their respective witness and vision.

Jesus and Paul before Christianity

A summary comparison could be made along many lines. I have chosen five that seem to me to be pertinent and constructive: geography, education, religion, historical horizon, and vision.

GEOGRAPHY

Place plays a significant role in human identity-formation, especially in agrarian societies. The social location of thought is now a truism among sociologists, anthropologists, and psychologists. If one can determine a person's geography, then their aims and aspirations and expressions of thought can be understood as growing out of that context. By "geography" I do not mean an address merely, the name of the place where a person lives. Geography is a broad term that implies the character of the place where people go about their daily lives: the land as food base, water resources, rural-urban, economy, political climate, religion, language, crafts, access to benefits, opportunities for employment, community, etc. People in the ancient world—less so in modern times—were often identified simply by their geography: Jesse the Bethlehemite, Elijah the Tishbite, Judas the Galilean, the Egyptian who incited a revolt, Jesus of Nazareth, Paul of Tarsus, etc.

Jesus lived most of his thirty-year life in Lower Galilee, more specifically in the small rural village of Nazareth. As he matured he would have travelled into the surrounding districts, including pilgrimages south to the religious center in Jerusalem for the festivals. There were five festivals altogether, Passover being very important. As expected of him, he would have returned to his native Nazareth to be among his relatives and friends. Nazareth was one of many such hamlets in the area. The residents were mostly peasants, day laborers and tenant farmers. (Josephus estimates three million altogether, an exaggeration no doubt). Galilean Jewish peasants lived off their plot of land that the Lord their God had given them. Jesus was Jewish, as were his family and friends. He knew the meaning of the land. It was a practical source of food, to be sure, but it was above all the gift from God for sustaining the human life of the elect people. Regardless of what a Jewish person did for a living, respect for the land that produced food was always uppermost. The land, for Israel, symbolized God's promise of salvation: the land was life giving.

But Jesus witnessed the peasants lose their land to elite absentee landowners, often living in the cities. Land could be lost through debt or taxation, or a combination of both. Forgiveness of debts to peasants was viewed as a gift from God, as "The Lord's Prayer" affirms. The peasant plots of land could not support all members of families, so some developed a trade or craft. Jesus was a *tektōn*, a craftsman of some sort, but always a village craftsman. There is some suggestion that Jesus travelled, possibly as far as Egypt, to find work. During his ministry he went as far north as the region of Caesarea Philippi, and east to Syrophoenicia. But he always returned to his rural community, and his familiar Galilean surroundings, which included the Sea of Galilee on which he sailed many times with friends.

Conclusion

Cities in Galilee were the arenas of politics, pleasure, education, specialization, and entertainment. Herod Antipas, son of Herod the Great, was the ruler of Galilee and Perea at the time of Jesus. Antipas built two important cities in the region, Sepphoris and Tiberias. Sepphoris had a history before Antipas decided to make it his political home base. The city had fallen into a state of ruin as a result of battles. Antipas reconstructed it and made it his seat of power for almost twenty years. Sepphoris was only a few miles from Nazareth. Yet there is nothing on record to suggest that Jesus visited that great city, "the ornament of all Galilee," during his lifetime. The same is true for the city of Tiberias on the west coast of the Sea of Galilee, which Antipas built from scratch. One might expect Jesus to have brought his message to the urban population of Galilee, but that seems not to have happened. His life and ministry were among the peasant people, the unemployed, the poor, the widows, the sick, and the marginalized. Being a rural Galilean himself, Jesus could identify with the hardships of his rural people and offer them words of hope and acts of kindness.

Taxes levied by the city authorities were high, and went to support the massive building projects of Herod Antipas, on the one hand, and the Roman imperial institution on the other. In addition, the two-drachma Temple tax, a kind of poll tax, went to Jerusalem to support the elaborate priestly system. Costly offerings were also presented at the Temple of Jerusalem as an act of worship. Faithful Jewish people felt obliged, perhaps honored, to pay the Temple tax and present offerings out of reverence to their God in hope of maintaining their righteous standing.

Language was also part of geography. Living in Canada, as I do, I am very aware of the two official languages—French and English— and the respective provinces with which they are associated. Jesus, being a Jewish Galilean, would have spoken Aramaic as his primary language. Aramaic was a first cousin to Hebrew, and marked the Palestinian Jewish people off from their Greek-speaking neighbors. But Galilee had many non-Jewish residents, all of whom spoke Greek. Jesus would have known enough conversational Greek to function as a tradesperson, but his language at home, among Jewish friends, and in synagogue was Aramaic.

Paul's geography was quite another matter. However much Paul understood and appreciated the land of promise, he did not live there, nor was his thought shaped directly by his life-experience in that location. From Acts we learn that Paul was born and reared in the important city of Tarsus, capital of Cilicia. Geographer, Strabo, claims that Tarsus was a city of learning as well as commerce and wealth. It lay on a major east-west trade route. Those who were educated in Tarsus were thereby able to make their way in any other city of Greco-Roman society. Most of those who left did not return to Tarsus. That description of Tarsus and its people fits Paul. Neither Acts nor Paul's letters suggests that he conducted any missionary activity in his home city. Even though Acts claims Paul was a citizen of Tarsus, probably by birth, he himself makes no mention of such citizenship. But he was clearly urban in orientation, as one enculturated in a city setting.

He mentions the city of Damascus of Syria more than once in his letters, as though Damascus were his adopted city. That city was the center of his synagogue discipline

Jesus and Paul before Christianity

imposed on the Jewish Christ-followers, and to Damascus also he returned after his revelation of the risen Jesus. Paul's urban orientation was most clearly displayed in his missionary activity in the name of Jesus. He moved westward from the city of Antioch in Syria to major urban centers in Asia Minor and Europe. The urban destinations of his letters confirm his focus on cities for preaching Jesus Christ, and for forming new communities in that name. Paul may have adopted urban mission as a strategic measure to reach as many non-Jewish people as possible, but it seems more likely that Paul simply felt at home in cities, more so than in rural hamlets. In this respect Paul is quite unlike Jesus. Despite his devotion to Jesus, there is no indication that Paul made a pilgrimage to Nazareth, as Christians do today.

From the tradition in Acts, we learn that Paul developed the craft of tent making from which he supported himself (Acts 18:3; 20:34; 1 Thess. 2:9). Both Jesus and Paul knew the meaning of manual work. Yet Paul came to understand Jesus, not as a rural craftsman from Galilee, but as one who put his earthly life on the line for the sake of others. Paul adopted the life of the crucified Jesus, and presented himself thus in word and deed to the people of the many cities he visited. One could say, then, that Paul translated Jesus out of a Galilean village environment into an urban one in the larger Greco-Roman world. In fairness, though, others had already launched that translation project ahead of Paul. He carried it forward aggressively.

Paul's primary language was Greek, not Aramaic. He lived in a thoroughly Hellenistic city, and probably worshipped in a Greek-speaking synagogue. His complete familiarity with the Greek translation of the Hebrew Bible is testimony to the primacy of Greek in his communication. He wrote his complex arguments in his letters in Greek, as one completely at home in that language. If Paul knew Aramaic, or Hebrew, it would have been simply enough to get by on his pilgrimages to Jerusalem. This is the reverse of Jesus. Paul's mission, moreover, was to translate the mind and spirit and work of Jesus out of it original Aramaic milieu in Galilee and Judea into the Greek-speaking cities of the world.

EDUCATION

An estimated ninety percent of the population of Galilee was non-literate at the time of Jesus. By that I mean the large majority of people could not read or write. That does not mean that the people were thereby socially dysfunctional or intellectually naïve. On the contrary, the culture was predominantly oral, and the people were disciplined in remembering and recalling information and stories. Many of them were adept at creating stories for oral communication.

Those who could read would lead in worship, read from Scriptures, and give homilies. The rest listened and learned from the *speech* of the readers. Memory was keen by necessity, unlike the present time when memory is not as necessary in the midst of multiple means of storing and retrieving information. Jesus was educated in an oral culture in a village setting. City people, especially the elite, had opportunity to become literate. Teachers set themselves up in cities. Persons interested in learning to read and write would hire the services of a teacher-scribe if they could afford the service. Some may have found favor with a patron who paid for the education.

Once educated in the skills of reading and writing, a person could then find work as a scribe in the patronage of a person of high rank. Theophilus of Luke 1:4 was such a patron. The writer of Luke (and Acts) had gained a first-rate education in a city in the empire, as evidenced in his two-volume work, and then imagined Jesus as no less fortunate than himself. Hence Jesus' ability, in Luke 4:16, to read from the scroll of Isaiah. More likely Jesus would have *recited* a selected text from Isaiah.

The likelihood of Jesus having learned to read and write in the manner of Luke or Paul is marginal. His rural village life simply did not require it, nor did his ministry, conducted mainly among his fellow Galileans. Had Jesus attached himself to a master-scribe in a city, surely some mention of the city and/or the scribe would appear in the gospel narratives. But nothing of the sort is recorded. Furthermore, Jesus *announced* his message of the kingdom of God. He did not write it down for posterity. If he did, not a scrap of the manuscript has survived. The task of recasting the acts and words of Jesus in literary form went to later devotees who had learned to read and write, and that in the Greek language.

A characteristic form of speech in the ministry of Jesus was the parable. Parables flourish in the soil of oral culture. Jesus' parables grew out of that soil, and were returned to it for further germination. "The parables of Jesus exhibit his rhetorical art at its finest."[1] The earliest gospel writers would have found the parables circulating in communities years after Jesus' death, and then committed them to written form. One has to remember when *reading* the parables of Jesus in the synoptic gospels that they were first *spoken* to an audience. Audience participation in the telling of a story is dynamic, much more so than in the private or public reading of a text.

Paul, on the other hand, received a literary education. He was a man of the city, an important city at that. The opportunity to learn was more readily available in the city. The author of Acts has Paul boldly present himself as having sat "at the feet of Gamaliel" (22:3)—a position of learning in ancient societies. Even without such a note, we have clear evidence from Paul's letters that he was well acquainted with literary skills. His creative rhetoric suggests that he may have attended one of the schools of Greek rhetoric, or was at least acquainted with rhetorical conventions of the day.[2]

Rhetoric was designed for formal oratory, although not exclusively. The persuasive speech could be committed to writing. Paul's opponents at Corinth accused him of having greater ability in written rhetoric than in oratory. He learned what the opponents were saying about him, perhaps from one his friends who brought a report from Corinth: "For they say, 'His letters are weighty and strong, but his bodily presence is weak, and his speech contemptible'" (2 Cor. 10:10). Paul did not demonstrate skill in creating parables in the manner of Jesus' parables. Nor did he cite a single parable of Jesus in his letters. He was more adept at argumentation of various sorts, including

---

1. Meyer, "Language," 82.
2. Betz, *Galatians*, 1, 14–15.

the use of irony, satire, sarcasm, analogy, etc. Such argumentation was at home in city settings where philosophers plied their trade. Paul's urban congregations may have struggled to understand his arguments in his letters, as modern interpreters do, but they treasured them nonetheless, collected them, and passed them down to posterity. As the later epistle of Second Peter attests, "There are some things in [Paul's letters] hard to understand, which the ignorant and unstable twist to their own destruction" (3:16). The "ignorant" (*amatheis*) implies those without formal training in reading the literary creations of the educated class.

RELIGION

Jesus and Paul shared one important characteristic, one that remained with them to the end of their lives: *the religion of Judaism*. This does not imply that Judaism in the first century was homogenous throughout the Greco-Roman world. In Palestine itself Judaism was multifaceted. Sadducees did not believe exactly as Pharisees did. Another group took offence at the way the priests of the Temple of Jerusalem were colluding with Rome, so they formed a community of their own in the Judean desert far away from the Temple. Those Qumran covenanters considered themselves the true representatives of Israel. The largest Jewish group in Palestine was the ordinary non-sectarian Jewish people of the land.

Beyond the various groups that made up Palestinian Judaism was Hellenistic Judaism. These Judeans all spoke Greek at home, in the marketplace and in the synagogue. They used the Greek translation of the Hebrew Bible as their scripture. Most of them lived outside Palestine. Despite the variation from one Jewish group to the other, the shared pattern of religion was still Judaism. E. P. Sanders, among others, investigated the available Jewish sources of the period and found a common pattern of religion among the different Jewish groups. Even when one group separated from the rest, the central tenets of the religion remained. Sanders called the pattern of the religion of Judaism throughout the Greco-Roman period "covenantal nomism": covenantal, depicting the pledge-agreement between God and the elect people; nomism, from the Greek word, *nomos*, meaning "law."

Covenantal nomism has eight facets, according to Sanders:

> (1) God has chosen Israel and (2) given the law. The law implies both (3) God's promise to maintain the election and (4) the requirement to obey. (5) God rewards obedience and punishes transgression. (6) The law provides for means of atonement, and atonement results in (7) maintenance or re-establishment of the covenantal relationship. (8) All those who are maintained in the covenant by obedience, atonement and God's mercy belong to the group which will be saved. An important interpretation of the first and last points is that election and ultimately salvation are considered to be by God's mercy rather than human achievement.[3]

---

3. Sanders, *Palestinian Judaism*, 422.

Conclusion

As with all essentialist statements about belief and practice, this one scarcely captures the day-to-day religious experience of everyone and everything Jewish. Plenty of questions come to mind. What were the elements of a synagogue service? Was the Shema recited every day in Jewish households? How were the festivals celebrated outside Palestine? How important was the Temple of Jerusalem to the life and thought of Hellenistic Jewish people? Were the Hellenistic Judeans outside Palestine more lax in obeying the law? How important was pilgrimage to the Land and the Temple? Many more could be added no doubt.

On the matter of Jesus and Judaism, and Paul and Judaism, different pictures emerge. Jesus was law-observant, despite some opposition to his social and religious behavior. He was not executed for breaking Jewish law. Nor did he teach his disciples to break any Jewish law. According to the Gospel of Matthew, Jesus upheld the Law of Judaism: "Do not think that I have come to abolish the law or the prophets; I have come not to abolish but to fulfill" (5:17). Nowhere does Jesus recommend setting aside circumcision, Sabbath keeping, or kosher observance. The same cannot be said for Paul. But why not, if the two were faithful to their religious confession? The answer, I believe, must come from understanding the *context* of each of them.

Jesus' ministry was primarily among his own Jewish people of Galilee and Judea. He did not move beyond the borders of the traditional Land of Israel, and he did not deliberately preach to non-Jewish people in Palestine. Paul, on the other hand, felt compelled to gather people from the nations into new communities in the name of Jesus Messiah. That commission pushed him to open up parts of the Law to admit non-Judeans to full membership in the covenant that God made with Abraham. Jewish people of faith in Jesus Christ could continue to observe the Law as they had done before believing. But the new communities of non-Judeans were not obliged to be circumcised, or keep Sabbath or observe kosher rules. Those communities were not thereby second-class members of God's covenant of salvation. They were as much chosen people of God through the faithfulness of Jesus Christ as native Judeans were.

The notion that Paul abandoned Judaism to create a new religion after his encounter with the risen Jesus is misguided, if not absurd. Paul's letters simply do not support such a view. They were the byproduct of his mission to bring non-Jewish converts into the Abrahamic covenant through faith in Messiah Jesus. The letters should be read in light of that missionary context. Paul had not discarded his Jewish faith or heritage any more than he had abandoned his Jewish scripture. And he certainly had not done that. Paul continued to attend synagogue services, sometimes suffering sever discipline in doing so. He maintained his respect for Jerusalem also, reflected especially in his presentation of the offering from the nations in that city.

In short, I suggest that Paul, after his call, adhered to his Jewish faith-heritage, as Jesus had done after launching his ministry about the in-breaking kingdom of God. Paul's conviction about the saving grace of God in Jesus' death and resurrection did not vitiate his commitment to Judaism. If we should acknowledge that covenantal nomism was at the heart of Judaism, then Paul, being Jewish, continued to live within that religious conviction as surely as he breathed the Mediterranean air. We witnessed

Jesus and Paul before Christianity

his deep commitment to Judaism in our survey of Romans 9–11. Of course, his new call and mission to the non-Jewish world led him to reinterpret the parameters of his religion in light of Jesus Christ. But reinterpretation is far from abandonment. Paul's most telling sentence confirming his allegiance to Judaism is short and to the point: "we uphold the law" (Rom. 3:31). He states this after turning his angle of vision on the Law this way and that. The key to understanding his reinterpretation is to keep an eye on his mission to the non-Jewish world. He opened a door to allow believers from the nations to enter into the new covenant-community of Jesus Christ, not as God-fearing guests, and not as proselytes to Judaism, but as members in full standing in God's covenant with Abraham. In that sense they were equal with Judeans without becoming Judeans in the usual way. Once inside the covenant-community, however, the members were expected to fulfill "the just requirement of the law" (Rom. 8:4).

HISTORICAL HORIZON

The image of "horizon" is a shorthand way of describing how a person understands life and its purpose in the world, given the time and place and circumstance in which that person thinks and lives. Who has not climbed a mountain and looked down over the region below in amazement at how the small pieces of landscape fit together in a majestic mosaic? The vision from the top is very different from the vision below.

The historical horizon of Jesus was not quite that of Paul. As we discovered under the topic of geography, the life-and-thought location of Jesus and Paul was unique to each of them. The same with the historical vistas: they too were different. Even though Jesus probably knew that his preaching about the kingdom of God, his subversive demonstration in the Temple, along with his other actions and words, could lead to his death, his ministry among the Galileans and Judeans did not revolve around his death by crucifixion at the hands of the Romans. Simply put, his self-sacrificial death was not a historical reality during his ministry.

The same was true for God's vindication of Jesus by the resurrection. Jesus did not preach his own resurrection as a mark of the coming kingdom of God in the world. The appearances of Jesus resurrected obviously had not happened during his earthly life, so his audience could not have conceived of him in that post-crucifixion form. It is possible, even likely, that the people of Galilee who heard Jesus speak in parables about the kingdom of God, who watched him heal the sick, who followed him here and there in the villages, who sailed the Sea of Galilee to be with him on the other side, all remembered him in that way. Suppose they did not all go to Jerusalem for that fateful Passover. They did not witness the trial or crucifixion of Jesus, nor did they experience him in resurrected form. Did they then forget him? I suggest they remembered him, remembered his provocative sayings, his unconventional behavior among the outcasts, and preserved that memory in oral form. I believe we have much of that remembered material, that time-honored treasure, in the written gospels. But there is only a smidgen of it in Paul's writings, understandably. The gospels were not yet written in Paul's lifetime, and the oral tradition about Jesus was fluid, moving piecemeal among the communities. And in any case, Paul was not driven to find and use the words and actions of the historical Jesus before his death in Jerusalem.

Paul lived within a different historical horizon. After the crucifixion and resurrection of Jesus in Jerusalem, believers began to preach about the saving grace of Jesus who gave "his life a ransom for the many," whom God raised from the dead. Paul entered the scene and heard the word about the crucified Messiah of the Judeans, and did his best to squelch the movement. Within two or three years after Jesus' death Paul had an epiphany, a vision of the same crucified Jesus he had heard preached among his Hellenistic Jewish contemporaries. That vision changed his horizon, setting him on another course with a message about a crucified Messiah whom God raised from the dead. It was not simply that the crucifixion and resurrection of Jesus were two pieces of information about Jesus among many others. The crucifixion and resurrection of Jesus became "the truth of the gospel" for Paul (Gal. 2:5, 14), the centerpiece around which the Christ-life was lived and Christ-communities formed.

In summary, the historical horizons of Jesus and Paul were not in conflict, neither were they identical. Jesus lived and ministered in Galilee. He communicated a message about the kingdom of God in the occupied province of Palestine. His audiences did not hear him speak about his crucifixion and resurrection as having happened already for the salvation of Israel, much less for the whole world. Paul's audiences, on the other hand, heard precisely that message: "that Christ died for our sins in accordance with the scriptures, and that he was buried, and that he was raised on the third day in accordance with the scriptures" (1 Cor. 15:3–5). This was Paul's horizon of meaning, and also his unwavering message to the nations of the world, including his own Jewish people.

VISION

Vision is not easy to map precisely, even one's own vision. How much more difficult the vision of someone who lived two thousand ago. A major hurdle to overcome is the interpreter's knowledge and experience of the shape that vision took in the hands and minds of people living many years afterward, up to the present time.

I shall begin with a negative assessment, which seems easier. Jesus did not intend to found a new religion separate from Judaism, a worldwide religion that developed an anti-Jewish perspective, a religion that would influence some adherents to bring pain and death to millions of Jewish people, a religion that hoped to displace Judaism and the Jewish people, of whom Jesus was one.

The same can be said of Paul: he did not envision Christianity. More than a few people have proposed that Paul was the real founder of Christianity. Yet there is nothing whatever in Paul's correspondence with his Christ-communities to suggest that he envisioned a non-Jewish religion under the name of Jesus Christ that would encircle the world and displace Judaism. Any such scenario for Jesus or Paul grows out of a much later experience and understanding from within Christianity, and distorts the vision of the historical Jesus, and also that of the historical Paul.

Jesus and Paul before Christianity

On the positive side, Jesus preached the kingdom of God among his Jewish people of Palestine. He called disciples to follow him, and identified twelve men specifically. Twelve male disciples represented the twelve sons of Israel, signaling —not so subtly— the beginning of a restored Israel.

Jesus engaged his audiences with parables about the character of the kingdom of God compared to the current oppressive kingdom of imperial Rome to which the current Temple of Jerusalem was beholden. By his words and actions Jesus challenged the existing systems of religion and politics by his announcement of the kingdom, and kingship, of God. He envisioned Israel restored, delivered from oppression, practicing justice, caring for the weak and marginalized, and reflecting the glory of God. He seems to have imagined a new Temple, not one tied in with Roman political power. He witnessed many people of Israel lost in a sea of debt, unemployment, poverty, and death. His mission, according to Matthew, was to reach "the lost sheep of the house of Israel" (15:24).

Implicit in Jesus' vision and message concerning the restoration of Israel was a "promise" to the nations, according to Jeremias.[4] (In the Gospel of Matthew, written after a successful mission to the nations, the "promise" became an overt command from the resurrected Christ [28:18–20]). However that may be, the followers of Jesus after Easter, saw in his cruel death for the sake of others a message of hope for oppressed people beyond Israel. Sure enough, more and more non-Jewish people received the message and formed new communities in the name of Jesus Christ.

Paul became a chief spokesperson of that message. His vision was shaped in large part by his understanding of "the fullness of time": God had acted in the death of Jesus to bring about the turn of the ages. Paul saw himself as living and working at the end of the old age and the beginning of the new. A resurrection had happened already. A new creation was under way (2 Cor. 5:17). The Spirit of Messiah was active in Paul, empowering him to gather in the people of the nations into covenant-relationship with God through Jesus Messiah crucified and raised. His vision was not long-term, and certainly not two thousand years and counting. He expected the complete number of people from the nations to be gathered in during his lifetime, or shortly thereafter (1 Cor. 7:29). With that feat accomplished, then "all Israel will be saved" (Rom 11:26).

---

4. See Jeremias, *Jesus' Promise to the Nations*.

Bibliography

Adams, Edward. "First-Century Models for Paul's Churches: Selected Scholarly Developments Since Meeks." In *After the First Urban Christians: The Social-Scientific Study of Pauline Christianity Twenty-five Years Later,* edited by Todd D. Still and David G. Horrell, 60–78. New York: T. & T. Clark, 2009.

Allison, Dale C. "The Pauline Epistles and the Synoptic Gospels: The Pattern of the Parallels." *NTS* 28 (1982) 1–32.

Arndt, William F. and Gingrich, F. Wilbur. *A Greek-English Lexicon of the New Testament and Other Early Christian Literature.* Translation and adaptation of Walter Bauer's *Griechisch-Deutsches Wörterbuch zu den Schriften des Neuen Testaments und der übrigen urchristlichen Literatur.* Fourth Edition (1952). Chicago: The University of Chicago Press, 1957.

Badenas, Robert. *Christ the End of the Law: Romans 10:4 in Pauline Perspective.* Journal for the Study of the New Testament Supplement Series 10. Sheffield: JSOT Press, 1985.

Barrett, C. K. *Paul: An Introduction to His Thought.* Louisville: Westminster John Knox, 1994.

———. *The Second Epistle to the Corinthians.* Black's New Testament Commentary. Peabody, MA: Hendrickson, 1973.

Beker, J. C. "Contingency and Coherence in the Letters of Paul." *USQR* 33 (1978) 141–51.

———. *Paul the Apostle: The Triumph of God in Life and Thought.* Philadelphia: Fortress, 1980.

Betz, Hans Dieter. *Galatians: A Commentary on Paul's Letter to the Churches in Galatia.* Philadelphia: Fortress, 1979.

———. *2 Corinthians 8 and 9. A Commentary on Two Administrative Letters of the Apostle Paul.* Philadelphia: Fortress, 1985.

Bickerman, Elias J. "The Name of Christians." *HTR* 42 (1949) 109–24.

Bonnington, Mark. "Review Article: *Galatians,* by Philip F. Esler." *Tyndale Bulletin* 50.1 (1999) 141–55.

Borg, Marcus J., and John Dominic Crossan. *The First Paul: Reclaiming the Radical Visionary Behind the Church's Conservative Icon.* New York: HarperOne, 2009.

Bornkam, Günther. *Jesus of Nazareth.* Translated by Irene and Fraser McLuskey with James M. Robinson. London: Hodder and Stoughton, 1960.

Boyarin, Daniel. *A Radical Jew: Paul and the Politics of Identity.* Berkeley: University of California Press, 1994.

———. *Border Lines: The Partition of Judaeo-Christianity.* Divinations. Philadelphia: University of Pennsylvania Press, 2006.

Bultmann, Rudolf. *The History of the Synoptic Tradition.* 1963. Reprint, Peabody, MA: Hendrickson, 1994.

———. "The Significance of the Historical Jesus for the Theology of Paul." In *Faith and Understanding,* 220–46. Translated by L. P. Smith. New York: Harper and Row, 1969.

Cadbury, Henry. J. *The Peril of Modernizing Jesus.* 1937. Reprint. London: SPCK, 1962.

Cameron, Ron, editor. *The Other Gospels: Non-Canonical Gospel Texts.* Philadelphia: Westminster, 1982.

Campbell, William S. "The Addressees of Paul's Letter to the Romans: Assemblies of God in House Churches and Synagogues." In *Between Gospel and Election: Explorations in the Interpretation of Romans 9—11,* edited by F. Wink and J. Ross Wagner, 171–95. Wissenschaftliche Untersuchungen zum Neuen Testament 257. Tübingen: Mohr Siebeck, 2010.

———. *Paul and the Creation of Christian Identity.* Library of New Testament Studies 322. London: T. & T. Clark, 2006.

Bibliography

———. *Paul's Gospel in an Intercultural Context: Jew and Gentile in the Letter to the Romans.* Studien zur interkulturellen Geschichte des Christentums 69. Frankfurt: Peter Lang, 1991.

———. "Romans III as a Key to the Structure and Thought of Romans." In *The Romans Debate*, edited by Karl P. Donfried, 251–64. Peabody, MA: Hendrickson, 1991.

Chadwick, Henry. *Origen: Contra Celsum.* Translated with notes by Henry Chadwick. Cambridge: University Press, 1953.

Chilton, Bruce. *Pure Kingdom: Jesus' Vision of God.* Grand Rapids: Eerdmans, 1996.

———. *Rabbi Jesus: An Intimate Biography.* New York: Doubleday, 2000.

———, and Jacob Neusner. *Judaism in the New Testament: Practices and Beliefs.* London: Routledge, 1995.

Conzelmann, Hans. *1 Corinthians.* Hermeneia: A Critical and Historical Commentary on the Bible. Translated by James W. Leitch. Philadelphia: Fortress, 1975.

Crossan, John Dominic, *The Historical Jesus: The Life of a Mediterranean Jewish Peasant.* San Francisco: HarperSanFrancisco, 1991.

———. *In Parables: The Challenge of the Historical Jesus.* Eagle Books. Sonoma, CA: Polebridge, 1992.

———. *Jesus: A Revolutionary Biography.* San Francisco: HarperSanFrancisco, 1994.

———. "The Parables of Jesus." *Int.* 56.3 (2002) 247–59.

———. *Who Killed Jesus? Exposing the Roots of Anti-Semitism in the Gospel Story of the Death of Jesus.* San Francisco: HarperSanFrancisco, 1995.

———, and Jonathan L. Reed. *Excavating Jesus: Beneath the Stones, Behind the Texts*, Revised and Updated. New York: HarperOne, 2002.

Danby, Herbert, translator. *The Mishnah.* London: Oxford University Press, 1938.

Das, A. Andrew. "Paul and the Law: Pressure Points in the Debate." In *Paul Unbound: Other Perspectives on the Apostle*, edited by Mark D. Given, 99–116. Peabody, MA: Hendrickson, 2010.

Davies, Philip R. *Scribes and Schools: The Canonization of the Hebrew Scriptures.* Louisville: Westminster John Knox, 1998.

Davies, W. D. *Paul and Rabbinic Judaism.* London: SPCK, 1965.

———. *The Gospel and the Land: Early Christianity and Jewish Territorial Doctrine.* Berkeley: University of California Press, 1974.

Dix, Gregory. *Jew and Greek: A Study in the Primitive Church.* New York: Harper and Brothers, 1953.

Dodd, C. H. *Gospel and Law: The Relation of Faith and Ethics in Early Christianity.* New York: Columbia University Press, 1951.

———. *The Parables of the Kingdom.* London: Charles Scribner's Sons, 1961.

Donahue, John R. *The Gospel in Parable.* Philadelphia: Fortress, 1988.

Donaldson, Terence L. *Paul and the Gentiles: Remapping the Apostle's Convictional World.* Minneapolis: Fortress, 1997.

Dungan, D. L. *The Sayings of Jesus in the Churches of Paul: The Use of Synoptic Tradition in the Regulation of Early Church Life.* Oxford: Basil Blackwell, 1971.

Dunn, James D. G. *A New Perspective on Jesus: What the Quest for the Historical Jesus Missed.* Grand Rapids: Baker, 2005.

———. *The Partings of the Ways: Between Christianity and Judaism and their Significance for the Character of Christianity.* London: SCM, 1991.

Eisenbaum, Pamela M. *Invitation to Romans.* Participant Books. Nashville: Abingdon, 2006.

———. *Paul was not a Christian: The Real Message of a Misunderstood Apostle.* New York: HarperOne, 2009.

Elliott, Neil. *Liberating Paul: The Justice of God and the Politics of the Apostle.* Maryknoll, NY: Orbis, 1994.

Esler, Philip F. *Galatians.* New Testament Readings. New York: Routledge, 1998.

———. *The First Christians in their Social Worlds: Social-scientific Approaches to New Testament Interpretation.* New York: Routledge, 1994.

Eusebius. *The Life of Constantine.* Translated with Introduction and Commentary by Averil Cameron and Stuart G. Hall. Oxford: University Press, 1999.

Fallen, Francis T. *2 Corinthians.* New Testament Message. Wilmington, DE: Michael Glazier, 1980.

Farris, Michael. "A Tale of Two Taxations (Luke 18:10–14b)." In *Jesus and His Parables: Interpreting the Parables of Jesus Today*, edited by V. George Shillington, 23–33. Edinburgh: T. & T. Clark, 1997.

Bibliography

Fitzmyer, Joseph A. *Romans*. The Anchor Bible. New York: Doubleday, 1993.
———. *The One Who is to Come*. Grand Rapids: Eerdmans, 2007.
Fredriksen, Paula. *From Jesus to Christ: The Origins of the New Testament Images of Jesus*. New Haven: Yale University Press, 1988.
———. *Jesus of Nazareth, King of the Jews: A Jewish Life and the Emergence of Christianity*. New York: Vintage Books, Random House, 1999.
Freyne, Seán. *Galilee: From Alexander the Great to Hadrian 323 BCE to 135 CE: A Study of Second Temple Judaism*. London: Continuum, 1988.
———. *Galilee, Jesus and the Gospels: Literary Approaches and Historical Investigations*. Philadelphia: Fortress, 1988.
———. *Jesus, a Jewish Galilean*. London: T. & T. Clark, 2005.
———. "Jesus of Galilee at Thirty: What Have We Learned?" A paper presented at the Society of Biblical Literature in New Orleans, November 2009.
———. "The Geography of Restoration: Galilee-Jerusalem Relations in Early Jewish and Christian Experience." *NTS* 47 (2001) 289–311.
Funk, Robert W. *Honest to Jesus: Jesus for a New Millennium*. San Francisco: HarperSanFrancisco, 1996.
———. *Parables and Presence: Forms of the New Testament Tradition*. Philadelphia: Fortress, 1982.
———, and Roy W. Hoover. *The Five Gospels: The Search for the Authentic Words of Jesus*. New York: Macmillan, 1993.
Furnish, V. P. "The Jesus-Paul Debate: From Baur to Bultmann." *BJRL* 47 (1965) 342–81.
———. "On Putting Paul in His Place." *JBL* 113/1 (1994) 3–17.
Gager, John G. *Reinventing Paul*. Oxford: University Press, 2000.
Gaston, Lloyd. "Paul and Jerusalem." In *From Jesus to Paul: Studies in Honour of Francis Wright Beare*, edited by Peter Richardson and John C. Hurd, 61–72. Waterloo, ON: Wilfrid Laurier University Press, 1984.
———. *Paul and the Torah*. Vancouver: University of British Columbia Press, 1987.
Hanson, K. C., and Douglas E. Oakman. *Palestine in the Time of Jesus: Social Structures and Social Conflicts*. Second Edition. Philadelphia: Fortress. 2008.
Hays, Richard B. *Echoes of Scripture in the Letters of Paul*. New Haven: Yale University Press, 1989.
———. *First Corinthians*. Interpretation: A Bible Commentary for Teaching and Preaching. Louisville: John Knox, 1997.
Hengel, Martin. *Between Jesus and Paul: Studies in the History of Earliest Christianity*. Translated by John Bowden. Philadelphia: Fortress, 1983.
———. *The Charismatic Leader and His Followers*. Translated by James Greig. New York: Crossroad, 1981.
———. *Crucifixion: In the Ancient world and the Folly of the Message of the Cross*. Philadelphia: Fortress, 1977.
———. "Paul in Arabia." *BBR* 12.1 (2002) 47–66.
———. *Property and Riches in the Early Church: Aspects of a Social History of Early Christianity*. Translated by John Bowden. London: S.C.M. Press, 1974.
———, with Roland Deines. *The Pre-Christian Paul*. Translated by John Bowden. Philadelphia: Trinity, 1991.
Herzog II, William R. *Parables as Subversive Speech: Jesus as Pedagogue of the Oppressed*. Louisville: Westminster John Knox, 1994.
Hickling, C. J. A. "Centre and Periphery in the Thought of Paul." In *Papers on Paul and Other New Testament Authors*, edited by Elizabeth A. Livingstone, 199–214. Studia Biblica 1978. Journal for the Study of the New Testament, Supplemental Series 3. Sheffield: JSOT Press, 1980.
Horrell, David. "The Label *Christianos*: 1 Peter 4:16 and the Formation of Christian Identity." *JBL* 126 (2007) 361–81.
Horsley, Richard A. *Archaeology, History and Society in Galilee: The Social Context of Jesus and the Rabbis*. Valley Forge, PA: Trinity, 1996.
———. *Galilee: History, Politics, People*. London: Continuum, 1995.
———. *Jesus and the Spiral of Violence: Popular Jewish Resistance in Roman Palestine*. Minneapolis: Fortress, 1993.

Bibliography

Jeremias, J. *Jesus' Promise to the Nations*. Translated by S. H. Hooke. Philadelphia: Fortress, 1982.

———. *The Eucharistic Words of Jesus*. Translated by Norman Perrin. London: SCM, 1966.

———. *The Parables of Jesus*. Translated by S. H. Hooke. 2nd ed. New York: Charles Scribner, 1972.

Jervell, Jacob. "The Letter to Jerusalem." In *The Romans Debate*, edited by Karl P. Donfried, 53–64. Peabody, MA: Hendrickson, 1991.

Jewett, Robert. "Following the Argument of Romans." In *The Romans Debate*, edited by Karl P. Donfried, 265–77. Peabody, MA: Hendrickson, 1991.

———. *Romans*. Hermeneia. Philadelphia: Fortress, 2007.

Johnson, Luke Timothy. *The Real Jesus: The Misguided Quest for the Historical Jesus and the Truth of the Traditional Gospels*. San Francisco: HarperSanFrancisco, 1996.

Josephus, Flavius. *Josephus: Complete Works*. Translated by William Whiston. Grand Rapids: Kregel, 1960.

Käsemann, Ernst. *Commentary on Romans*. Translated by Geoffrey W. Bromiley. Grand Rapids: Eerdmans, 1980.

Kasser, Rodolphe, Marvin Meyer, and Gregor Wurst, editors. *The Gospel of Judas*. Commentary by Bart D. Ehrman. Washington D.C.: National Geographic Society, 2006.

Kee, Howard Clark. *What Can We Know about Jesus?* Cambridge: University Press, 1990.

Klassen, William. "Authenticating Judas." In *Authenticating the Activities of Jesus*, edited by Bruce Chilton and Craig A. Evans, 409–10. Leiden: Brill, 1999.

Levine, Amy-Jill. *The Misunderstood Jew: The Church and the Scandal of the Jewish Jesus*. New York: Harper Collins, 2006.

Lieu, Judith M. *Christian Identity in the Jewish and Graeco-Roman World*. Oxford: Oxford University Press, 2004.

———. *Neither Jew nor Greek? Constructing Early Christianity*. Edinburgh: T. & T. Clark, 2002.

Lonergan, Bernard J. F. *Method in Theology*. New York: Herder and Herder, 1973.

Love, Stuart L. "Jesus, Healer of the Canaanite Woman's Daughter in Matthew's Gospel: A Social-Scientific Inquiry." *BTB* 32.11 (2002) 11–19.

Lüdemann, Gerd. *Early Christianity According to the Traditions in Acts: A Commentary*. Translated by John Bowden. Minneapolis: Fortress, 1987.

———. *Paul, Apostle to the Gentiles: Studies in Chronology*. Translated by E. Stanley Jones. Philadelphia: Fortress, 1984.

Malina, Bruce J., and Jerome H. Neyrey. *Portraits of Paul: An Archaeology of Ancient Personality*. Louisville: Westminster John Knox, 1996.

Marcus, Joel. "The Beelzebul Controversy and the Eschatologies of Jesus." In *Authenticating the Activities of Jesus*. Editors, edited by Bruce Chilton and Craig A. Evans, 247–78. Leiden: Brill, 1999.

Martin, R. P. *Carmen Christi: Philippians ii. 5–11 in Recent Interpretation and in the Setting of Early Christian Worship*. Cambridge: Cambridge University Press, 1967.

Mason, Steve. *Josephus, Judea, and Christian Origins: Methods and Categories*. Peabody, MA: Hendrickson, 2009.

McCane, Byron R. "'Where no One Had Yet Been Laid:' Participation in the Arrest of Jesus." In *Authenticating the Words of Jesus*, edited by Bruce Chilton and Craig A. Evans, 389–410. Leiden: Brill, 1999.

McFague, Sallie. *Speaking in Parables: A Study in Metaphor and Theology*. Philadelphia: Fortress, 1975.

McKnight, Scot. "Jesus vs. Paul." *Christianity Today*. 54:12 (2010) 26–29.

Meeks, Wayne A. *The First Urban Christians: The Social World of the Apostle Paul*. New Haven: Yale University Press, 1983.

Meyer, Ben F. *The Aims of Jesus*. London: SCM, 1979.

———. *The Early Christians: Their World Mission and Self-discovery*. Wilmington, DE: Michael Glazier, 1986.

———. "How Jesus Charged Language with Meaning: A Study in Rhetoric." In *Authenticating the Words of Jesus*, edited by Bruce Chilton and Craig A. Evans, 81–96. Leiden: Brill, 1999.

———. *The Man for Others*. New York: Bruce, 1970.

Miller, Robert J., editor. *The Complete Gospels: Annotated Scholars Version*. Sonoma, CA: Polebridge, 1994.

Bibliography

Modica, Joseph B. "Jesus as Glutton and Drunkard: The 'Excesses' of Jesus." In *Who Do My Opponents Say I Am? An Investigation of the Accusations Against Jesus*, edited by Scott McKnight and Joseph B. Modica, 50–75. Library of New Testament Studies 327. London: T. & T. Clark, 2008.

Moore, Anne. "The Search for the Common Judaic Understanding of God's Kingship." In *Common Judaism: Explorations in Second-Temple Judaism*, edited by Wayne O. McCready and Adele Reinhartz, 131–41. Philadelphia: Fortress, 2008.

Murphy-O'Connor, Jerome. *Jesus and Paul: Parallel Lives*. Collegeville: Liturgical, 2007.

———. *St. Paul's Corinth: Texts and Archaeology*. Collegeville: Liturgical, 1983.

Nanos, Mark D. "'Broken Branches': A Pauline Metaphor Gone Awry? (Romans 11:11–24)." A paper presented at the International Symposium: "Romans 9–11 at the Interface Between the 'New Perspective on Paul' and Jewish-Christian Dialog," 1–28. Göttingen: 2008.

———. "'Callused,' Not 'Hardened': Paul's Revelation of Temporary Protection Until All Israel Can Be Healed." In *Reading Paul in Context: Explorations in Identity Formation. Essays in Honour of William S. Campbell*, edited by Kathy Ehrensperger and Brian J. Tucker, 52–73. London: T. & T. Clark, 2010.

———. *The Irony of Galatians: Paul's Letter in First-Century Context*. Minneapolis: Augsburg Fortress, 2002.

———. *The Mystery of Romans: The Jewish Context of Paul's Letter*. Minneapolis: Augsburg Fortress, 1996.

———. "Paul and the Jewish Tradition: The Ideology of the Shema," 1–22. Online: http://www.marknanos.com/Paul-Shema-10-27-08.pdf, 2008.

———. "Paul and Judaism." In *Codex Pauli*, 54–55. Rome: Società San Paolo, 2009.

———. "Paul and Judaism: Why Not Paul's Judaism?" In *Paul Unbound: Other Perspectives on the Apostle*, edited by Mark D. Given, 117–60. Peabody, MA: Hendrickson, 2010.

———. "Paul's Reversal of Jews Calling Gentiles 'Dogs' (Philippians 3:2): 1600 Years of an Ideological Tale Wagging an Exegetical Dog?" *BI* 17.4 (2009) 448–82.

———. "A Torah-Observant Paul?: What Difference Could it Make for Christian/Jewish Relations Today?" 1–61. Online: http://www.marknanos.com/Boston-Torah-Obs-5-9-05.pdf, 2005.

Nietzsche, F. W. *The Antichrist*. Translated by H. L. Mencken. Torrence: Noontide, 1980.

Nolan, Albert. *Jesus Before Christianity*. New York: Orbis, 2001.

O'Neill, J. C. *Messiah: Six Lectures on the Ministry of Jesus*. The Cunningham Lectures 1975–76. Cambridge: Cochrane, 1980.

———. *Who Did Jesus Think He Was?* Leiden: Brill, 1995.

Origen. *Contra Celsum*. Translated with notes by Henry Chadwick. Cambridge: University Press, 1953.

Philo. *Philo*. Loeb Classical Library. Vols. I–X. Translated by F. H. Colson and G. H. Whitaker. Cambridge: Harvard University Press, 1930.

Rajak, Tessa. "'Torah Shall Go Forth from Zion:' Common Judaism and the Greek Bible." In *Common Judaism: Explorations in Second-Temple Judaism*, edited by Wayne O. McCready and Adele Reinhartz, 145–58. Philadelphia: Fortress, 2008.

Reed, Jonathan. *Archaeology and the Galilean Jesus: A Re-examination of the Evidence*. Harrisburg, PA: Trinity, 2000.

Remus, Harold. *Jesus as Healer*. Cambridge: University Press, 1997.

Rensberger, David. *Johannine Faith and Liberating Community*. Philadelphia: Westminster, 1988.

Rivkin, Ellis. *What Crucified Jesus?* London: SCM, 1984

Robinson, James M. *Jesus: According to the Earliest Witness*. Philadelphia: Fortress, 2007.

———. *The Sayings of Jesus: the Sayings Gospel Q in English*. Faucet Books. Minneapolis: Fortress, 2002.

Roetzel, Calvin J. *The Letters of Paul: Conversations in Context*. Third Edition. Louisville: Westminster John Knox, 1991.

Rohrbaugh, Richard L. "A Dysfunctional Family and its Neighbours." In *Jesus and His Parables: Interpreting the Parables of Jesus Today*, edited by V. George Shillington, 141–64. Edinburgh: T. & T. Clark, 1997.

Rousseau, John J., and Rami Arav. *Jesus and His World: An Archaeological and Cultural Dictionary*. Minneapolis: Fortress, 1995.

Rubenstein, Richard L. *My Brother Paul*. New York: Harper & Row, 1972.

Sanders, E. P. *The Historical Figure of Jesus*. London: Penguin, 1993.

———. *Jesus and Judaism*. Philadelphia: Fortress, 1985.

Bibliography

———. *Jewish Law from Jesus to the Mishnah: Five Studies*. Philadelphia: Trinity, 1990.
———. *Judaism: Practice and Belief, 63 BCE –66 CE*. Fourth Edition. London: SCM, 2004.
———. *Paul and Palestinian Judaism: A Comparison of Patterns of Religion*. Philadelphia: Fortress, 1977.
———. *Paul, The Law and the Jewish People*. Philadelphia: Fortress, 1983.
———. "Paul's Attitude Toward the Jewish People." *USQR* 33 (1978) 175–87.
Sandmel, Samuel. *The Genius of Paul: A Study in History*. Philadelphia: Fortress, 1979.
Schweitzer, Albert. *The Quest of the Historical Jesus: A Critical Study of its Progress from Reimarus to Wrede* (1910). Translated by W. Montgomery. London: A. & C. Black, 1956.
Scott, Ian W. "Epistemology and Social Conflict in *Jubilees* and *Aresteas*." In *Common Judaism: Explorations in Second Temple Judaism*, edited by Wayne O. McCready and Adele Reinhartz, 195–213. Minneapolis: Fortress, 2008.
Segal, Alan F. *Paul the Convert: The Apostolate and Apostasy of Saul the Pharisee*. New Haven: Yale University Press, 1990.
Sheets, Dwight D. "Jesus as Demon-Possessed." In *Who do my Opponents Say That I Am? An Investigation of the Accusations against Jesus*, edited by Scott McKnight and Joseph B. Modica, 27–49. London: T. & T. Clark, 2008.
Shillington, V. George. *2 Corinthians*. Believers Church Bible Commentary. Scottdale, PA: Herald, 1998.
———. "Atonement Texture in 1 Corinthians 5.5." *JSNT* 71 (1998) 29–50.
———. *An Introduction to the Study of Luke-Acts*. London: T. & T. Clark, 2007.
———. *The New Testament in Context: A Literary and Theological Textbook*. London: T. & T. Clark, 2008.
———. "Reading Jesus' Parables in Light of his Crucifixion." In *A Wandering Galilean: Essays in Honour of Seán Freyne*, edited by Zuleika Rodgers with Margaret Daly-Denton and Anne Fitzpatrick McKinley, 505–24. Leiden: Brill, 2009.
Smallwood, E. Mary. *The Jews Under Roman Rule: From Pompey to Diocletian*. Studies in Judaism in Late Antiquity 20. Leiden: Brill, 1976.
Smith, Morton. *Clement of Alexandria and a Secret Gospel of Mark*. Cambridge: Harvard University Press, 1973.
Stemberger, Günter. *Jewish Contemporaries of Jesus: Pharisees, Sadducees, Essenes*. Translated by Allan W. Mahnke. Philadelphia: Fortress, 1995.
Stendahl, Krister. *Paul Among Jews and Gentiles and Other Essays*. Philadelphia: Fortress, 1976.
Still, Todd D., editor. *Jesus and Paul Reconnected: Fresh Pathways into an Old Debate*. Grand Rapids: Eerdmans, 2007.
Stowers, Stanley K. *A Rereading of Romans: Justice, Jews, & Gentiles*. New Haven: Yale University Press, 1994.
Strabo. *The Geography of Strabo*. Translated by H. L. Jones. Cambridge: Harvard University Press, 1960–1969.
Suetonius. *Lives of the Caesars*. Translated by Catharine Edwards. Oxford: University Press, 2000.
Tacitus, P. Cornelius. *The Annals*. Translated by Alfred J. Church and William J. Broadribb. Whitefish: Kessinger, 2004.
Taylor, Justin. "Why Were the Disciples First Called 'Christians' at Antioch? (Acts 11, 26)." *Revue Biblique* 101 (1994) 75–94.
Toews, John E. *Romans*. Believers Church Bible Commentary. Scottdale, PA: Herald, 2004.
Trudinger, Paul. "Exposing the Depth of Oppression (Luke 16:1b–8a)." In *Jesus and His Parables: Interpreting the Parables of Jesus Today*, edited by V. George Shillington, 121–37. Edinburgh: T. & T. Clark, 1997.
Van Kooten, George H. *Paul's Anthropology in Context: The Image of God, Assimilation to God and Tripartite Man in Ancient Judaism, Ancient Philosophy and Early Christianity*. Wissenschaftliche Untersuchungen zum Neuen Testament 232. Tübingen: Mohr Siebeck, 2008.
Via, Dan Otto, Jr. *The Parables: Their Literary and Existential Dimension*. Philadelphia: Fortress, 1967.
Von Harnack, Adolf. *What is Christianity?* Translated by T. B. Saunders. New York: Harper and Row, 1957.
Wedderburn, A. J. M., editor. *Paul and Jesus: Collected Essays*. Journal for the Study of the New Testament, Supplemental Series 37. London: T. &T. Clark, 2004.

Bibliography

Wernle, Paul. *The Beginnings of Christianity*. Vol. 1. Translated by G. A. Bienemann. London: Williams and Norgate, 1903.

Wire, Antionette Clark. *The Corinthian Women Prophets: A Reconstruction through Paul's Rhetoric*. Minneapolis: Fortress, 1995.

Wise, Michael, Martin Abegg Jr., and Edward Cook. *The Dead Sea Scrolls: A New Translation*. San Francisco: HarperSanFrancisco, 1996.

Witherington III, Ben. *The Many Faces of the Christ: The Christologies of the New Testament and Beyond*. New York: Crossroad, 1998.

Wohlgemut, Joel. "Entrusted Money (Matt. 25:14–28)." In *Jesus and His Parables: Interpreting the Parables of Jesus Today*, edited by V. George Shillington, 103–120. Edinburgh: T. & T. Clark, 1997.

Wright, N. T. "Five Gospels but no Gospel: Jesus and the Seminar." In *Authenticating the Activities of Jesus*, edited by Bruce Chilton and Craig A. Evans, 83–120. Leiden: Brill, 1999.

———. *Justification: God's Plan & Paul's Vision*. Downers Grove, IL: IVP Academic, 2009.

Zannoni, Arthur E., editor. *Jews and Christians Speak of Jesus*. Philadelphia: Fortress, 1994.

Zeitlin, Irving M. *Jesus and the Judaism of His Time*. Boston: Polity, 1988.

Zerbe, Gordon. "Jews and Gentiles as People of the Covenant: The Background and Message of Romans 11." *Direction*, 12.3 (1983) 20–28.

———. *Non-retaliation in Early Jewish and New Testament Texts: Ethical Themes in Social Context*. New York: Continuum, 1993.

Zetterholm, Magnus. "Jews, Christians and Gentiles: Rethinking the Categorization Within the Early Jesus-Movement." In *Reading Paul in Context: Explorations in Identity Formation. Essays in Honour of William S. Campbell*, edited by Kathy Ehrenspereger and Brian J. Tucker, 242–54. London: T. & T. Clark, 2010.

Ziesler, John. *Paul's Letter to the Romans*. London: SCM, 1989.

———. *Pauline Christianity*. Oxford: University Press, 1983.

Ancient Documents Index

OLD TESTAMENT/HEBREW BIBLE

Genesis
1–2	197
1:26–27	117
1:27	168, 197, 204
3:16	196
17:7–8	161
17:9–14	148, 180
17:18–23	172
18:1–8	99

Exodus
3:8	43
8:19	78
9:16	210
16:18	200
20:3–4	176
20:12	70
27–30	143
32:32	207

Leviticus
16	192
18:2–17	191
20:11	191
20:24	43

Deuteronomy
6:4	168
21:23	39, 146
25:3	145
32	56

1 Samuel
10:1	114

2 Samuel
7:14	116
12:1–10	65

1 Chronicles
16:1	65
16:12–13	115

Ezra
1:2–11	44
6:3–5	44

Nehemiah
2:17–20	44

Psalms
2:7	116
10:16	65
17:50	171
89:27–28	116
117:1	171

Isaiah
2:2	199
9:1	45
8:14	208
10:22–23	207
11:10	171
11:11–12	73
11:28–29	213
28:16	208
35:5	78
40:3	56
42:6	168
45:14, 22	80
49:1–6	158

Ancient Documents Index

Isaiah (continued)
49:6, 23	80, 168
53	152
56:6–8	80
56:7	121
59:20–21	213
66:18	171, 199
66:19	80

Jeremiah
1:5	158
3:17	171
7:1–11	121
31:9	20, 116
50:2	171

Ezekiel
2:3	117
2:6	117
2:8	117
17:22–23	19
33:7	117

Daniel
7	118
7:13–14	115, 117

Hosea
11:1	116

Joel
3:2	171

Amos
4:1–2	44

Micah
4:1, 13	80
12:2	73

Zephaniah
2:9	80
3:11–13	73

Haggai
2:6–9	199

Zechariah
2:11	80
8:20–23	80
9:9	119
6:12	159

Malachi
2:13–16	106

APOCRYPHA

Wisdom
2:17–18	116

Tobit
14:6–7	80

1 Maccabees
2:19–22	44
5:14	47

PSEUDEPIGRAPHA

1 Enoch
90:30–33	80

Psalms of Solomon
17:32–36	115

NEW TESTAMENT

Matthew
1:1—2:23	91
1:18–25	53
1:19	92
2:1–15	47
2:2	118
3:7–10	58
3:11–12	58
3:13–15	59
3:15	92
4:3, 6	116
5:3	79
5:5	94
5:6	92
5:10, 20, 45	92
5:13	95
5:17–18	35
5:32	106
5:39–42	107
5:43–44	106

Ancient Documents Index

6:10	42	23:35, 37	92
6:12	95, 106	24–25	118
6:14–15	106	24:13	188
6:19–20	94	24:1–2	98
6:24	72, 103	25:12	98
6:25–30	102	25:14–30	104
6:33	92	25:46	92
8:5–10, 13	80	26:25	68
8:19–20	70	26:33	115
8:21–22	69	26:47—27:5	123
8:29	116	26:56	113
9:13	92	26:63	115
9:32–34	83	26:69	31
10:2–4	72	27:11	118
10:5–6	74	27:19	92
10:7	74	27:37	125
10:10	74	28:7, 16–17	137
10:37–39	72	28:9	128
10:41	92	28:16–17	128
11:7–11	63	28:18–20	226
11:11	62		
11:12	63	*Mark*	
11:16–19	84, 122	1:1	116
11:28	88	1:5	58
12:42	22	1:9	59
13:33	99	1:4	59
13:39	188	1:11	59
13:43	92	1:14	61, 69
13:46	88	1:14–19	62
13:55	53	1:15	61
15:21–28	80	1:16	41, 53
15:24	47, 97, 226	1:16–20	68
15:31	77	1:19	53
16:28	100	1:20	54
18:23–35	106	1:34	77
19:16–23	71	1:40–44	78
19:28	72	2	86
19:30	100	2:10	118
20	103	2:13–17	86
20:1–15	94	2:22	102
20:16	100	2:17	89, 97
20:20–23	119	2:18	62
21:2–11	119	3	82, 83
21:12–16	120	3:9	54
21:23–42	98	3:11	116
21:32	92	3:14	68
22:1–10	108	3:16–19	72
22:17–22	105	3:20–30	82
23:5–7	101	3:21, 31–35	71, 72
23:27	14	3:28–30	83

Mark (continued)

4:1, 36–37	54
4:3–8	99
4:26–29	99
4:30–32	99
5:1–13	82
5:2, 18, 21	54
6	53
6:3	51, 53
6:4	167
6:16–18	47
6:18–27	61
6:32, 45	54
6:34	54
6:38	54
6:45	54
7	14
7:19	14
7:24–30	80
8:27	41
8:30	115
8:27–30	115
8:31–33	115
9:1	100
9:2	42
9:5	24, 68
9:38	77
10:5–9	106
10:7–11	74
10:17–19	71
10:20	71
10:23, 25	101
10:30, 31	100
10:35–40	119
10:41–45	101
10:45	138
10:46–51	79
11:1–10	119
11:9–10	119
11:15–18	120
11:21	24
11:25	106
12:1–11	95
12:13–17	105
12:28–43	33
12:37	88
12:38–39	101
12:44	94
13:1–2	98, 138
13:28–30	99
14:22–24	122
14:32–36	37
14:43–45	123
14:50	113
14:53–65	125
14:57–58	121
14:58	98, 138
14:61–62	115, 116, 117
14:66–71	124
15:1–15	125
15:2	118
15:13	39
15:16–20	38
15:26	125
15:40, 47	71
15:42	25
15:43	127
16:1	71
16:7	137

Luke

1:4	221
1:5	47
1:26–38	91
2:1–39	91
2:21	53
2:40	52
2:52	52
2:41–50	40
2:48–51	52
3:23–38	91
3:38	117
4:3, 9	116
4:16	221
4:41	116
5:1	41
5:27–32	86
5:33	62
6	25
6:14–16	72
6:15	46
6:20	103
6:21	92
6:30	101
6:32	107
6:37	106
7:11–16	79
7:33	107
9	70
9, 10	76

Ancient Documents Index

9:2	74	7:31–35	84
9:27	100	7:34	122
10:1	75	9:57–58	70
10:7	74	9:59–60	69
10–18	26	11:2–4	26
10:30–37	26, 96	11:4	95, 106
11:2–4	26	11:31	22
11:5–8	109	11:44	49
11:14–15	83	12:22–29	102
11:20	78, 100	13:20–21	108
12:16–29	94	14:26	72
13:18:19	99	16:13	72, 103
13:24	98	16:16	63
13:32	47	16:18	106
15:11–32	26, 108	19:12–27	104
16:1–8	104	22:28	47
16:19–29	79	22:30	47
17	118		
17:11–17	78	*John*	
17:21	100	1:1–18	91
18:2–5	109	1:6–9	60
18:18–23	71	1:20–21	60
18:9–14	96	1:29	60
19:29–38	119	1:32	60
19:45–47	120	1:37	60
20:9–17	95	1:45	53
21:5–6	98	1:49	24, 68
22:47–49	123	2:13–22	120
22:59	31	2:16–22	138
22:69	116	2:22	120
23:3	118	2:18–20	98
23:38	125	3:2, 26	24
23:49	113	3:30	60
24:15–16, 30–31	128	4:9	97
29:19–26	105	4:31	24
		6:1	41, 49
Q = Matthew-Luke Sayings		6:21	49
3:3:7–9	58	6:25	24
3:16–17	58	6:68	90
6:20	50, 79	7:52	31
6:27	106	8:44	14
6:32	106	9:2	24
6:34–35	107	11:8	24
7:1	47	12:12–15	119
7:1–10	80	13:1	33
7:3	47	13:1–30	122
7:6–9	47	13:23	72
7:18–23	61	18:1–6	123
7:24–28	63	18:28—19:16	125
7:28	62	18:33	118

Ancient Documents Index

John (continued)

18:36	119
19:14, 31	25
19:13, 17, 20	140
19:16	125
19:19	53, 125
19:25–27	113
20:19–20	128
20:26–29	128
20:30–31	25
21:1	49
21:7, 20	72

Acts

1:4	137
1:8	75
1–13	76
1–15	75
1:15–23	123
2:5	138
4:32–34	137
5:37	46
6	147
6:1	139, 140, 160
6:1–5	140
6:6–15	141
6–7	29
6:11	142
6:13–14	142
7	29
7:2–53	142
8:1	145
8:1–3	217
8:4–8	144
9	172
9:3–19	155
9:29	140
9:30	165
10:15	35
11:19–20	147
11:26	7
13:1—14:28	148
13:46	203
14:1	138
14–18	76
15	148
15:1	148
16:13	51
16:14	146
17:7	9
18:1–4	165
18:3	220
18:4	138
18:6	203
18:17	146
19:10, 17	138
19:19	77
20:21	138
21:21–28	141
20:34	220
21:39	164, 166
21:40	140
22:3	164, 221
22:6–16	155
22:21	203
22:25	166
23:27	166
26	7
26:12–18	155
26:18	156
28:28	203
26:28–29	7

Romans

1:1–2	171
1–8	202
1:3	192
1:3–4	151
1:4	129
1:14	138
1:16	81, 138, 203
1:17	186
1:18—3:20	169
1:23–24	177
2:5	19
2:9	138, 203
2:9–11	169
2:13	185
3	202
3:1–3	204
3:3	174
3:9	138
3:13	186
3:21	179
3:22	186
3:21–22	174
3:21–26	202
3:23	169
3:26	169
3:27	173

Ancient Documents Index

3:28	177, 185	12–16	202
3:31	189, 224	13:1–7	214
4	159	13:9	186
4:6	177	13:9–10	188
4:9–10	177	13:11	170
4:9–12	204	13:12	170
4:25	151	14	35
6:4	181–82	15	199
6:18–20	200	15:7	204
7	216	15:9–18	171
7:7–12	162	15:16–31	200
7:7–24	205	15:24–28	201
7:12	185, 191	15:25	199
7:14	178, 185	15:26	200
8:1–17	205	16:22	166
8:2	178, 184		
8:3–4	187	### 1 Corinthians	
8:4	180, 184, 186, 192, 200, 224	1:8	188
8:9	184	1:13	185, 188
8:14	184	1:17–23	34
8:19	170	1:23	37, 39, 146, 209
8:23	170, 178	1:24	138
8:33	204	1:26	166
8:34	151	2:2	130
9:1–5	14	2:8	24
9:5	192	3:17	192
9–11	163, 201, 202, 206, 212, 216, 224	4:16	69
9:1–5	162, 206	5	191, 194
9:6	73	5:10	190
9:33	209	6:11	186
10:4	185, 188, 189	7:2–5	198
10:9	181	7:10–11	17, 24, 106
10:17–11	213	7:10	24
11	211, 213	7:11–15	106
11:1	73	7:12	17
11:1–2	162	7:14–15	198
11:11	209	7:18	162
11:13	204	7:18–20	180
11:13–14	209	7:19	17
11:15–16	207	7:25	17
11:17–24	81, 211	7:29	170, 226
11:24–26	14	7:31	15, 170
11:25–26	171, 201, 206, 209, 212	8	148
11:25–32	212	8–10	189
11:26	226	8:1–6	14
11:26b–27	213	8:6	168
11:29	216	8:7	189
12:1–2	195	9:1	159
12:4–8	177	9:4–18	17
12–15	215	9:10	2

Ancient Documents Index

1 Corinthians (continued)

Reference	Page
9:12	199
9:14	17, 24, 74
9:16	164
9:19–23	189
10	148, 197
10:4	184
10:11	170
10:14	176
10:20	168
10:20–21	177
10:25–30	14
11	150
11:1	69
11:3–16	195–96, 198
11:17	182
11:17–33	197
11:20–22	166
11:21–22	194
11:23	24, 124, 149
11:23–25	17, 24, 149
11:23–26	194
11:27	200
12	185
12:12–13	191
12:13	177
12:27	194
13	3
13:4–8	188
14	185, 198
14:34–35	196, 198
15	129
15:3	19, 149
15:3–4	183
15:3–5	127, 150, 225
15:5	72
15:5–8	128
15:8	159, 169
15:9	145
15:20–27	204
15:51–2	170
16:2	182
16:8	179

2 Corinthians

Reference	Page
3:3	183
3:6	184, 213
3:15–18	183
4:4	117
4:13	183
5:5	178, 193
5:16	16
5:17	170, 226
8–9	198–99
8:1–2	199
8:8–15	195
8:14	199–200
8:15	200
10:10	221
11	167
11:5	160
11:22	73, 140
11:22–23	160
11:24	145, 160
11:25	213
11:24–26	167
11:32	145
11:32–33	172
12:2	118
12:11	160
12:14–15	199

Galatians

Reference	Page
1–2	138
1:2	176
1:13	145, 147
1:13–17	157
1:15	158–59
1:16	13, 135
1:17	145, 171
1:18	13, 24, 171
1:18–2:1	138
2	35
2:1–2	148
2:1–10	148
2:5	225
2:6	169
2:7	204
2:6–10	138
2:10	13
2:11–14	147, 149
2:14	225
2:15	155
2:16	173–74, 177, 186
2:19	134, 174, 195, 200
2:19–20	34
2:20	33
3:2	173
3:5	173
3:6–9	177

Ancient Documents Index

3:10	173, 185	4:15	17
3:12	173		
3:13	39, 146	*1 Timothy*	
3:16	73, 159	2:11–15	198
3:16–29	177		
3:21	185, 205	*Philemon*	
3:22	174	19	166
3:24	185		
3:26–29	195	*1 Peter*	
3:28	138, 191, 195, 197	4:15–16	7
3:29	159		
4:4	15, 24, 179	*Revelation*	
4:30	183	1:5	33
5:6	73		
5:11	172	## DEAD SEA SCROLLS	
5:14	186, 188		
5:19	192	1QM 12:13–14	80
5:22	184	1QS 5	56
5:25	184	4QFlorilegium	115
6:2	16, 178	4Q458	115
6:11	157, 166		
6:15	170	## RABBINIC/JEWISH WRITINGS	
6:16	159		
		Josephus	
Ephesians		*Ant.* 3.212	88
5:2	33	*Ant.* 13.297	87
		Ant. 13.14.2.380	37
Philippians		*Ant.* 14.22–24	77
2:1	184	*Ant.* 18.1.1.1	46
2:5	185	*Ant.* 18.2.1.27	48
2:6	159	*Ant.* 18.2.3..36	50
2:6–11	37, 151	*Ant.* 18.3.3.63	30
2:13	185	*Ant.* 18.5.4.136	47
3:5	140	*Ant.* 18.23	46
3:6	145	*Ant.* 18.63	113
3:5–9	161–62	*Ant.* 20.9.1.200	30
3:7–10	167	*Ant.* 116–19	57
3:9	174	*J. W.* 1.14.4.284	38
3:20	167	*J. W.* 1.16.2.304	48
4:5	170		
		Philo	
Colossians		*Confusion of Tongues* 63	159
1:15	117	*In Flaccum* 83–85	38
1 Thessalonians		*Mishnah*	
1–2	136	*Shebiith* 9:2	41
1:6	69	*Taanith* 3:8	77
1:9	176		
2:9	220	*Talmud*	
2:14	69, 167	*Berakoth* 3:1	70

Ancient Documents Index

GRECO-ROMAN WRITINGS

Celsus
I, 28	51

Strabo, Geography
8.6.20	199
14.5.13	165

Tactius
Annals 15:44	144

EARLY CHRISTIAN WRITINGS

Eusebius
Constantine 37–41	9

Gospel of the Ebionites
4:1	59

Gospel of the Hebrews
2	59

Gospel of the Nazorenes
2	59

Gospel of Peter
7	113

Gospel of Thomas
20:1–4	99
21:9	99
36	102
46	62
47:1–2	103
47:3	102
55	72
64:1–12	108
65:1–7	95
69	92
95:1–2	107
96	99
100:1–4	105

Author Index

Badenas, R., 188
Barrett, C. K., 161
Baur, F. C., 13
Beker, J. C., 156, 184, 213
Betz, H. D., 158, 195
Borg, M., 19, 136, 159, 166, 173
Bornkamm, G., 52
Boyarin, D., 154
Bultmann, R., 15-16, 52
Cadbury, H., 3-4, 77
Conzelmann, H., 189
Crossan, J. D., 11, 19, 52, 54, 57-58, 63, 78, 84, 91, 103, 112, 119, 126, 136, 159, 166, 173
Davies, W. D., 16, 94, 176
Dix, Gregory, 15
Dodd, C. H., 16, 92, 108
Donaldson, T., 154, 157, 169
Drescher, R., 14
Dungan, D. L., 17
Eisenbaum, P., 6, 154, 157, 176, 206
Esler, P., 127, 187, 194
Farris, M., 96
Fredriksen, P., 60, 73, 120, 123, 145-47, 154
Fitzmyer, J., 209
Freyne, S., 31, 42, 46, 54, 72
Gager, J., 154, 160, 210-11
Harnack, Adolf von, 13-14
Hengel, M., 37, 39, 69-71, 100-101, 105-6, 135, 139, 141-42, 172-73
Herzog, W., 96, 105
Hickling, C. J. A., 169-70
Horrel, D., 8
Horsley, R., 41, 45-46, 96
Jervell, J., 201
Jewett, R., 151, 188, 206, 213
Käsemann, E., 151
Klassen, W., 124

Lohmeyer, E., 152
Lüdemann, G., 144, 171
Martyn, J. L., 16
McCane, B., 127
Meyer, B. F., 15, 27, 33-34, 69, 90, 101, 149-50, 152
Meyers, E., 48
Neusner, J., 29
Modica, J., 85, 122
Nanos, M., 81, 154-55, 161, 179-80, 190, 203, 206, 210
Nietzsche, F., 3
Oakman, D. E., 32
Reed, J., 11, 32, 52, 54, 126
Remus, H., 76-77
Rensberger, D., 125
Rivkin, E., 60, 83-84, 120
Robinson, J. M., 26, 103
Roetzel, C., 164
Rohrbaugh, R., 79, 81-82, 108
Rousseau, J., 126
Sanders, E. P., 29, 35-36, 55, 62, 67, 74, 79, 86-87, 90-91, 119, 123, 155, 186, 197, 212
Schweitzer, A., 12
Sheets, D., 83
Shillington, V. G., 8, 34, 75-76, 160, 191, 199
Smallwood, M., 45
Stendahl, K., 154-56, 206
Toews, J. E., 188, 206
Trudinger, P., 104
Wedderburn, A. J. M., 17, 19
Weiss, J., 15
Wernle, P., 14
Wrede, W., 15, 232
Wohlgemut, J., 104
Wright, N. T., 4, 155, 187, 229, 233
Zerbe, G., 206

Subject Index

Abraham, 42, 58, 143, 157–58, 159–62, 163, 172–74, 177, 179–81, 196, 201, 204, 210–13
Adam, 62, 117, 204–5
adultery, 60–61, 106
agrarian/agriculture, 28, 88, 94
allegorical/allegory, 93, 95, 108
Alexandria, Egypt, 10, 27, 29, 38, 45, 75, 139, 142–43, 147, 159, 165, 232
anachronistic, 4, 6, 14, 158
Anthony, Mark, 38
aniconic monotheism, 176
anointed, 5, 7, 114
anti-Jewish, 11, 112, 154
Antioch, 7, 76, 112, 146–50, 152–53, 220, 232
Antipas, Herod, 31, 47–50, 56–58, 60, 63, 65, 112, 172
apocalyptic, 57–58, 117–18, 156, 158, 170
apostate, 155, 209
apostleship/apostolate, 148, 159, 163, 207
Aquinas, Thomas, 23
Aramaic language, 27, 29, 52–53, 64–65, 76, 92, 94, 98, 100, 103, 114, 126, 139–41, 145, 149–51, 160
archaeology, 32, 43, 45–46, 48, 229–31
Athanasius, Bishop, 10
Augustine, Saint, 23
atonement, 29, 87, 191–93, 200, 202
Augustus, Caesar, 47, 116, 159, 167
Babylonia, 29, 44–45, 73, 148
baptism, 55–62, 64, 177, 181, 194–95
Baptizer, John, 55–57, 60, 64
Beelzebul, 82–83
Bethlehem, 52–53
betrayal/betrayed/betrayer, 24, 111, 124–25, 149–50, 193
borderlines/borders 11, 31, 125, 153

burial, 49, 111, 126–27, 178
Byzantine, 51
Caesar, Julius, 147
Caesarea Philippi, 41–42
Caiaphas, High Priest, 115–16, 120–21, 125
canon/canons 8, 10, 18
Capernaum, 47, 80
census of 6 or 7 BCE, 46
charismatic, 65, 69–7, 83, 123, 197
Christendom, 10–11
Christianity, 3, 5–12, 14–15, 17–19, 113, 122, 124, 137, 152–54, 157–58, 173, 178
Christians, 3, 5–7, 9–12, 14, 90, 113, 127, 155, 158, 178
Christology, 59–60, 115–16, 152
circumcision, 53, 146, 148–49, 162, 170, 172, 177, 179–81, 187, 204
citizenship, 166–67
coherence, 33–34, 111, 227
collaboration with Rome, 66, 85–86
collection for Jerusalem, 199, 201
commandments, 44, 70–71, 176, 180, 194
Constantine, emperor, 9–10, 15, 126
conversion/convert, 6, 9, 15, 55–56, 154–58, 161, 171–73
covenant, 29, 42, 44, 55–56, 67, 81, 85–87, 89, 94, 96, 122, 125, 144, 148–49, 156–58, 160–63, 168, 172–74, 177, 180–81, 194, 200–201, 206, 208, 211, 213
covenantal nomism, 29, 222–23
creation/Creator 15, 42, 65, 116–17, 137, 155, 163, 168, 170, 176, 197, 203–5
creed, 9–10, 168
crowds, 57–58, 60, 60–61, 63–64, 82–84, 89, 120, 127

247

Subject Index

crucifixion, 15, 25–26, 33–39, 67, 71, 111–12, 114, 120, 125–30, 135, 137–38, 146, 150, 171, 217, 224–25,
Damascus, 145, 152, 155–56, 158, 167–69, 171–72
David, messianic King, 17, 43–46, 53, 65, 81, 115, 119, 138, 151
deliverance/delivered 14, 18–19, 27, 30, 87, 115, 140, 143, 193, 159, 200
demons, 74, 76, 81–83, 100, 116, 168, 177
desert, 44, 55–58, 60, 63, 172, 192
destitute/destitution, 64, 83, 88, 94, 103, 108
deviance, 52, 110
Diaspora, 138–41, 143, 145–46, 178–79, 183
Diocletian, emperor, 9
discipleship, 62, 68–69
distribution of resources, 94–95, 104, 137, 139–40
divorce, 24, 28, 106
Easter, 10, 24–26, 34, 72, 75, 91–92, 113–16, 119, 121–22, 130, 149–50, 152–53
education, 4, 29–30, 41, 49, 52, 101, 139, 164–67, 189
Egypt, 27, 29, 38, 45, 51, 59, 75, 77, 116, 122, 139–40, 142–43, 147, 210
elite/elitism, 34, 49, 51–52, 83, 85, 87, 94, 101, 108, 116, 118, 166, 200
emperor/empire 8–9, 15, 49, 112, 116, 126, 131
epiphany, Paul's, 156, 225
equality, 151, 194, 198, 200
eschatological, 15, 57–58, 72, 74, 79–82, 138, 143, 148, 151–53, 163, 170, 199, 204, 210, 212–14
Essenes, 87–88
ethnicity, 47, 140
eucharist/eucharistic, 24, 27, 122, 124, 150, 194–95
Eusebius, 9, 112
excommunication, 192
execution, 25, 28, 34–35, 37–38, 56, 60–62, 64, 83, 85, 111–12, 125, 138, 144, 146
exorcism, 64, 100, 110
faithful/faithfulness 19, 86–87, 114, 156–57, 162–63, 169, 173–75, 177, 179–81, 184–86, 187, 189–91, 198, 200, 202–5, 207, 211–13
farmers, 49–51, 54, 94–96, 99, 102–3
fasting, 84

fellowship, 12, 79, 84–85, 87, 89, 107, 122, 146, 166, 175, 178, 183, 185, 188–91, 193–95, 197, 199
forgiveness, 57, 59, 69, 74, 86, 89, 96, 106, 110
Freud, Sigmund, 77
gender, 4, 188, 191, 194, 196–97, 200
Ginnosar, 54
gnostic/gnostics 124
government, 36–38, 42, 44, 52, 66–67, 96, 117, 167, 175
guests, 84, 107–8, 179–80
guilt/guilty 33–34, 83, 86, 89, 143
Hadrian, emperor, 8
harmonization, 3, 16, 26, 112–13, 124
Hasmonean/Hasmoneans 31, 37–38, 45–47, 66–67
healing/healings 61, 64, 71, 74, 76–82, 89, 110, 130, 210
Hebraioi, 139–40, 142, 144, 145
Hebrews, 25, 56, 59, 122, 139–40, 160–61
hellenism/hellenistic, 5, 17, 29, 31, 48, 50, 76, 82, 116, 141–42, 176
Hellenistai/Hellenists 139–41, 143–44, 147, 149–50
heresy/heretical/heretics, 9, 124, 198
Herod the Great, 31, 45, 47–48, 219
hierarchy, 75, 77–78, 84, 127, 144, 197–98
Hillel, Rabbi, 35
honor, 7–9, 31, 33, 39, 49, 60, 70, 100–101, 107, 109–10, 120, 126, 129–33, 167, 169, 175
hospitality, 74, 107, 109
ideological/ideology 13, 18, 78
idolatrous/idolatry/idols, 19, 103, 148, 176–77, 179–81, 190, 194–95, 197
impure/impurity, 28, 80, 85, 89, 108, 110, 176, 200
indebtedness, 43, 88, 94–95, 104, 106, 110, 135, 218, 226
individualism, 11, 182, 192
injustice, 57–58, 62, 103, 107, 110, 116, 207
insurrection, 39
interpolation, 198
interpretation/interpreter, 32, 39, 45–46, 57, 62, 66–67, 70, 90, 93, 110, 113, 122, 144–45, 150, 154–55, 157, 161–62, 183, 206, 210, 213–14
intertexture, 202
Israel, 3, 15, 29–31, 34, 41–47, 49, 53, 56–58, 65, 72–74, 77, 80–82, 85–89, 93–94, 96–97, 99, 102, 114–18, 121–22, 125, 136,

Subject Index

138–39, 143–44, 146, 148–52, 155–63, 168–71, 173, 176, 179–81, 186–88, 191–92, 195–96, 201–4, 206–14

Israelites, 43–47, 57, 73, 85–86, 94, 155–56, 160–63, 168–69, 176, 184, 203, 207–8, 211

Irenaeus, 124

Jerusalem, 8–9, 13, 18, 24–25, 28–32, 34, 36–40, 44–46, 48, 53, 55–58, 66–67, 73, 75–76, 78, 80, 82–83, 87, 91, 93, 96–98, 102, 105, 108, 111, 113, 115, 117–23, 125–27, 129, 137–45, 147–51, 153, 158, 165, 169, 171, 173, 179, 199–203, 212, 214

Josephus, 30, 37–38, 41, 46–49, 51, 56, 60–61, 77, 87–88, 113–14

Judas, disciple of Jesus, 44, 46, 53, 72, 83, 123–25

judgment, 15, 17, 19, 35, 56–58, 61, 76, 85–86, 98, 100, 105, 118, 137, 142, 144, 152, 161, 164, 170, 192, 194, 197, 209

jurisprudence, Roman, 35, 67

justice, 28, 42, 88, 91, 93, 103–4, 107, 109–10, 115, 117–18, 120, 174–75, 177, 186, 202, 207, 210

justify/justifying, 186–87, 204–5

kosher, 53, 148, 179, 181, 187, 191

label/labeling, 8, 31, 47, 85–86, 110, 140–41, 204

lament, 206–7

landowners, 49–50, 94, 96, 100, 103

leprosy, 77–78

Law, Jewish, 14, 16, 24, 29, 35–36, 46–47, 52, 55–56, 67, 74, 86–87, 96–97, 105–6, 139–46, 154–55, 162, 171, 178–79, 183, 185–91, 193, 200, 205

literal/literally 16, 35, 68–69, 74, 114, 117, 158, 161, 174, 184, 192–93

loyalists/loyalty, 140, 141, 145, 147, 155–56, 161, 174

Luther, Martin, 23, 173, 187

Maccabees, 44

magic, 77–78

mammon, 101, 103, 110

Marcion, 8, 184

marriage, 28, 60–61, 98, 106, 108

martyrdom, 37

Mary, mother of Jesus, 10, 25, 51, 53

meals, 107, 122–23, 175

Messiah, 5, 7–9, 13–15, 19, 24–25, 30, 37, 39, 62, 65, 69, 71, 84, 114–17, 135–37, 146, 150–53, 155–60, 162–67, 169, 171–73, 175–97, 199–202, 204, 206–8, 211–13

metaphor/metaphoric, 3, 26, 92, 95, 97, 108, 116, 123, 159, 210–11

miracles, 76, 78

Mishnah, 27–29, 41–42, 48, 77, 146

moneychangers, 123

monotheism, 168, 176

Moses, 27, 44, 46, 56, 77–78, 87–88, 141–43, 146, 161–62, 207

mystery, 12, 39, 171, 198, 201–2, 207–9, 212–14

myth/mythical, 154, 192

narrative/narrator, 7, 14–15, 24–27, 29, 35–36, 40, 43, 59–60, 63, 71–72, 75–76, 80, 83, 92–93, 101, 104, 108, 112–13, 116, 118, 136–37, 140–42, 144–45, 148, 157

nations, 5, 13–16, 19, 30, 44, 47, 65, 73–74, 79–81, 89, 108, 115, 121, 130, 141, 146, 148–49, 153, 155–59, 162, 164–65, 167–71, 173, 175, 179–81, 195, 199–207, 209–13

Nazareth, 6, 10, 16, 18, 41–42, 45, 48–49, 51–55, 59, 66, 71, 78, 91, 125, 130, 142–43, 163–64, 166–67, 172

Nicea, Council of, 9–10

obedience/obey, 12, 44, 67–68, 70, 87, 97, 179–80, 202

observant, 39, 49–50, 52–53, 86, 88–89, 97, 146, 162, 166, 189–91

occupied, land and people, 19, 24, 30–31, 40, 43, 45, 65, 67, 83, 88–89, 93–94, 102, 110, 147, 152, 185

opponents of Jesus and Paul, 14, 82–83, 107, 117, 122, 144, 159–61, 211

oppression, 58, 115, 193

orthodoxy, 9

Palestine/Palestinian, 8–9, 17, 20, 24, 27–30, 32, 34–35, 37–38, 47, 52, 56, 62, 67–69, 75, 77, 79, 83, 85, 87–89, 92–94, 97, 101–3, 110–11

parable, 26, 36, 79, 92–100, 102–10, 211

Passover, 25, 40, 53, 99, 120–23, 138, 193, 200

Patronage/patrons, 166, 221

pax romana, 47

peasants, 42–44, 88, 94, 105

penitence/penitent, 56, 97, 108, 109, 193

persecution, 8–9, 28, 144–47, 155, 161–62, 171, 172

Subject Index

Pharisees/Pharisaic, 24, 28, 37–39, 45, 52, 67, 87–88, 96–97, 121, 142, 156, 158, 161
Philo of Alexandria, 29, 38, 159
Pilate, Pontius, 11, 35, 65, 112–14, 118–22, 125–27
pilgrimage/pilgrims, 53, 88, 120, 123, 138, 218, 220, 223
polytheism, 179, 190
Pompey, 37, 45, 141
poverty, 51, 83, 88, 101, 103
priesthood/priests, 29, 36, 44, 55–57, 67, 78, 82, 87–88, 96, 98, 113–14, 116, 120–23, 139
priest-king system, 37, 45, 66
privilege, 52, 71, 166, 194, 212
prophecy/prophetic/prophet, 31, 44, 47, 56, 58, 63, 73, 75, 77, 80, 85, 105–6, 112, 115–17, 119–21, 144, 155, 157, 158, 159, 161, 163, 169, 171, 199, 207–8, 213
proselytes, 157, 160, 162, 179–80, 202, 211
prostitutes/prostitution, 86, 97
purity, 28, 36, 56, 63, 80, 85, 88, 115, 121–23, 156, 191, 193
Quelle, 26
Qumran, 29, 45, 55, 57, 87, 106, 115
rebellion/rebels 8, 36, 39, 44, 46, 48, 57, 78, 83, 89, 106
redemption/redemptive, 15, 37, 85, 87, 120, 124, 138, 170, 183, 188, 192–93, 202–3, 211
Reformation, 10–11, 155, 161–62, 173
remnant, 73, 129–30, 201, 207–8
repentance, 56–59, 61, 74, 85–87, 89, 96–97, 110, 155, 161, 179
restoration, 31, 47, 58, 61, 73–74, 77, 79, 97, 138, 149, 179, 201–5, 207–9, 211, 213
retainers, 95, 105
retrojection, 14, 119
revelation, 135, 143, 152–53, 158–63, 168–71, 212, 214
revolutionary/revolts, 30, 44–46, 48, 57, 64, 71, 83–84, 119
rhetoric, 136, 157, 160, 163, 165, 194, 196–97, 201
righteous/righteousness, 19, 59–60, 77, 85, 87, 89, 92, 96–97, 115–17, 150, 161–62, 168, 174, 177, 184–88, 177, 192, 200, 202–5
ritual, 48, 56, 67–68, 80, 87, 109, 122, 143, 175, 177–78, 182, 192–95

Rome, 8–9, 30–31, 38, 46–48, 50, 66–67, 73, 82–83, 85–86, 93, 96, 111, 114, 121, 125, 141, 147, 151, 163, 166–67, 176–77, 189, 195, 201–4, 210, 212, 214
sacrifice, 28, 33, 57, 74, 87–89, 96–98, 105, 109–10, 121–23, 138, 143, 175, 177, 193–95, 200, 202
salvation, 7, 9, 15, 80–81, 85–87, 94, 110, 112, 118, 124, 130, 151–52, 155, 161, 168–71, 173, 175, 180, 186–87, 191, 193, 199, 201, 203–4, 206, 208–14
sabbath, 25, 28, 118, 179, 181, 187
Sadducees, 87–88
Samaria/Samaritans, 26, 36, 44–46, 74, 96–98, 107–8, 110, 144–45
Sanhedrin, 30, 121, 127, 142, 144
Satan, 83, 115, 156, 191–93
scribes, 52, 67, 75, 82, 86, 142
sectarianism, 11, 55–56, 112, 142
Seleucids, 44, 45
Sepphoris, 31–32, 40–41, 45, 47–51
Septuagint/LXX, 27, 75
sexuality, 176–77, 190–91, 193, 200
Shamai, Rabbi, 35
shame, 7, 37, 39, 107, 109–10, 126, 130, 208
Shema, 70, 156
Sinai, 143, 171–72, 190
slavery/slaves, 37, 48, 50, 63, 95–96, 104, 122, 141, 152, 166, 177, 180, 189–90, 196, 200, 205, 210
socialization, 84
Stephen of Acts, 29, 141–45, 147
Strabo, 165, 199
subversion, 8, 9, 58, 64, 66, 78, 83, 117, 123, 143, 167, 214
symbolism, 9, 31, 53, 66–67, 72–73, 75–76, 87, 90, 98, 99, 111, 119, 121, 142, 177, 193
synagogue, 8, 27, 48, 50–52, 75, 80, 101, 138–43, 145–47, 156, 159–62, 165, 172–73, 178–84, 203
talents, 104–5
Talmud, 28–29, 70
targum, 29, 52, 65, 68
Tarsus, 41, 164–67
taxation, 42–43, 46, 49–50, 67, 88, 94, 105, 190, 214
temple of Jerusalem, 8, 27–29, 31, 35–36, 40, 44–46, 53, 55, 57, 66–68, 73, 77–78, 82, 85, 87–88, 91, 93–94, 96–98, 102, 105, 111, 113, 116–18, 120–27, 138–45,

Subject Index

    147, 151, 155, 160-61, 163, 179, 183, 192-93, 195, 200, 208
tenant farmers, 50, 95-96
Tiberias, city in Galilee, 31, 40-41, 49-51, 63
Tiberius, Caesar, 49, 114
tithe, 67, 96
Torah, 27-28, 35, 67, 70, 155, 162, 165, 178-80, 190-92, 196, 201, 205, 210
traitor/traitors, 85-86, 96, 123
tribute, 26, 42
uncircumcised/uncircumcion, 141, 148, 170, 180, 191, 204
universality, 168, 204-6
urban, 48, 166-67, 175, 178
viceroy, Jesus as, 97, 116, 119, 125

victim, 37, 39, 97-98, 144, 146
village, 32, 50-52, 68, 73-74, 166
vindication of Jesus, 13, 114, 150-51, 224
violence/non-violence, 32, 39, 64, 96, 120, 190
weak/weakness, 63, 125, 130, 189-90, 221, 226
wealth, 43, 48-49, 52, 55, 88, 95, 101-5, 114, 199
widows, 137, 139-41
wisdom, 28, 52, 71, 100, 104, 109, 115, 140, 214
wives, 37, 196
women, 28, 62, 98-99, 113, 177, 196-98, 200
worship, 8, 10, 42, 121, 139-40, 143, 146, 156, 161, 163, 167-68, 176-80, 196-98, 208
Zealots/zeal, 46, 87-88, 145, 161, 188

www.ingramcontent.com/pod-product-compliance
Lightning Source LLC
Chambersburg PA
CBHW080612230426
43664CB00019B/2870